Cyber Resilience Best Practices

AXELOS.com

GLOBAL BEST PRAC

Published by TSO (The Stationery Office), part of Williams Lea,
and available from:

Online
www.tsoshop.co.uk

Mail, Telephone, Fax & E-mail
TSO
PO Box 29, Norwich, NR3 1GN
Telephone orders/General enquiries: 0870 600 5522
Fax orders: 0870 600 5533
E-mail: customer.services@tso.co.uk
Textphone 0870 240 3701

TSO@Blackwell and other Accredited Agents

First published 2015

ISBN 9780113314638

Printed in the United Kingdom for The Stationery Office
Material is FSC certified and produced using ECF pulp, sourced from fully sustainable forests.

P002707537   06/15

Contents

List of figures

List of tables

Foreword

SO WHAT DOES GOOD LOOK LIKE?

We've all heard about the problem of 'one' – that our information security and risk management needs to be right 100% of the time, while our adversaries only have to be right once. The more I hear this expression, the more it feels like an excuse. We know from many annual breach reports that approximately 80% of breaches require a low- to medium-skill level to succeed, so perhaps we should focus on being good, as a starting point, versus trying to be perfect.

So how do you know what good is? It's been my experience that good starts with creating an organization of people who are cyber-aware, who are curious, who ask the right questions and who are always looking for a better way. It's an organization which knows that, regardless of how good its people, processes and technologies are, it will never be bullet-proof. It knows that, despite its best efforts to identify, detect and protect the enterprise from its adversaries, it will also be called upon to respond and recover from cyber-attacks in the most effective manner possible. Even with an enviable level of maturity in its technology and process capabilities, a successful organization knows that it must always be evolving the awareness and support of its people in the face of a growing number of cyber-attacks.

The experience AXELOS has from owning and growing global best management practices will be leveraged in the new RESILIA™ Cyber Resilience Best Practices portfolio. It will become a tremendous asset for information security, upon which risk leaders will be able to build effective programs. It will also help those of us in the information security and risk management fields to answer that key question, 'So what does good look like?'

Gary Warzala

Gary has been a chief information security officer (CISO) for more than 15 years. He is currently an information security executive at a US financial institution. He has worked as a trusted CISO adviser with the Verizon Research, Investigations, Solutions, Knowledge (RISK) team on the target corporation breach response and previously was the chief information security officer of Visa where he had organizational accountability for the development of programs designed to protect in excess of 2 billion unique personal account information records and more than $6 trillion in annual global payment card transactions. Before Visa, Gary was the CISO at the Aon Corporation in Chicago, and at GE Aviation in Cincinnati.

Foreword

KEEPING THE VALUE OF YOUR BUSINESS IN YOUR BUSINESS

The digital age has provided all organizations with vast opportunities to grow and innovate. But it has also brought a new world of risk, especially to one of our most precious assets – information. The information that is critical to our future success is also valued by a wide range of adversaries and, with the emergence and rapid development of a globally networked information environment, it is now easier than ever before to target and attack that information.

However, inside any organization there is a powerful force that can protect its reputation, safeguard its information and keep its customers close – people. The majority of cyber-attacks are successful because of the unwitting actions of one of us. Organizations don't detect and protect us from cyber-attacks, nor do they respond and recover from them – people do. And every person in an organization, and its wider ecosystem, has a vital role to play in dealing with cyber-attacks.

Applying cyber resilience best practices across the enterprise will enable organizations to tackle their cyber risks with renewed confidence. It will help define what good cyber resilience looks like for them, guide them in effectively managing cyber risks, and enable them to bounce back following an attack with minimal reputational or financial damage. For organizations to harness this opportunity they have to adopt an enterprise approach that encompasses people, process and technology.

These best practices provide practical and pragmatic guidance that can be used to support and enhance an organization's use of existing cyber resilience frameworks or standards – ultimately strengthening its ability to keep the value of its business in its business.

I recommend this guidance to all organizations looking to fully exploit the opportunities of operating in the digital age whilst managing their cyber risks effectively.

Peter Hepworth
CEO
AXELOS Global Best Practice

Preface

The resilience of information systems has always been vital to the sustainability of businesses and other organizations. The secure use of information technology has for many years been the topic of guidance and standards describing controls to prevent the loss of critical information. However, the emergence and continuing rapid development of the global networked information environment that we call cyberspace has changed the nature of the problem. While this connectivity offers unparalleled opportunities and benefits, the very same mechanisms create complex and continually evolving risks. This guide offers a practical approach to cyber resilience, reflecting the need to detect and recover from incidents, and not rely on prevention alone.

This publication provides organizations with a methodology for implementing cyber resilience. However, detailed and prescriptive instructions on the application of individual cyber resilience controls will depend upon the risks arising from the nature of each business, the environment in which the organization is operating and other factors described in this publication.

The risk-based design and implementation of cyber resilience controls can only be delivered successfully through the organization's management system, which is in turn driven by its strategic goals. This publication uses the ITIL® framework, which provides a proven approach to the provision of services that align with business outcomes. Developed originally for the delivery of effective, business-focused IT services, ITIL is now used successfully for the management and provision of other services. *Cyber Resilience Best Practices* covers a range of cyber resilience practices and activities across the ITIL lifecycle and describes how some of the processes and activities described by ITIL can be used to support an organization's cyber resilience strategy.

This publication is relevant for any organization using technology to manage information that is critical to its success. It is aimed at those who are responsible for staff and processes that contribute to the cyber resilience of the organization, whether designing, operating, supporting or acting as the end users of those information systems.

Contact information

Full details of the range of material published under the RESILIA and ITIL banners can be found at:

https://www.axelos.com/resilia

https://www.axelos.com/itil

If you would like to inform us of any changes that may be required to this publication, please log them at:

https://www.axelos.com/best-practice-feedback

For further information on qualifications and training accreditation, please visit:

https://www.axelos.com/training-organization-benefits

For all other enquiries, please email:

Ask@AXELOS.com

Acknowledgements

AXELOS Ltd is grateful to everyone who has contributed to the development of this guidance and in particular would like to thank the following:

AUTHORS

Stuart Rance

Stuart is a consultant, trainer and author, and owner of Optimal Service Management Ltd. Stuart works with a wide variety of clients in many countries, helping them use ideas from IT service management and information security management to create business value for themselves and their customers. He is a Chartered Fellow of BCS (FBCS CITP), a Fellow in Service Management at prISM (FSM), and a Certified Information Systems Security Professional (CISSP).

Stuart shares his expertise widely, regularly presenting at events and writing books, white papers, blogs and pocket guides on all aspects of IT. He is the author of *ITIL Service Transition* (2011 edition), and co-author of the *ITIL V3 Glossary*. He has written many pocket guides for *it*SMF and for the official ITIL portfolio.

Mike St John-Green

Mike St John-Green is an independent consultant in cybersecurity, currently working with a range of clients, primarily in the City of London and Europe. Mike also works with the Information Security Forum, which publishes the internationally recognized *Standard of Good Practice*. He was on the steering board of the recently published cybersecurity standard, PAS-555, and supports the IET's work on cybersecurity, principally by chairing committees and conferences. He is a frequent speaker and writer on the topic of cybersecurity.

He retired in 2013 after more than 39 years working for the UK government, mainly at GCHQ and most recently in the Office of Cyber Security and Information Assurance in the Cabinet Office. His Cabinet Office responsibilities included international relations and the role of standards in improving cybersecurity. He had a range of roles in GCHQ, including deputy director CESG, the Information Assurance arm of GCHQ. Mike is a chartered engineer and was made a Fellow of the IET in 2000.

Moyn Uddin

Moyn is an independent information and cyber risk practitioner with nearly 30 years in IT, networking, IT security, information security, governance risk and compliance. He has extensive practical hands-on experience of applying security best practice, both in government and in the private sector, on some of the largest IT-led transformation and change programmes in the world.

Moyn is a CISSP, CISM, CISA, CRISC, CLAS, ISO/IEC 27001 lead auditor and TOGAF-certified enterprise architect. He is a member of the Institute of Information Security Professionals (IISP) and the Association of Enterprise Architects. He is accredited by the CESG through its CLAS scheme as a CESG Certified Professional (CCP) to risk assess and provide information security risk management advice to UK government departments.

REVIEWERS

Appreciation is due to the following (amongst many others) for the time and effort they have put into reviewing various drafts of this publication:

Nathan Cooper, Capita; Ian Davies, deputy chairman of BMT Group and senior independent director at the Institute of Chartered Accountants in England and Wales (ICAEW) and Harvey Nash; Alan Field, Highdown Management Services Ltd; Darren Hampton, iSolutions, University of Southampton; Noel Hannan, Capita; Alexander Hernandez, KPMG; George Judd and the team at CASK LLC; and Gary Warzala.

Contents summary

Cyber Resilience Best Practices comprises:

- **Chapter 1 Introduction** Introduces the concept of cyber resilience.
- **Chapter 2 Risk management** Describes an approach to risk management.
- **Chapter 3 Managing cyber resilience** Explains the need for a single management system that will ensure the delivery of cyber resilience alongside other business goals.
- **Chapter 4 Cyber resilience strategy** Addresses the strategy stage of the cyber resilience lifecycle.
- **Chapter 5 Cyber resilience design** Explains the design stage of the cyber resilience lifecycle.
- **Chapter 6 Cyber resilience transition** Concerns the transition stage of the cyber resilience lifecycle.
- **Chapter 7 Cyber resilience operation** Discusses the operation stage of the cyber resilience lifecycle.
- **Chapter 8 Cyber resilience continual improvement** Addresses the continual improvement stage of the cyber resilience lifecycle.
- **Chapter 9 Cyber resilience roles and responsibilities** Describes roles and responsibilities necessary to achieve cyber resilience.
- **Further research** Provides useful references for further research.
- **Abbreviations and glossary** The glossary is a full version of the terms used in this guide.

CASE STUDIES

This publication uses three fictitious companies to illustrate how to implement good practice and the consequences of getting it wrong. The three companies are described in section 1.2, and their story will continue in colour-keyed text boxes throughout the publication. Actions and incidents involving the three companies are described in detail in the 'Scenarios' sub-sections towards the end of Chapters 4–8.

GLOSSARY TERMS

Please note that certain terms are emboldened in the main text. This is to signify their inclusion in the glossary. They are emboldened on first mention only.

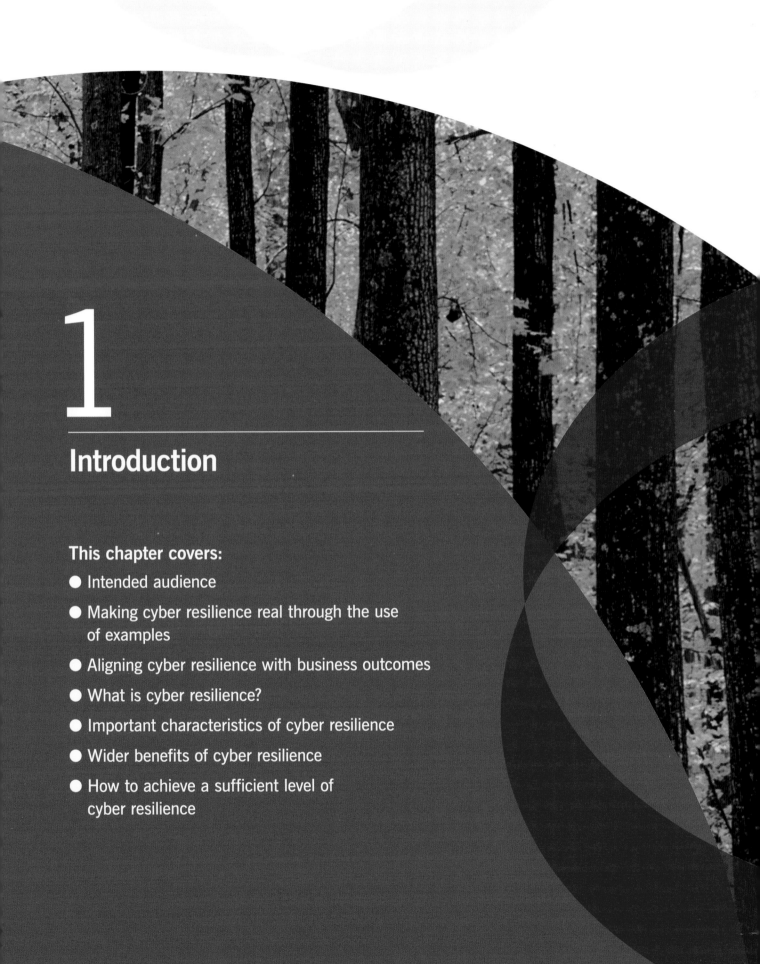

1

Introduction

This chapter covers:

- Intended audience
- Making cyber resilience real through the use of examples
- Aligning cyber resilience with business outcomes
- What is cyber resilience?
- Important characteristics of cyber resilience
- Wider benefits of cyber resilience
- How to achieve a sufficient level of cyber resilience

1 Introduction

The global digital **environment**, comprising the internet and other forms of digital information technologies, has become the principal nervous system upon which social and economic activity now depends. It has inspired a revolution in the way **organizations operate** internally and communicate with their **customers** and **suppliers** – reinventing business **models** while increasing the speed and reducing the **cost**s of day-to-day interactions.

Individuals, organizations and countries are now dependent on cyberspace for their everyday activities. Yet there is a complex and shifting **risk** landscape that jeopardizes its **operation**, its **effectiveness** and the trust we place in it. Retail companies have been fined heavily for allowing personal **data** to fall into the wrong hands, and there is now a wider sensitivity about privacy online. Nation states have been accused of stealing intellectual property on an unparalleled scale, particularly from high-tech industries. Many organizations have felt the pain of successful cyber-attacks whether that results in loss of private customer data, **release** of commercially sensitive **information** or intellectual property, or the disruption of critical business **system**s. The **impact**s can be significant – damage to corporate reputation or loss of competitive advantage.

Good **cyber resilience** provides the necessary measures to address these risks effectively, giving organizations the confidence to exploit the digital age to deliver the opportunities for growth and innovation on which they rely. There will always be a balance between opportunity, cost and risk for the board of any organization to manage. Increasingly these trade-off decisions rely on having an informed position on cyber resilience across the organization from the board to those responsible for managing IT and all staff who have access to IT.

1.1 INTENDED AUDIENCE

This publication is relevant to all organizations that operate in the digital age and use systems to manage information – for example, organizations that:

- Rely on networked **information system**s for their operations
- Handle personal data about their customers and their employees
- Possess and employ valuable intellectual property
- Use outsourced **IT service**s
- Provide IT services, either internally or externally.

The primary audience is those who will actively use and reference this publication for their Foundation and Practitioner course/exams and as part of their day-to-day jobs, so these will include:

- Managers who are responsible for staff and **process**es where cyber resilience **practice**s are required – for example, those processing payment card information, sensitive commercial data or customer communications
- **IT service management** teams, IT development and security teams, cyber teams and relevant team leaders – those who operate the information systems that the organization relies on
- IT designers and architects – those responsible for the **design** of the information systems and the **control**s that provide resilience
- The chief information security officer (CISO), the chief security officer (CSO), IT director, head of IT, IT managers.

The introduction of effective cyber resilience requires a top-down approach with strong support from the board and C-suite executives. One of the benefits of the way in which this publication has been written is that it can also be read and understood by others in the business. This additional audience will include:

- Executives and managers who are accountable for or responsible for cyber resilience – for example, the board lead on cyber resilience and those designing suitable **governance** and approving **strategy** and **policy**
- Other heads of lines of business – for example, risk, procurement, HR, marketing/customer management, the chief information officer (CIO).

● Those responsible for information ownership and management and the policies concerning the use of that information – for example, the director of HR for employee personal data, the director of procurement for contractors that process sensitive intellectual property and/or the general counsel/head of legal.

1.2 MAKING CYBER RESILIENCE REAL THROUGH THE USE OF EXAMPLES

As mentioned in the contents summary, this publication uses three fictitious companies to illustrate how to implement good practice and the consequences of getting it wrong. Their story will be developed in colour-keyed text boxes throughout the publication.

Retail example: SellUGoods

The SellUGoods' risk department is responsible for **compliance** with the various relevant regulations, working with the business continuity plans where there is synergy and with the IT department to implement technical controls. Within the risk department, the information security manager wants to know more about the need to prepare for **incident**s and is no longer willing to assume that **preventative controls** will be successful.

Medical example: MedUServ

MedUServ has outsourced all its IT services to a large and reputable provider. The **contract** is managed by the small finance office that also looks after payroll. MedUServ is in the process of negotiating a contract with a new customer, a very large hospital. The contract includes some specific clauses about assuring the cyber resilience of any IT systems where patient data is held. The finance officer has been reading up on the subject.

Manufacturing example: MakeUGoods

One of MakeUGoods' non-executive directors has become concerned about cyber resilience and wants to see whether MakeUGoods is adequately prepared.

1.3 ALIGNING CYBER RESILIENCE WITH BUSINESS OUTCOMES

The purpose of cyber resilience is to ensure that an organization can confidently continue to deliver its business strategy and desired **outcome**s. Cyber resilience measures must therefore be aligned to those outcomes.

The cyber resilience **lifecycle** described in this publication is based on the **ITIL** service management lifecycle, which offers a proven approach to the provision of **service**s that align with business outcomes. Developed in 1989 and famous for the delivery of effective, business-focused IT services, ITIL is now used successfully for the management and delivery of other services, making the ITIL **service lifecycle** a natural choice for the delivery of cyber resilience.

Cyber Resilience Best Practices covers a range of cyber resilience practices and activities across the ITIL lifecycle and outlines how the processes and activities described by ITIL can be used to support an organization's cyber resilience strategy. However, it must be stressed that this guidance is relevant to all organizations, not just those that use ITIL as a basis for their IT **service management**.

1.4 WHAT IS CYBER RESILIENCE?

1.4.1 Evolution from computer security to cyber resilience

The rapid growth in the power of the silicon integrated circuit, since its development in the 1960s, has led to today's modern computer revolution. By connecting computers in what amounts to a single global network, the internet, the impact of the computer revolution has, since the 1990s, been magnified many times further.

As dependence on information and communications has increased, the **scope** of security practice has also had to evolve: from computer security to IT security, then to information security and now to cybersecurity and on to cyber resilience.

Before networks were significant, computer security was largely based on maintaining a physically and technically enforced boundary around the computer, limiting ordinary **users'** access to **resource**s and privileges to the minimum necessary to allow them to complete their tasks. With the advent of early corporate networked IT, computer security continued to rely on a boundary. It was mainly focused on the hardware, software and networking **component**s, and was largely based on an assumption that good technical controls could deliver the required level of security.

With the arrival in the 1980s of personal computing, for the first time the user had a computing device that was not under tight corporate configuration control, and the user became a key part of delivering effective IT security. As users demanded the flexibility and freedom to innovate, they became a significant source of insecurity. Although IT did a good job of managing the security of technology components, it did not provide sufficient coverage of the people and process aspects and often failed to address the security of non-IT business processes. At this point, the topic became known as 'information security', reflecting the value of the information rather than the technology itself. Information security was no longer just something the IT department did: it involved the whole business to varying degrees in the protection of their business processes and information. However, for many organizations, there remained a widespread belief that information security was the sole responsibility of the IT department. The expressions 'cyberspace' and 'cybersecurity' have entered the common lexicon in the past decade, reflecting the impact of the digital age and the recognition that cyberspace has changed the way in which businesses operate. Accordingly, the new term of cyber resilience has also entered the common lexicon. The tendency to leave cybersecurity to the IT department has not, unfortunately, changed for many organizations.

1.4.2 The porous boundary – importance of the external environment

The internet has allowed organizations to reinvent their business practices. **Supply chain**s have become more complex and more closely integrated with the business to offer greater **operational** efficiencies. Organizations trust their supply chains with sensitive information in order to achieve better mutual business understanding, improve **efficiency** and deliver cost savings. Many organizations have outsourced key parts of their operation to partners, or rely on the professional services of lawyers and auditors, thereby sharing their most precious commercial secrets.

Customer engagement with many organizations is largely online, and new organizations exist entirely using this model, for example Amazon. The brand presence of an organization may now be dominated by its online presence. Consequently, security is no longer just concerned with protecting processes, information and data within the perimeter of the business but reaches out across the internet, to the supply chain, to customers, partners and to society as a whole. This does not reduce the need for traditional **information security management**, but it does change the boundaries and scope of what organizations must do in order to achieve a sufficient level of cyber resilience. 'Bring your own device' (BYOD) adds a further twist; consumer products can offer greater functionality and better **performance** than corporate products.

What is BYOD?

Bring your own device (BYOD) is the expression used for the trend for employees to use personal devices for work purposes.

Organizations need to consider the impact of everything they do in this wider context and evaluate how the actions of others might affect their own interests. Commercial organizations need to work together, with governments and with private citizens to achieve cyber resilience.

1.4.3 The internet of things: operating in a hyper-connected world

The '**internet of things**' offers the promise of measuring and controlling many aspects of people's lives: cyberspace is now moving from being purely an information space to controlling the very environment in which people live.

Key definition

The 'internet of things' is a proposed development of the internet in which everyday objects have network connectivity, allowing them to send and receive data.

Oxford English Dictionary

More and more products now have embedded IT or communications that make them resemble a computing device on a network. Within the office environment, routers and printers are an obvious example, but security cameras, door access mechanisms and heating, ventilation and air conditioning (HVAC) systems are appearing on the network; they are sometimes visible from the internet due to poor network **configuration**.

This makes these devices vulnerable to attack and in turn available to be used in launching attacks on other devices. Outside the office, new generations of cars, TVs and smart meters are being connected to networks.

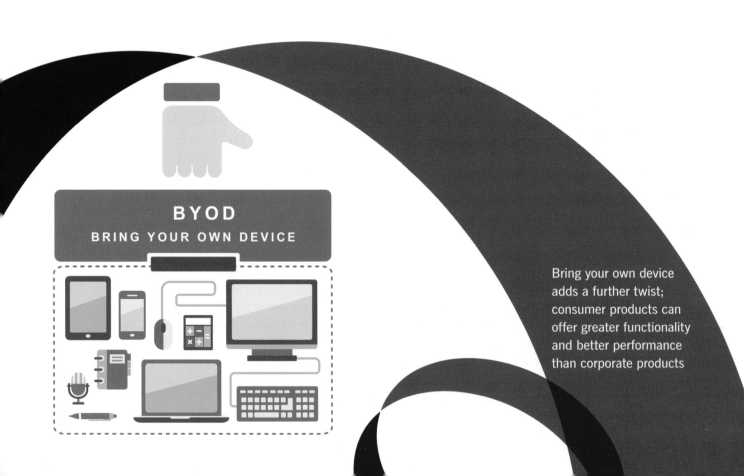

BYOD
BRING YOUR OWN DEVICE

Bring your own device adds a further twist; consumer products can offer greater functionality and better performance than corporate products

The providers of power, water and other critical national infrastructure services represent a more important area of concern as components in the critical national infrastructure, such as water pumping stations and traffic light controllers, are connected to the network and, again, sometimes to the public internet. This is the beginning of the internet of things; it creates a need for cyber resilience in areas of the business that were previously completely unaware of these **requirement**s and contributes to a further increase in the scope of cyber resilience over traditional information security.

1.4.4 Resilience is more than prevention alone

Traditional cybersecurity has tended to focus on prevention, albeit with an acknowledgement of the need to monitor operations of people and technology, reflecting the risk appetite and expectation that proper controls will prevent security incidents. However, many will recognize the **problem** that as the nature of the **threat** increases, agility and innovation can be hindered by ever more stringent security controls.

The threat landscape has developed along with the global internet to the point where the preventative approach is considered inadequate. It is no longer possible to treat IT systems in isolation because they are all connected one way or another to the global digital environment, even if only occasionally, such as when using portable media for routine maintenance, which represents a channel for malicious software.

Key message

Recognizing that 100% risk mitigation is not possible in any complex system, the overarching goal of a risk-based approach to cybersecurity is system **resilience** to survive and quickly recover from attacks and accidents.

Partnering for Cyber Resilience World Economic Forum, January 2013

Any connection can provide the route for malicious software, which can currently defeat the best technical and procedural protection, given sufficient commitment on the part of the adversary. For this reason, cyber resilience cannot rely entirely on defensive procedural and technical controls to prevent an incident: organizations must also make the necessary preparations to detect an incident promptly and correct its effects successfully. This philosophy reflects a change that has emerged in the past few years as the network connectivity offered by cyberspace has become more significant.

The advantage is often with the attacker and, in addition to investing in proportionate preventative security controls, an organization should devote some resources in anticipation of a successful attack in order to detect the incident and correct quickly. This change also demands more effective **risk management** and governance – capabilities which will become critical for successful organizations.

Resilience is defined by the *Oxford English Dictionary* as 'the quality or fact of being able to recover quickly or easily from, or resist being affected by, a misfortune, shock, illness etc.; robustness; adaptability'. In cyberspace, this demands characteristics to prevent an incident and to bounce back after an incident.

Security is defined as 'the state of being free from danger or threat' and involves the protection of what is important, often with more emphasis on prevention and less emphasis on **recovery** from an incident. Both terms – security and resilience – are used with varying scope in expert literature. In this publication, resilience is used to encompass prevention, **detection** and correction.

1.4.5 A definition of cyber resilience

Good cyber resilience is a complete, collaborative approach driven by the board but involving everyone in the organization and extending to the supply chain, partners and customers. To balance the cyber risks faced by the business against the opportunities and competitive advantages it can gain, effective cyber resilience requires an enterprise-wide risk-based strategy that proactively manages the vulnerabilities, threats, risks and impacts on its critical information and supporting **asset**s. It also involves moving away from strategies that seek solely to prevent attacks on assets to ones that include preparing for, and recovering from, a cyber-attack.

Key definition

Cyber resilience is the ability to prevent, detect and correct any impact that incidents have on the information required to do business.

The critical elements of effective cyber resilience include:

● Clear board-level ownership and responsibility for cyber resilience
● The adoption of tailored learning and development for all staff.

This in turn will establish:

● A clear understanding of what the organization's critical assets are, especially with regard to information
● A clear view of the organization's key threats and vulnerabilities arising from their environment, including that of their customers, partners and supply chain
● The adoption of a common language used by all **stakeholder**s in the organization
● An **assessment** of the organization's cyber resilience **maturity** and design of appropriate, prioritized and proportionate plans using best-practice guidance
● An appropriate balance of controls to prevent, detect and correct.

1.4.6 Using the management system to achieve balance in cyber resilience

For effective cyber resilience, an organization must strike the right balance between three types of control **activity**: preventing, detecting and correcting incidents that jeopardize the cyber resilience of the organization:

● Preventative controls are intended to prevent incidents that jeopardize cyber resilience.
● **Detective control**s are intended to identify the occurrence of an incident that jeopardizes cyber resilience, so that the organization can respond appropriately.
● **Corrective control**s are intended to respond to the incident and recover from the situation.

This is illustrated in Figure 1.1. These definitions are expanded in more detail in Chapter 7 of this publication. This type of distinction between controls is reflected in international publications such as the National Institute of Standards and Technology (NIST) Framework for Improving Critical Infrastructure Cybersecurity (more information about this NIST framework can be found in section 8.5.2 of this publication). NIST sets out a sequence of activities comprising 'identify – protect – detect – respond – recover', and the need for balance is implicit in their advice.

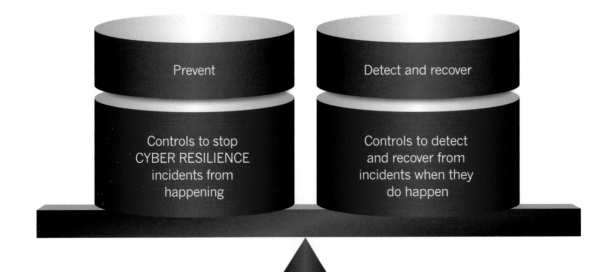

Figure 1.1 Achieving a balance of controls

Figure 1.2 The ITIL
management lifecycle

In selecting the appropriate balance between prevention, detection and correction, an organization must consider whether cost-effective prevention is viable and whether instead rapid detection and correction can be achieved with an acceptable short-term impact on cyber resilience. In determining the degree of controls to be imposed, an organization must reconcile the often competing demands to deliver the needs of the business, including controlling costs and maintaining user convenience while also mitigating risks to cyber resilience. Different balance points will be appropriate for different systems, assets etc.

These decisions must be made as part of a single, coherent risk-based strategy, judged against the risk appetite of the organization.

All organizations have management systems, whether formal or informal, to control their activities. The risk-based design and implementation of cyber resilience controls will be achieved only by delivery through the organization's management system, driven by the organization's **strategic** goals. There are a number of different models available for organizations to base their management system on. *Cyber Resilience Best Practices* will use the management lifecycle of 'strategy – design – **transition** – operation – continual improvement', which is defined by ITIL (more information about the ITIL service lifecycle can be found in section 3.2 of this publication). This is illustrated in Figure 1.2.

Alternative lifecycles can be used equally well and a foremost example is 'context – leadership – planning – support – operation – performance evaluation – improvement', which is defined by **ISO/IEC 27001**:2013. (More information about ISO/IEC 27001 can be found in section 3.1.2 of this publication.)

Chapters 4 to 8 of this guide are structured around a cyber resilience lifecycle based on the stages of the ITIL service lifecycle. Each chapter starts with an explanation of the purpose of that stage of the cyber resilience lifecycle. These are summarized here to provide a context for the rest of the publication:

● **Cyber resilience strategy** Ensures that all cyber resilience activity is based on clearly understood **objective**s and helps to achieve the intent of the organization's governance. The strategy work identifies critical assets – what information, systems and services matter most to the organization and its stakeholders – and it identifies what vulnerabilities and risks they face.

● **Cyber resilience design** Designs a management system and controls that will meet the intention of the strategy. The design work selects appropriate and proportionate controls, **procedure**s and training to prevent harm to what matters most, where practical to do so. It also identifies who has what authority to decide and act.

- **Cyber resilience transition** Moves the output of design into operational use. The transition work will **test** the correct operation of the controls and refine how to detect an incident, to know when something is not right with a critical asset, whether through malicious action or accident, and whether this has resulted from internal or external action.

- **Cyber resilience operation** Operates the controls, and detects and manages cyber resilience **event**s and incidents. This includes continual testing of controls to ensure that they are effective, efficient and consistent. During operation, the organization must be ready to respond when an incident is detected, to follow a well-rehearsed plan, acting in a timely manner to contain the consequences when something goes wrong and to provide a remedy.

- **Cyber resilience continual improvement** Ensures that cyber resilience continues to provide the protection needed in a constantly changing environment. As the organization recovers from an incident, it must learn from its experience, modifying its procedures, its training, its design and even its strategy accordingly.

Cyber resilience has to be organization-wide – a complete, collaborative approach driven by the board but including everyone, extending to partners, supply chain and customers. For large and complex organizations with many internal interdependencies, this will represent a considerable challenge. For organizations comprising different companies with distinct environments or **culture**s, separate initiatives may represent a more practical approach.

1.5 SOME IMPORTANT CHARACTERISTICS OF CYBER RESILIENCE

The world has changed. We all now live and work in the digital age, and cyberspace provides its global fabric. Distance and quantity are no longer barriers to the sharing of information. The rapid growth of computing power and connectivity make what was impossible a decade ago now commonplace, but as organizations become ever more reliant on cyberspace, they need it to be resilient.

Information is increasingly a valuable and sensitive commodity. Individuals are demanding greater controls over their individual privacy because cyberspace makes it much more easily invaded. An organization that is instrumental in the invasion of someone's privacy, even by accident, will suffer increasingly severe financial and reputational consequences. Similarly, organizations are finding that cyberspace makes the theft of their vital intellectual property considerably easier. Organizations that lose their trade secrets will jeopardize their commercial position. Some will go out of business as a result.

1.5.1 No absolutes and no certainties – balancing risks and opportunities

There is no specific point at which absolute cyber resilience is achieved, and there is generally a law of diminishing returns in the extra resilience arising from additional investment balanced against the exposure to risk that remains. An informed choice about the right level of investment to achieve sufficient cyber resilience requires a good grasp of what and where your critical assets are, the relevant vulnerabilities and risks faced by the organization, and the use of effective risk management techniques. This **cost benefit analysis** can be hindered by the intrinsic difficulty of expressing these risks in financial terms.

It is unfortunately the nature of business that security and other resilience controls can add cost and inconvenience to users. Increased cyber resilience may reduce the efficiency and effectiveness of staff, how quickly and easily tasks can be performed and how long it takes for decisions to be made. Furthermore, if an organization seeks to achieve sufficient cyber resilience by placing burdensome controls on its users without explanation of their purpose and importance, it may find those rules circumvented and widely discredited. For example, if staff find their organization's security measures too difficult to access, they will use their own devices to navigate around them. The solution is a combination of risk management and the intelligent application of controls.

Organizations also require a balance between protection of their assets and the ability to respond to innovative ideas. Each organization has to understand this balance according to its particular business needs, considering for example:

- Increased sharing of data can result in new business opportunities and increased efficiency, but can also lead to increased data protection risks.
- Modern technology may enable new business processes, but it will also introduce new vulnerabilities and the need for new security controls.
- Encouraging staff to be creative and imaginative in how they do their work may be vital to revenue and growth but may also demand mitigating controls to manage increased security risks.
- **Outsourcing** and offshoring may result in significant cost reduction for the business, but the risks must be properly understood and some of the cost savings re-invested in order to reduce the consequent security risks.

SellUGoods and BYOD

When most information resources were located in their offices, SellUGoods could invest in strong perimeter controls to protect the organization. Many people now work outside traditional offices, and computers are as likely to be carried around as to be hosted in dedicated data centres. The increase in the use of cloud services and personal phones and laptops to access business data – BYOD – has led to a reduction in the effectiveness of traditional security controls such as locked doors, security guards and network firewalls, and increased the need for more distributed controls, implemented for example on personal phones and laptops.

MakeUGoods and industrial control systems

Even highly secure computing equipment with no connection to other networks and rigid access controls can be subject to security **breach**es. Industrial control systems (ICS) responsible for sensitive factory automation have been compromised by a sophisticated attack that propagated across the internet to infect systems from which ICS updates were loaded onto USB storage devices.

Traditional technology controls were not able to protect the organization from this sophisticated attack. People and **process control**s play a vital **role** in the implementation of cyber resilience.

Domestic devices can be connected to the user's network making it vulnerable to attack

Every organization is unique in determining the optimum balance, though the approach is always the same: understand the risk appetite, establish policy and principles, and then implement and manage appropriate security controls. The details of how controls will be applied to an organization will be quite specific to that organization; there is no single set of controls that is appropriate for every organization in every situation. Risk management will be addressed in detail in Chapter 2.

1.5.2 Common cyber resilience threat sources and their methods

There are many different sources of threat to an organization that can be mitigated by effective cyber resilience (see HMG IA Standards No.1 and No.2, now known as IS 1&2). They can be categorized in many ways, including:

- **Cyber crime** Serious and organized crime, generally motivated by financial reward either directly (stealing money) or indirectly (acquiring the means to steal money). Employees and competitors may also commit these crimes.

- **Cyber 'hacktivism'** Hackers and activists generally motivated by a cause or a belief to achieve a range of outcomes: for example, to cause harm for revenge.

- **Cyber espionage** Nation states, generally motivated to gain strategic and economic advantage in trade, diplomacy or through warfare.

- **Business continuity management** Natural hazards, including the consequences of the acts of nature, accidental consequences of human action such as operator **errors**.

Increasingly, these different threat sources exchange techniques and tradecraft or build on one another's actions to enact more damaging, sophisticated attacks. In one example a large number of usernames and passwords for a UK supermarket were used to perpetrate a fraud. These had been discovered simply by trying usernames and passwords that had been obtained from security breaches at other organizations. In this case, the combination of weak protection of usernames and passwords combined with the reuse of passwords by users helped criminals to compromise the more secure systems of the supermarket. This illustrates how incidents can comprise a sequence of activities known by some as a 'kill-chain'. Also, any attacker can cause unintended consequences and collateral damage through their acts, such as thieves who steal cable and disrupt the rail network, causing massively disproportionate unintended economic harm to the wider economy.

Within the cyber environment, there are many techniques that can be used by attackers. These too can be categorized in different ways, including:

- **Malicious software** Known by many names, such as viruses, worms, trojans and rootkits, having subtle distinctions of method but with a common goal of causing the device (phone, tablet, PC, **server**, network device, printer etc.) to perform a malicious action that may be covert and persistent. Some are used to collect information such as bank account details or usernames and passwords; some simply cause damage and loss of service; others may demand money to **restore** encrypted or deleted data; some are used to create botnets.

- **Hacked websites** A perfectly legitimate but vulnerable website may be modified covertly so that the browser of an unwitting visitor will execute hidden malicious code, achieving the same outcome as above. Many browsers will warn users that they have asked to visit an infected site, where this is known.

- **Botnets** These are groups of computers that are performing a common malicious, often covert action. The name derives from a 'robot network' of computers. Controlled by a remote 'command and control centre', botnets are often used in 'distributed denial of service' attacks or to send massive volumes of spam email.

- **Denial of service attacks** These burden and try to overwhelm a legitimate service, such as a website, with a large number of pointless messages to render it incapable of normal operation. A distributed denial of service (DDoS) attack uses a large number of different machines to mount the attack, usually by means of a botnet.

- **Socially engineered attacks** Phishing is a common form of this type of attack, attempting to trick a user into trusting a message and then performing an action to the attacker's benefit. For example, an email claiming to be from a bank might ask for **authentication** credentials. Fake websites, twitter feeds etc. can also be used. Spear-phishing is a sophisticated form of phishing in which the social engineering is targeted at a specific individual using research, often from social media.
- **Network penetration** This is the traditional form of attack as portrayed in popular media in which access is gained across a network to systems, defeating the authentication. This may employ password-guessing, based on lists of stolen passwords, or using knowledge obtained through other means such as simple deception over the telephone, persuading a user to reveal their password.

1.5.3 The insider – usually accidental, sometimes malicious, often damaging

A large proportion of techniques for malicious action in cyberspace rely on deception of a legitimate user at some point: for example, responding to a convincing phishing email. Almost all attacks can be assisted by an insider and some attacks can only be conducted by an insider.

Furthermore, most technically based attacks will seek to masquerade as a user at some point and to operate using the user's authentication credentials within the systems being attacked, in order to avoid detection. Clearly, there is a limit to the protection that purely technical measures can offer to prevent the legitimate user performing malicious acts, whether unwittingly malicious or intentional. However, measures to detect such acts and **alert** management should be proportionate and effective. For example, if a colleague makes an unusual request for access to contract negotiation information, the organization's culture should encourage a challenge to that request.

Pre-employment screening of employees where possible, an effective security culture, training and awareness, continuing personnel security and corresponding arrangements for contractors, partners and suppliers collectively provide controls for reducing the exposure to the insider threat. (For more information on the insider threat, see the Centre for the Protection of National Infrastructure (CPNI) advice pages at www.cpni.gov.uk)

1.5.4 Legal and regulatory requirements

There are many different laws and regulations pertinent to the information that an organization handles. Its cyber resilience framework will form a central part of the organization's compliance measures. These are quite likely to be preventative controls, required to reduce the risk of penalty. Those controls may also overlap with controls an organization needs in order to manage its other business risks.

An organization must take professional legal advice to identify all prevailing laws and regulations. These examples serve to illustrate their range:

- Country-specific laws such as HIPAA (the US Health Insurance Portability and Accountability Act) or the European Data Protection Directive (enacted into law slightly differently in each EU country, for example as the UK Data Protection Act).
- Extra-territorial regulations. Some laws affect organizations outside the country where the legislation was enacted. For example, the **Sarbanes-Oxley Act** is a US federal law that affects organizations which have registered securities with the US Securities and Exchange Commission. In practice, this means all organizations that are listed and traded on a stock exchange in the USA, even if they are based in other countries. Although this act is about financial controls, it has significant impact on cyber resilience since it requires controls to ensure the **integrity** of financial **record**s.
- Industry-specific regulations such as the payment card industry regulations (PCI-DSS), which are enforced by the credit card industry to ensure that retailers provide suitable controls to protect credit card data.

1.5.5 Characteristics of confidentiality, integrity and availability (CIA)

At the core of information security are the three main characteristics of **confidentiality**, integrity and **availability** of information, which confer requirements on information systems and processes. These characteristics apply equally to cyber resilience.

Key message

The payment card industry data security standard (PCI-DSS) was developed to encourage and enhance cardholder data security and facilitate the broad adoption of consistent data security measures globally. PCI-DSS provides a baseline of technical and operational requirements designed to protect cardholder data. PCI-DSS applies to all entities involved in payment card processing – including merchants, processors, acquirers, issuers and **service provider**s, as well as all other entities that store, process or transmit cardholder data (CHD) and/or sensitive authentication data (SAD).

PCI-DSS Requirements and Security Assessment Procedures, Version 3.0, November 2013

1.5.5.1 Confidentiality

Confidentiality is the most common characteristic associated with security in the minds of many people: 'keeping a secret' or 'having a private conversation' are everyday examples of the need for confidentiality. Cyber resilience relies on maintaining the confidentiality of critical information. For example, the loss of confidentiality of commercially sensitive pricing information in merger talks could damage an organization's ability to secure an **agreement**.

Key definition

Confidentiality is a characteristic of information that ensures it is not made available or disclosed to unauthorized entities. Confidentiality, integrity and availability are the three core characteristics which confer requirements on information security systems and processes.

Any portable media used represents a channel for malicious software

1.5.5.2 Integrity

The integrity of information is the **quality** of it being correct: integrity is important for a user to be able to trust and act on the information. Cyber resilience relies on the integrity of critical information being maintained. For example, loss of integrity of information controlling an industrial process could jeopardize the integrity of the process that uses that information and cause significant harm – even loss of life. The Sarbanes-Oxley Act places demands on the integrity of an organization's financial data.

Key definition

Integrity is a characteristic of information that ensures it is accurate and can only be modified by authorized personnel and activities.

1.5.5.3 Availability

Availability means that the information can be used when required: the information system will process the information and the user can trust that it will be there when needed. Cyber resilience relies on availability of information. For example, if the medical results of an urgent test are not available when required, harm or loss of life could result.

Key definition

Availability is a characteristic of information that ensures it can be used when needed by authorized persons.

1.5.6 Authentication, non-repudiation and links to privacy and data protection

There have been a number of suggested extensions to the three characteristics described in section 1.5.5: in particular, authentication and **non-repudiation**.

Key definition

Authentication is **verification** that a characteristic or **attribute** which appears to be true, or is claimed to be true, is in fact true: for example, that a specific user is who they claim to be.

1.5.6.1 Authentication

To take a simple example, authentication concerns establishing a person's **identity**, often using a username and password. The password is a secret that should be known only to the parties who use it. There are many issues with the management of traditional passwords, and there are very large numbers of staff who still use passwords as their only means of authentication. There are alternative authentication methods but these can be difficult to implement and manage.

Cyber resilience depends on effective authentication. If implemented badly, authentication by demanding knowledge of a user's identity can convey more information about that user to the other party than is absolutely necessary, which can invade their privacy. Authentication should allow one party to establish the validity of the claim made by the other party: for example, that they have the means to pay for a service or that they are old enough to enter a contract. It should not require access to needless detail, for example about their wider purchasing power and past purchases, their gender or age. As people do more online, companies and governments can build up a picture that might constitute an invasion of privacy.

Key definition

Non-repudiation is providing undeniable proof that an alleged event actually happened or an alleged action was actually carried out, and that this event or action was carried out by a particular entity.

1.5.6.2 Non-repudiation

Non-repudiation refers to someone being unable to deny (repudiate) having done something: for example, posting a message or sending an email.

Cyber resilience can depend on effective non-repudiation controls: for example, ensuring that a purchaser cannot deny that they made a purchase and thereby defraud an online vendor.

Non-repudiation is closely associated with authentication but concerns the persistent data that parties hold concerning **transaction**s. As more and more transactions move to the internet, this becomes increasingly important.

Clearly there is a balance between the legitimate need for authentication and non-repudiation on the one hand and the reasonable expectation of privacy and data protection on the other. Many countries have laws or regulations about privacy and data protection, which dictate in particular the **rights** of individuals regarding the confidentiality of their personal information. To some extent this is simply legal and regulatory enforcement of confidentiality of personal data, but many organizations have stringent data protection requirements which can have as much impact on a cyber resilience **programme** as the protection of corporate secrets.

1.5.7 The security incident – when things do go wrong

It is no longer practical and realistic to put in place sufficient control measures to guarantee to prevent a breach of information security, though effective preventative controls will reduce the probability. Even a single security incident can have a high cost to financial wellbeing, to reputation and to the careers of an organization's most senior executives. In extreme cases, it can threaten the survival of the organization.

Most organizations will suffer many low-level information security incidents. It is important to reduce the impact of a breach by having adequate controls to detect and correct the breach promptly with a scaled response and well-exercised **escalation** procedures. This prompt response and a focus on apparently low-level breaches can also help to reduce the damage from more advanced persistent malicious activity, which will manifest subtle indicators for vigilant operators and users. The corrective controls and **incident management** response must be aligned with the business continuity planning activities for information assets and corresponding information services. It is also important to have in place incident management procedures that include senior managers who have been trained and have regular exercises in incident management, including management of the press and protection of the organization's reputation.

1.6 WIDER BENEFITS OF CYBER RESILIENCE – BUILDING TRUST

Good cyber resilience can provide significant benefits beyond mitigation of threats and consequent reduction in exposure to risk.

Some customers will ask for **certification** to the international information security management **standard** ISO/ IEC 27001 before they will allow an organization to bid for work. Compliance to the PCI-DSS standard is a prerequisite for an organization processing payment cards such as credit cards. However, there is as yet no universal and ubiquitous standard for cyber resilience that can be applied without expert judgement. It is possible to be compliant with the best-designed standard and still suffer a cyber-incident. Equally, an organization will want to look beyond the bald assertion that a partner or supplier is compliant with a particular standard. Good cyber resilience demands, amongst other things, good governance, good risk management, a good understanding of data ownership and effective incident management. Assessment of these characteristics demands experience and judgement.

The benefits of a well-run organization with these characteristics extend beyond mitigating risks arising from cyberspace. Similarly, organizations that develop management systems based on **best practice** such as ITIL are likely to **optimize** the value that they create for their customers and increase their competitive advantage through a more effective operation.

1.7 HOW TO ACHIEVE A SUFFICIENT LEVEL OF CYBER RESILIENCE

1.7.1 Information – the life blood of the organization

The first step to achieving sufficient resilience in an organization's use of cyberspace is to understand what information it holds and to identify what needs to be protected, in **priority** order. Every organization has valuable information that must remain confidential, whether intellectual property, employee personal data or sensitive commercial agreements. Some organizations will have information whose integrity is important, such as industrial process control instructions. Similarly, the availability of near real-time medical data in an operating theatre is vital. An organization should not seek to protect all information to the same degree, and it will have a different appetite for particular risks to particular categories of information. There may be tensions and trade-offs to be made. This discussion must involve the business, not just the technology teams, and organizations may find it helpful to assign ownership of information assets to those parts of the business for which the information is most vital. For example, the director of HR may be the best placed to identify critical HR information, to decide how it is labelled and handled in a way that achieves the right balance of cyber resilience against cost and user inconvenience.

1.7.2 Business awareness and understanding

Over the course of the evolution from computer security to cyber resilience, the community of stakeholders has broadened massively, yet in many organizations the key policy decisions regarding information security activities are still delegated to the IT department. Cyber resilience requires the active participation of the business in the same way that the business manages the balance of other risk-benefit choices.

For many organizations, this involvement in a subject hitherto left to the IT department still needs to be explained to the business in a conscious programme of business **change**, using a compelling narrative. Part of that change includes putting in place the effective governance arrangements necessary to achieve sufficient cyber resilience, which will bring the consideration of risk-benefit choices into the mainstream of business decision-making. This requires a top-down approach with strong support from the board. It also requires close alignment with an organization's risk management process. In a large organization, there may be a group risk **function** while in a small organization this may be implicit in the general governance activities.

Delivery of effective cyber resilience requires attention to all aspects of how an organization's operation handles its information, including its customers, suppliers and partners. This means agreeing requirements for proportionate cyber resilience preventative controls, detective controls and corrective controls with every supplier, and through them with their own suppliers. Addressing these needs requires the close cooperation of an organization's procurement function. Rarely should an organization demand precisely the same cyber resilience requirements from all its suppliers, as this will be disproportionate and will increase costs and hidden risks, particularly when dealing with small and medium enterprises.

Most organizations are themselves part of someone else's supply chain and are likely to be obliged to have in place equivalent arrangements. Many organizations will hold **client** information, some of which can be very sensitive and its loss very damaging: organizations expect their suppliers to look after their information, just as their customers expect them to look after theirs. Addressing these needs may require the close cooperation of an organization's sales and marketing function.

Cyber resilience can also benefit from cooperation between organizations. For example, when financial institutions share information about the activities of attackers, it helps them to mount effective defences. If each bank has to detect and analyse the latest cyber-attack for itself, the attackers will have greatly increased success. Such business-to-business cooperation is often facilitated by government agencies.

Stakeholders

Cyber resilience should involve many different stakeholders, both internal to the organization and external. As discussed in this section, these stakeholders include:

- Governors and board members who represent the interests of the owners of the organization
- Risk management or compliance management departments who must ensure that risks to information are well managed
- Everybody within the organization who owns, or uses, information
- IT departments or any other parts of the organization that manage information on behalf of others
- Customers, clients, or other people or organizations who entrust their information to the organization with an expectation that it will be well managed
- Partners or suppliers who process information on behalf of the organization
- Competitors and other organizations operating in the same industry who may wish to share information about threats and vulnerabilities
- Government and regulatory authorities who expect the organization to conform to legal and regulatory frameworks.

1.7.3 Cyber resilience relies on people, process and technology

Cyber resilience relies on the right balance between people, processes and technology as illustrated in Figure 1.3. A common mistake is to become over-reliant on technology and neglect the vital contribution to cyber resilience of well-informed people and well-designed processes. Weaknesses in one area, for example technology, can be mitigated in other areas, for example with stronger process or people controls.

The three must be considered so that the components of cyber resilience fit together in a complementary way, without gaps. Cyber resilience will also rely on physical security and personnel security measures to ensure completeness.

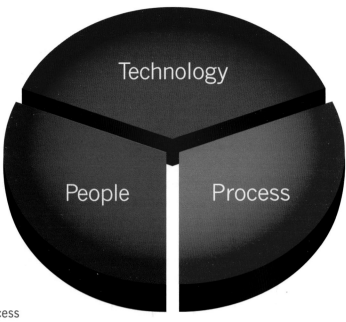

Figure 1.3 The right balance of people, process and technology

1.7.3.1 People and cyber resilience

The nature of most threats to cyber resilience will involve a legitimate user at some point. An ill-informed user can represent a **vulnerability** through their unwitting actions. Providing tailored training and improving awareness reduces this likelihood and delivers further cyber resilience through improved user vigilance – being aware of potential incidents and acting promptly to remediate.

Cyber resilience should be a consideration for any individual who handles information using technology associated with their organization – that covers just about everybody to some degree. Depending on the nature of the organization, its users may be employees, clients, suppliers or members of the public, over whom it will have varying degrees of influence.

Within an organization, the people providing leadership, governance and management have a unique and vital role in improving and maintaining cyber resilience. They will require their own tailored programme of education and awareness-raising.

1.7.3.2 Processes and cyber resilience

The processes of an organization include the formal 'rule book' and the implicit 'how we do things here'. Some organizations are run strictly according to detailed rules, while others operate under loose guidance against a set of principles or values. Designing and implementing suitable processes to deliver cyber resilience must take into account the culture of the organization. The nature of the processes must also reflect the organization's risk appetite and consciously adjust the balance between reducing risks to cyber resilience and reducing efficiency and convenience. Frequently, a risk can be reduced by restricting users' flexibility and freedom in the manner in which a job is done. There is a tendency for those charged with reducing risks to do just this. Whilst this choice is not always a zero-sum game, the business may frequently have to make a conscious trade-off between on the one hand taking an unpopular action to mitigate a risk and on the other hand accepting the risk. These choices should be made with awareness of their effect on the entire business.

Cyber resilience will be a consideration for any process that involves handling of information using technology – and that covers just about every activity in most organizations today.

1.7.3.3 Technology and cyber resilience

The history of cyber resilience, starting in computer security, means that many organizations will expect the IT department to be entirely responsible for all technology measures to deliver cyber resilience, which is not a sufficient strategy. In a manufacturing plant, it will include the industrial control systems and involve engineers who have previously not been concerned with cyber resilience.

It extends to employees' own devices where BYOD is permitted, and to clients' and suppliers' equipment where they share data. For a bank with public-facing systems the end-user devices used by the general public may be poorly maintained with out-of-date software and infected with malicious code. With the proliferation of consumer and industrial devices now connected to the internet, the scope of technology for inclusion in cyber resilience is widening rapidly.

1.8 SCOPE OF THIS PUBLICATION

This publication covers all aspects of cyber resilience. It provides organizations with a methodology for its implementation but does not provide detailed and prescriptive instructions on the implementation of individual cyber resilience controls. The choice of specific controls depends on the risks arising from the nature of the particular business, the environment in which the business is operating and other factors described in this first chapter. For proportionate cyber resilience measures, effective risk management is a key foundation.

1.9 INTRODUCTION QUESTIONS

Here are some of the critical questions you should address during the journey to cyber resilience best practice.

1. Who is responsible for cyber resilience in your organization, covering the complete business context with an effective balance of people, process and technology? If that overall role is not assigned, who should it be in your view and how can you communicate the need for action, using language the board will understand and respond to? Who are your allies? Who shares your concern about this topic?

2. In order to prioritize your cyber resilience activities, how well do you know what comprises your organization's critical information and where it is located? If you do not know, who does?

3. What is the top threat to information and cyber-enabled activities in your organization? How do you keep on top of the latest threat picture for your organization?

4. How well do your board and senior management embrace the concept of risk management for cyber resilience, accepting that there are no certainties? If there is still a view in your organization that the IT department is responsible for preventing information breaches and consequent loss in business performance, what steps should you take to remedy this?

For a bank with public-facing systems, the end-user devices used by the general public may be poorly maintained with out-of-date software and infected with malicious code

2

Risk management

This chapter covers:
- Management of Risk
- Assets, threats, vulnerabilities and risks
- Actions to address risks and opportunities

2 Risk management

Management of cyber resilience is largely about managing risks: identifying things that might happen, assessing how likely they are to happen and what impact they might have, and deciding what action to take. This action typically includes implementing balanced controls to prevent incidents where possible, detect incidents that couldn't be prevented and take corrective action to protect the business where needed. People usually think of risks as being possible negative outcomes, due to something bad that may (or may not) happen, but there are also positive risks due to good things that may (or may not) happen. An example of a risk with a negative outcome is that a thief might break into the office and steal some valuable equipment. An example of a risk with a positive outcome is that an investment in a new business opportunity may result in the positive outcome intended. This uncertainty results in a need for attention and formal risk management. Something that is certain to happen or has already happened is not a risk, and risk management is not an appropriate response. Managing risks requires identifying, understanding and controlling exposure to risks which may have an impact on **business objectives**.

Every organization manages its risk, but not always in a way that is visible, repeatable and consistently applied to support decision-making. In the worst case, risk management might be completely informal, based on organizations making poorly judged decisions or acting irrationally without considering the costs and benefits of the actions they are taking. The purpose of formal risk management is to enable better decision-making based on a sound understanding of risks and their likely impact on the achievement of objectives. An organization can gain this understanding by ensuring that it makes cost-effective use of a risk framework that provides a well-defined approach for managing risks. Decision-making should include determining any appropriate actions to manage the risks to a level deemed to be acceptable by the organization.

Each organization will have a different tolerance for risk, and it is the responsibility of the board of directors (or equivalent) to define the risk appetite and the approach to be taken to managing risk.

A number of different methodologies, standards and frameworks have been developed for risk management. Some focus more on generic techniques widely applicable to different levels and needs, while others are specifically concerned with risk management relating to important assets of the organization in the pursuit of its objectives. Some of these methodologies are described in Table 2.1.

Each organization should determine the approach to risk management that is best suited to its needs and circumstances, and it is possible that the approach adopted will leverage the ideas reflected in more than one of the recognized standards and/or frameworks.

Table 2.1 Risk management methodologies

Management of Risk (M_o_R®)	Framework for managing risk at all levels through an organization, to help the organization take informed decisions (see section 2.1 for more information on M_o_R).
ISO 31000	International standard defining risk management principles and **guidelines**. Defines a risk management process at a high level. Unlike many other international standards it is intended to be adopted and adapted and there is no certification to this standard.
ISO/IEC 27001	International standard for an **information security management system**. This is not a risk management standard, but it includes many requirements relating to risk management. The risk management approach described in section 2.3 is aligned with the requirements in ISO/IEC 27001.
NIST Framework for Improving Critical Infrastructure Cybersecurity	This US framework describes itself as 'a risk-based approach to managing cybersecurity risk'. The NIST framework is described in section 8.5.1. The risk management approach described in section 2.3 is similar to the approach described in the NIST framework.
COBIT 5	COBIT 5 is a business framework for governance and management of enterprise IT. Although it is not about risk management, it includes aspects of risk management at many levels of the framework. More information about COBIT 5 can be found in section 3.1.7.

Many of these methodologies, standards and frameworks cover a much broader scope than just risk management, and more detail about these is provided elsewhere in this publication. M_o_R is solely concerned with **management of risk**, and is further described in section 2.1.

2.1 MANAGEMENT OF RISK

Management of Risk (M_o_R) is intended to help organizations put in place an effective framework for risk management. This will help them make informed decisions about the risks that affect their strategic, programme, **project** and operational objectives.

M_o_R provides a route map of risk management, bringing together principles, an approach and a process with a set of interrelated steps and pointers to more detailed sources of advice on risk management techniques and specialisms. It also provides advice on how the principles, approach and process should be embedded, **review**ed and applied differently depending on the nature of the objectives at risk.

The M_o_R framework is based on four core concepts:

- **M_o_R principles** Principles are essential for the development and maintenance of good risk management practice. They are informed by corporate governance principles and the international standard for risk management, ISO 31000: 2009. They are high-level and universally applicable statements that provide guidance to organizations as they design an appropriate approach to risk management as part of their internal controls.

- **M_o_R approach** Principles need to be adapted and adopted to suit each individual organization. An organization's approach to the principles should be agreed and defined within a risk management policy, process guide and strategies.

- **M_o_R process** The process is divided into four main steps: identify, assess, **plan** and implement. Each step describes the inputs, outputs, tasks and techniques involved to ensure that the overall process is effective.

- **Embedding and reviewing M_o_R** Having put in place an approach and process that satisfy the principles, an organization should ensure that these are consistently applied across the organization and that their application undergoes continual improvement in order for them to be effective.

There are several common techniques which support risk management, including a summary risk profile. A summary risk profile is a graphical representation of information normally found in an existing risk register, and helps to increase the visibility of risks. For more information on summary risk profiles and other M_o_R techniques, see *Management of Risk: Guidance for Practitioners* (OGC, 2010).

2.2 ASSETS, THREATS, VULNERABILITIES AND RISKS

In the world of cyber resilience, we use the terms assets, threats, vulnerabilities and risks with very specific meanings. It is important to understand these terms when managing risks.

2.2.1 Assets

Assets are things that have value to an organization. An organization must determine if (and how) to protect them. Assets might be IT systems, people, information, business processes, intellectual property or anything else which has a value. An asset can be a physical thing like a building, or it can be an intangible thing such as a company's reputation. If it has a value to the organization then it is an asset that should be suitably protected.

Examples of assets that might need to be protected include:

- A tablet computer on the kitchen table
- Credit card data stored on a PC
- Confidential patient information stored on a server in a hospital
- A bank debit card that allows cash to be withdrawn from a bank account.

The value of an asset is not fixed: it depends on how the organization uses the asset. For example, a computer that is used by passengers to browse the internet in an airport may have a much lower value to the business than an identical computer that performs a vital function in the air traffic control centre. Note that the value of the asset that we are discussing here is not the same as the financial value that might be recorded in a **fixed asset register**. The value here refers to the ability of the asset to produce an outcome for the business.

2.2.2 Threats

The formal definition of a threat introduces the concept of a vulnerability, which we will discuss in the next section. Informally, a threat is a circumstance or event that might have an impact on an asset. This impact could vary from complete destruction of the asset, to the ability to obtain a copy of the asset, or the ability to modify the asset (see Figure 2.1). Threats to an information asset are usually considered in terms of their potential impact on the confidentiality, integrity or availability of the asset (see section 1.5.5 for explanations of confidentiality, integrity and availability).

Examples of threats might include:

● A burglar might steal from someone's home.
● A criminal organization might send large numbers of emails containing links that download malware when they are clicked.
● Someone might buy a server that is no longer needed from an organization and discover confidential data on the disk drive.
● A thief might watch someone using an ATM, hoping to steal from them.

Threats exploit vulnerabilities to have an impact on assets.

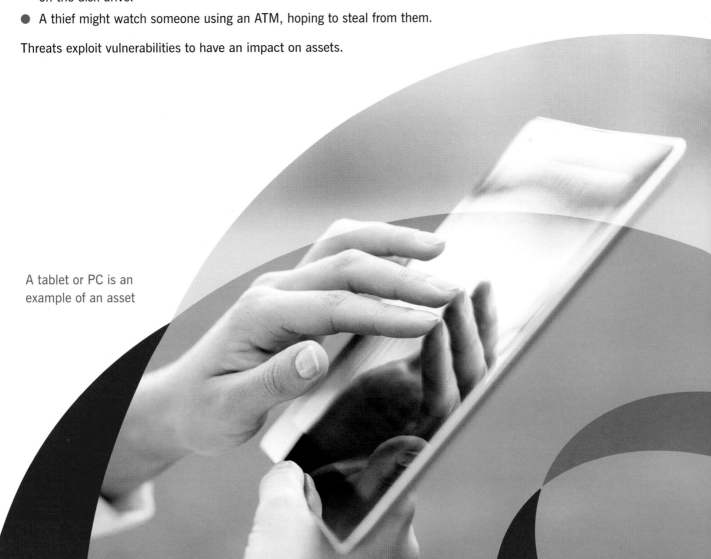

A tablet or PC is an example of an asset

2.2.3 Vulnerabilities

A vulnerability is a flaw or weakness in security protection that can be exploited by a threat, allowing an attack to succeed. By managing vulnerabilities people are able to reduce the likelihood or impact of threats.

> ## Retail example: SellUGoods
>
> Vulnerabilities that could be exploited by criminals attempting to steal payment card data from the customer-facing website at SellUGoods include:
>
> ● Vulnerable software due to patches for the website not being kept up to date
>
> ● Insufficient security training for staff who create website code
>
> ● Weak website software due to lack of code reviews to detect weaknesses in website code.
>
> The following examples of vulnerabilities correspond to the sample threats above:
>
> ● Leaving the kitchen window open provides a thief with easy access to burgle your home
>
> ● Out-of-date anti-virus software allows downloaded malware to successfully take over a PC
>
> ● Lack of encryption allows someone with physical access to a disk drive to access all of the information on that drive
>
> ● Lack of awareness of the risk of shoulder surfing results in a debit card PIN being entered without attempting to hide the keys being pressed, so the person standing behind can see the PIN.

Key message

There is not a simple **relationship** of one threat and one vulnerability for each asset. Each asset could be compromised by many different threats, and each of these threats could exploit a range of different vulnerabilities.

2.2.4 Risks

A risk is a possible event that could cause harm or loss, or affect the ability to achieve objectives. A risk is measured by the probability of a threat, the vulnerability of the asset to that threat, and the impact it would have if it occurred. Risk management considers the value of the asset, the impact on the asset if the threat succeeds, and the likelihood of the threat succeeding based on understanding the vulnerabilities it could exploit.

The examples of risks shown in Table 2.2 are based on the threats and vulnerabilities described above.

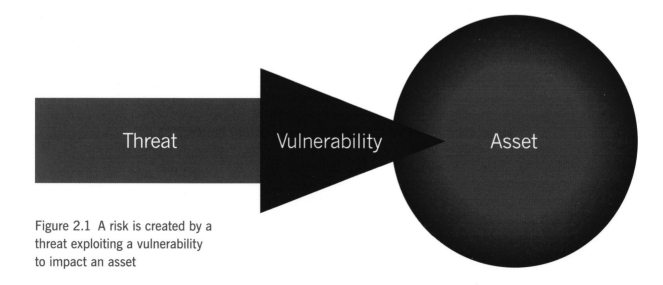

Figure 2.1 A risk is created by a threat exploiting a vulnerability to impact an asset

Table 2.2 Examples of assets, threats, vulnerabilities and associated risks

Asset	Threats	Vulnerabilities	Risks
A tablet computer on the kitchen table	A burglar might steal the tablet	The kitchen window is open	The burglar might climb through the kitchen window and steal the tablet
Credit card data stored on a PC	An email arrives with a link that could download malware	The anti-virus software is out of date	The user may click the link and credit card data may then be transferred to a criminal organization
			The organization's reputation may suffer
		Users have not been trained to never click links on unsolicited emails	The financial regulator may impose a fine
Confidential patient information stored on a server in a hospital	Someone might buy a server that is no longer needed from our organization and discover confidential data on the disk drive	An employee is unaware of the IT policy that states that all data on disk drives must be erased before that equipment is released from use	Newspapers may report that the hospital has not protected patient data properly, and the hospital's reputation may be severely impacted
		Confidential patient information is not encrypted	Patients may sue the hospital for breach of their privacy
A bank debit card that allows cash to be withdrawn from a bank account	A thief might watch someone using an ATM, hoping to steal from them	The bank debit card user is not aware of the risk of shoulder surfing and enters their PIN without sufficient care	If the thief withdraws money from the bank account, the bank may say it is the bank account holder's responsibility since their PIN was used and they may lose the money

2.3 ACTIONS TO ADDRESS RISKS AND OPPORTUNITIES

It is essential to identify and manage risks. This does not mean that an organization has to invest in controls to manage every risk, but it does have to understand the risks being faced, make a decision about how to treat each risk, document the risk treatment plan, and verify that the plan is being followed.

Every organization has a limited **budget** for investing in cyber resilience, and an organization that does not use a formal risk management process is likely to protect against the wrong risks and waste money and resources. **Failure** to protect against actual risks may have a major impact on an organization's continuing existence. Every year thousands of organizations suffer security breaches, and many businesses do not survive as a result of the losses incurred. The National Cyber Security Alliance estimates that '60% of small businesses will close within six months of a cyber attack'. Investing in the right security controls can significantly reduce the risk of a security breach happening.

There are many different approaches to managing risk. Some focus on assets, threats and vulnerabilities, others on more general business risk, or on scenarios that could lead to business impact. Descriptions of some of these approaches can be found in Table 2.1. Every organization should adopt an approach to risk management that is appropriate for its circumstances. Selection of a risk management approach is often a governance decision, and the selected approach may be mandated for use throughout the organization.

The following methodology describes an approach to risk management based on understanding assets, threats and vulnerabilities. This methodology is similar to the approaches described in ISO/IEC 27001:2013 and in the NIST Framework for Improving Critical Infrastructure Cybersecurity. The approach described below is a good methodology for understanding security risks, but if an organization is already making effective use of a different risk management methodology then it might be appropriate to use or adapt this to manage its cyber resilience risks. Whatever approach is used, it should cover all of the activities described here.

There are a number of distinct phases required to address risks, as shown in Figure 2.2 and described below. Figure 2.2 illustrates the activities that are required, the order in which they should be carried out, and the main feedback loops.

2.3.1 Establish context

There are some actions that need to be taken before starting to assess and manage risks. These include:

● Understanding the organization and its context, including any internal or external issues that are already known to be relevant to cyber resilience. This could include asking questions like 'why are we starting a cyber resilience project?' or 'what are we worried about?'

● Understanding the needs and expectations of stakeholders, including legal and regulatory requirements and contractual obligations (see section 1.7.2 for a discussion of stakeholders).

● Identifying the scope of the security management system, and understanding how this maps to the overall management system (see section 3.1 for a discussion of management systems).

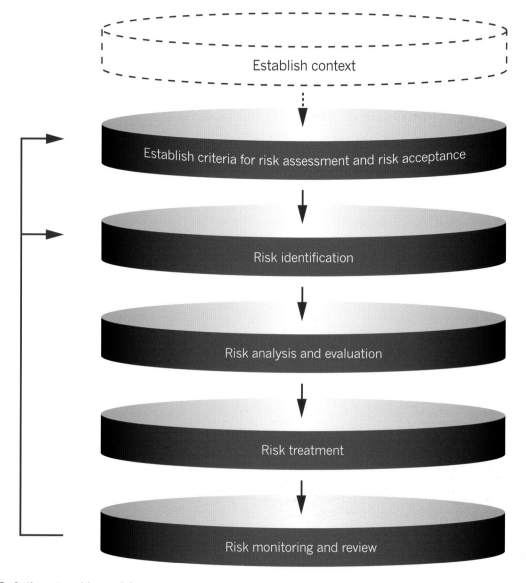

Figure 2.2 Actions to address risks

Many of these actions should be defined and managed as part of the governance of the organization. Chapter 4 looks in more detail at the strategy stage of the service lifecycle, which includes these activities. The context should be re-evaluated on a regular basis to ensure that risk management continues to be aligned with the needs of the organization.

2.3.2 Establish criteria for risk assessment and risk acceptance

Every organization should document criteria to ensure that people carrying out **risk assessment**s use consistent methods.

- **Risk assessment criteria** Define how risk assessments should be carried out.
- **Risk acceptance criteria** Define which risks should be accepted (and which risks therefore require action to be taken to reduce the likelihood or impact of the risk).

Risk assessment criteria should be defined to ensure that assessment results are consistent, that comparisons between assessments are meaningful, and therefore that assessments can be used for ongoing management of security risks.

Cost of security controls

An organization could decide to control access to a building by using turnstiles operated with an ID card and PIN. This would increase security by making it much harder for an intruder to access the building.

The cost of the new system would include:

- Financial cost of the new equipment
- Costs of the implementation project and team
- Costs of staff awareness communication and training
- Increased time for staff to arrive at work in the morning due to queues at the turnstiles
- Ongoing cost of resetting PINs when users forget them
- Ongoing cost of maintaining the turnstiles and card readers.

Using PIN and ID card access to an organization's office requires the involvement of all staff members

Risk **acceptance** criteria should be defined to support the governance goals of the organization and to ensure consistent decisions regarding what risks are considered acceptable.

It is not possible for any organization to completely eliminate all risk. Even after extensive controls have been put in place there will always be some residual risk. Security controls also have costs. This is not limited to the cost of implementing the control itself. There is also often the cost of working with the effect of the control – for example it may slow down a business process or require more people to be involved in an activity.

Each organization needs to consider the level of risk that it is prepared to accept, and to document its risk appetite and risk acceptance criteria in a form that people actually carrying out risk management can use. This will help to ensure consistent decision-making that is aligned with the needs of the organization.

2.3.3 Risk identification

Risk identification starts by identifying the assets that need to be protected, and the ownership of those assets. The scope of the management system should help to identify which assets must be considered (see section 3.1 for a discussion of management system scope). It is important to remember that these assets include intangible assets such as business processes and the reputation of the organization, as well as physical assets such as people, IT systems and buildings. Section 6.1 discusses **asset management** in more detail.

Key message
The purpose of cyber resilience risk management is to protect valuable information assets. Start by identifying the assets that need protecting.

Risk identification considers what threats might impact these assets, what controls are already in place to protect the assets, and what vulnerabilities still remain. Consideration is given to threats that might impact the confidentiality, integrity or availability of assets.

Risk identification should use a wide range of inputs to help ensure that all significant risks have been considered. Subsequent steps will establish the significance of risks, but any risks that are missed at this stage are unlikely to be identified later. It is essential to identify an owner for each asset to ensure that decisions are made based on the business value of the asset, and that someone is accountable for understanding that value.

Inputs which could help with risk identification include:

- Outputs of previous risk assessments
- Current or **retired** risks that have been documented on a risk register
- Information about common threats and vulnerabilities provided by vendors, partners or other organizations
- Information about risks that have been identified by other parts of the organization
- Checklists based on standards such as ISO/IEC 27001, the NIST cybersecurity framework, or best practices such as this publication
- Output of technical tools such as firewall logs or reports from intrusion detection tools or intrusion prevention tools
- Interviews with customers.

Each identified risk should be assigned a risk owner, who is accountable for ensuring that the risk is understood and appropriate action is taken.

The list of risks and risk owners should be documented in a risk register, which should include details of the assets, the threats to those assets, and the vulnerabilities that might lead to the threats successfully compromising the assets. This risk register should be maintained to ensure that up-to-date information about risks is available in a consistent form and that the **status** of each risk is always understood.

2.3.4 Risk analysis and evaluation

Risk analysis and evaluation is required for each identified risk.

Risk analysis considers all the available information about the asset, the threat and the vulnerabilities to provide answers to the following questions:

- How likely is the risk to materialize?
- What impact would the risk have on the asset?
- What impact would the risk to the asset have on the business?

Risk analysis can be quantitative or qualitative. Quantitative risk analysis considers financial and other impacts in strict numerical terms. It also uses numerical estimates of probability to result in projections of the actual cost of a risk. This risk is commonly expressed as an **annualized loss expectancy** (ALE), and is calculated by multiplying the **single loss expectancy** (SLE) by the **annual rate of occurrence** (ARO).

ALE is often compared with the cost of mitigating a risk, to provide information that can be used in return on investment (ROI) calculations and to justify investment in suitable controls to modify the risk.

Qualitative risk analysis uses a simple scale, such as high, medium, low, to distinguish different levels of likelihood and impact. Qualitative risk analysis often makes use of a table which is used to derive an overall risk level from levels of impact and likelihood.

Example of a loss expectancy calculation for a retail organization: SellUGoods

SellUGoods Ltd has heard about incidents where customer data has been breached at other retail organizations, and the information security manager has been analysing the potential cost if this happened at SellUGoods.

The calculation for annual loss expectancy is:

ALE = SLE * ARO

where ALE is the annual loss expectancy, SLE is the single loss expectancy, and ARO is the annual rate of occurrence.

In our example:

- The information security manager estimates that the cost of an incident where a large number of payment cards are leaked would be $800 million. This figure includes lost sales, lost share value, the cost of compensating customers and other costs that have been identified in other similar breaches. This is the single loss expectancy, so SLE = $800 million.

- The information security manager has researched the frequency of this kind of data breach, and thinks that every year approximately one large retailer in every 2,000 suffers a data breach of this sort. In other words a retailer like SellUGoods can expect to see a data breach once every 2,000 years. This is the annual rate of occurrence, so ARO = 1/2000 = 0.0005.

- The annual loss expectancy is the average amount that SellUGoods can expect to lose each year. In this case it is calculated, according to the formula above, as $800 million * 0.0005 which gives a value of $400,000.

This figure of $400,000 represents the upper limit of what SellUGoods should consider spending each year to prevent or mitigate this kind of event.

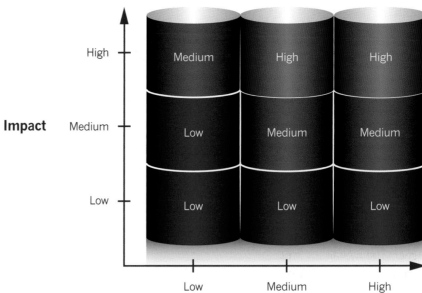

Figure 2.3 Example of a matrix
for defining qualitative risk levels

The output of the risk analysis is a determination of the level of risk, which is documented as part of the risk assessment. In the example in Figure 2.3, something that has a medium likelihood and a high impact would be rated as a high risk. What this means is specific to the organization; something that is high risk in one organization might be medium or low in another. This particular example has a simple high/medium/low scale but some organizations use a five-point scale on each axis of the matrix. There is no 'correct' matrix – it just needs to be used consistently within the organization. Therefore, the output of qualitative risk assessment cannot usually be compared across organizations.

Risk evaluation compares the results of risk analysis with the documented risk acceptance criteria, and then prioritizes risks to ensure that investment is focused on the most important risks.

Qualitative risk assessment requires much less time and effort than quantitative risk assessment, and often provides sufficient information to enable the organization to decide which risks should be addressed.

A combination of qualitative and quantitative approaches may be appropriate for some organizations. This usually involves carrying out an initial qualitative assessment to prioritize risks, followed by a quantitative risk assessment for medium- and high-impact risks, to provide data needed to support the business case for addressing those risks.

> ## Retail example: SellUGoods
>
> If criminals obtained copies of payment card data from SellUGoods the impact would be high.
>
> If SellUGoods did not implement controls to prevent criminals stealing payment card data, then the likelihood of this would be high and therefore the risk would be high.
>
> Even after implementing controls the residual likelihood might be medium, so the risk would still be high. This is likely to be an unacceptable residual risk, so more controls would be needed.

2.3.5 Risk treatment

There are many different things that an organization can choose to do about a risk. It is not always necessary to reduce or eliminate risks: a judgement on what to do will depend on the nature of the risk, the cost of any action required to mitigate the risk, the likelihood and impact of the risk, and the organization's risk acceptance criteria. Actions that can be taken to handle a risk include risk avoidance, risk modification, risk sharing and risk retention, as described in Table 2.3.

Table 2.3 Methods of treating risk

Risk avoidance	Prevent the risk by not carrying out the business activity
Risk modification	Implement controls to reduce the likelihood or impact of the risk
Risk sharing	Reduce the impact by passing some of the risk to a **third party**
Risk retention	Intentionally decide to accept the risk because it is below an acceptable **threshold**

These are described in more detail in sections 2.3.5.1 to 2.3.5.4

The decision about how to treat each risk should be agreed with the risk owner, and documented in a risk treatment plan. There must be appropriate communication about how each risk will be treated. Decisions about who needs to know about each risk should be based on the likelihood and impact of the risk and defined as part of the agreed criteria for risk assessment (see section 2.3.2). Some major risks may need to be discussed at board level, whereas many smaller risks only need to be understood by the assigned risk owner. The overall risk treatment plan should also be communicated, reviewed and approved by someone with appropriate authority.

2.3.5.1 Risk avoidance

Risk avoidance can be achieved by not carrying out the activity that could lead to the risk. For example:

● The risk of data being compromised by a third party could be avoided by never allowing other organizations to have access to sensitive data. This may be difficult and expensive, but in some circumstances it may be appropriate in order to avoid a risk.

● The risk of an investment in a new business opportunity not delivering the required ROI can be avoided by deciding not to invest in the business opportunity. This type of risk avoidance is actually very common when business investments are seen to have significant risk; it is often better to invest in a different opportunity that has lower risk of failure.

Retail example: SellUGoods

SellUGoods may choose to avoid the risk of a third party exposing their payment card data, by only allowing their own staff to have access to this data.

Alternatively they could make use of third parties to do some processing of payment card data, but they would then need additional controls to mitigate this risk.

Risk avoidance can certainly be very effective in removing risks, but it can also result in the organization failing to capitalize on opportunities. Risk avoidance is a common response for managing positive risks such as entering a new market or seizing a new business opportunity, but this can result in significant long-term negative risk if competitors take advantage of these opportunities. This means that organizations must consider alternatives to risk avoidance if they want to be successful.

The purpose of cyber resilience risk management is to balance the risk against the costs and opportunities. It is not possible to eliminate all risk, so some residual risk will have to be accepted; this is why the organization should establish a risk appetite and risk acceptance criteria. Risk can also be a good thing: an organization that takes no risks is unlikely to be competitive or to succeed in the long term.

2.3.5.2 Risk modification

Risk modification involves implementing controls that will change the likelihood or impact of a risk. For a negative risk this will usually be to reduce the threat's likelihood or impact – but remember that risk management also applies to positive risks as well as negative ones, so risk modification could make a positive risk more likely. Controls that reduce the likelihood of a risk are often thought of as cybersecurity controls, whereas controls that reduce the impact of a risk may be seen as cyber resilience measures.

Key definition

Defence-in-depth uses multiple independent security controls to provide **redundancy**. If one control fails, or a vulnerability is exploited, then assets will be protected by alternative controls.

It is common for a threat to require more than one vulnerability before it can successfully compromise an asset. This is why many cyber resilience designs are based on the idea of defence-in-depth, so that if a threat is able to exploit one vulnerability there will be further security controls that can still prevent the risk from occurring, or reduce the impact of the risk if it does occur.

Examples of controls include:

● **Encrypting all confidential data** This reduces the vulnerability of the data to many risks such as theft or accidental disclosure.

● **Acceptable use policies and awareness training** These can be used in many areas, for example to reduce the likelihood of staff following links that would install malware onto PCs.

Risk modification is the most common response to security risks, and many examples of controls that are intended to reduce the likelihood or impact of threats are described throughout this publication.

Retail example: SellUGoods

Some things that SellUGoods could do to modify the risk of criminals stealing payment card data are:

● Ensuring that they comply with the payment card industry data security standard (PCI-DSS)

● Training software development staff in how to prevent SQL injection and buffer overflow attacks

● Carrying out code reviews of all website code

● Ensuring that patches for the customer-facing website are installed very soon after they are released

● Only storing the absolute minimum amount of data and deleting this as soon as it is no longer needed.

2.3.5.3 Risk sharing

Risk sharing may be achieved by insuring against the loss that the risk would cause, or by contractually passing responsibility for the risk to another organization. 'Risk sharing' is sometimes known as 'risk transfer', but 'risk sharing' is a better term as the risk cannot normally be completely passed to a third party. For example, if an organization has fire insurance, this will provide financial compensation when there is a fire, but the fire may still have an enormous impact on the organization.

Many services are designed to transfer risks between organizations. For example, if an organization purchases **IT infrastructure** as a service (IaaS) from another organization, then many of the risks involved in operating that IT infrastructure are also transferred. The organization purchasing the IaaS is charged for the service and effectively pays the other organization to share the operational risks.

Accountability for a risk can never be transferred to a third party: even if the third party has agreed to accept the risk, the outsourcing organization is still accountable for it. This means that the outsourcing organization has to ensure that the third party is managing the risk effectively, and that the contract covers every eventuality. Service providers often word contracts in a way that avoids responsibility for things that the outsourcing organization might think are covered.

2.3.5.4 Risk retention

Risk retention is a deliberate decision to accept a risk without taking any measures to avoid, modify or share it. This may be appropriate for risks that have a very low impact, or a very low probability. The decision to retain a risk should always be based on previously agreed criteria for risk acceptance (see section 2.3.2) and must be clearly documented and communicated to appropriate stakeholders. Retained risks should be documented in a risk register, so that they can be monitored in case the probability or potential impact changes.

When risks have been avoided, modified or shared, it is likely that there will still be some level of residual risk. This residual risk must be compared with the organization's risk acceptance criteria and formally retained, to ensure that sufficient controls have been put in place to meet the organization's governance requirements.

2.3.6 Risk monitoring and review

It is not sufficient to just carry out an assessment, document risk treatments and pass these to people to implement. There must be a process in place to monitor and review risks to ensure that:

● Risk treatments documented in the risk treatment plan are carried out as defined.

● The actual effect of implementing risk treatments is understood, compared with the effect predicted by the risk treatment plan, and any deficiencies are identified and acted on.

● New threats are identified and result in updated risk assessments.

● Residual risks are transferred to a risk register which provides a consolidated view of risks.

● New vulnerabilities are identified and result in updated risk assessments, and new entries in the risk register.

● Changes in the likelihood or impact of specific threats are identified and result in updated risk assessments.

● New, changed or removed assets are identified and added to (or removed from) the risk treatment plan as appropriate.

● Changes in the business environment are understood and result in modified risk assessment criteria or risk acceptance criteria where appropriate.

Risk **monitoring** and review are discussed in more detail in Chapters 7 and 8, as they make a significant contribution to operation and continual improvement.

Many risks will be managed by controls (a risk modification measure), and these controls should be constantly monitored to ensure they are effective, efficient and consistent. There are many different types of control, such as policies, procedures, standards, training and technical controls, and the effectiveness, efficiency and consistency of these controls needs to be verified. In this context:

● Effectiveness is the ability of the control to achieve its purpose.

● Efficiency is a measure of the amount of resource required.

● Consistency is a measure of how completely the control has been applied to all appropriate assets. For example, a required security patch may have been installed on 99% of vulnerable servers, but a threat to the remaining 1% of vulnerable servers may have a major impact.

When security breaches are reported it is very common to discover that controls which should have been in place would have prevented the breach, but lack of verification meant that the organization did not discover that the controls were not consistent until after the breach. This is why it is essential to carry out regular reviews and **audits** of all cyber resilience measures.

2.4 RISK MANAGEMENT QUESTIONS

1. How do you identify the assets that you need to protect? What could you do to identify additional assets that should be within the scope of your cyber resilience management?

2. How do you identify threats and vulnerabilities that might affect your assets? What additional sources of information could you use and how would these help? What else could you do to improve this?

3. How do you record information about cyber resilience risks? What information do you record? What additional information could you record and how would this help?

4. How do you measure the effectiveness of your controls? What improvements could you make in this area?

5. How effective is your risk treatment plan? How could you improve it?

6. Who knows about the cyber resilience risks within your organization? Who should know? What can be done to communicate cyber resilience risks more effectively?

An example of a control: allowing staff to log in to their work network remotely enables them to work outside office hours

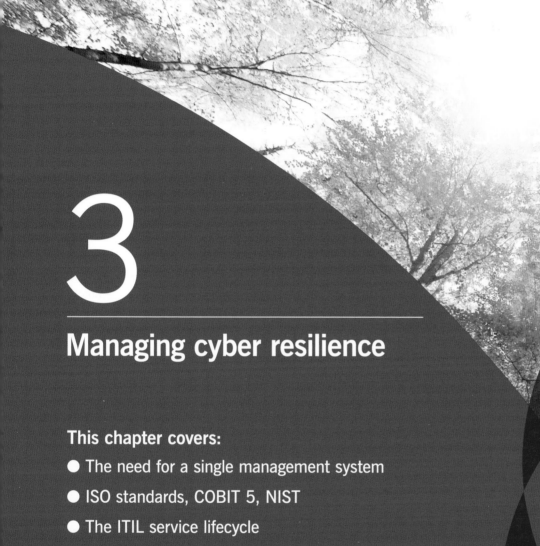

3 Managing cyber resilience

This chapter covers:

- The need for a single management system
- ISO standards, COBIT 5, NIST
- The ITIL service lifecycle

3 Managing cyber resilience

3.1 THE NEED FOR A SINGLE MANAGEMENT SYSTEM

What is a system?

A system could be defined as 'any number of things working together to achieve an overall objective'.

Some systems are based on technology, but when we refer to a 'management system' we are using the word 'system' in a wider context. It includes all the things that are needed to manage and govern what an organization does.

Every organization has a management system that is used to guide and control the work it carries out. This may be a formal management system or simply an informal set of activities, measurements and guidelines that ensure people know what they are supposed to do. There can be multiple management systems if they have different scopes, but only one management system should be responsible for controlling any particular set of activities. This management system must deliver the level of cyber resilience needed by the organization as well as enabling the organization to meet all its other objectives.

The scope can be limited by geography (separate management systems in each territory or continent), by organization design (separate management systems for each **business unit**), or by any other factor that makes sense in the context of the organization. In any case the scope must be well defined, clearly documented and understood by the stakeholders involved. Defining the scope of the management system is one aspect of governance, which should oversee and direct the activities of management.

Typically a management system will include:

- **Governance activities** To evaluate the business environment, to direct management to carry out required activities, and to monitor to ensure that expectations are met. Governance is the highest level in the management system. It specifies and communicates the **mission** and vision of the organization, defines the decision makers and ensures that management decisions taken throughout the organization support the intent of the governing body.

- **Management activities** To plan, build, run and improve the business. Management allocates resources, makes **tactical** and operational decisions and oversees activities to ensure they are carried out efficiently and effectively. Figure 3.1 shows the relationship between governance and management.

- **Policies** Set out management intent and ensure that staff understand what is required of them. There can be many different policies within an organization, each focused on requirements for a specific area.

- **Processes** Document activities, inputs, outputs, interfaces etc. Processes are typically documented using flowcharts and explanatory text, and can be used to guide activities and to identify requirements for tools and other supporting systems.

- **Roles** Define the responsibilities, activities and authorities assigned to people or teams. It is important to distinguish roles from **job descriptions**. One person may carry out multiple roles: for example, a risk manager may also be an information security manager; or one role may be assigned to multiple people: for example, there may be an information security manager in each business unit.

- **Organization design** Defines the structures for directing staff and reporting activity and results throughout the organization.

- **Metrics, key performance indicators (KPIs) and critical success factors (CSFs)** These measure, report, and plan improvements for the management system and for any outputs that are created.

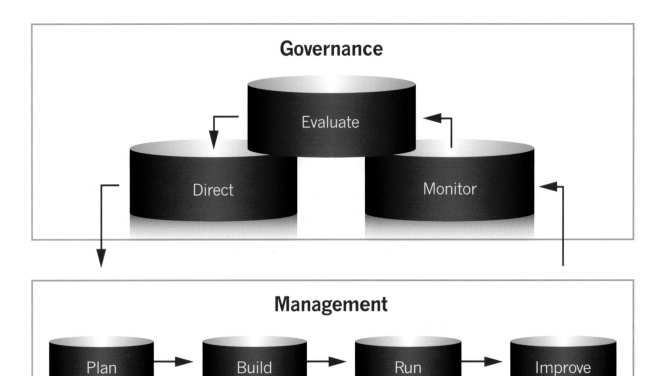

Figure 3.1 Governance and management

There are a number of standards and frameworks that organizations can use to help them design and implement a management system. These standards and frameworks are NOT management systems – they are ideas that can be adopted by organizations as inputs to the design of a management system. Each of these standards and frameworks has a different focus, and it is likely that a combination of these will be needed to achieve the goals of any particular organization. An organization that designs its management system around only one of these is likely to miss some important areas. The best approach to take is to understand all the different standards and frameworks, and then to use ideas from all of them to help design a management system that meets the needs of the organization.

Examples of standards and frameworks that may help organizations to improve how they manage cyber resilience include:

- ITIL
- ISO/IEC 27001
- **ISO/IEC 20000**-1
- **ISO 9001**
- ISO 31000
- ISO 22301
- COBIT 5
- NIST Framework for Improving Critical Infrastructure Cybersecurity
- Management of Risk (M_o_R).

You may recognize some of these frameworks and standards from Table 2.1, where we introduced risk management methodologies. Risk management is one of the areas that should be considered in the design of your management system, but this list includes other standards and frameworks because your management system will need to cover much more than just risk management.

3.1.1 ITIL

Why use ITIL as part of a management system?

ITIL is the most widely accepted approach to managing IT services worldwide. It has support from a large number of organizations that provide training, consulting and supporting tools. Managing IT services well can make a significant contribution to cyber resilience, as many cyber resilience threats involve IT.

ITIL is a best-practice framework for IT service management. It is a very different style of guidance from the international standards described below. ITIL is not an auditable standard, and organizations cannot be certified to show that they comply with ITIL; it is a set of practices that organizations can adopt and then adapt to suit their own particular circumstances. ITIL has extensive adoption, and is the most widely recognized set of practices for managing IT services.

ITIL uses a lifecycle model consisting of five stages of the service lifecycle: **service strategy**, **service design**, **service transition**, **service operation** and **continual service improvement**. This lifecycle model can also be used to help think about the management system needs of cyber resilience, since cyber resilience also requires design to be informed by well-thought-out strategy, transition to take the output of design and implement it into an operational environment, and continual improvement of every aspect to ensure that it remains **fit for purpose**. Chapters 4 to 8 of this guide expand on how the ITIL lifecycle model can be applied to cyber resilience.

More information about the ITIL service lifecycle and the practices that it describes can be found in section 3.2.

3.1.2 ISO/IEC 27001

Why use ISO/IEC 27001 as part of a management system?

ISO/IEC 27001 is commonly used as an approach to information security management in Europe and Asia, and is increasing in popularity in other regions.

Cyber resilience has a wider scope than information security management, but ISO/IEC 27001 can help to manage this core aspect of cyber resilience.

Like other **ISO** standards, ISO/IEC 27001 certification can help to demonstrate information security **capability** to potential customers and partners.

ISO/IEC 27001:2013 defines requirements for information security management systems. It is relevant to any organization that wants to preserve the confidentiality, integrity and availability of information by applying a risk management process. It is an international standard which describes requirements for establishing, implementing, maintaining and continually improving an information security management system.

The ISO/IEC 27001:2013 standard itself is quite short. As an international standard it includes requirements which can be used in an audit to demonstrate that an organization's information security system meets the internationally agreed ISO standard. It describes how an information security management system should operate, and includes sections on scope, normative references, terms and definitions, context of the organization, leadership, policy, planning, support, operation, performance evaluation and improvement.

Half of the ISO/IEC 27001 publication is in an Annex titled 'Reference control objectives and controls' (also known as Annex A) which, as the name suggests, provides a list of suggested information security objectives and controls for reference purposes. These are often used as a checklist to help organizations plan and check their information security controls. More detailed controls can also be found in ISO/IEC 27002:2013, the code of practice for information security management systems.

ISO/IEC 27001 is one of a series of publications that cover many different aspects of information security management. There are more than 20 publications in the ISO/IEC 27*** series, including:

- ISO/IEC 27000: Overview and vocabulary
- ISO/IEC 27002: Code of practice
- ISO/IEC 27032: Guidelines for cybersecurity.

This series of standards is being actively developed, and other publications are due for release.

Like other ISO standards, ISO/IEC 27001 is commonly used in two distinct ways:

- As an audit standard, with certification from an external certifying body, to provide evidence to customers and other stakeholders that the organization's management system is fit for purpose. This may be required by some customers as a condition of being allowed to bid for work, or it may be required by management to provide a competitive advantage.

- As an internal checklist, to ensure that required areas have been considered and that the organization's management system does not have any significant omissions. One common way that ISO/IEC 27001 is used is for organizations to compare their information security controls to the controls listed in the 'Reference control objectives and controls' Annex (Annex A) of the standard, to help them identify potential vulnerabilities.

In practice, many organizations use ISO/IEC 27001 for both of these purposes.

3.1.3 ISO/IEC 20000-1

Why use ISO/IEC 20000 as part of a management system?

ISO/IEC 20000 is an auditable standard for management of IT services. Managing IT services well can make a significant contribution to cyber resilience, as many cyber resilience risks involve IT.

Like other ISO standards, ISO/IEC 20000 certification can help to demonstrate IT service management capability to potential customers and partners.

ISO/IEC 20000-1:2011 defines requirements for an **information technology** service management system. It is relevant to any **IT service provider** that delivers services to customers, whether they deliver these services to external paying customers or to internal customers within their own organization.

ISO/IEC 20000-1 is an international standard for service management systems which describes requirements for the design, transition, delivery and improvement of services. It describes a management system based on the **Plan-Do-Check-Act** (PDCA) methodology. Figure 3.2 shows an overview of a management system based on Plan-Do-Check-Act (see section 8.2.1 for more detail about PDCA). Like ISO/IEC 27001 this standard includes requirements that can be used in an audit to demonstrate that a service provider meets the required standard.

ISO/IEC 20000-1 includes sections on scope, normative references, terms and definitions, service management system general requirements, design and transition of new or changed services, service delivery processes, relationship processes, **resolution** processes and control processes. The processes defined in ISO/IEC 20000-1 are very similar to the processes described in ITIL (see section 3.2), but they are described in less detail; the standard defines requirements for what must be done rather than descriptions of how things should be done.

ISO/IEC 20000-1 is Part 1 of a series of publications that cover many different aspects of IT service management.

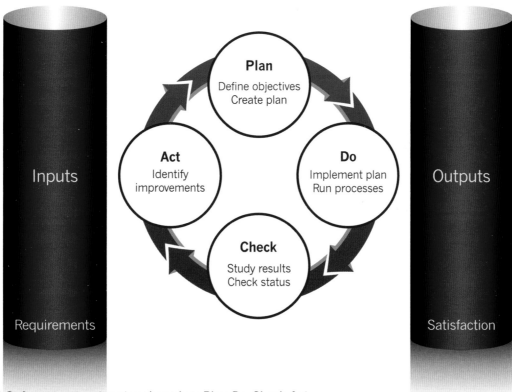

Figure 3.2 A management system based on Plan-Do-Check-Act

3.1.4 ISO 9001

Why use ISO 9001 as part of a management system?

ISO 9001 is an auditable standard for quality management which is appropriate for any size of organization and any industry.

Like other ISO standards, ISO 9001 certification can help to demonstrate quality management capability to potential customers and partners.

ISO 9001:2008 is a customer-focused, process-based **quality management system** based on PDCA principles (see Figure 3.2). It is widely implemented and externally assessed throughout the world. A new version of the standard, ISO 9001:2015, is expected to be published later in 2015. ISO 9001:2008 can be combined or integrated with other management systems such as ISO/IEC 27001.

3.1.5 ISO 31000

Why use ISO 31000 as part of a management system?

ISO 31000 provides guidance on risk management, which is an important aspect of cyber resilience.

ISO 31000:2009 provides principles and generic guidelines on risk management. This international standard is not specific to information security risk, or to IT risk: it can be applied to any type of risk whatever its nature.

ISO 31000 is intended to provide a common approach that can be used by standards dealing with specific risk or industry sectors. Unlike the other ISO standards described here, ISO 31000 is not intended for the purpose of certification and an organization cannot claim to be 'compliant' with this standard.

ISO 31000 describes a process-oriented approach to risk management. This high-level approach to risk management can be combined with reference controls from a standard such as ISO/IEC 27001 to provide a comprehensive approach to risk management.

3.1.6 ISO 22301

Why use ISO 22301 as part of a management system?

ISO 22301 provides guidance on **business continuity management**, which is an important aspect of cyber resilience.

ISO 22301:2012 specifies requirements for business continuity management systems. This standard includes requirements to plan, establish, implement, operate, monitor, review, maintain and continually improve a management system, which will help to protect the organization against disruptive incidents as well as reduce the likelihood of these incidents, while helping the organization to plan, respond and recover when they do occur.

This standard is relevant to the field of cyber resilience because cyber resilience must support business continuity planning, and also because invoking a business continuity plan may be an appropriate response to certain types of security events.

3.1.7 COBIT 5

Why use COBIT 5 as part of a management system?

COBIT 5 considers both governance and management of enterprise IT.

Good governance and management of enterprise IT are essential to achievement of cyber resilience goals because many cyber resilience threats involve IT.

COBIT 5 is a business framework for the governance and management of enterprise IT. It is based on a number of principles, including:

- **Meeting stakeholder needs** COBIT 5 describes processes and enablers required for the enterprise to use IT to create value for stakeholders.
- **Covering the enterprise end-to-end** COBIT 5 covers all governance and management functions and processes within the enterprise.
- **Applying a single, integrated framework** COBIT 5 is aligned with other standards and best practices at a high level, so it can be used as an overarching framework for governance and management of enterprise IT.
- **Enabling a holistic approach** COBIT 5 takes into account seven categories of enablers that can help to achieve the objectives of the enterprise. These are:
  - Principles, policies and frameworks
  - Processes
  - Organizational structures
  - Culture, ethics and behaviour
  - Information
  - Services, infrastructure and **applications**
  - People, skills and competencies.
- **Separating governance from management** COBIT 5 makes a clear distinction between governance and management.

For historical reasons COBIT 5 is most commonly used for audit and compliance purposes; this can be contrasted with ITIL, which is commonly used to help design practices and processes.

3.1.8 NIST Framework for Improving Critical Infrastructure Cybersecurity

This framework was published by the US National Institute of Standards and Technology (NIST) in February 2014. It is described in section 8.5.2, but it is mentioned here as it can make a significant contribution to cyber resilience. NIST approaches are commonly adopted in the USA.

3.1.9 Management of Risk

Management of risk (M_o_R) provides a framework for risk management that can be incorporated into a management system to improve decision-making by ensuring that risk is properly considered.

M_o_R is described in more detail in section 2.1.

3.1.10 Combining multiple management system approaches

Organizations typically need to incorporate ideas from more than one of these standards or frameworks into the design of their management system. This may be because they wish to be certified as compliant with more than one standard, or simply because there are important ideas that they wish to use in more than one of these standards and frameworks. Organizations wishing to be certified against multiple standards (for example ISO/IEC 27001 and ISO/IEC 20000-1) will need to be confident that the single management system they **build** provides evidence that they meet the requirements of each standard. It is unlikely that an organization would want to adopt all of the standards and frameworks described here. Selection of which standards and frameworks to include as inputs to the design of a management system will depend on the countries and industries the organization operates in, as well as the existing knowledge and preferences of the people designing the management system.

If an organization creates a management system that incorporates aspects from multiple standards or frameworks, it should ensure that it has understood any conflicting requirements. These conflicts might, for example, involve definitions of terms (such as 'risk' or 'threat'), required outputs of processes, or any other aspect of the standard or framework. The organization must ensure that its single management system meets all requirements of each standard or framework, resolving any conflicts as necessary. It will also need to clearly demonstrate how these conflicts have been resolved, and how the management system meets each requirement in order to achieve certification.

When an organization is implementing a single management system, requirements may come from a variety of sources, including information security management, service management, quality management, personnel management etc. This may include auditable requirements from multiple standards. But whatever else it includes, a single management system must include cyber resilience requirements as well as all of the others; it is not possible to have an effective cyber resilience management system that is separate from all the other activities involved in running an organization.

Figure 3.3 illustrates some of the many things that might contribute to an organization's management system. It would be unusual for a single organization to include requirements from all of these inputs, but some organizations do use a large number of them.

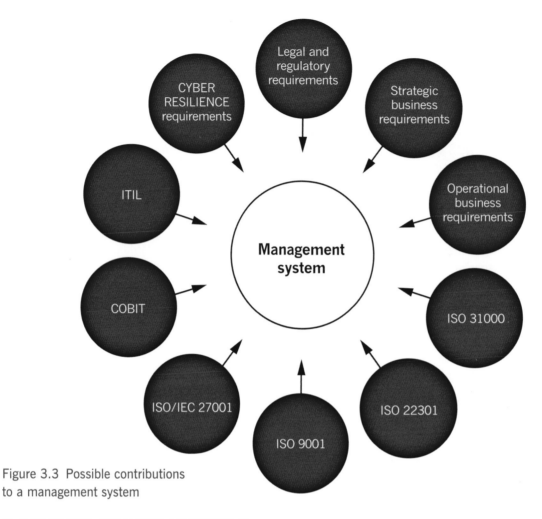

Figure 3.3 Possible contributions
to a management system

3.2 THE ITIL SERVICE LIFECYCLE

Although cyber resilience has a much wider scope than security of IT systems and services, one area where cyber resilience is especially relevant is in the management and use of IT. Whether IT services are managed in-house or sourced from a third party, every organization must ensure that its IT services are able to support all of the organization's cyber resilience requirements.

Isn't ITIL just about IT operations?

There is a common belief that ITIL is just about operating IT systems, but as ITIL has evolved over the years it has moved to be much more comprehensive than this.

ITIL considers every aspect of IT services throughout their entire lifecycle – starting with setting the overall strategy and understanding how IT can create value for customers, it then considers how services are designed, built and transitioned to **live** operation, as well as how they can be continually improved.

ITIL is used by many thousands of organizations around the world to help them design and operate a management system for the creation, delivery and improvement of IT services. ITIL defines a lifecycle for IT service management that has five stages: service strategy, service design, service transition, service operation and continual service improvement. ITIL has a set of five core publications, each covering one stage of the service lifecycle, plus a range of complementary publications. These publications provide extensive guidance and advice on how to implement the processes and practices needed to manage IT services. The ITIL service lifecycle is illustrated in Figure 3.4, and the five lifecycle stages are described in more detail in sections 3.2.1 to 3.2.5.

Figure 3.4 The ITIL
service lifecycle

3.2.1 *ITIL Service Strategy*

ITIL Service Strategy (Cabinet Office, 2011) describes how service providers create value, how they decide which customers and markets to work with, and what IT services to deliver. Processes described in this publication include:

- **Strategy management for IT services**
- **Service portfolio management**
- **Financial management for IT services**
- **Demand management**
- Business relationship management.

Strategy is discussed in more detail in Chapter 4.

3.2.2 *ITIL Service Design*

ITIL Service Design (Cabinet Office, 2011) describes how to design new or changed IT services to ensure that they meet the evolving requirements of the business. Processes described in this publication include:

- **Design coordination**
- **Service catalogue management**
- **Service level management**
- **Availability management**
- **Capacity management**
- **IT service continuity management**
- Information security management
- **Supplier management.**

Design is discussed in more detail in Chapter 5.

3.2.3 *ITIL Service Transition*

ITIL Service Transition (Cabinet Office, 2011) describes how a service provider can ensure that new, modified or retired services meet the expectations of the business, as defined in the strategy and design. Processes described in this publication include:

- **Transition planning and support**
- **Change management**
- **Service asset and configuration management**
- **Release and deployment management**
- **Service validation and testing**
- **Change evaluation**
- **Knowledge management.**

Transition is discussed in more detail in Chapter 6.

3.2.4 *ITIL Service Operation*

ITIL Service Operation (Cabinet Office, 2011) describes how to deliver agreed levels of service to users and customers, while managing the infrastructure and applications required to deliver this. Processes described in this publication include:

- **Event management**
- Incident management
- **Request fulfilment**
- **Problem management**
- **Access management.**

Operation is discussed in more detail in Chapter 7.

3.2.5 *ITIL Continual Service Improvement*

ITIL Continual Service Improvement (Cabinet Office, 2011) describes how to maintain value for customers by continually evaluating and improving services and the underlying processes and technology. The process described in this publication is:

- The **seven-step improvement process**.

Continual improvement is discussed in more detail in Chapter 8.

Manufacturing example: MakeUGoods

The IT department at MakeUGoods has some IT service management (ITSM) processes that are based on ITIL. These processes are from the service transition and service operation stages of the service lifecycle, and include incident management, request fulfilment, change management and release management. MakeUGoods is a fairly new company and has not thought about how ITIL could help with strategy, design or continual improvement. Now might be a good time for the company to start thinking about how adoption of more ideas from the ITIL framework might help it improve its cyber resilience.

3.2.6 ITIL and cyber resilience

Many of the practices described in ITIL are directly relevant to cyber resilience, and integrating cyber resilience into a management system based on ITIL can be very effective. Organizations that use ITIL as the basis for their management system can incorporate cyber resilience into all stages of the service lifecycle, and can be confident that a project to implement or improve cyber resilience management should work with their existing service management system to ensure that the organization has one integrated management system.

Even organizations that have chosen not to adopt ITIL as a framework for managing their IT services could find that the service lifecycle makes a very effective framework for thinking about cyber resilience. This is because effective cyber resilience management requires a complete lifecycle approach to managing risks. It is essential to start with an overall strategy for cyber resilience, and then to design everything needed to turn that strategy into reality. This should be followed by a transition stage to test and deploy the cyber resilience solution, which will then be operated to ensure that it meets the cyber resilience needs of the organization. Continual improvement has to be used at all stages to ensure that the cyber resilience solution is appropriate for the organization's needs, is effective at meeting these needs, makes efficient use of resources, and continues to be appropriate, effective and efficient as the organization responds to changes in context.

More detail on how this can be done is included in Chapters 4 to 8.

3.3 MANAGING CYBER RESILIENCE QUESTIONS

1. How well integrated is the management of cyber resilience with other areas of management in your organization? How could you improve the integration between cyber resilience management and other areas of management?

2. What is the scope of the management system that helps you to achieve your cyber resilience goals? How does your organization ensure this is the right scope? How do you think the scope could be improved?

3. What are the major inputs to your management system design? Which standards or sources of best practice do you think might help to improve your management system? How would these result in improvements?

4. What benefits could your organization get from being certified to a management system standard such as ISO/IEC 27001, ISO 9001 or ISO/IEC 20000? What difficulties might there be in achieving this certification?

4

Cyber resilience strategy

This chapter covers:

- Objectives and controls for a cyber resilience strategy
- Aligning with IT service strategy
- Strategy scenarios

4 Cyber resilience strategy

A cyber resilience strategy ensures that activities carried out to protect an organization's information assets are coherent. It makes sure that cyber resilience objectives are understood and are aligned with the needs of stakeholders. It provides a common understanding to ensure that people in the organization are working together to achieve these objectives, and it ensures that the resources needed to achieve the objectives are made available.

The development of strategy should be carried out by governors and management. This is a critical part of the management system, and everything described in this chapter (and subsequent chapters) will be part of that management system.

A strategy is more than just a plan. It also provides a framework within which the organization can adapt to a changing environment. This means that appropriate responses to previously unknown threats and vulnerabilities can be made in a way that aligns with the goals and intents of the organization.

Without a strategy, cyber resilience activities are likely to be disjointed, with no clear objectives, no understanding of how cyber resilience contributes value to the organization, and no ability to adapt to changing circumstances.

A cyber resilience strategy helps the organization and its stakeholders to understand:

● What cyber resilience is
● The importance of cyber resilience to the organization, and to its customers
● How cyber resilience will be managed and funded
● The organizational capabilities required to deliver the necessary cyber resilience
● What assets will be used to manage cyber resilience and how performance of these assets can be optimized
● How cyber resilience will be integrated into all aspects of value creation for an organization, ensuring the business processes that the organization depends on, and the data and information that these processes use, are properly protected
● The approach the organization will take to manage cyber resilience
● The cyber resilience objectives that the organization will work towards
● The cyber resilience constraints within which the organization must work.

Strategy does not by itself provide the cyber resilience that the organization needs. Rather it defines the context, results and oversight that are needed to enable cyber resilience to be designed, transitioned, operated and improved. This chapter describes how to create a cyber resilience strategy; subsequent chapters describe design, transition, operation and improvement activities that are needed to realize this cyber resilience strategy.

Section 2.3 described how controls can be used to manage risks. Section 4.1 describes controls that are required to support a cyber resilience strategy, and section 4.2 discusses how these controls could be integrated into an overall IT service strategy.

4.1 CONTROL OBJECTIVES AND CONTROLS FOR A CYBER RESILIENCE STRATEGY

The controls described in this section make a significant contribution to establishing and maintaining the cyber resilience strategy of an organization. Many of these are examples of administrative controls, which contribute to cyber resilience in the way that they influence people and the design of other controls, rather than having a direct impact on specific technical risks. All of these controls are particularly relevant to the strategy stage of the cyber resilience lifecycle but they are also active during other stages.

4.1.1 Establish governance of cyber resilience

Governance was introduced in Chapter 3. It is the set of activities that ensure the organization understands and meets the expectations of the owners and other stakeholders, and protects their interests. It helps to ensure that the organization does the right things and complies with relevant legal and regulatory frameworks.

Governance has a much wider scope than cyber resilience, and governance of cyber resilience should be part of the overall governance of the organization. At the highest level, corporate governance is the responsibility of the board of management (or equivalent), who are accountable to the owners and to other stakeholders such as government or regulatory authorities. Governance provides oversight of cyber resilience, and ensures that all aspects of cyber resilience are appropriate for the organization.

Key message

Not all staff will fully understand strategic governance goals but they should appreciate the reasons behind the controls they operate or supervise.

Even the smallest organization needs to establish governance of cyber resilience, as this provides an overall context, prioritizes the needs of different stakeholders, and ensures that everyone in the organization understands these needs. If governance is not put in place then decisions will be made that conflict with each other, and with the expectations of the owners and other stakeholders.

In a very small organization governance may simply be the steps an owner takes to ensure that staff understand what stakeholders need and to ensure that they do what is required to protect the company and its clients. In a large organization, the establishment of governance may involve the creation of many organizational structures, committees and reports, as well as communication and training to ensure that staff understand what is expected of them, and compliance audits to ensure that they follow the rules. In either case, governance decisions must be clearly documented. This ensures that there can be no ambiguity about what the governing body requires from management.

Organizations that operate in multiple countries may need to balance the conflicting needs of different legal and regulatory systems. For example, the privacy laws in one country may conflict with government demands for access to data from another country. Part of the responsibility of governance is to define responsibility for deciding how these different, potentially conflicting, requirements will be managed.

The key activities that should be established as part of governance of cyber resilience include:

- Evaluating the needs and expectations of stakeholders, prioritizing these and deciding on the overall requirements from cyber resilience
- Providing direction to management about what cyber resilience should achieve
- Defining who makes cyber resilience decisions and how those decisions should be made
- Ensuring that cyber resilience risk is adequately addressed
- Monitoring the performance and outcomes of cyber resilience and intervening if necessary to ensure that the specified direction is followed.

Figure 4.1 illustrates the key governance activities: evaluating the requirements and expectations of owners and other key stakeholders, directing management, and monitoring to ensure that required activities are carried out.

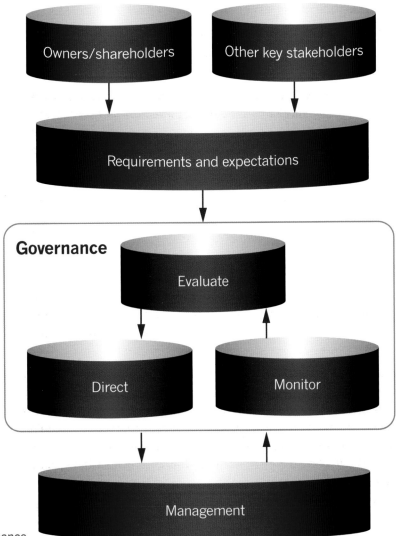

Figure 4.1 Key activities of governance

4.1.1.1 Vision and mission

The vision and mission of the organization are short but clear summaries of the intentions of the owners and major stakeholders. The vision and mission of the organization can be very useful in helping to manage governance of cyber resilience.

- Vision is what the organization plans to achieve in the future. The vision will change occasionally as the organization develops. For example, in May 1961 President John Kennedy stated that America would put a man on the Moon by the end of the decade. That vision has now been replaced by an intention to send humans to Mars.

- Mission is the purpose of the organization. For example, the mission of the National Aeronautics and Space Administration (NASA) is to 'Drive advances in science, technology, aeronautics, and space exploration to enhance knowledge, education, innovation, economic vitality, and stewardship of Earth'.

Vision and mission can be used to guide management decisions, and in the context of cyber resilience they can be used as a basis for evaluating every policy, process, procedure and control to ensure that they are aligned with the expectations of the key stakeholders.

4.1.1.2 Cyber resilience governance roles

Many organizations appoint a chief information security officer (CISO) to oversee the governance and management of cyber resilience within the organization. This role includes responsibility for all aspects of cyber resilience, including:

- Supporting governance of cyber resilience (but remember that accountability for governance rests with the board of management or equivalent)
- Managing stakeholders
- Managing cyber resilience policies
- Oversight of risk analysis and management
- Oversight of all cyber resilience controls
- Management of major cyber resilience incidents
- Audit and compliance (these may be done by an independent department in some organizations, if there is a need for separation of duties or centralized audit and compliance).

Depending on the size and complexity of the organization, this work may be distributed to a number of people, or it may all be carried out by the CISO. It is likely that the CISO will retain oversight of many of these activities even if they are delegated to other people.

Large organizations may appoint a cyber resilience steering committee to discuss and agree on matters relating to cyber resilience. This committee would normally be chaired by the CISO and include representatives from IT, HR, finance and legal departments, risk and audit departments, and business managers. It is often a sub-committee of the executive board.

4.1.2 Manage stakeholders

Key definition
A stakeholder is a person who has an interest in an organization, project, IT service etc. Stakeholders may be interested in the activities, targets, resources or deliverables. Stakeholders may include customers, partners, employees, shareholders, owners etc.

Understanding and managing all the different stakeholders who have an interest in cyber resilience is an important part of cyber resilience strategy. Stakeholders include anyone who might gain a benefit or suffer a loss from a cyber resilience incident, as well as anyone who might be involved in helping to prevent, detect or correct incidents.

Cyber resilience strategy should include the following stakeholder management activities:

- Identifying and categorizing stakeholders
- Gathering stakeholder requirements
- Planning stakeholder communications.

4.1.2.1 Identifying and categorizing stakeholders

Before stakeholder requirements can be gathered and a plan for communicating with stakeholders prepared, it is vital to understand who the stakeholders are. Stakeholders will need to be categorized so that plans for how to communicate with each type of stakeholder can be prepared. This section includes an example of stakeholder categorization, but each organization will define its own categories depending on its specific needs.

Even a very small organization should create **document**ation to assist in stakeholder management. A simple spreadsheet might be sufficient, but larger organizations might prefer to integrate stakeholder management into a customer relationship management (CRM) system. There are also a number of specialist tools available to assist with stakeholder management.

After stakeholders have been identified and categorized it is important to maintain this information so that it can be used in support of other strategic activities. Maintenance activities should include carrying out regular reviews (typically annually) and creating interfaces with other processes, such as supplier management, to detect changes in stakeholders.

Some common categories of stakeholder that should be considered include:

- **Owners and investors** In the private sector this will include shareholders; in the public sector it may include elected or appointed officials, or committees appointed by them. The requirements of these stakeholders are usually given very high priority.

- **Customers and clients** If there are external customers or clients then their needs will usually be represented in contracts, which may be written or implied. Customers may require very high levels of confidentiality, integrity or availability for some services or information that an organization manages on their behalf, and they may expect the organization to meet the conditions of a standard such as ISO/IEC 27001. The needs of internal customers are often specified less formally, but these requirements may still be critically important to them, and to governance of the organization.

  If customers include members of the public then it is important to consider issues such as how old they are, and how to ensure that they give informed consent to use of their information.

- **Suppliers** Many organizations depend on the activities of their suppliers to ensure they meet their customers' goals for confidentiality, integrity and availability. This means that strategic decisions about which suppliers the organization will work with, and which activities they will always carry out themselves, are critical. If a supplier needs to behave in particular ways to ensure it meets cyber resilience goals, then it is important to consider their requirements, along with those of all other stakeholders. Contracts with suppliers often specify things that must be done by the contracting organization as well as by the supplier, and this can include cyber resilience requirements. The most important aspect of managing suppliers is considering how to manage the risks they pose to the organization's cyber resilience. This is discussed in Chapter 6.

- **Employees** Management of cyber resilience is critically dependent on the attitudes, behaviour and culture of employees. This means that it is essential to think of employees as stakeholders – indispensable participants in helping to meeting an organization's cyber resilience goals. Their needs must be taken into account and communication with them planned. Some organizations may have formal employee representatives in the form of trades unions, staff councils or similar bodies: but even if this is not the case it is still important to understand employees and think about how best to engage them.

- **Legal and regulatory authorities** Many cyber resilience requirements come from legal or regulatory authorities, and many organizations have to report to these authorities on a regular basis. It is important therefore to identify which authorities are relevant to the organization, and what the authorities expect from it.

- **Competitors and industry bodies** In some industries there are formal or informal arrangements for organizations to share knowledge of cyber resilience threats, to assist in the management of cyber resilience. This may involve the organization in working with competitors, and strategic decisions must be taken about what level of information sharing is appropriate in this context.

Key message

One of the functions of strategy is to decide who the stakeholders are and what influence, if any, they will have in the governance and management of the organization. With cyber resilience, the behaviour of employees and their understanding of controls is a key factor in supporting cyber resilience strategy.

4.1.2.2 Gathering stakeholder requirements

At a strategic level it is important to understand the high-level requirements of stakeholders, so that these can be taken into account when defining governance of cyber resilience and goals for cyber resilience management. Detailed requirements analysis, which is also necessary, is carried out as part of cyber resilience design and is discussed in section 5.1.2.2.

There are a number of different approaches that can be used to gather strategic requirements from stakeholders. These include:

- **Discussions and interviews** This can be a great way to understand customers and employees, and to allow them to offer insight into their needs. It is essential to formally document the requirements after the discussion and to then review these with the stakeholders to ensure they have been understood.

- **Contracts and agreements** It is common for strategic requirements from external customers, and from suppliers, to be captured in contracts or formal agreements. Ideally the strategic requirements should be discussed at an earlier stage to help influence the content of these formal agreements, but it is also wise to review the actual contracts to ensure that all requirements are understood and included in strategic decision-making.

- **Laws and regulations** Many requirements are not negotiated with employees but are given to them in the form of laws and regulations. Organizations should ensure that every law and regulation that might impact their cyber resilience has been identified and that employees are aware of their responsibilities and know what is required from them. This would often be carried out by a legal department, or in a very small organization by the legal adviser (see section 4.1.4.2 for further discussion of compliance management).

An organization's cyber resilience strategy may also have a part to play in managing conflicting requirements from different stakeholders. For example, different customers may have conflicting requirements for confidentiality of data, and this could even result in a decision to design two completely distinct services to meet those conflicting requirements.

It is important to document all the cyber resilience stakeholder requirements identified. This will enable an organization to review the requirements with the stakeholders, to get confirmation that it has correctly understood its stakeholders' needs, and to facilitate sharing the requirements with other people – where appropriate – to ensure that they are carried forward into the design of governance, services, processes and controls.

Making sure organizations understand stakeholder requirements is not something that can be done once and then forgotten, because requirements are not static. All requirements should be reviewed at least annually, and changes in requirements should be taken into account as part of continual improvement (see Chapter 8 for further discussion of continual improvement).

4.1.2.3 Planning stakeholder communications

Regular communication with each group of stakeholders is a key aspect of stakeholder management. This communication needs to be planned, based on the needs of each stakeholder group. It should continue throughout the entire cyber resilience lifecycle, and a strategic communication plan should be created to ensure that it remains both sufficient and appropriate.

A strategic communication plan should include information about:

- Frequency of communication
- Target audience for each communication
- Purpose of each communication
- Media or channels to be used
- Expected content of the communication.

The purpose of a communication might be to:

- Ensure that cyber resilience requirements have been understood, and identify when requirements change
- Inform stakeholders of their cyber resilience responsibilities, and ensure these have been understood and accepted
- Identify the impact of operating cyber resilience controls on the organization, to identify improvements that might be needed
- Provide assurance to stakeholders to build trust in the cyber resilience of information and systems
- Report on the effectiveness of cyber resilience and the cost of implementation to management and governors (for example, to an executive committee of the board of management).

Communication is not just a one-way channel from the organization to the stakeholders. Organizations need to listen to their stakeholders, as well as talk to them. For example:

● If an organization is carrying out an annual review to understand whether any requirements have changed, it may need to set up discussion sessions with key customers, or provide a survey for them to complete, or invite them to a forum where they can discuss their needs with other customers.

● If an organization is communicating the need to follow a particular control to employees, then it needs to ensure they have understood, and are going to comply with, the requirement. An organization should never just send out a communication and assume that the job is complete. This communication may therefore include tests or requests for positive confirmation to ensure that employees have been properly engaged. Compliance is discussed in section 4.1.4.

4.1.3 Create and manage cyber resilience policies

Policies are a type of administrative control, which can help to reduce risk by ensuring that people understand what is expected from them. Policies are an important tool for communicating with stakeholders: they state what is expected, usually in the form of rules or high-level requirements.

Some cyber resilience policies are strategic in nature, and these are typically produced by the CISO or cyber resilience steering committee (or equivalent body at a similar level in the organization), and approved by the governing body. An example of this method would be a risk management policy that defines what approach will be taken to identifying and managing cyber resilience risks.

Other cyber resilience policies may be more tactical in nature. These could be created by technical staff who have designed specific controls, which will typically be approved by the CISO. An example of this kind of policy would be a firewall management policy. There may also be a need for standards to support the policies: for example a firewall configuration standard. These standards would normally be produced during the design stage of the cyber resilience lifecycle.

Policies provide the information needed by people designing cyber resilience processes, procedures and controls to ensure that these will meet the expectations of the governors. Policies also ensure that people responsible for following the processes, procedures and controls understand what is expected from them.

The policies that are needed in any specific organization will vary. Some organizations may have a single cyber resilience policy that covers all requirements; others may have a large number of different policies for each area of concern. What is important is that each policy is clear and unambiguous, is easy for people to read and understand, has an appropriate level of detail for its intended audience, and sets out what is required rather than detail of how it should be done. It is very important to consult with the right stakeholders to gain their commitment when producing (or amending) a policy.

Examples of policies that are used by many organizations include:

● **Information security policy** This defines the overall objectives and provides a framework for the governance and management of information security.

● **Risk assessment and management policy** This defines how risks will be identified, assessed and managed. It may be a cyber resilience policy, or may be a wider organizational risk management policy. The risk management policy is often used to communicate the organization's risk appetite and risk acceptance criteria.

● **A policy for classifying information and other assets** This defines security categories for assets (such as confidential, secret etc.) and how these should be applied to different types of asset. It also often includes a requirement for every asset to have a named owner.

● **Secure systems and software development policy** This defines security requirements for development of IT systems and software.

● **Removable and portable media policy** This defines requirements for management of portable media such as USB drives and CDs.

- **Mobile device policy** This defines policy requirements for laptops, smartphones, tablets and other mobile computing devices.

- **Bring your own device (BYOD) policy** This defines policy requirements for people who use their own personal productivity devices (typically smartphones and tablets) to access the organization's resources.

- **Remote-working policy** This defines cyber resilience requirements for staff working from remote locations. Including, for example, what equipment and software they should use, how they should connect to corporate resources, and what information they are allowed to access when working remotely.

- **Access control policy** This defines how decisions will be made about which entities are allowed to access which resources, and how these decisions should be enforced.

- **Backup policy** This defines what data should be backed up, how frequently, and how the backed-up data should be stored and managed.

- **Cryptographic controls policy** This defines how encryption should be used to protect information, by specifying for example what type of information should be encrypted and how encryption keys should be managed.

- **Clear-desk and clear-screen policy** This defines a requirement for information to be removed from desks and screens before they are left unattended.

- **Supplier security policy** This defines the requirements for managing cyber resilience when working with suppliers.

- **Information lifecycle policy** This defines how information should be managed across its lifecycle. It might include requirements for **validation** of information when it is received; secure storage and transfer to protect the confidentiality, integrity and availability of the information; and secure destruction of information when it is no longer needed. Typically, the requirements of this policy will be different depending on the **classification** of the information.

- **Log management policy** This defines how system and device access logs should be created, stored, protected and archived, to ensure that data required for investigations, audits or evidence is available when needed.

- **Cyber-incident response policy** This defines requirements for responding to cyber resilience incidents. It provides information needed by people designing and implementing processes, tools, training or testing of cyber resilience incident management.

This is not a definitive list of policies that organizations should create. Other commonly required policies cover HR, physical security, business continuity, compliance and audit. Some of these might not be appropriate for every organization, but each of the policies should at least be considered and a decision made on whether it is needed. Some organizations will combine some of these suggested policies into higher-level policies: for example, there may be a single policy that covers clear-desk, BYOD and remote working.

Deciding what policies are needed is a significant part of what should be done when establishing a cyber resilience strategy, and there are many areas that have not been mentioned here which might require a defined policy. Other policies may be required to help treat risks that have been identified by a risk assessment. No matter what policies an organization decides it needs, some of their content will be defined as part of the strategy; further detailed content may be developed in the design stage of the cyber resilience lifecycle.

4.1.3.1 Structure of cyber resilience policies

It is important that policies are as short as practical and written in simple language, so that people can easily read and remember them. A policy that is long and complex is unlikely to be effective.

The information that should be included in each policy is not fixed or externally defined. It depends on the culture of an organization, and on how the organization intends to use the policies. Things that are often included in policies include:

- Title of the policy
- Version number

- Owner
- Approver
- Validity dates (from and to)
- Next review date
- Location of a definitive copy of the policy
- Document history
- Purpose of the policy
- Scope and applicability (Does this policy apply to the whole organization or just some locations/people/assets?)
- Responsibilities and requirements defined by this policy – this forms the bulk of the policy.

4.1.3.2 Management of cyber resilience policies

If policies are simply created and then stored away on a shelf (or hard drive), they will deliver very little value. A clear process for managing policies that covers the whole lifecycle of the policy is required.

- **Policy creation** It is essential to consult with appropriate stakeholders, to review applicable laws and regulations, and to ensure that the policies are well written and fit for purpose. Ideally, organizations should have a policy template that is used for all policies. This ensures that all critical information is provided in a standard way and makes the policies easier for people to read and understand.

  Every policy must be reviewed and formally approved by an appropriate authority, and stored in an agreed location so that it can be referenced when needed.

- **Policy communication** It is not sufficient to simply create the policy and store it away. Organizations must ensure that people who are expected to follow the policy are aware of its existence and understand its requirements.

  It may be appropriate to create a **RACI** matrix, showing who is 'responsible, accountable, consulted and informed' for each policy. This can help to ensure that the correct stakeholders have been engaged.

  The target audience for each policy must be identified, and then decisions made about how to communicate the requirements of the policy to that audience. For a policy that is just directed at a small number of senior management it may be sufficient to simply tell them about it or supply a copy. This is unlikely to be adequate for a policy that is applicable to all staff, or for a policy that requires evidence for compliance purposes. In this case it may be necessary to include information about the policy in induction training for new employees, and in periodic refresher training for all staff. This could be followed up by regular reminders or tests, to ensure that people have understood and remembered the key points of the policy.

  If the policy is going to require significant change in the attitudes, behaviour or culture of staff then consider the ideas in section 6.2.8 'Management of organizational change'.

- **Policy review and update** Every policy must be regularly reviewed, at least annually, to ensure that it is still fit for purpose. This should include a review of any inputs such as stakeholder requirements to identify if these have changed. Policies must also be reviewed if at any time it becomes apparent that the requirements may have changed: for example if there is a change to a relevant law or regulation, or a significant change to the technology being used to process information.

  If this review identifies a need to update the policy then this update should include the same consultation, approval and communication steps as have been described for a new policy.

4.1.4 Manage cyber resilience audit and compliance

The purpose of audit and compliance is to ensure that policies are followed, that controls are implemented and operated as intended, and that legal and regulatory requirements are being met. Audit provides assurance that the management system conforms to the organization's requirements for cyber resilience and to any external standards that the organization has elected to implement. Compliance management helps to avoid breaches of legal, regulatory or contractual obligations.

Even if an organization designs and implements the best possible set of cyber resilience controls, including well-crafted policies and processes, and uses brilliant technology, it is unlikely that it will be able to maintain the level of protection it intends without regular and effective audit and compliance management. This is because:

- IT changes may lead to technology controls not being applied to all assets as they should be. For example, a PC may be introduced without the appropriate **endpoint** protection, or a server rebuild may result in some required parameters being set to the wrong values.

- Personnel changes or poor discipline may lead to people taking shortcuts rather than following the required processes.

- New technology may result in the designed controls being no longer able to provide the level of protection that was intended. For example, an operating system upgrade or a newly discovered vulnerability may make some controls ineffective.

- Changes in business processes may lead to controls no longer having the desired effect: for example, a new supplier may be engaged for payment processing and this may require different controls to be in place.

- People may forget about things they are supposed to do if these are infrequent and not part of their natural behaviour. For example, users may have been trained not to follow hyperlinks in email messages, but if that training took place a long time ago they may no longer react appropriately.

- Changes in laws, regulations or contracts can lead to non-compliance if compensatory changes are not made to the cyber resilience controls.

4.1.4.1 Audit

Audits are used to verify that the management system conforms to the requirements established for it. The results of an audit can be used to provide assurance about the cyber resilience status of the organization, and to identify opportunities for improvement.

Every organization should carry out internal audits to satisfy itself of the status of its cyber resilience. Many organizations are also subject to external audits; this may be because they want certification to show that they comply with a management system standard such as ISO/IEC 27001, or it may be a requirement in a customer contract or from a regulator.

Audits should not be so frequent as to consume significant resources: nor should they be too infrequent, as this might allow issues to remain unidentified. The cyber resilience strategy should determine the type and frequency of audits.

Audit planning should include:

- The type and frequency of audits; for example, it is likely that internal audits will be carried out before any required external audits
- The scope for each audit
- The audit criteria to be used
- Who will carry out the audit
- Who the audit report will be delivered to
- Who will be accountable for managing any issues identified by the audit.

It is rarely sufficient to rely on infrequent audits to ensure that controls are in place. This is why some organizations have a multi-level approach that includes:

- Allocation of responsibility for implementing controls
- Frequent assurance testing to check regularly that controls are in place – often carried out monthly
- Internal audits to ensure that the organization is fully prepared for external audit, and to help prevent undetected issues between external audits. These may be annual, or more frequent where appropriate.
- External audits to provide formal confirmation – typically carried out annually.

4.1.4.2 Compliance management

Compliance management is used to help avoid breaches of legal, regulatory or contractual requirements. Compliance management usually has a much wider scope than cyber resilience, but there are often many compliance requirements that depend on cyber resilience.

The starting point for effective compliance management is an understanding of all the legal, regulatory and contractual requirements that must be met. This may demand a very large and ongoing effort, depending on the nature of the organization and the context in which it works. It is important to document all of the requirements, and to maintain this documentation as the requirements change.

Demonstrating that all compliance requirements have been met may call for the collection and management of significant amounts of evidence. For each requirement, documentation should be available to show which cyber resilience controls ensure that it is being met. Organizations may need to include information about how controls operate and how they are audited. System logs, device logs and transaction records are often essential – either because they are specified in a requirement or because they provide evidence that a requirement has been met. Compliance management should ensure that controls are in place to protect the integrity and availability of these records.

When designing and implementing compliance management, it is important to ensure that it delivers real value by ensuring that cyber resilience controls are in place and effective. It is very easy to implement a 'tick box' approach to compliance, which gives the appearance of value but does not properly protect the business.

4.2 ALIGNING CYBER RESILIENCE STRATEGY WITH IT SERVICE STRATEGY

IT service strategy considers how service providers create value. During this stage of the IT service lifecycle, organizations define objectives and expectations; they identify, select and prioritize the markets they want to work in, the customers they want to supply, and the opportunities they want to pursue. An effective cyber resilience strategy must take all these activities into account. In other words IT service strategy and cyber resilience strategy must be considered together and not independently. This is the same issue that was identified in section 3.1 'The need for a single management system'.

Organizations that use ITIL as a basis for their IT service management system can integrate cyber resilience strategy into the service strategy stage of the service lifecycle. Organizations that are not using ITIL to manage their IT services may find it helpful to adopt some of the processes and activities described in *ITIL Service Strategy* to support their cyber resilience strategy.

There are many cyber resilience activities that should be integrated with the strategy stage of the service lifecycle, including:

- Defining an overall strategy for cyber resilience
- Identifying the stakeholders who have an interest in cyber resilience, and understanding their needs and expectations
- Understanding the business requirements for cyber resilience
- Defining high-level goals and **critical success factor**s for cyber resilience
- Defining roles and responsibilities for governance and management of cyber resilience
- Providing funding for cyber resilience activities.

ITIL Service Strategy describes a number of processes that are particularly relevant to the strategy stage of the service lifecycle. Every one of these processes needs to include appropriate aspects of cyber resilience; it is not possible to run cyber resilience processes that carry out similar activities to the IT service management processes in isolation from each other. They must be integrated, or at the very least aligned, to ensure that there is no conflict. Many of the controls described in section 4.1 can be implemented effectively through such integrated processes. This can enable an organization to achieve both its IT service strategy objectives and its cyber resilience strategy objectives efficiently and effectively.

Cyber resilience activities should be integrated with each of the processes described in *ITIL Service Strategy*, as follows.

4.2.1 Strategy management for IT services

Strategy management considers many different things that could influence the organization, including for example all stakeholders (internal and external), what resources are available, the environment (laws, regulations, business strategy etc.) and competitive pressures. Based on understanding all these different factors it defines overall objectives, policies, plans, governance structures, markets and customers.

Figure 4.2 illustrates the key inputs and outputs for the strategy management for IT services process.

Strategy management for IT services is an IT service management (ITSM) process that ensures that service strategy is defined, maintained and achieves its purpose. Strategy management is the responsibility of the executives of the organization and incorporates many aspects of governance, to ensure that the service strategy is aligned with the business strategy and the needs of the stakeholders. This process includes understanding the environment in which the organization operates, selecting markets and customers, and deciding how the organization will create distinctive value within its chosen markets. Every service provider needs to understand how they are special: for example, they may have deep understanding of the industry their customers operate in, they may be very low cost, they may be able to demonstrate very high-quality services, or they may be able to adapt very fast to changing requirements. Understanding what is special or distinctive about a service provider is essential to enable it to compete with alternatives.

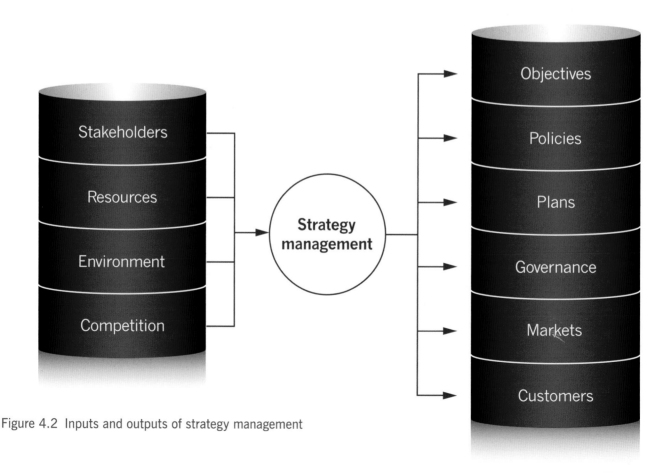

Figure 4.2 Inputs and outputs of strategy management

Strategy management also considers how the organization fits into a **value network**. No organization can exist by itself, and part of the strategy includes an understanding of how value is created for customers by an entire network of organizations. Detailed consideration of supplier security management can be found in section 5.1.3, but high-level decisions about whether to do things ourselves or source them from other organizations may be part of the overall strategy, even though most sourcing decisions are taken during the design stage of the service lifecycle.

All these aspects of strategy management apply equally to internal IT departments and to external IT service providers. An **internal service provider** that does not understand this will not be in a position to demonstrate to its customers what is distinctive about the IT services it offers. In this case it is highly unlikely that the customer will understand the value their service provider brings to the organization, and the continued existence of the internal service provider will be at risk.

Many aspects of the strategy management for IT services process should be integrated with cyber resilience strategy:

● Cyber resilience governance should be part of the overall governance of the enterprise. Governance of cyber resilience, like governance of IT, should come from the owners, not from the people doing the work. Cyber resilience governance and governance of IT should work together to ensure that the cyber resilience needs of the organization are achieved.

● The work done to understand business needs and create an IT strategy that supports these should include making sure employees understand the cyber resilience needs of the business, so that the strategy created applies to both IT service management and cyber resilience.

● When analysing markets and customers it is important to include an analysis of the differing cyber resilience risks and opportunities that these markets and customers represent; understanding these risks and opportunities should help to inform decisions about which markets to enter and which customers to work with.

● Strategic considerations of what work to do in-house and what could be sourced from other organizations must consider cyber resilience as well as other factors. Risk from suppliers can be a very big factor in overall cyber resilience risk.

● Creation of strategic plans for IT services should include cyber resilience aspects of those services, and creation of strategic plans for cyber resilience should include understanding of plans for IT service management.

4.2.2 Service portfolio management

The ITSM service portfolio management process ensures that organizations can offer the right mix of services to meet their overall service strategy. This process is not about administrative management of the **service portfolio**, but is a strategic process that makes sure the service portfolio is fit for purpose. In other words service portfolio management concerns itself with governance. It ensures that organizations invest in a portfolio of services designed to deliver their strategic intent. Service portfolio management analyses potential services in an organization's **service pipeline** to understand the costs, benefits and risks, and it then decides whether to fund development of these services.

ITIL Service Strategy describes four distinct activities for the service portfolio management process. These activities are shown in Figure 4.3:

● **Define** Document and understand existing and potential new services.

● **Analyse** Understand the value of each service, the demand for it, and the cost and ability to supply the service. Prioritize investments (and disinvestments).

● **Approve** Check for conflicts with other planned changes and authorize the investment required to add, change or remove a service.

● **Charter** Formally initiate development of the new or changed service.

ITSM service portfolio management can make significant contributions to cyber resilience by:

● Ensuring that cyber resilience requirements for new or changed IT services are considered when the services are being analysed for possible inclusion in the service portfolio

● Ensuring that funding for new and changed services includes sufficient funds to meet the cyber resilience needs of stakeholders.

Cyber resilience can contribute to ITSM service portfolio management by:

● Providing clear requirements for all cyber resilience aspects of new or changed services in sufficient time that they can be considered during analysis for possible inclusion in the service portfolio

● Providing information about the costs and benefits of cyber resilience measures that are appropriate for new or changed services.

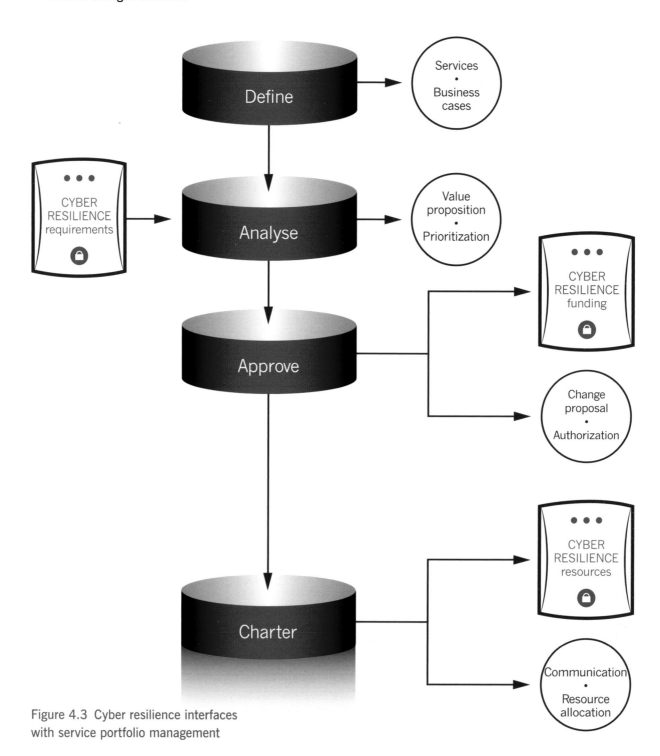

Figure 4.3 Cyber resilience interfaces with service portfolio management

In an ideal world cyber resilience would never be an add-on to a new or changed service at a late stage of the design but would be a fundamental aspect of strategic planning for the service; in practice there is often a need to add new cyber resilience capabilities to existing services, but wherever possible this should be included as part of the strategic planning for the new or changed service.

4.2.3 Financial management for IT services

The ITSM financial management for IT services process enables organizations to manage their IT **budgeting**, **accounting** and charging requirements, and helps them to quantify the value that IT services contribute to the business. Definitions are as follows:

● **Budgeting** is the process of predicting, and planning for, income and expenditure.

● **Accounting** is the process of tracking actual income and expenditure, comparing these to budgets and taking corrective action as necessary.

● **Charging** is the process of billing customers for services supplied to them and managing the collection of billed monies.

All aspects of **financial management** for cyber resilience should be integrated into one overall **enterprise financial management** process. This process is not part of ITSM or cyber resilience, but is defined as part of the governance of the organization. It sets policy and standards for financial management and allocates budgets to different areas. Budgeting and accounting for cyber resilience should be part of this overall budgeting and accounting. If organizations charge their customers for IT services then this charging should cover the cost of providing cyber resilience as well as all other aspects of the service. This does not of course cover all costs of cyber resilience, only those costs related to specific IT services. It would be unusual for cyber resilience to be directly charged to individual business units, other than as part of an IT service. When organizations quantify the value that IT services contribute to the business, they should include analysis of the value created by cyber resilience aspects of the services.

Who paid for the link?

A UK hospital had a link to a local social services department, which enabled them to share confidential data. This was a fairly slow link with limited **capacity** for expansion. When a request arrived to add more users, the technology needed to be upgraded. Junior staff trying to deal with the request discovered that nobody knew who had funded the link, who was responsible for it or who was allowed to request that additional users be added.

Good integration between cyber resilience, financial management and service portfolio management can help to avoid situations like this arising.

Many organizations see cyber resilience as a significant cost, but they rarely analyse the value created by investments in cyber resilience. This can make it very difficult to get the required investments. Good financial analysis can help to demonstrate the value of cyber resilience, to ensure that this is understood by people making investment decisions.

A major input to budgeting for cyber resilience should be the risk treatment plan, described in section 2.3.5. This plan identifies all investments required in cyber resilience controls. Financial management can also help to analyse the return on investment (ROI) in cyber resilience, which may be needed to obtain funding to implement the risk treatment plan.

Figure 4.4 depicts the relationship between enterprise financial management, IT service management, cyber resilience and other **cost centre**s in an enterprise. Every department must follow the centrally defined enterprise process for budgeting, accounting and understanding value (for example ROI calculations). Any department that charges for its services should also follow the centrally defined enterprise-wide process, but many departments do not charge for their services, they simply act as cost centres. Note that this diagram shows the normal situation where cyber resilience is centrally funded, and there is no separate charging for it.

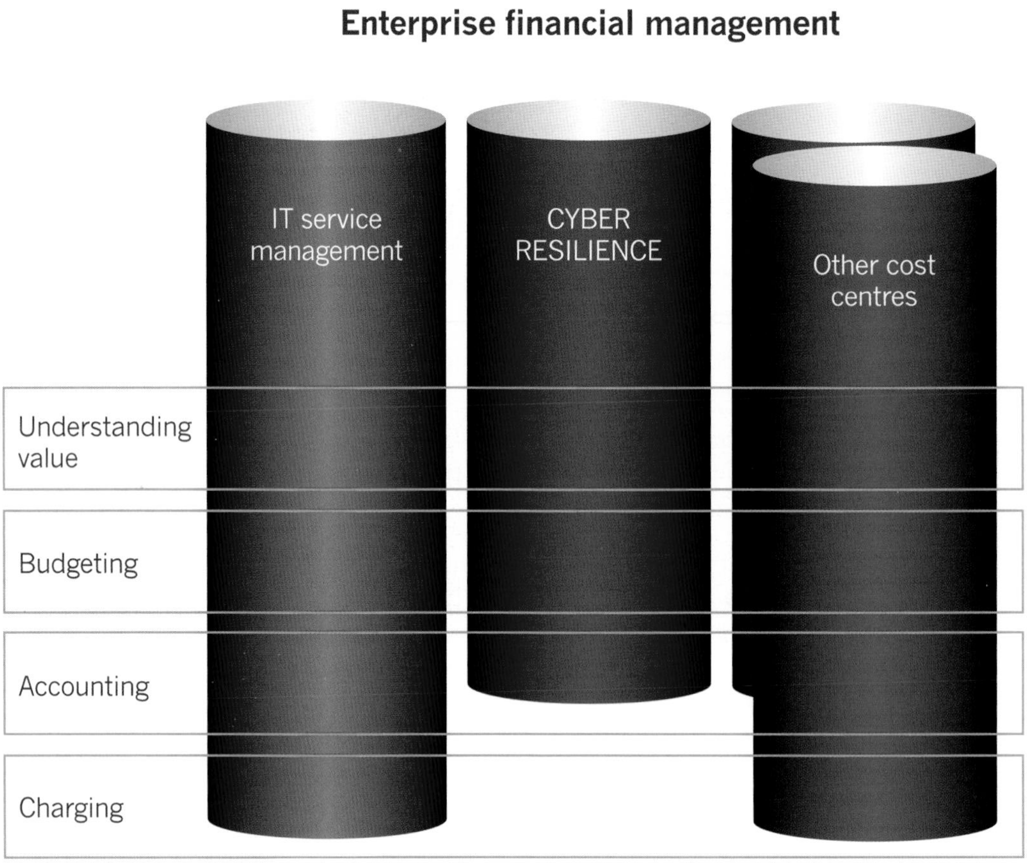

Enterprise financial management

	IT service management	CYBER RESILIENCE	Other cost centres
Understanding value			
Budgeting			
Accounting			
Charging			

Figure 4.4 All cost centres must follow enterprise financial management standards

4.2.4 Demand management

Who pays for cyber resilience demand?

One important aspect of demand management for cyber resilience is ensuring that customers understand what cyber resilience they need, why they need it, and what it costs to provide this.

A customer may know that they could buy a 1TB disk drive for their home PC for less than £40. This same customer may be surprised to learn that the cost of 1TB of storage on a server at work is more than £400, because of the need to provide reliable hardware with additional integrity protection, monitoring, **backup**, archiving and other high-availability features.

Demand management should provide the customer with the information they need to understand the cost and value of the service provided.

The ITSM demand management process enables organizations to understand, anticipate and influence customer demand for services, and helps them to work with other parts of IT to ensure the provision of capacity to meet these demands. Poorly managed demand can be a significant risk for any service provider. Over-provision of service can result in excessive costs: under-provision can result in poor performance or poor availability of services.

All aspects of an organization's demand management process should include consideration of cyber resilience. This means that an organization must ensure it understands its customers' requirements for cyber resilience in the same way as it understands their need for any other aspect of the service. A service provider should anticipate its customers' future demands for cyber resilience, and where appropriate it should influence those

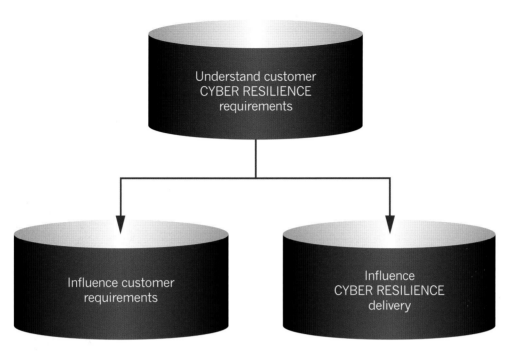

Figure 4.5 Cyber resilience demand management activities

demands. Demand management should work with other parts of IT to ensure the provision of cyber resilience to meet customers' demands, in the same way as for any other aspect of the IT services.

ITSM demand management can make significant contributions to cyber resilience by:

● Ensuring that cyber resilience demand is included in customer discussions about demand for IT services

● Helping customers to understand the need for cyber resilience, and the cost of delivering this, as part of their requirements for IT services.

Cyber resilience can contribute to ITSM demand management by:

● Providing information about how cyber resilience can contribute to new or changed IT services

● Providing information about the costs and benefits of cyber resilience to facilitate customer discussions of demand.

As shown in Figure 4.5, demand management has three distinct aspects. Firstly customer requirements must be understood, then based on this, both the customer requirements and the delivery of services can be influenced to ensure that customer expectations are met.

4.2.5 Business relationship management

The ITSM business relationship management process provides links between an organization and its customers at a strategic and tactical level. These links ensure that an organization understands the business requirements of its customers and engages with those customers appropriately. Business relationship management also assists in managing customer satisfaction.

Business relationship management should include cyber resilience in all aspects of the process. Cyber resilience should be discussed in regular customer meetings, to ensure that IT understands customers' cyber resilience needs, and to ensure that customers understand how IT is meeting these needs. This process should also be used to help understand how cyber resilience contributes to customers' business success and communicate this to both customers and IT staff.

Cyber resilience can make a significant contribution to customer satisfaction, both in a positive and a negative way. The business relationship management process should be used to help communicate cyber resilience risks and issues, ensuring the customer is appropriately informed, helping to manage any potential impact on customer satisfaction, and improving customer awareness of cyber resilience.

4.2.6 Information risk management and risk treatment

ITIL considers risk management to be an integral part of many practices and processes. It does not recommend a specific risk management methodology but says that 'each organization should determine the approach to risk management that is best suited to its needs'. Each ITIL publication includes an appendix on risk assessment and management, which describes a number of different approaches that can be used.

When integrating cyber resilience into the service strategy stage of the service lifecycle, it will be appropriate to select a risk management methodology that can be applied across both service management and cyber resilience. If the organization already has a preferred methodology for identifying and managing risks to IT services then this methodology can be adopted for managing cyber resilience risks; otherwise the process described in section 2.3 may be used for this purpose.

4.2.7 Aligning cyber resilience controls with IT service strategy

Section 4.2 has considered the integration of cyber resilience and IT service management by considering how each ITSM process can be integrated with cyber resilience. An alternative way to consider integration of cyber resilience and IT service management is to look at how each of the strategic cyber resilience controls described in section 4.1 can be integrated with ITSM.

4.2.7.1 Cyber resilience governance, audit and compliance management

ITIL Service Strategy describes activities needed to establish governance and to set up a management system. Governance is not described as a process within ITIL, but as a set of activities. The ITIL description of governance is based on the activities evaluate/direct/monitor and includes compliance management as part of the monitoring. Cyber resilience governance and audit and compliance should be integrated with the overall organizational approach to governance and compliance management.

4.2.7.2 Stakeholder management

This control should be integrated with the 'business relationship management' and 'demand management' processes and with 'service portfolio management'. All of these service management processes consider customer needs from different perspectives, and all of them need to include cyber resilience considerations.

4.2.7.3 Policy management

IT strategy, policies and plans are defined by the 'strategy management for IT services' process. These policies and plans need to align with cyber resilience policies and plans as an integral part of how IT is managed, rather than as an afterthought.

4.3 STRATEGY SCENARIOS

This section of the publication looks at some aspects of strategy for the three fictitious organizations. As you read through these descriptions you should think about:

- Who are the key cyber resilience stakeholders in each organization?
- How well has each organization implemented the strategic controls described in this section? Which controls need further investment?
- What are the major risks that each of these organizations should be protecting themselves against?

Retail example: SellUGoods Ltd

The in-house magazine for **SellUGoods** publishes an interview with a different manager each month. Here the interviewer (I) is interviewing the information security manager (ISM).

I   Can you tell me a bit about information security at SellUGoods Ltd?

ISM   Well, information security at SellUGoods Ltd is one of the responsibilities of the risk management department.

I   Not the IT department?

ISM   No, we're part of the business; I report to the head of risk management and she reports to the finance director.

I   Can you tell me a bit more about the risk management department?

ISM   OK. There are three sections: financial risks and controls, business continuity, and information security.

I   And they work together?

ISM   Yes. We are the people responsible for identifying and managing business risks.

I   That sounds like quite a big responsibility. How do you even decide where to start?

ISM   It's not as hard as you might imagine. There are a lot of legal and regulatory requirements – they tell us quite a bit about what we have to do.

I   Which are the most important?

ISM   They're all important, but we're a US-owned company, listed on the New York Stock Exchange, so I'd have to say Sarbanes-Oxley.

I   What's that?

ISM   It's a US law intended to ensure the accuracy of corporate financial statements. Most aspects of Sarbanes-Oxley relate to how we manage and report our financial results. Obviously our IT systems play a massive role in managing this information, so Sarbanes-Oxley has a significant impact on information security management.

I   But you don't just leave compliance up to the IT manager?

ISM   No we don't. Our financial risks and controls section takes responsibility for ensuring that we comply with Sarbanes-Oxley, and we in the information security section implement many of the necessary controls.

I   And how do you ensure compliance with Sarbanes-Oxley?

ISM   Amongst other things, we work closely with the financial risks and controls section to ensure that appropriate technical controls are in place. And they carry out regular audits.

This month it is the turn of the information security manager

I	Audits?
ISM	Yes, to prevent and detect financial irregularities across the business.
I	[smiles] And do they?
ISM	That would be privileged information.
I	So that's Sarbanes-Oxley. Is there anything else?
ISM	PCI-DSS. Oh – and the European Data Protection Directive.
I	Let's take them one at a time shall we? PCI-DSS?
ISM	Anyone who has anything to do with payments made using payment cards – credit or debit cards – knows about this one. We certainly do, since 75% of purchases from our company are made using payment cards. It's the payment card industry data security standard (PCI-DSS), and all the major payment card companies – Visa, MasterCard, American Express and so on – require any organization that processes payment cards to comply with it.
I	I see. And I'd guess that the information security section implements the controls for this one too?
ISM	You've got it.
I	And what about the European Data Protection Directive? I suppose that affects us because we have stores all over Europe, to say nothing of a huge online presence there. Is it a law?
ISM	No, it's not actually. But it does require each EU country to pass laws covering the protection of personal data. We have to comply with the data protection laws in all EU countries, so we've developed a standard approach that we use for handling personal data everywhere in Europe. There's a replacement for this directive due to come into force quite soon: it's called the European General Data Protection Regulation, but everyone abbreviates that to GDPR. When it's been passed we'll have two years to transition to the new rules.
I	And which of your risk management sections is responsible for making sure that you comply with European data protection laws?
ISM	This is not one of ours at all. It belongs to the legal department! But of course information security still deals with the controls side of things.
I	So we've talked quite a bit about what information security does, and a bit about what financial risks and controls does. What about business continuity?
ISM	Oh, business continuity's the section that defines policy for business continuity, creates templates to help with creation of business continuity plans and runs regular business continuity tests.
I	Just the templates for creating plans across the organization? They don't create all the continuity plans themselves?
ISM	That kind of detailed planning is much better done by the people who actually do the work. Every department creates and tests its own business continuity plans. But of course, business continuity reviews the plans and audits the tests.
I	And does this apply to IT service continuity too? I must ask, because after all, almost every department's business continuity plans are going to depend on IT services. Anything that goes wrong there…well.
ISM	We know, which is why we work so closely with them.
I	What about the future plans? I've heard there are some changes coming?
ISM	Changes to the way we manage business continuity? You're exceptionally well informed. We're already well aligned to the requirements of ISO 22301, and so our business continuity manager has been talking to the head of risk management about the possible benefits of assessment and certification to this standard. Watch this space.
I	So – information security. We've talked a fair bit about the role of information security in implementing controls. What else does your information security management team do?
ISM	We're responsible for all aspects of information security across the organization. We define information security policies which apply to all departments. We conduct regular awareness training (mostly web-based). And we carry out audits to ensure that the policies are being complied with.
I	How many information security policies are we talking about?
ISM	Currently? Only five.

I　Only? And what are they?

ISM　Well, there's the risk assessment policy, which defines the types of information security risk assessment we do and says how often they should be carried out. Then there's the data classification policy, the data centre security policy, the remote-working policy, and the web application security policy.

I　Can you convince our readers that we need quite so many different policies?

ISM　I can try. The data classification policy: I'm grateful for the chance to talk about this one actually, because so many staff members don't seem to be aware that it exists or that it's important. It's not that surprising, I suppose. In practice most of our data isn't classified, but we do need to do a bit more work to make sure people understand this one. This is the policy that defines our classification categories: sensitive, confidential, personal and company secret.

I　And if I was ever in any doubt that a data classification policy's important, those names are as much explanation as I need.

ISM　Yes. And then it describes how we should be managing the different types of data. And don't forget, we're not just talking about data we have stored on our IT system. We're talking about paper-based and voice-based data too – chats in the cafe, telephone conversations, Skype…

I　Careless talk costs lives?

ISM　Not quite, but that's the general idea!

I　You mentioned a data centre security policy?

ISM　That one defines the information security controls we need for our data centres, and for the servers, storage and networking equipment in the data centres. We apply the same policy to all of our data centres to make sure we can meet all of our legal and regulatory obligations, even if data is moved around. Then there's the web application security policy, which defines the controls we need to protect our external-facing websites. Then there's the remote-working policy, which defines the equipment and communication methods that can be used by staff who are working outside a SellUGoods location. I'd say the need for these is pretty self-explanatory too.

I　All of this is about tech we already have…what about new IT equipment?

ISM　That's an excellent point. We're considering introducing a policy to cover acquisition of new IT equipment. There's someone working on a draft as we speak.

I　Tell us a bit more about the relationship between the risk management department and the IT department.

ISM　We do work very closely together, especially those of us in the information security section. We can't manage risk effectively without IT systems that do what we need them to do. Obviously we delegate technical controls such as firewall configuration, patch installation and anti-virus measures to IT. There are frequent changes to firewall rules, and other technical security controls; though we do review some of them we mostly just let the technical staff in the IT department, who are very knowledgeable about the technology, get on with it. In the information security section we retain overall responsibility though.

I　I see. We've heard a lot about continual improvement recently. How does risk management deal with that?

ISM　Well, first off, we know what we're already good at. That's the starting point. The approach to cyber resilience at SellUGoods is mainly based on prevention; our policies and audits ensure that controls are in place to defeat security attacks. But there are things we need to work on.

I　For example?

ISM　We've all heard about major security breaches involving payment card data at other retail organizations. Obviously we already have a process for security incident management in place, but we've been reviewing security incident management and we'll be making recommendations for how to move forward shortly.

I　Are you saying there's a problem with our security incident management?

ISM　No, not at all. Part of our PCI-DSS compliance requires us to have a security incident plan that we test annually. It's just that we haven't needed to use it to deal with any significant events. Maybe we could do things to make it a little more…robust.

I	Anything else?
ISM	Our research tells us that what we need next is to develop a more balanced approach, with a greater emphasis on detecting and recovering from incidents, but without compromising the need to prevent security incidents wherever possible. We're already reviewing security incident management and we'll be making recommendations for how this could be improved before too long.
I	What's the scope of the review?
ISM	The scope?
I	Will the review be looking at how security incidents are detected, or just at how they are handled after they become known?
ISM	You know, I'm not sure. Thanks for pointing that out to me. I'll have to get back to you.
I	One last thing. Do you have any thoughts you would like to share about the IT department?
ISM	The IT department has a technical focus. They have a very effective **service desk**, and a good process for reviewing changes before they go live.
I	But?
ISM	Other IT service management processes are less formal.
I	Who plans the IT strategy? Is it something risk management would like to be more involved with?
ISM	The IT director owns the IT strategy, and technical teams take responsibility for areas such as availability management and capacity management, but at the moment there are no formal processes or measurement of these and there are no availability plans or capacity plans. There's an **IT steering group** (ISG), which includes the IT director, the IT development manager and the heads of key business departments. The ISG helps to define overall IT strategy, reviews the IT budget and approves spending on major IT projects.
I	Are there any changes you are hoping to see?
ISM	Yes. I have been talking to the IT director recently about approaches to integrating cyber resilience into an improved IT service management framework. The ISG has already approved a project to look at how this could be done. So watch this space.

Medical example: MedUServ Ltd

MedUServ Ltd is a small, private, UK-based company that tests medical samples.

There are five board members – the two co-founders, the company secretary (who is a lawyer), a managing director and a technical director. The technical director, who has a medical background, manages the labs. The finance manager, who reports to the managing director, manages any projects, including the outsourcing contract for all of MedUServ's IT.

MedUServ has ISO 9001 certification for its labs. The company set out to obtain this certification because a potential customer wanted it to demonstrate that its processes for handling medical samples were reliable and repeatable. MedUServ has benefited greatly from the certification work. ISO 9001 certification has helped the company to win several contracts. It has also ensured that the company maintains well-documented processes for most business activities, and that the people who work for the company are good at following formal written policies. MedUServ's outsourced IT services were not included in the ISO 9001 assessment and certification.

Every medical sample that arrives at MedUServ for testing comes with a paper form, which has been printed by the doctor requesting the test. The form contains some information about the patient, space for test results and a barcode that can be used to access an electronic version of the same form online. The form includes 'personally identifiable information' which is subject to the UK Data Protection Act.

MedUServ's ISO 9001-compliant management system means that there are well-documented, well-understood, and reliably executed procedures for managing medical samples and the written forms that accompany them. MedUServ's lab technicians analyse the samples reliably and enter results on the paper forms accurately. The barcodes are scanned to access the patients' electronic forms, the patients' results are entered online and the paper forms are archived. MedUServ's staff take all the steps necessary to maintain the confidentiality, integrity and availability of patient data.

MedUServ's finance manager has been appointed as the data controller for the company; he is the person responsible for ensuring that MedUServ complies with the requirements of the UK Data Protection Act. He knows the people who work in the labs very well: he has confidence in them and in the company's processes. However, he relies on the IT outsourcer to provide appropriate levels of protection for IT systems and data. Like everyone else in the company he assumes that the IT outsourcer does the right things to protect the confidentiality, integrity and availability of information; there are no checks in place to make sure that this is the case.

MedUServ is in the process of negotiating a contract with a new customer – a very large hospital. The contract includes some specific clauses about assuring the cyber resilience of any IT systems where patient data is held. This has prompted the finance manager to contact the outsourcing supplier to ask them to provide the assurance the new contract will require.

MedUServ Ltd is a small, private UK-based company that tests medical samples

Manufacturing example: MakeUGoods

MakeUGoods is a relatively small company that specializes in the manufacture of novel petroleum products. MakeUGoods has developed methods and recipes for the bulk production of materials that are unusually light and strong. These are extremely valuable in manufacturing components for military applications. MakeUGoods has also established an enviable reputation for **reliability**. Consequently, MakeUGoods has lucrative contracts to supply its products to a number of defence manufacturers. The company is aggressively pursuing new contracts in both foreign and domestic defence markets, and the new company chairman is anxious to ensure that challenging growth and efficiency targets are met.

The new chairman knows that MakeUGoods has many strengths:

● The company's manufacturing processes are highly innovative.

● The company supplies superior products at lower prices than its competitors.

● The company has a reputation for reliability.

● The company has a wide range of customers who buy in bulk.

● The company has an excellent health and safety record.

● There is good availability and integrity of IT services.

However, MakeUGoods will only remain a market leader if it can manage threats to its position effectively. The company has taken appropriate measures to address the most urgent threats – industrial espionage and the risk of sabotage.

The manufacturing process developed by the research and innovations team at MakeUGoods is unique, clever, difficult to implement and highly reliant on IT. It is the company's most valuable asset, and if the details were to become known to other companies, MakeUGoods would lose its competitive edge. The company is determined to protect its intellectual property.

MakeUGoods also needs to take into account the fact that many of its contracts are with defence manufacturers, and this may attract security attacks from well-resourced hackers. As a relatively small company MakeUGoods is particularly vulnerable to the long-term effects of a successful attack. Significant loss of manufacturing capability for whatever reason would leave the company unable to fulfil its contracts and could shatter its reputation for reliability. Naturally enough, MakeUGoods goes to great lengths to protect its plant against industrial espionage and other security threats.

There is a SCADA control system (see box) that controls all manufacturing. This has dedicated connections to MakeUGoods' factory equipment but no other network access. This is designed to eliminate the risk of remote attacks. The most highly innovative aspects of manufacturing take place in closed rooms, to which only a small number of specially vetted people have access. This limits the possibility of information about critical processes being leaked. The SCADA systems at MakeUGoods are managed by the engineering team, which is completely separate from the IT organization.

What is SCADA?

SCADA stands for 'supervisory control and data acquisition'. It's a system that provides control of equipment by sending signals to the equipment and collecting status information from it.

SCADA is used at MakeUGoods to programme and monitor all the manufacturing equipment in the factory.

It is important to protect SCADA systems, as a security breach could enable an attacker to completely take over the factory automation.

Despite the fact that MakeUGoods is a relatively small company, it must comply with all relevant health and safety legislation. It must also ensure that its manufacturing processes avoid putting the surrounding population and environment at risk.

The new chairman has been told that the IT department at MakeUGoods bases much of its ITSM on ITIL; specifically processes from the service transition and service operation stages of the service lifecycle, including incident management, request fulfilment, change management and release management. The change management process in particular is very robust, which is part of the reason for the company's reputation for reliability.

The chairman has identified that the IT department has a conservative attitude towards change. While being slow and careful ensures the integrity and availability of IT services, it can take an inordinate amount of time to approve and implement even simple changes. This is already causing friction, with some departments within the organization talking quite seriously about bypassing the internal IT department completely and procuring routine IT services from the cloud. With a period of rapid growth ahead, relationships between IT and other departments may deteriorate unless steps can be taken to improve matters.

4.4 CYBER RESILIENCE STRATEGY QUESTIONS

1. How effective is governance of cyber resilience in your organization? Are the right people involved? What could be improved?

2. In what ways do your stakeholders contribute to defining your cyber resilience objectives? What improvements could you suggest?

3. How do you know that the stakeholders in your organization understand your cyber resilience objectives?

4. What is the scope of cyber resilience policies in your organization? What additional policies are needed? How easy are the policies for people to understand? How appropriate is the level of detail for the audience?

5. What obstacles stand in the way of achieving your cyber resilience objectives? What could you do to overcome them?

6. How closely aligned are the processes and organizational units that run IT service management and cyber resilience in your organization? How well do they work together? How could this be improved?

7. Do your cyber resilience policies work effectively to help protect your organization from threats? What could you do to improve the effectiveness of these policies?

8. What monitoring would help to ensure your cyber resilience policy is working effectively?

9. Do your cyber resilience audits provide the level of assurance that is needed? What improvements could be made to the type or frequency of audits?

10. How effective is your cyber resilience compliance management? How confident are you that all legal, regulatory and contractual requirements are being met? How could compliance management be improved?

5

Cyber resilience design

This chapter covers:

- Objectives and controls for cyber resilience design
- Aligning with IT service design
- Design scenarios

5 Cyber resilience design

When the strategy has been defined, the next step is to design everything needed to turn that strategy into reality. It is not possible to just implement controls and processes to deliver the strategy, because a detailed design that identifies what is needed must first be created, with details of how it can be implemented. Once the cyber resilience design is created it will not provide the protection and resilience for an organization's needs by itself; however, a good design will provide a solid underpinning to ensure that the processes and controls that can be implemented later will meet the organization's needs.

Cyber resilience design ensures that an organization's management system and security controls are designed in a way that will realize the cyber resilience strategy. Good cyber resilience design will enable an organization to achieve the required level of cyber resilience efficiently and cost effectively, ensuring that risks are understood, that the negative impact of security controls is minimized, and that everything required can be efficiently transitioned into the operational environment.

If cyber resilience is not designed, security controls will evolve on an ad hoc basis to meet the demands of specific risks and issues. This will provide controls that meet some specific cyber resilience risks that have been identified, but without a holistic design it is likely that these controls will fail to address many important risks and issues. Good cyber resilience design can result in a management system and controls that are flexible enough to meet the changing cyber resilience needs of the organization, giving the right level of protection with minimal gaps while minimizing the negative impact on the business. Unless the whole threat landscape is considered at the design stage, it is likely that controls will be missing and that the management system will not provide the required level of resilience. Good design can also help to prevent duplication of functionality in controls, although a requirement for defence-in-depth may require controls to have overlapping functionality, to ensure that failure of a single control does not result in exposure to significant risk.

A cyber resilience design will help organizations who work with third-party vendors to manage and protect intellectual property

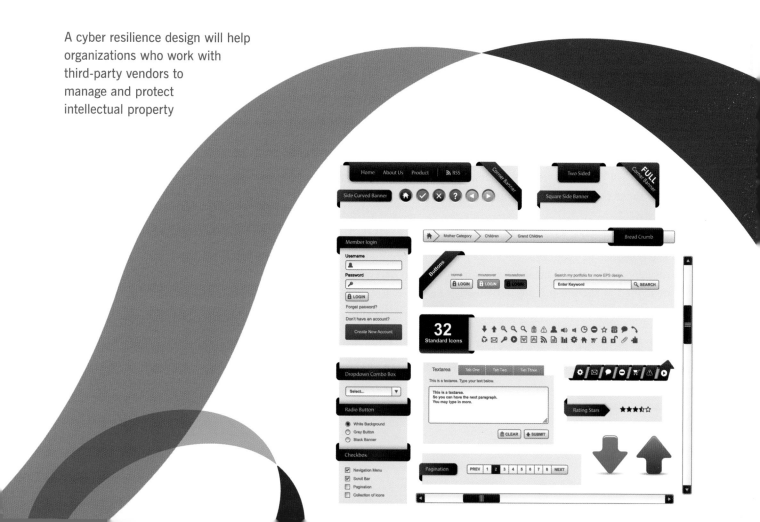

Cyber resilience design helps an organization to:

- Ensure that the design of the organization's management system is able to meet the requirements defined in the cyber resilience strategy
- Design cyber resilience controls that will deliver the required level of cyber resilience
- Understand the cyber resilience risks posed by people, processes and technology, and design solutions that will manage these appropriately
- Achieve an appropriate balance between preventative controls that will help to prevent security incidents from occurring, detective controls that will detect security incidents when they do occur, and corrective controls that will enable recovery after a security incident has occurred
- React to changing threats and vulnerabilities to ensure that the strategic intent is met even as the environment changes
- Create layers of security controls that provide defence-in-depth, to ensure that failure of one security control does not expose the organization to immediate loss in the event of a threat occurring.

Cyber resilience design identifies:

- How cyber resilience will be integrated into all appropriate aspects of the organization's management system
- What cyber resilience controls are needed to deliver the organization's cyber resilience strategy
- How information will be classified and what controls are required for each classification. For example there may be specific controls that are applied to payment card data, or to personally identifiable information, or to corporate financial data
- How to design cyber resilience into IT services, rather than providing security controls as a later add-on
- How cyber resilience will be included in the design of processes and procedures so that these meet the cyber resilience requirements of the organization as well as other requirements
- How cyber resilience will be included in the definition of roles and responsibilities, in training and in all aspects of people management.

Cyber resilience should be designed into all areas where it might be required, including for example:

- Business processes and systems
- IT services and systems
- Physical and environmental systems
- **Architecture**s and standards for any of the above
- Attitudes, behaviour and culture throughout the organization.

Section 5.1 describes controls that are required to support cyber resilience design, and section 5.2 discusses how these controls could be integrated into an overall IT service management system design.

5.1 CONTROL OBJECTIVES AND CONTROLS FOR CYBER RESILIENCE DESIGN

The objective of cyber resilience design is to ensure that controls are appropriately designed to manage cyber resilience risks to the business objectives through carefully designed and planned controls. All of the controls described in section 5.1 are particularly relevant to the design stage of the cyber resilience lifecycle but they are also active during other stages.

5.1.1 Human resource security (people, HR, awareness and training)

The objective of designing controls in human resources is to manage the risk from employees (and contractors) during hiring, whilst they are in employment and when they leave the organization. The consideration here is slanted towards cyber resilience and not meant to be a general description of HR practices.

People are an organization's greatest asset and also the weakest link when it comes to cyber resilience. People – the general staff, managers, technicians, system administrators, researchers, engineers, scientists, doctors, sales and marketing personnel – are examples of the users of IT systems. Some of them can also be the people who administrate, manage and maintain these systems. This means that they will invariably have privileged access to IT and information systems that contain the organization's critical and sensitive assets.

Equally, people can also be the hackers – the threats that an organization's valuable assets require protection from. For example, many organizations face what is commonly known as insider threats from dishonest, disgruntled and disaffected employees. Insider threats can lead to deliberate exfiltration of information, fraud, theft and misuse of assets, and cyber resilience incidents. These employees can also be targets of malicious influence and coercion. This is a pre-eminent vulnerability to organizations due to the fact that these people are already inside the organization, have access to systems and physical locations, and may have privileges (in the case of administrators) that are difficult to monitor or manage. This is a common and growing threat to organizations. Recent surveys on insider threats show that it is a real and growing exposure for many organizations.

On the other hand, poorly trained and unaware employees can inadvertently disclose information, lose assets or cause system failures – not forgetting the well-intentioned employees who circumvent controls or cut corners that may also result in unintended exposure to risks for the organization.

These are all HR- or people-related risks to cyber resilience that can be managed through a well-thought-out and designed HR management process. In cyber resilience, HR management does not end with the recruitment of the resource. Like many other areas for cyber resilience there needs to be a holistic and lifecycle approach to HR management, from the initial identification of the need for an employee to the job **specification**, skills matching, induction training, in-job training and line management through to termination.

5.1.1.1 Recruitment process

The recruitment process starts with the definition of the role, the responsibilities and the skills required. Cyber resilience should be central when considering these elements. For example, when defining the role, any security or cyber duties should be considered. Where the role has direct cyber resilience responsibilities, these should be specifically noted alongside the specialist skills and **qualification**s that are required for the role, including any clearance requirements if the individual will be working for or in government organizations.

Employees with weaknesses can be susceptible to coercion and malicious influence

These would typically be documented in a job specification or description. However, the level of screening and vetting that can be carried out will largely depend on where the organization is operating. Organizations will have to consider the local legal and cultural constraints and design their screening and vetting policies and processes accordingly. The idea is to manage risks to an acceptable level; it may not always be possible to totally eliminate the risks. For example, multinationals operating in multiple jurisdictions may have screening policies that are aligned with national laws and processes of the countries they are operating in.

5.1.1.2 Pre-employment

It is important that the right person is recruited for the right role. Pre-employment or contract checks provide an opportunity for employers to get some assurance about the person being recruited before a final commitment to employ is made. The pre-employment checks should include verification of:

● Qualifications and skills

● Employment history through references

● Right to work – for example any restrictions on employment due to immigration

● Criminal and financial record status

● Qualifications

● Identity

● Security clearances

● Health issues.

Best practice

Pre-employment checks must be made to verify the prospective employee's claims made on the application and CV. This is an early check on the integrity of the person. False claims or gross exaggeration of skills and experience will point to possible future issues.

Any discrepancies should be followed through. Employment should not be granted before the checks are complete.

If recruitment agencies are used, ensure they are carrying out preliminary screening of candidates.

Although past history is not an indicator of future behaviour, financial problems or heavy debt for example may point to susceptibility to bribery; falsification of qualifications may suggest lack of integrity; and poor health, like alcoholism, addiction or other indiscretions, can be exploited by others for coercion and blackmail. From a cyber resilience perspective, organizations should ensure that people with access to sensitive assets are not susceptible to influence, corruption, bribery or blackmail. Organizations should be careful to ensure that their pre-employment checks are not used to discriminate against people with a disability or medical condition (or perceived to be used in this way) and such checks should be aligned to the local disability and employment laws.

5.1.1.3 During employment

Pre-employment checks and clearances are a barometer of an employee's past; however, it is not a prediction of their future conduct. People's personal and financial situations change over time, hopefully to the good but they can also worsen. These are matters for line management to monitor and identify before they lead to the aforementioned susceptibility. Line managers should ensure that any significant changes to employee behaviours are noted. An unhappy or disgruntled employee can be just as dangerous as a coerced employee. Many insider attacks are carried out by disaffected or disgruntled employees who have grievances against their employers and unlimited means of exfiltration for doing this. Small, cheap and ubiquitous storage devices can easily store whole databases of information that can be simply concealed or exfiltrated;

high-resolution cameras on phones can be used to take photos of documents and screens. With the proliferation of remote working, mobile devices, camera phones, miniature cameras and perimeter-less networks, the opportunity for exfiltration of information is vast.

Key message

Ensure that people with cyber resilience responsibilities and privileged access are not susceptible to blackmail, coercion and external influence.

Line management duties should include a review of employee wellbeing, welfare and clearances.

Sudden changes in employee behaviours such as working late, increased spending, requesting additional access or other uncharacteristic activities are usually signs that need further scrutiny.

Line management practices should include regular review and appraisal of the employee's work performance and, if possible, their personal situation. Providing employees with work–life balance, job satisfaction, employee engagement, recognition and reward, complemented with monitoring controls to ensure that wrongdoings do not go unnoticed, are good line management practices that can help to mitigate these risks. One way of incentivizing employees is to reward secure behaviour by linking performance and reward schemes. Conversely, bad behaviour and deliberate breaches of policy should be dealt with through a formal disciplinary process, and continual deliberate breaches should lead to swift dismissal.

Additionally, at the technical level, judiciously designed and allocated access rights based on employees' roles (role-based access) and regular reviews of those access rights, with monitoring and logging activities, are good technical measures that should be implemented.

5.1.1.4 Exit and termination of employment

HR processes include smooth and contentious exit from employment. As employees or contractors leave the organization their exit should be planned and controlled. The leavers' process needs to be designed to include cyber resilience controls such as asset retrieval, termination of systems and network access, and a reminder of any post-employment or contract obligations such as requirements for confidentiality.

Organizations should design their **joiners, movers and leavers** (JML) process to include a lifecycle approach to HR, which includes the initial hiring, role changes, review of access rights during employment and the exit and termination of employment. A fully functioning JML process is essential to cyber resilience. The JML process is used to track the employee's journey within an organization, which includes the allocation of new access rights, review and modification as their roles and access requirements change, and finally how their access is terminated when they leave employment. The JML process includes review of rights and authorization of access at each stage of a user's journey.

5.1.1.5 Training and awareness

Not all cyber resilience breaches are malicious. A combination of poorly trained employees and sophisticated or complex IT systems can lead to errors. Induction training should include users familiarizing themselves with the organization's security policies and procedures: ensure that they read and understand them, and if possible formally retain a record of their acceptance of the policies, as this may be required for compliance or regulatory purposes. Cyber resilience-specific training, including information and data protection training, must be provided to employees on a regular basis. Training should be designed and tailored to specific roles where possible. For example, cyber resilience-specific roles should include professional training: incorporate certification, accreditation and continual professional development (CPD) that ensures continual improvement of knowledge and skills. Behavioural and cultural change should be nurtured and conveyed through leadership and vision including slogans such as 'Cyber resilience is everyone's duty'. This could be executed throughout the organization, possibly built into **charter**s, vision statements and mandates from senior management.

Key message

Design training to address risks that the organization is facing, and make it specific to the roles and responsibilities of employees.

Awareness campaigns should be designed to raise awareness and address specific risks or issues.

New systems, whether developed or acquired, should include user training and operating procedures as part of their transition process into service operation. The threat profile of a system can be used to design training for the system. For example, if a new call centre is likely to be the target of social engineers who would try to get inside information by phoning the call centre, then provide the call centre staff with anti-social-engineering training. The incident management team for instance may need training on responding to incidents on the new system.

Organizations should identify the competencies and skills required for each role and align their training to match these. The skills, competencies and training requirements should be reviewed to ensure that organizations have the right set of skills as technologies and risks evolve.

Separately, a generic skills matrix such as the Skills Framework for the Information Age (SFIA) can be consulted and adapted to suit the organizational need. SFIA defines nearly 100 professional IT skills, arranged in six categories, each of which has several subcategories. It also defines seven levels of attainment, each of which is described in generic, non-technical terms.

5.1.2 System acquisition, development, architecture and design

The control objectives of cyber resilience in system acquisition, architecture and design are to ensure that cyber resilience controls are considered at the earliest stage of system design, development and acquisition, as well as throughout the system development lifecycle so that vulnerabilities in software are minimized.

5.1.2.1 System acquisition and development

Like information, information systems too have a lifecycle within which they are perceived, defined, designed, developed, tested and transitioned into operations, used, maintained and ultimately disposed of at the end of the lifecycle when they are no longer required. At each stage of development and acquisition, cyber resilience must be considered. Software developed or acquired without cyber resilience consideration is likely to be vulnerable to cyber-attacks, have back-doors, get infected by malware and not be as robust in the face of system failures.

Key message

Incorporate cyber resilience controls into the system at an early stage. Bolt-on controls are expensive and disruptive to implement and may not be as effective as those designed from inception.

There are many software development lifecycle (SDLC) methodologies, including 'Waterfall', 'Spiral', 'Agile', 'RAD' etc. Each can be fitted to a cycle. Table 5.1 shows a conceptual SDLC model and how cyber resilience controls can be integrated.

System acquisition and development starts with the identification of a business problem that needs to be resolved – a business objective. This is then converted into technical requirements, starting with functional and non-functional requirements. Security requirements should form part of this requirements capture. There are some cyber resilience requirements that are easy to derive, such as the basic need for authorization, authentication and accounting. Generally stated, all systems will require some sort of access control and auditing. Other specific control requirements, such as the type of access control and authentication, will require detailed consideration.

Table 5.1 How cyber resilience controls can be integrated into the software lifecycle

System development lifecycle							
Initiation	Requirements analysis and capture	System design	System development	Testing	Implementation	Operations and maintenance	Decommissioning or disposal
Cyber resilience control integration							
Control objectives	Control requirements, business and privacy impact assessments	Initial controls, and KPI design	Threat **modelling** and control development	Cyber resilience security testing	Control implementation	Audit review and improvement of controls	Secure disposal of system and data
			Secure coding standards, OWASP top 10	Application security testing			

A good example of a way to ensure that cyber resilience controls are considered from the beginning is to incorporate these in an organization's project and programme management methodology. For example, gateways or checkpoints can be established in the project plan where security requirements are tested and refined. For instance, a **PRINCE2**® project initiation document (PID) could include high-level security requirements that can be refined and expanded later as the project progresses.

In Agile development, each 'epic' (or smaller 'sprint') could include a set of security deliverables alongside the functions. User stories could be designed to test for positive and negative outcomes (the so-called 'evil' stories).

5.1.2.2 Requirements analysis

The requirements analysis process is normally used to capture what the stakeholders expect from a system. Requirements analysis is usually incorporated in business or systems analysis, and it is used to understand and document the overall business problem and requirements. It is an important process that is part of many matured development methodologies. From a cyber resilience perspective this is a critical stage and invariably the starting point in the security control development process. Alongside the functional and non-functional requirements, cyber resilience requirements must also be captured. Non-functional requirements are usually where security requirements are captured; there are, however, some security requirements that should be functional requirements of any system. For example, the control objectives for a system could be captured as functional requirements, with the non-functional requirements detailing the more abstract requirements. Including cyber resilience requirements as functional requirements gives prominence to cyber resilience and ensures that these important requirements are not relegated to the status of non-functional requirements, which are perceived to be less important. This is crucial if systems are to be resilient by design.

Requirements can be gathered either from stakeholders or from security best practices, policies and standards. For example, it is certain that most systems will require some level of confidentiality, integrity and availability, which could be initially translated through:

● Authorization

● Authentication

● Auditability

● Validation and verification

● Backup and restore

● Resilience.

These could form the basis of the functional cyber resilience requirements. A more formal and detailed requirements gathering exercise would expand on these and include them, as either functional or non-functional requirements.

Table 5.2 Security requirements should be captured alongside system requirements in functional and non-functional form

FR = functional requirement; NFR = non-functional requirement

Requirement	Functional requirement – security
FR1	The system must require users to be authenticated before being allowed access
FR2	The system must support remote connections
FR3	The system must support **multi-factor authentication**
FR4	The system must support encryption
FR5	All system activities must be auditable
FR6	The system must be PCI-DSS compliant
Requirement	**Non-functional requirement – security**
NFR1	The system must require unique credentials for each user
NFR2	The system should support multiple encryption algorithms
NFR3	The system must support alphanumeric passwords
NFR4	The system should support digital certificates
NFR5	The system should support hardware encryption
NFR6	The system must support session time-out
NFR7	The system should be maintainable and supportable both locally and remotely

The scope of cyber resilience is wider than just security requirements: it also includes complementary controls, which are not usually considered as security requirements. However, these can also support the resilience of a system – for example:

● **Reliability** System uptime and resilience requirements

● **Maintainability** Supportability – how easy is it to support, maintain and upgrade the system

● **Usability** User interface and ease of use

● **Extensibility** How easy is it to extend and enhance the system

● **Performance** The performance expectation

● **Portability** Support for other platforms.

Table 5.2 shows a typical way of capturing security requirements in functional and non-functional form.

As well as documenting control objective requirements for a system, captured requirements can act as records of agreement between the project and the stakeholder. From a cyber resilience perspective, the requirements can also be used to design security testing and **key performance indicator**s (KPIs) to assess the effectiveness of the controls that will be tested later in the lifecycle.

The cyber resilience requirements will largely be driven by the confidentiality, integrity and availability requirements of the system. These are generally derived by carrying out a **business impact analysis** (BIA) – assessing what would be the consequences to the business if the confidentiality, integrity and/or availability of the information being processed by the system were to be compromised. BIA is traditionally associated with business continuity planning (BCP). In cyber resilience, BIA can be used as a precursor to risk assessments. Other cyber resilience considerations should include where the system will be used, when it will be used, who will be using the system, the service uptime requirements and the classification of the data to be processed. The BIA should also take legal, contractual and regulatory impacts into consideration. These can form the mandatory security requirements on top of which other requirements can be built.

For example, a system processing credit card transactions will need to comply with the PCI-DSS. The PCI-DSS requirements can be derived from the requirement of compliance or the applicable self-assessment questionnaire (SAQ). An HR system, or any system that processes personal data, will need to consider data protection compliance requirements. The data protection and privacy impacts are generally derived through a privacy impact assessment (PIA). Indeed, some government system developments and acquisitions require PIA to be carried out before a system is developed or acquired so that privacy requirements can be incorporated from the beginning.

Requirements capture is an iterative process because complete requirements are difficult to capture or implement at once. Formal requirements analysis and capture methods should be used and the requirements documented. Sign-off from stakeholders must be obtained before implementation.

5.1.2.3 Architecture design and development

Enterprise and security architecture are disciplines that are ways of developing structured and controlled system development. There are many established architecture methodologies. **TOGAF**® is the most widely used of these because of its open framework and extensibility: since it is a framework it can incorporate other architecture methodologies. TOGAF's architecture is hinged around its **Architecture Development Method** (ADM), which is an iterative model that includes business, application, data and technology domains. Requirements for each of the domains are gathered and refined in each iteration of the ADM and validated in each domain. A repository of architecture artefacts is built and this can be reused. Although TOGAF does not specifically address security requirements, it can be adapted to cyber resilience and used to gather cyber resilience requirements in a formalized architectural framework that considers business, application, data and technology. 'Sherwood Applied Business Security Architecture' (SABSA®) is another architecture method specifically dedicated to security, which is gaining popularity. It can be integrated into the TOGAF ADM to provide the security architecture component missing in the TOGAF ADM. Figure 5.1 shows how this can be achieved.

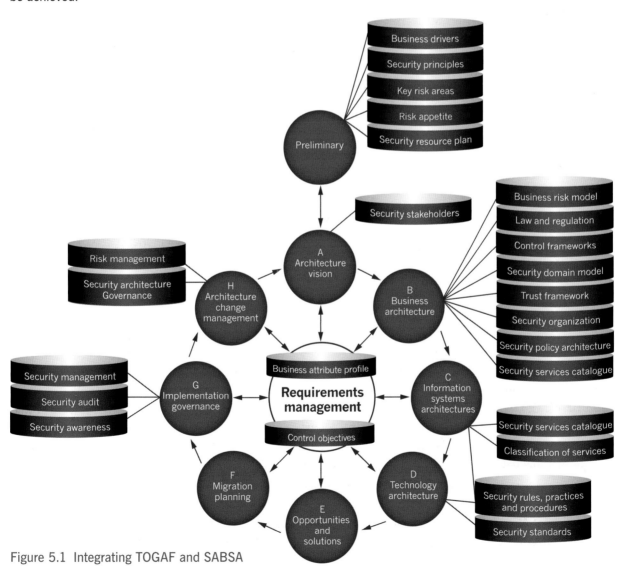

Figure 5.1 Integrating TOGAF and SABSA

Key message

Enterprise architecture offers a method of supporting system design, development and acquisition. It can provide established policies, taxonomy, artefacts, baseline architecture artefacts and design patterns that can be reused and modified, and enhanced to suit an organization's requirements. Enterprise architecture can be used to support and build cyber resilience.

5.1.2.4 Threat and vulnerability modelling

Once an organization has the baseline requirements, further controls can be developed through threat modelling or threat and vulnerability assessment. Threat modelling should assess the likely threats, their capability, skills and motivation to attack the systems. Threat assessments should not be limited to just the external threats but also address insider threats that the system may face. Threat modelling helps to derive system-specific and granular controls. The modelling should also take into account any inherent vulnerabilities of the system that could be exploited by the threats. Threat modelling may be followed by a more formal risk assessment.

The modelling can be as simple as listing generic threats based on the information that the system is to process – for example personal information, credit card information – or modelling can be based on the perceived or known threats to organizations operating in a particular sector. Some good sources of threat information are the many annual breaches, surveys and reports published by security research organizations. Some of these break the threats down by industry and sectors, such as finance, pharmaceuticals, manufacturing etc.

The more discerning organizations can commission specialist security providers to research and tailor threat assessments for their specific needs. Vulnerability modelling can be based on the type of software being used, testing, known vulnerabilities, hosting, support and management model etc. Many vulnerability databases such as the US National Vulnerability Database (http://nvd.nist.gov) and the Common Vulnerabilities and Exposures Database (https://cve.mitre.org) provide a catalogue of reported vulnerabilities by software and applications. The **Open Web Application Security Project** (OWASP) organization (https://www.owasp.org) is another good source for threat modelling to consider (see Table 6.3): this could be a good source for input into an organization's vulnerability modelling.

Not to be confused with risk assessment, threat and vulnerability modelling provides a quick way to understand the security requirements of a system before a more detailed risk assessment is carried out. It is a good source for designing security testing and controls, and it can be applied at different phases of the software development lifecycle.

Hints and tips

Threat and vulnerability modelling should be used to initially assess threats and vulnerabilities of a system before a more detailed risk assessment is carried out.

5.1.2.5 Secure system design and development

Many breaches are due to software vulnerability through poor, or non-existent, secure coding and testing. Once the requirements have been captured, the next phase in the lifecycle is to start designing and developing the system securely. At this stage the development methodology, software development framework, and platforms are selected. Cyber resilience design should consider secure software and hardware platforms for the development. Consider whether the software development framework is well supported, extensible, and supported by vendor or other secure coding standards and programming libraries (for example NIST, CIS, DISA, OWASP). At the minimum, the vendor's security standards for the choice of development framework or programming language should be followed.

5.1.2.6 Systems acquisition

Not all systems are developed in-house. Development is an option for larger organizations, which often require bespoke and tailored software applications to support complex business processes. Smaller organizations may want to procure commercial of-the-shelf software (COTS) that either meets their core requirements out of the box or is extensible through configuration and can be adapted to meet their functional requirements. It is becoming common for systems to be acquired from external software vendors rather than being developed from scratch. This is certainly the case with new cloud-based service models such as **software as a service** (SaaS), where the pay-per-use model is becoming more common. SaaS is often used for software that supports common business processes, such as customer relationship management or enterprise resource management.

Even in the new software acquisition models, security requirements still have an important part to play: more so because organizations are no longer fully in control of their own data but are trusting third parties with their valuable assets. This is even riskier when using shared or multi-tenanted hosting facilities, as cloud-based services may be hosted in data centres which are in separate legal jurisdictions, thus complicating legal and regulatory compliance such as the data protection or privacy laws of the data owner. In some countries such as those in the European Union (EU) it is even illegal to transfer data outside the EU without demonstration of what is called the 'adequacy' requirement. The United States' Safe Harbor is an example of implementation of the adequacy requirement.

When procuring cloud-based facilities, organizations should assess services to be procured against their cyber resilience requirements. Requirements will of course need to be refined to address the new model but most will still be applicable. A good starting point for building a requirements catalogue is the cloud control matrix from the **Cloud Security Alliance** (https://cloudsecurityalliance.org/), which provides a list of good-practice security checks for organizations to use when procuring cloud-based services. These should be supplemented with the organization's own requirements and independent validation, accreditation and certification of the offerings.

5.1.2.7 Cyber resilience security testing

Once systems have been designed and developed, they should be security tested before transitioning into service. As well as the traditional functional and non-functional testing, the system must also undergo rigorous security testing against the control objectives and the requirements.

Security testing, whether code verification, application testing or infrastructure testing (for example, through penetration testing) must be carefully designed to ensure that the controls are working as designed before and after they are in operational service. Code validation and verification should have been part of the system testing. Security testing should concentrate on testing the cyber resilience controls, perhaps using ethical hackers. The design and development phase provides a unique opportunity to test the system in a controlled environment before transitioning into a live or operational environment. Organizations should design their development, test and **production environment**s and keep them separate, through logical, physical or managerial control, so that development and testing is not carried out in a **live environment**.

Testing should be based on scenarios, emulating the threats identified in the risk assessment and known vulnerabilities. Additional testing should include anti-scenario and evil testing, where not only the expected result is tested but also the unexpected results.

Organizations should have a strategy for remediating the findings of the security testing, in the form of **remediation** plans. A risk-based approach to remediation should be taken, as it may not be practical to attempt to resolve all the issues before transitioning into operation. Management should review and analyse the quick wins – the issues that must be fixed before transitioning into operational service; these are usually the high- and medium-impact issues considered in the context of the organization's business and infrastructure. The remediation plan should include ownership and a timeline to remediation for the remaining issues post-transition.

Key message

Cyber resilience should be designed into the system at the beginning – starting with business objectives and requirements capture. A SDLC approach to cyber resilience controls should be taken so that controls are designed, refined and tested at each stage of the system development. If systems are acquired then the security requirements will still apply and the security requirements should be included in any procurement process.

Cyber resilience requirements should be formed from business requirements, as well as being informed by legal, regulatory and compliance policies, threat and vulnerability assessment, and best-practice standards.

Once the system has been developed, test rigorously against the control objectives and controls. If issues are found, remediate any critical issues before transitioning into service.

5.1.3 Supplier and third-party security management

5.1.3.1 Supply chain risk management

The control objective of supply chain risk management is to ensure that the organization's supply chain is robust and does not present cyber resilience risks in terms of availability of the products and services they provide. ITIL supplier management provides a set of processes which ensure that suppliers are managed. This is covered in section 5.2.7.

To many organizations, the supply chain presents significant unknown risks. This is simply because many are not aware of the extent or the nature of their supply chain dependency.

The ever-extending supply chain carries many risks for organizations. There are contractors and sub-contractors, who also have sub-contractors. Many organizations have fully outsourced their IT and business processes to third parties who may have many other customers relying on them for the same services. With the new enthusiasm for cloud-based services and white-labelling of services, it is difficult to understand where an asset is and where the risk lies. Small specialist suppliers may be critical to the cyber resilience of a business, and any of these suppliers might not have the security resources, knowledge or skills required to protect themselves or the assets they are entrusted with. Some suppliers may not follow the minimum security good practices such as having a firewall and an adequate level of access control in place.

An organization's supply chain is as strong as the weakest link in the chain. Without a proper assessment and understanding of the supply chain, organizations will not understand where the risk lies and therefore cannot strengthen it. For example, the smallest company of a single-person supplier could be vital to its cyber resilience; if it fails it may not be able to get a vital component or support to recover its system. In such cases, organizations must assess the risk and ensure that there is an alternative supplier which can provide the necessary components or services within the recovery timeframe. If the risk is understood, then supply chain risk management can be supported by cyber resilience, IT service continuity and business continuity planning.

These risks must be considered and managed from the outset. When procuring services, careful consideration should be given to how and where the risks lie, and how these risks will be managed. Supply chain risks should be assessed and due diligence carried out, along with cyber resilience, before the supplier is trusted with assets or relied upon for critical components that support the business.

Often in complex supply chains, where there may be multiple suppliers (e.g. for end-user computing, for the local area network (LAN), for the wide area network (WAN), for the service desk and for the data centre), the demarcation between suppliers and their responsibilities is not always clear. This is a risk to cyber resilience when rapid response to events is required: the suppliers may not know who should be dealing with a particular incident and some incidents may not be reported or responded to.

Supply chain roles and responsibilities must be clearly defined so that each supplier understands what they are responsible and accountable for, so that suppliers do not blame one another if things go wrong or if they simply do not know that they are responsible for certain controls.

Cyber resilience requirements, such as compliance with security or certification to standards, should be mandated as the baseline for security requirements and complemented with specific requirements from the organization's risk assessment, cyber resilience requirements and/or due diligence. Contracts should reflect as closely as possible cyber resilience policies. If suppliers and third parties do not sign up to policies, then include specific security requirements in their contracts, starting with baselines. Often, requiring suppliers to sign up to policies delays procurement of services, as the supplier will invariably want to review and evaluate the cost of compliance. Furthermore, the policies may contradict their own policies.

A practical way forward is to assess suppliers' cyber resilience posture in questionnaire form using a carefully designed set of questions, and then assess the risks from their responses. These responses could be followed up by a risk-based set of cyber resilience requirements in the contract, binding the questionnaire responses to the contract. In this way specific services and risks can be targeted. For example, there is no point requiring the supplier to comply with an infrastructure security policy if they are only providing the software to the organization and the infrastructure is managed by the organization itself.

ITIL proposes that the supplier management process should include the management of all suppliers and contracts needed to support the provision of IT services to the business. Each service provider should have formal processes for the management of all suppliers and contracts. However, the processes should adapt to cater for the importance of the supplier and/or the contract and the potential business impact on the provision of services. Many suppliers provide support services and products that, when considered independently, have a relatively minor and fairly indirect role in value generation; however, collectively they make a direct, and important, contribution to value generation and the implementation of the overall business strategy. The greater the contribution the supplier makes to business value, the more effort the service provider should put into the management of the supplier, and the more that supplier should be involved in the development and realization of the business strategy. The smaller the supplier's value contribution, the more likely it is that the relationship will be managed mainly at an operational level, with limited interaction with the business. It may be appropriate in some organizations, particularly large ones, to manage internal teams and suppliers, where different business units may provide support for key elements.

The supplier management process should include:

- Implementation and enforcement of the supplier policy
- Maintenance of a contract **management information system**
- Supplier and contract categorization and risk assessment
- Supplier and contract evaluation and selection
- Development, negotiation and agreement of contracts
- Contract review, renewal and termination
- Management of suppliers and supplier performance
- Identification of improvement opportunities for inclusion in the **continual service improvement (CSI) register**, and the implementation of service and supplier improvement plans
- Maintenance of standard contracts, terms and conditions
- Management of contractual dispute resolution
- Management of sub-contracted suppliers.

Although it is IT- and service-focused, ITIL supplier management nevertheless provides organizations with an established and trusted platform to build its cyber resilience supplier management upon.

Key message

A robust supply chain is essential to cyber resilience. Many supply chains are extended and may have weaknesses, such as smaller, risky or unviable suppliers providing a key component for the organization. Organizations must be able to manage the supply chain risk as part of their cyber resilience through supply chain risk assessment and management. Ensure that:

- When procuring services, proper due diligence is carried out: include cyber resilience requirements but also the right to audit the supply chain.
- There are clear and robust contracts in place with suppliers, which includes cyber resilience backed up by robust contract management and enforcement.
- Suppliers are included in the organization's resilience planning.
- Suppliers have a business continuity plan and their BCP testing includes the organization.
- Suppliers have an effective incident response team.
- Critical suppliers are identified and any weaknesses in the supply chain are clearly understood.
- Suppliers know whether they are the critical suppliers.
- Suppliers are resilient to their supply chain failures.
- Suppliers are aware of the recovery objectives and can meet them.
- Suppliers can support an organization as a priority even if they have other clients affected at the same time.
- **Service level agreement**s (SLAs) and KPIs for supplier performance are set and are appropriate.

5.1.3.2 Managing third-party risks

Many organizations allow their suppliers and partners to integrate into their in-house IT systems. This accelerates business data flow and information sharing. However, this also presents risks to the organization from semi-trusted or untrusted sources. Where such needs exist, there should be an unambiguous understanding of the code of conduct that is expected of the third party.

This can be achieved through an agreed protocol in the form of **codes of connection** (CoCo) and information sharing agreements. CoCos set out the minimum set of standards in terms of cyber protection that the third party must adhere to, the compliance and audit requirements, and sanctions for failure to comply.

Often, organizations use the services of third-party consultancies and contractors, support personnel who may be located in the organization's own offices, and may be privy to internal information or systems material. Risk from these third parties needs to be managed. For example, consultants working on their own equipment should not be allowed to connect to the organization's internal networks: they should connect to a 'call-home' type of network that only allows outward connection. This may create a separate issue with regard to sharing sensitive information, as the organization's policy will not be enforceable on the consultant's company computers or network. The consultancy agreement should clearly state who owns the information and whether it will be retained, returned or disposed of.

5.1.3.3 Confidentiality and non-disclosure for suppliers and third parties

Where sensitive information is to be shared with third parties, use non-disclosure or confidentiality agreements before information is discussed or shared with them. Include confidentiality clauses in supplier contracts and ensure that confidentiality is maintained during and after relationships.

Codes of connection should at the minimum require:

- Endpoint protection – minimum build and configuration standards for devices that will access an organization's systems
- Vulnerability management – endpoints and supplier systems
- Perimeter protection – protection of a third party's networks from other connected networks
- Incident management and reporting
- Personnel security – a minimum level of screening for persons accessing the organization's IT systems
- Technical assurance – initial and annual technical assurance through security/penetration testing of third-party networks and connections
- Right to audit – including spot checks and annual audit
- Sanctions for non-compliance – including penalties and disconnection
- Liability clauses – financial penalties for major breaches
- Confidentiality clauses – for the organization and for users of the service.

5.1.3.4 Compliance and auditing of the supply chain and third parties

Organizations need continual assurance that their supply chain is durable and intact. Contractual obligations and codes of connections are all very good. However, without assessment to check that the controls remain effective, assurance cannot be gained. Contract clauses for key suppliers and third parties that have access to an organization's systems or assets should include the right to audit against the CoCos and contractual obligations.

Best practice

- Include security and cyber resilience in contracts with suppliers. These contracts should specify resilience and recovery timing.
- Carry out supplier due diligence and cyber resilience risk assessment.
- Have a risk-based set of baseline resilience requirements.
- Agree a governance structure with clear roles and responsibilities for each supplier.
- Have a cyber resilience and contingency plan for the supply chain.
- Test the plans with the supply chain, at least annually.
- Ensure that key suppliers are included in risk assessments and testing.
- Implement an incident management and reporting process. Include the right to audit in contracts for key suppliers and in the supply chain.
- Create a supply chain risk management and audit plan.
- Ensure that a policy exists for sharing information with external parties.
- Build a separate network for visitors and suppliers to connect out. Do not let third parties connect to the internal network.

5.1.4 Endpoint security

The objective of endpoint security is to ensure that endpoint devices are built and configured to be secure – to ensure that endpoints are not compromised and used to infiltrate the organization's network.

An endpoint or an endpoint device is any device that can be used to access an information resource over a network. Examples of endpoints are PCs, laptops, smartphones, tablets etc.

Proliferation of mobile devices and operating systems and the changing culture towards flexible and mobile working has introduced new opportunities and new security challenges to organizations. De-perimiterization has diminished the organization's traditional technical fortress: the network boundary protected by big firewalls is no longer appropriate. A consequence of this de-perimiterization and adoption of new ways of working with associated risks introduced by things like BYOD has been to elevate the protection of the endpoint to top priority for the cyber risk manager.

Endpoints can store and process huge amounts of data and can be used to connect remotely to the organization's network – hopefully over secure connections such as IPsec VPNs or SSL/TLS encrypted sessions. These connections protect the data-in-transit but not the **data-at-rest** on the endpoint. The endpoint has become an extension of the organization's network – a target for attackers and a new opportunity for them to access the internal networks from trusted endpoints. If the endpoint is compromised, it can provide an avenue for attackers into the organization's network.

Whilst endpoint protection for laptops and desktops is common, protection for mobile smart devices is still maturing. Organizations can protect their endpoints by implementing a policy on mobile working, **mobile device management** (MDM) and BYOD that clearly sets out the operating systems permitted, the secure build and the services that can be provided on the endpoints. This should be backed up by MDM and **network access control** (NAC) technology (see section 7.1.1.10) for scanning, authentication and authorization of devices for use on the organization's network. At the minimum, organizations should ensure that mobile devices are configured to enable the following:

● Hardened build-only to allow minimum services

● Integrated host firewall and IDS/IPS managed by the organization

● Malware protection that is updated from the organization's servers

● Encryption for data-at-rest and date-in-transit

● Strong device authentication using digital certificates and password policy

● Facility for remote management using MDM so that policy can be enforced

● Inclusion of a container for organizational data on BYOD or a policy covering full ownership of BYOD and management via MDM, including deletion of all data on devices, if required

● An incident management policy and a process for reporting lost/stolen devices

● A policy for devices to be treated as untrusted until they have passed minimum standards, verified using NAC.

Best practice

● Secure endpoints by encrypting the disk/storage and the connection to the organization's network.

● Implement host firewall, host IDS/IPS and anti-malware software that is automatically updated before a connection is permitted.

● Authenticate all endpoints.

● Use MDM technology to manage endpoints, especially tablets and smartphones.

● Have a policy on BYOD that outlines the management of the devices and ownership of data.

5.1.5 Cryptography

The objective of cryptography or encryption is to protect the confidentiality of information by preventing access by unauthorized persons. However, this can also be used to authenticate and assure integrity and non-repudiation of actions. Both cryptography and encryption are used synonymously in this publication.

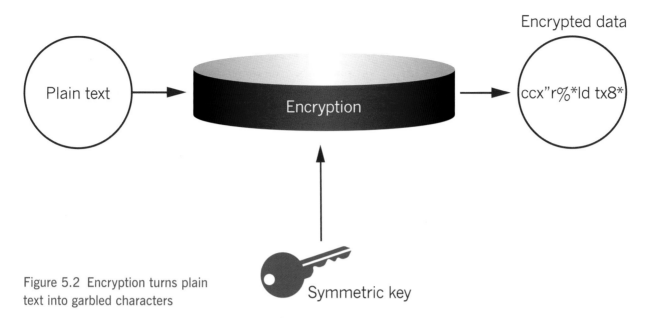

Figure 5.2 Encryption turns plain text into garbled characters

Cryptography or encryption is a valuable tool for protecting sensitive data from unauthorized access both at rest and in transit. An example of encrypting data-at-rest is the encryption of hard disks so that the data stored on the disk is protected from unauthorized access. Protecting a payment system's data flows using encryption is an example of protecting **data-in-transit**. Other uses for cryptography are authenticating access and supporting accountability of actions (non-repudiation). Organizations should have clear policies and standards on the use of encryption covering when, where and how to use encryption, the ciphers or algorithms that should be used, the key sizes and key management requirements.

In the simplest form, cryptography or encryption is the act of turning **plain text** (readable text) into unintelligible code. The process involves taking plain text that users want to hide, transforming it through a complex mathematical process called a cipher or algorithm using a secret (the key) and then receiving an output which is **cipher-text** or encrypted code. The scrambled output is meaningless to anyone without the original key to decipher or decrypt it. The algorithms are not secret; indeed their security is assured through the fact that they have been scrutinized by mathematicians and cryptanalysts for years. The secret is the encryption key. This simple process is depicted in Figure 5.2.

There are two approaches to encryption. One uses the same key, which is known as a **symmetric key** (also known as a secret key). In symmetric key encryption the same key is used to encrypt and also decrypt the encrypted data. The second approach is known as asymmetric or **public key encryption** (PKE). In PKE, the data is encrypted and decrypted using two separate but mathematically related keys. The keys are known as the private and **public key** pair. Symmetric and asymmetric encryption are explained below.

5.1.5.1 Symmetric encryption

In symmetric key encryption (also known as 'secret key encryption') the same key is used to encrypt as well as decrypt the encrypted data.

The problem with symmetric encryption is the difficulty in securely distributing the key to the recipient to decrypt the encrypted message. If the original encrypted message has been intercepted and the key is intercepted too, the message can be deciphered or decrypted by the adversary. To keep the key secure from interception, the key has to be sent securely to the recipient. This is done either by a secure channel that is separate from the encrypted message, or in a face-to-face meeting so that the adversary cannot intercept the key. Sending the key by a separate channel usually works but there is no guarantee that the separate channel is secure.

Sharing and protection of the encryption key becomes a major issue in symmetric key encryption. Symmetric encryption is very fast and efficient and is ideal for low-volume encryption, but it is cumbersome and difficult to manage in a dynamic, high-volume system or where one-to-many and many-to-many communications are

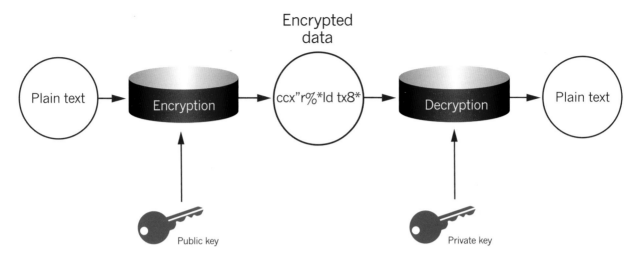

Figure 5.3 Public key encryption

required (especially if keys have to be changed often). If a shared key is compromised, all the instances of the key have to be changed and redistributed.

Private key/symmetric encryption still plays a part in one-to-one secure communication and in public key encryption (see Figure 5.3). For example, it is quite common to encrypt a file and attach it to an email to send to the recipient, followed up by texting or phoning over the password. Imagine, however, doing that for a thousand recipients, every day with a different password, or thousands of senders sharing their keys. Organizations can use a key server but key management still remains an issue. Managing keys and sharing them securely becomes nearly impossible. This is where asymmetric key encryption helps. PKE or public key encryption was invented to overcome this challenge. The advantage of symmetric encryption over asymmetric key encryption is the relative speed of symmetric encryption due to the smaller key size it uses.

5.1.5.2 Asymmetric encryption

In asymmetric key encryption (also known as public key encryption (PKE)) sender and the receiver use a pair of separate but mathematically related keys for encryption and decryption. Although the keys are related, one cannot be derived from the other. The keys form a public and private key pair. The message is encrypted using the recipient's public key and decrypted using their private key. Only the private key needs to be kept secret; the public key can be shared publicly. There is no need to have a pre-shared secret nor any need to exchange a shared secret key. PKE also includes a method for exchanging keys securely.

Key exchange

PKE removes the challenges of sharing keys with communicating partners and forms the foundation for the protection of online commerce and **public key infrastructure** (PKI). Encryption keys can be automatically exchanged securely using a key exchange method in PKE (for example, Diffie-Hellman Key Exchange). Once the keys are exchanged securely, the actual encryption uses symmetric encryption.

SSL and TLS, the protocols that protect internet banking and other secure communication on the web, rely on PKE.

PKE, when used in a PKI, can support additional services such as authentication using digital certificates and non-repudiation of actions using a **digital signature**.

5.1.5.3 Ciphers and algorithms

Both symmetric and asymmetric encryption require ciphers or algorithms to facilitate encryption. Ciphers or algorithms are complex mathematical functions that are used to convert plain text into cipher-text. They require a key to be able to do this. **Advanced encryption standard** (AES), RSA (named after Ron Rivest, Adi Shamir and Leonard Adleman), Triple DES (3DES) and Elliptic Curve (Diffie-Hellman) are some of the more well-known ciphers in use today. DES and AES are types of ciphers or algorithms: RSA and Elliptic Curve on the other hand are asymmetric ciphers.

There are also other types of encryption called 'hashes' or 'message digests'. These include:

● MD5

● SHA-1 – there has been speculation about SHA-1 being prone to weaknesses

● SHA-2

● SHA-3.

Hashing provides a one-way mathematical function; once the information is hashed the original information cannot be derived (reversed) from the result of the hashed data to discover the original text. The result of the hashing is known as the message digest. A hash can be used as a form of checksum to provide assurance about the integrity of the message. Once a message is hashed it can be verified later to see if the message has been altered. In simple terms, hashes do not require a key, only the plain text and the hashing algorithm.

Hashes have many uses in cryptography, including providing integrity of information and in digital signatures (see section 5.1.5.6).

Hints and tips

If assurance of integrity of the data-in-transit or in storage is required then hashes can be used to provide the data using one of the mentioned hashes in a message digest. If the data changes in transit or during storage, it can be easily verified by rehashing the data using the same algorithm and comparing the newly calculated message digest to the one calculated earlier. Hashing tools are feely available for doing this.

5.1.5.4 Key length or strength

The strength of the encryption is denoted by the strength of the key, this is the key length or the size of the key used to encrypt. The larger the key the stronger the encryption; however, the cost is in poor performance as it takes more computer processing to encrypt and decrypt. Therefore a balance should be made between the value of the information to be encrypted and the length of time for which the data needs to be protected (the crypto-period). For example, data encrypted using AES and a key size of 256 bits (often expressed as AES256) is predicted to be resilient for another 20 years, and AES128 for another 10 years, at least. However, any cipher with a key size of less than 128 bits is no longer strong enough to withstand determined attacks. The AES' predecessors DES and 3DES are still in use but are nearing their end of life and should not be used for new systems that require a long crypto-period (a long period of encryption protection).

The predicted crypto-periods of different key sizes are based on current and predicted computing power. If there is a leap in the processing power, the crypto-period should be re-evaluated. That aside, organizations should have a policy covering selecting key sizes and the renewal of keys and ciphers.

Key message

● Digital certificates can be used to authenticate and protect servers and for communication between the end user and the servers on VPNs.

● Organizations generate their own certificates to use locally but these will not provide the trust required externally.

● It is important to obtain digital certificates from well-known and established external certification authorities (CAs).

● Digital certificates can also be used to authenticate end devices such a smartphones and tablets. These are especially useful in securing BYODs.

5.1.5.5 Digital certificates

Digital certificates (also referred to as SSL or TLS certificates) are tied to an organization's public/private key and issued as proof of identity of the organization. These are commonly installed on a web server that needs to be authenticated. The certificates are generated by a trusted third party known as a 'certification authority' (CA) after verification of the applicant's identity and signed using the CA's private key to provide the stamp of trust required by users. Basically, the CA vouches for the authenticity of the organization and the server on which the digital certificate is installed. Self-signed certificates can be generated locally but these have little, or no, trust value to an external user, and internet browsers will not recognize them.

The certificate is installed on the server, which the browsers interrogate to set up a **secure sockets layer** (SSL) session. If a browser's URL starts with https:// then the session being used has been authenticated using a digital certificate and is protected by the SSL and TLS protocols.

Digital certificates are most commonly used to authenticate the web server users connect to, such as internet banking or when paying for something by credit card on an e-commerce site. However, there are other less common uses of digital certificates, such as in endpoint authentication where user devices can be authenticated by similarly installing a certificate on the device. This is used where end-user devices need to be authenticated. For example, an organization may have a large mobile workforce that uses BYOD so digital certificates can be installed on each BYOD to authenticate these devices before they are allowed to connect to the organization's networks.

5.1.5.6 Digital signatures and non-repudiation of action

Digital signatures are a way to prove the authenticity of a message or a document. Online activities can often be denied or repudiated by users. For example, sent emails can be claimed to have been forged or intercepted. A digital signature on the other hand, if used correctly between parties, cannot be repudiated (non-repudiation).

PKE can support non-repudiation: content signed with the recipient's private key (only known to the signer) is used to tie the owner to an action so they cannot deny carrying it out. This is known as a digital signature. Organizations can use digital signatures to provide electronic signatures for contracts and legal documents. Software companies sign software distributed over the internet so the authenticity and integrity of the software can be verified. Because the digital signature is tied to the private key of the signatory used to sign the software, the integrity and origination of the software is proven. The public key of the signer can be used to check digital signatures. Organizations installing signature software downloads should check the authenticity of the software before installing it on their systems.

Digital signature algorithm (DSA) is a US federal digital signature standard (DSS) that is endorsed by NIST. RSA, as well as being a PKE cipher, can support digital signatures too. This is a simplification of the process to provide an illustration of a complex subject. NIST special publications provide a number of standards on the subject and should be consulted.

5.1.5.7 Cryptographic key management

Cryptographic key management is an important aspect of cryptography. Key management includes the generation, distribution, renewal, recovery, revocation (for example, if the key is compromised) and destruction of keys. Key management ensures that keys are protected from inception to disposal, and if they are compromised or lost they can be recovered or retired and replacement keys generated. Key management forms the backbone of any public key infrastructure.

5.1.5.8 Virtual private networks

Virtual private networks (VPNs) are encrypted channels that can be set up to protect communication between sites or between computers. Basically, VPNs are used to secure communication between two points. There are various types of VPNs but the most common is Internet Protocol Security (IPsec). IPsec has a built-in key exchange mechanism, authentication, integrity checks and support for digital certificates.

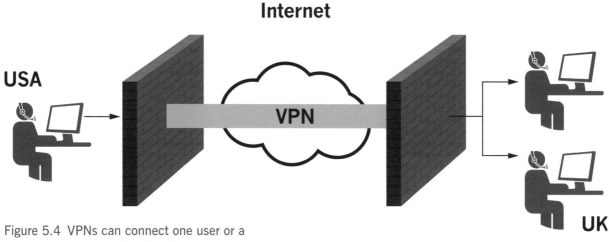

Internet

USA

UK

Figure 5.4 VPNs can connect one user or a
whole location to another location

Figure 5.4 shows a simplistic VPN between two remote sites.

IPsec can be set up to act as virtual point-to-point 'tunnels' over insecure networks such as the internet. All traffic within the 'tunnel' is encrypted and this method is particularly suited to situations where permanent high-volume data encryption between sites is required. It is often used for connecting two remote offices or a remote satellite office to headquarters over the internet. However, IPsec is also used for connecting single remote devices.

Secure session layer (SSL) and transport layer security (TLS) can also provide VPN services, but at the session layer of the open systems interconnection (OSI) reference model, meaning this information is encrypted at protected session level and not at network level. SSL and TLS are best suited to application-to-application encryption: unlike IPsec, the whole connection does not have to be encrypted. They are therefore suitable for intermittent point-to-multi-point communication rather than site-to-site connections. SSL VPN gateways can also be created to provide site-to-site encryption.

5.1.5.9 Secure shell

Secure shell (SSH) is an application-level VPN protocol that can encrypt point-to-point connections. It is primarily used for remote logins to servers for administration. It can support authentication through password or digital certificates. SSH2 is the latest version (SSH1 is no longer recommended for use).

Best practice

- Have a policy for encrypting sensitive information to protect it from unauthorized access, tampering and non-repudiation.
- Encrypt sensitive information at rest and in transit.
- Protect sensitive communications, such as logons, with encryption.
- Design a key management system to manage keys.
- Source external certificates from a reputable and accessible certification authority.
- Test encryption keys, and test that encrypted backups are still accessible.
- Ensure that private keys are secure.
- Use encryption to protect communication over untrusted networks.
- Ensure that there is a policy and training on the use of encryption, and understanding of legal requirements and trans-border restrictions in certain countries.

5.1.6 Business continuity management

Business continuity management (BCM) is an essential part of cyber resilience. Cyber resilience is not only about preventing attacks but also about an organization's ability to be resilient to cyber-attacks and its ability to recover from attacks if they crystallize. BCM involves much more than disaster recovery, which is about recovering from disaster events. BCM is about an organization's ability to continue its operation in the event of any threats to its operation. Without a continuity strategy and a plan, an organization may not have the ability to recover from a high-impacting continuity event.

Many organizations often make assumptions about their resilience and recoverability which prove to be incorrect in a disaster or continuity event. Successful BCM requires strategy, design, planning, testing and updating to ensure that strategy and plans remain valid. In ITIL the IT service continuity management (ITSCM) process provides a set of best practices for managing IT service continuity that can be incorporated into the overall BCM process.

BCM is a holistic approach to managing a business continuity event. This could include recovering from disaster or an IT service outage. From a cyber resilience perspective, the role of BCM is to identify potential harm that can affect an organization. It should also provide a holistic strategy with a planned set of activities supported by documented and tested processes to respond to and recover from adverse events. The aim is to do this with the minimum of disruption to operational services, whilst protecting the reputation of the organization and its stakeholders. BCM is a business-driven process, designed to protect the organization and its assets and its ability to meet its objectives. The process starts with the identification of all the important business-supporting functions (and processes) within an organization. These are then ranked by using business impact analysis (BIA).

5.1.6.1 Business impact analysis

The purpose of a business impact analysis (BIA) is to quantify the impact to the business that a loss of a business function would have. This impact could be a tangible impact that can be precisely identified (such as financial loss), or an intangible impact (such as brand image damage, health and safety problems or loss of competitive advantage). The BIA will identify the most important functions to the organization and will therefore be a key input to the strategy.

The BIA identifies the form that the damage or loss may take – for example:

● Lost income
● Additional costs
● Damaged reputation
● Loss of goodwill
● Loss of competitive advantage
● Breach of law, health and safety regulations
● Risk to personal safety
● Immediate and long-term loss of market share
● Political, corporate or personal embarrassment
● Loss of operational capability – for example in a command and control environment.

To ensure that the critical functions are identified and ranked in order of importance, the functions and their dependencies (on people, IT, information, locations, documentation etc.) are also identified.

The systemic approach to BCM can include organizations adopting a BCM system (BCMS) such as ISO/IEC ISO 22301, which describes a management system for managing business continuity risks. The BCMS takes a business-driven approach by first understanding the business, determining the BCM strategies and developing and implementing a BCM response in the form of plans and processes, and exercising, maintaining and updating those plans to make sure they are effective and continue to improve. In this way cyber resilience is built into the business process.

Organizations should adopt the BCMS approach to BCM to provide a risk-based and systemic approach to business continuity and continual improvement. The idea is to embed cyber resilience into the organization's business processes by designing robust and durable functions, locations, processes and systems with built-in cyber resilience, and selecting reliable products and services, including suppliers.

At the minimum, an organization should have a strategy and a tested plan that identifies all the critical functions that sustain it. Organizations should carry out a BIA to help understand the impacts to these critical functions and the options for recovering from **major incident**s that would affect, for example:

- **IT services the business relies on** Computers, internet links, telephony, working from home
- **Key people** Loss of knowledge, leadership
- **Suppliers** Supply chain dependencies
- **Workplace** Workplace recovery
- **Information** Access to information.

Often organizations make assumptions that are not tested or true so they find in the advent of a major incident that they are unable to respond or recover and many do not survive major adverse events.

The strategy and plans should be documented and tested before they become operational, and then reviewed and improved – testing the plans tests the underlying assumptions. If the strategy and plans are not appropriate, then testing provides an opportunity to correct them.

Key message

- Organizations cannot afford to make assumptions about business continuity and cyber resilience.
- Organizations must identify and assess the impact to their business of failure of critical processes and document all the dependencies.
- Organizations must have strategy and plans for identifying, responding to and recovering from major incidents that affect business-critical functions.
- It is not good enough just to have a plan: plans must be tested, reviewed and updated as functions or risks change.
- A BCMS can provide a systemic, measurable, auditable, improvable and holistic approach to BCM.

Best practice

- Have a strategy and a BCM plan for all critical services that sustain the organization.
- Test and update the BCM plan regularly. Fully test it annually.
- Know the maximum outage the organization can tolerate and plan to meet this.
- Include key suppliers and ensure that key suppliers include the organization in their BCM plans and testing.

5.2 ALIGNING CYBER RESILIENCE DESIGN WITH IT SERVICE DESIGN

IT service design considers how service providers can design and develop both IT services and IT service management practices. During this stage of the service lifecycle, organizations take the high-level requirements of IT service strategy and turn them into detailed requirements and plans that can be executed to deliver the strategy.

The key output of IT service design is descriptions of IT service solutions that can meet the changing requirements of the business. The description of each solution is documented in a **service design package**

(SDP), which includes all the information needed to build, transition and operate the IT service throughout the service lifecycle. *ITIL Service Design* considers five aspects:

● Service solutions for new or changed services

● Management information systems and tools

● Technology architectures and management architectures

● The processes required

● Measurement methods and **metric**s.

All five aspects are relevant to cyber resilience, and integration between cyber resilience and IT service management should consider all five of them. These five aspects should all be considered whenever any one of them is subject to change: for example, the design of a new service should include the design (or at least review) of management systems and tools, architectures, processes, measurement methods and metrics. Similarly, if an architecture is changed then the other four aspects should all be reviewed to understand the implications and ensure that they are still appropriate.

We have already discussed the need to have a single integrated management system, and the same applies for each of the other aspects:

● Service solutions for new or changed IT services must be designed so that they deliver the required level of cyber resilience.

● Management information systems and tools for cyber resilience need to be integrated with those for ITSM so that they support all the organization's governance and management requirements. Cyber resilience requirements for management systems and tools also need to be part of the design: for example, availability requirements, user access permissions and data retention requirements should be taken into account when designing the tools.

● Technology architectures and management architectures must support cyber resilience requirements as well as other needs, and standards and architectures for cyber resilience will have to be developed: these should be integrated with other standards and architectures in use. Also, any change to a cyber resilience standard will require review of all five aspects of service design to understand the implications for delivery of IT services.

● The processes required to manage IT services must take account of cyber resilience as well as other service requirements. Every process needs to take cyber resilience requirements into account, and specific cyber resilience processes should be designed so that they integrate with the other processes in the organization.

● Measurement methods and metrics should deliver the information needed by cyber resilience, in addition to that needed by other aspects of the IT services. Also the cyber resilience requirements of metrics and reporting must be defined, taking into account for example the requirements for confidentiality of management reports, and the need for integrity of metrics that might identify potential security breaches.

Organizations that use ITIL as a basis for their IT service management system can integrate cyber resilience design into the service design stage of the service lifecycle. Organizations that are not using ITIL to manage their IT services may find it helpful to adopt some of the processes and activities described in *ITIL Service Design* to support their cyber resilience design.

Management of cyber resilience requires many processes and activities. The following cyber resilience activities should be integrated with the design stage of the service lifecycle:

● Designing cyber resilience processes and controls

● Ensuring that cyber resilience has been taken into account in the design of individual IT services

● Ensuring that the design of all IT service management practices takes cyber resilience needs into account.

ITIL Service Design describes a number of processes that are particularly relevant to the design stage of the service lifecycle. Every one of these processes should include appropriate aspects of cyber resilience; it is not

Table 5.3 Service design processes

ITSM process	What it is for?
Design coordination	Ensures that goals and objectives of service design are met by providing a single point of coordination and control for all activities and processes within the service design stage of the service lifecycle
Service catalogue management	Maintains a catalogue of all IT services, ensuring that it is correct and current, and that it is available when and where needed
Service level management	Ensures that current and planned IT services are delivered to agreed, achievable, targets
Availability management	Ensures that the level of availability delivered for every IT service meets the agreed availability needs of customers in a cost-effective and timely manner
Capacity management	Ensures that the capacity and performance of IT services, and supporting infrastructure, meet the agreed needs of customers
IT service continuity management	Supports business continuity management (BCM) by managing risks that could seriously affect IT services and ensuring that minimum agreed levels of service can always be provided
Supplier management	Ensures that suppliers and contracts support IT service targets and expectations
Information security management	Ensures that IT security is aligned with 'business security' and considers the need for confidentiality, integrity and availability of the organization's assets, information, data and IT services

possible to run cyber resilience processes that carry out similar activities to the service management processes in isolation from one another. They must be integrated, or at the very least aligned to ensure that there is no conflict. Table 5.3 shows the name and purpose of each of the ITSM service design processes.

Sections 5.2.1 to 5.2.8 provide brief descriptions of these processes and discuss how they can be aligned with cyber resilience. Many of the controls described in section 5.1 above can be implemented effectively through such integrated processes. This can enable an organization to achieve both its service design objectives and its cyber resilience design objectives efficiently and effectively.

5.2.1 Design coordination

The ITSM design coordination process ensures that the goals and objectives of service design are met by providing a single point of coordination and control for all activities and processes within the service design stage of the service lifecycle. Design coordination uses input from many sources to produce service design packages (SDPs), which provide the interface between service design and the other stages of the service lifecycle. The design coordination process works at two different levels:

● It coordinates all the activities needed to create each individual SDP.

● It defines and coordinates the overall service design effort. This includes defining and maintaining service design policies and methods, planning resources and capabilities, and managing overall service design risks and issues.

Cyber resilience should be integrated with both these levels of design coordination. Figure 5.5 shows the main activities of the ITSM design coordination process and indicates how cyber resilience activities interact with these.

5.2.1.1 Coordinating activities to create each SDP

Every time a new or changed service is designed, the design must ensure that the service is **fit for use** – including the ability to meet all cyber resilience requirements. The SDP should incorporate everything needed to establish the correct cyber resilience environment for the new service, covering people and process controls as well as technical ones.

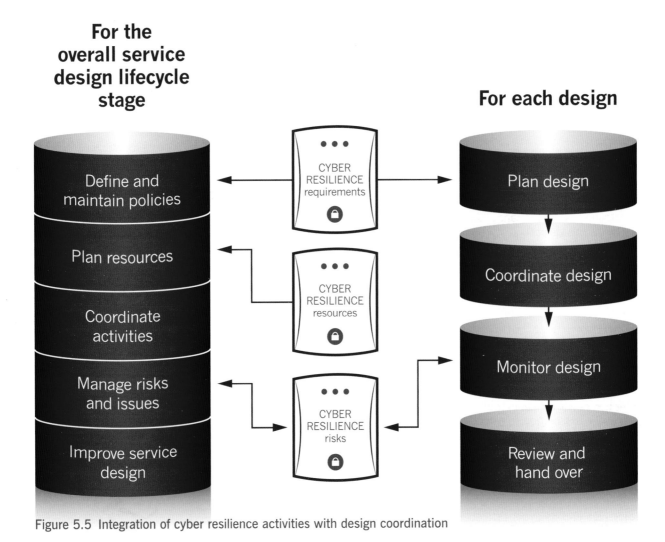

Figure 5.5 Integration of cyber resilience activities with design coordination

Cyber resilience requirements should be taken into account in designing every area of the new service to ensure that there is a coherent integrated solution that meets the cyber resilience needs of the organization as well as the business requirements for which the solution is being defined, plus the IT service management needs which will enable the IT organization to transition, operate and improve the service. Cyber resilience risks should be considered alongside all other risks and issues relating to the new or changed service, and potential new or changed cyber resilience risks should be identified.

> ## The cost of not providing clear cyber resilience requirements
>
> An IT organization was creating a new monitoring and control system for a technical customer. The customer had said they needed very high availability, so the design included clustering, RAID disks and many other **countermeasures** that would give high availability.
>
> Unfortunately, the customer and the IT organization had not agreed what 'high availability' meant. The solution was designed to recover from failure within 30 seconds to 2 minutes, whereas the real customer requirement was to recover in 300 milliseconds to prevent an expensive failure in the technology being monitored. The new solution had to be abandoned after $20 million had been spent on the project. This caused a delay of over a year in the introduction of a business innovation that would have provided a significant competitive advantage if it had been introduced when planned.

5.2.1.2 Coordinating the overall service design effort

At the overall design level, the policies and methods for service design must be suitable for the organization's cyber resilience requirements. Many different policies are needed within an IT organization and these must all take into account cyber resilience needs. Also the specific cyber resilience policies must be integrated with other policies to ensure complete coverage of all requirements with minimal overlap and no contradictions between different policies.

Planning to provide the correct resources and capabilities for the IT organization must include planning for the required cyber resilience resources and capabilities; and management of overall service design risks and issues must include the management of cyber resilience risks and issues. If the organization maintains a risk register then this must include cyber resilience risks as well as other risks. If the organization has a separate information security management team which takes responsibility for the design of cyber resilience aspects of new and changed IT services, then planning for this team should be integrated into overall design coordination planning.

5.2.2 Service catalogue management

The ITSM service catalogue management process maintains a catalogue of all IT services, ensuring that it is correct and current, and that it is available when and where needed. The **service catalogue** should be a single source of consistent information on all agreed services, and it should be used by all other service management processes as a source of information about those services. The service catalogue should also be used by customers who wish to know what IT services are available to them.

Effective cyber resilience makes use of the service catalogue to ensure that all IT services have been properly protected, and that risks relating to these services have been identified and appropriately managed.

What's in a service catalogue?

A service catalogue should include all the information that an organization's customers need so they can understand its services.

The required content in a service catalogue is the same as in any typical retail catalogue. The service catalogue should answer customer questions such as:

- What will I get?
- What will it cost me?
- How can I order it?
- What will I have to do to use the service?

Service catalogue management can make significant contributions to cyber resilience by:

- Providing a list of all services which are provided to the business. This is a great source of information to help identify assets which must be protected. The service catalogue should be used as an input to any risk assessment activities.

- Providing a structured mechanism for documenting and communicating cyber resilience risks, as well as user responsibilities. The service catalogue is used to communicate with the business about available IT services; therefore it can be used to communicate information about cyber resilience aspects of these services. The description of each service in the service catalogue should include information about what levels of availability, confidentiality and integrity will be provided for the service, as well as an overview of continuity arrangements and a description of user responsibilities, including user responsibilities for cyber resilience.

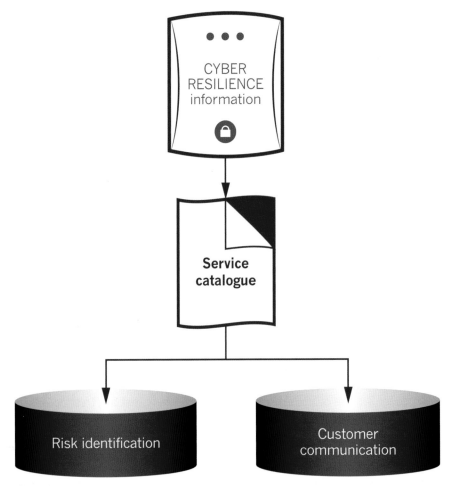

Figure 5.6 Integration of cyber resilience activities with service catalogue management

Cyber resilience contributes to service catalogue management by:

● Providing information about cyber resilience aspects of all services for inclusion in the service catalogue.

Figure 5.6 shows the major areas of integration between cyber resilience and service catalogue management.

5.2.3 Service level management

The ITSM service level management (SLM) process ensures that current and planned IT services are delivered to agreed, achievable targets. Service level management is responsible for understanding customer expectations and then negotiating and agreeing **service level target**s with customers, for recording these agreed targets in a service level agreement (SLA) and for monitoring, reporting and improving service level achievements. Each of these activities works within a feedback-and-improvement loop, as shown in Figure 5.7.

The SLM process helps to maintain customer satisfaction by ensuring that customer expectations are set appropriately and that services meet these expectations. Service level management is also responsible for ensuring continual improvement of services, even if agreed targets are already being met.

Service level management can make significant contributions to cyber resilience by:

● Ensuring that customers' requirements for cyber resilience are understood and that measurable targets for cyber resilience are agreed with those customers

● Making use of regular service level management meetings with customers as a forum where an organization and its customers can discuss cyber resilience risks and ensure that customers have understood these

● Helping to ensure that customers understand their own responsibilities and how their activities contribute to cyber resilience.

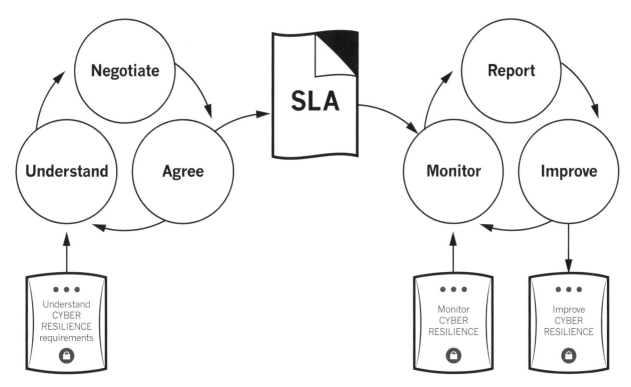

Figure 5.7 Integration of cyber resilience activities with service level management

Cyber resilience contributes to service level management by:

● Ensuring that information about cyber resilience requirements is available to service level management personnel in a form that they can understand and communicate to customers

● Helping to ensure that cyber resilience risks are managed in line with customers' expectations.

Figure 5.7 shows the major areas of integration between cyber resilience and service level management. Note that steps such as negotiate, agree and report will include cyber resilience aspects because these will have been incorporated into the requirements at the beginning of the process.

5.2.4 Availability management

The ITSM availability management process ensures that the level of availability delivered for every IT service meets the agreed availability needs of customers in a cost-effective and timely manner. Availability management is responsible for defining, analysing, planning, measuring and improving all aspects of availability of IT services, and the supporting infrastructure, processes, tools, roles and organization.

Availability management is an essential process for air traffic control centres

Availability is managed by planning appropriate levels of reliability (how long a service or component works without interruption) and **maintainability** (how quickly a service is restored after a failure). Availability management needs to include both proactive and reactive activities. Proactive availability management helps to plan availability and ensure that appropriate measures are in place to enable agreed targets to be met. Reactive availability management helps to monitor, measure, analyse and report availability.

Key activities of proactive availability management are shown in Figure 5.8. These include:

- **Risk assessment and management** There is a big overlap between this activity and cyber resilience risk assessment and management, as both should identify IT service availability issues and plan actions to deal with them. Each organization will need to resolve this overlap by assigning clear roles and responsibilities.

- **Helping to plan and design services** The design of new or changed services must take account of customers' availability needs. Many of these availability needs come from cyber resilience requirements, and the design should take account of all aspects of cyber resilience (as well as all other requirements).

- **Implementing cost-justifiable countermeasures** Even if agreed availability targets are reliably met, there may still be opportunities to improve availability at an acceptable cost. These availability countermeasures can be thought of as a subset of cyber resilience controls, focused on the availability of IT services and components.

- **Reviewing services and testing availability mechanisms** Tests should be carried out before the service goes into production, and regularly thereafter, to ensure that all availability and resilience countermeasures work effectively. Many of these tests can be integrated with cyber resilience testing.

- **Review and improve** Like all other ITSM activities, availability management should include continual improvement. Not only the process but also the availability of services and components should be reviewed and improved whenever this can be cost-justified.

The key activities of reactive availability management (as shown in Figure 5.8) are:

- **Monitor and review availability** Data should be collected and analysed to determine the availability of IT services and components, trends and issues should be identified, and reports should be created for customer and IT use. Some availability issues might be due to cyber resilience incidents and these may be identified and investigated by a cyber resilience team rather than as part of availability management.

- **Investigate and remediate availability issues** This may result in recommendations for changes to IT services to improve availability.

Availability management makes a major contribution to cyber resilience, since:

- Availability is one third of the CIA triad (confidentiality, integrity, availability) with which cyber resilience is concerned (see section 1.5.5 for an explanation of the CIA triad).

- Many of the plans developed by availability management should be included in cyber resilience controls to help defend against threats and vulnerabilities. These are effectively preventative controls.

- Planning to achieve appropriate levels of availability is critical to both availability management and cyber resilience. ITSM availability management should be integrated with cyber resilience to ensure efficient use of resources and prevent conflicting plans being developed.

- Monitoring availability can contribute to the *detective* controls needed by cyber resilience.

- Investigation and remediation of availability issues can contribute to the *corrective* controls needed by cyber resilience.

Cyber resilience makes a significant contribution to availability management since:

- Many of the threats and vulnerabilities identified in cyber resilience risk analysis are directly relevant to availability management.

- Both cyber resilience and availability management make contributions to a risk register, and this can be shared between them (and with other teams and processes) to provide a common view of business risk.

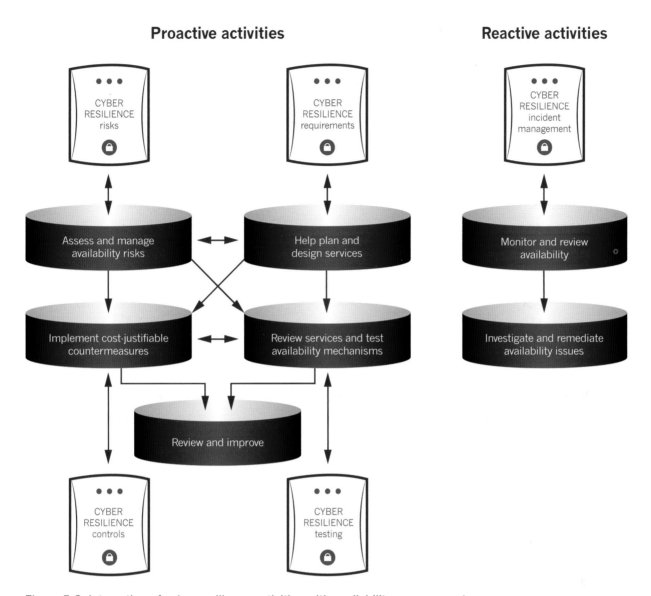

Figure 5.8 Integration of cyber resilience activities with availability management

5.2.5 Capacity management

The ITSM capacity management process ensures that the capacity and performance of IT services, and supporting infrastructure, meet the agreed needs of customers. This process considers capacity at three different levels:

- **Business capacity management** works with demand management to understand the changing needs of customers.

- **Service capacity management** plans to meet the end-to-end service requirements.

- Component capacity management analyses and understands the workload and **throughput** of individual infrastructure components.

Capacity plans identify expected levels of usage and performance and are used to identify when an organization will need to intervene – for example to upgrade components or manage demand. Like other service management processes, capacity management ensures that an organization delivers minimum agreed levels of service and identifies opportunities for improvement even when it is meeting agreed service levels.

Is planning for a DDoS attack availability management, capacity management or cyber resilience?

When we write about topics like cyber resilience, we tend to deal with things in separate, clearly distinct compartments. The real world is much more complex than this. A distributed denial of service (DDoS) attack is a good example of something that does not fit neatly into any single box.

- Capacity management should ensure that IT services are designed with sufficient capacity to deliver the agreed levels of service, even during a DDoS attack.
- Availability management should ensure that IT services deliver agreed levels of availability.
- IT service continuity management may be involved in planning how to respond to a DDoS attack, especially if invocation of recovery measures is a possible response.
- Cyber resilience considers how to prevent, detect and correct a DDoS attack.

In practice the people involved in all of these processes must work together to ensure that the response to a DDoS attack is appropriate for the needs of the organization. This is why it is so important to have a single integrated management system, rather than opting for a separate information security management system that is divorced from how other aspects of IT services (and business processes) are managed.

Capacity management can make a significant contribution to cyber resilience by:

- Contributing to the availability of services and information. If performance is too slow then the service may be considered unavailable by customers, so management of capacity is essential for management of availability.

Cyber resilience can make a significant contribution to capacity management by:

- Assisting in design of services that can cope with expected events such as DDoS attacks, which may appear as capacity-related issues
- Planning cyber resilience monitoring with a good understanding of the capacity impact of different monitoring approaches. For example, a ping every five minutes will have much less impact on performance than retrieving a web page every five seconds. Cyber resilience monitoring should try to achieve a balance between being responsive and able to detect events quickly and being a significant load on the services being monitored.

Figure 5.9 shows the major areas of integration between cyber resilience and capacity management.

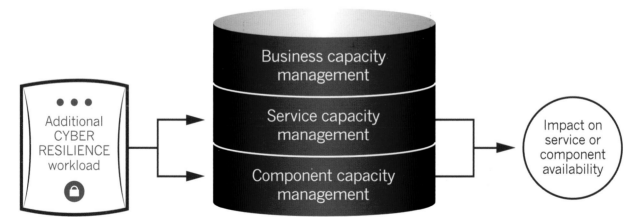

Figure 5.9 Integration of cyber resilience activities with capacity management

5.2.6 IT service continuity management

The ITSM IT service continuity management (ITSCM) process supports business continuity management (BCM) by managing risks that could seriously affect IT services. It helps to ensure that an organization can always provide minimum agreed levels of service. ITSCM uses business impact analysis (BIA) and risk management techniques to reduce risks to IT services and to plan for the recovery of IT services. This process creates, tests and maintains IT service continuity plans that support the organization's (or the customers') business continuity plans. Like other service management processes, ITSCM ensures that an organization delivers minimum agreed levels of service and identifies opportunities for improvement even when agreed service levels are being met.

The main activities of ITSCM are shown in Figure 5.10, and these include:

- **Initiation** Defining policies, agreeing scope and **terms of reference**, and initiating the ITSCM project
- **Requirements and strategy** Performing (or reviewing) BIA, carrying out risk assessment, deciding how to respond to risks, defining recovery options
- **Implementation** Creating detailed ITSCM plans in line with BCM plans. Implementing agreed risk reduction controls and service recovery arrangements, carrying out initial testing
- **Ongoing operation** Reviewing and updating BIA and risk assessment, education and training, testing, review and audit of continuity arrangements
- **Invocation** Activating the agreed continuity arrangements in response to an event.

Like most processes described in *ITIL Service Design*, ITSCM is active across the entire service lifecycle. Continuity plans are created during the design stage of the service lifecycle and implemented and tested during the transition stage; ongoing operation and invocation of continuity plans happens during the operation stage.

There are many different types of testing that are used in both ITSCM and BCM, and it is essential that testing includes a wide range of cyber-attack scenarios to ensure that the organization is prepared to deal with these. Common types of continuity test include:

- **Walk-through tests** These tests simply involve people reading the plan and discussing what they would do. A walk-through test is usually carried out before any other testing, as it is relatively low cost and will often identify significant issues that need to be addressed.
- **Full tests** These replicate an actual invocation of all recovery arrangements, including third parties where appropriate. They should incorporate recovery of the full business process, as well as supporting IT. A full test is often expensive and can cause significant disruption to the business. Many organizations never perform a full test, but this is risky as a full test is the only way to be absolutely sure that the continuity arrangements all work.
- **Partial tests** These typically involve recovery of just one IT service or one business process. They can be used in addition to full tests, but not as a replacement, as they do not confirm that all services and business processes can be recovered. Some organizations perform regular partial tests, with each test covering a different service. This can be combined with a much less frequent full test. For example, it may be appropriate to run a partial test every month and a full test once a year.
- **Scenario tests** These tests are used to see how the organization would react to specific conditions: for example, testing how the organization would respond to a major cyber resilience event such as a DDoS attack. In a typical scenario test, a third party will document a scenario and then provide information to participants as the test proceeds. Scenario tests are also commonly used in testing cyber resilience plans.

Whichever types of test are done, there are a number of aspects that must be considered:

- It is important to test the people and process aspects of recovery plans, as well as any technology.
- Every test should result in a report that identifies what was tested, what went well and what could be improved. This should result in improvements to the recovery plan and input to future testing.

- Testing should include many different kinds of test, to ensure maximum test coverage with minimum cost and minimum disruption to the business. A plan that has never been tested is extremely unlikely to work when it is needed.

ITSCM has a strong overlap with cyber resilience, which is also concerned with information security aspects of business continuity management.

ITSCM can make a significant contribution to cyber resilience by:

- Designing IT service continuity plans that can also be used for recovery after a cyber resilience event such as compromised integrity of a critical IT service. This means that these plans must take into account the types of scenario which might result from a cyber-attack, and that all aspects of the ITSCM process should include consideration of cyber resilience needs.
- Helping to protect the availability, confidentiality and integrity of assets (such as sensitive data) that are needed at recovery sites before, during or after testing or invocation of continuity arrangements.
- Sharing plans and resources for conducting scenario testing of potential cyber resilience events.

Cyber resilience can make a significant contribution to ITSCM by:

- Ensuring that cyber resilience aspects of ITSCM are appropriately considered. This may require consideration of how sensitive data will be made available at recovery sites, and how this data will be managed before, during and after testing and invocation of continuity plans.
- If there is no ITSCM process then cyber resilience design should implement controls which will effectively create an ITSCM process, since ITSCM plans are essential to maintain the required availability of information and services.
- Defining cyber resilience scenarios that can help to create realistic ITSCM scenario tests.

Figure 5.10 shows the major areas of integration between cyber resilience and IT service continuity management.

Who does risk assessment?

Risk assessment is needed as part of many different activities. As described in Chapter 2, it is a critical part of cyber resilience. We have also seen in this section that it is a critical part of IT service continuity management. It is also needed in availability management, supplier management, enterprise financial management and in many other areas of the business.

This is why it is so important to have a standard approach to identifying, analysing and reporting risks, so that risk analysis will be consistent, and so that governance decisions about where to invest can be based on a common view of risks throughout the organization.

5.2.7 Supplier management

The ITSM supplier management process enables an organization to manage its suppliers and the services they provide. It ensures that suppliers and contracts support IT service targets and expectations. Supplier management covers the whole lifecycle of supplier relationships, including appointment of suppliers, negotiation and agreement of services to be delivered, managing supplier performance and overseeing contract termination.

Supplier management ensures that the organization obtains good value for money, that contracts are aligned to business needs and SLA targets, and that suppliers deliver what is expected.

The main activities of supplier management are shown in Figure 5.11. These include:

- **Supplier and contract requirements** Understanding what is needed from the supplier, and from each contract with the supplier.
- **Supplier and contract evaluation and establishment** Defining evaluation criteria, evaluating options, selecting suppliers, negotiating and agreeing contracts.

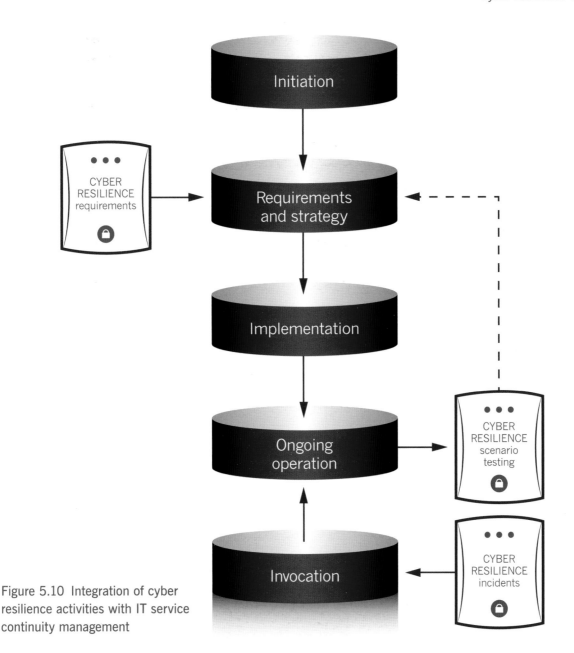

Figure 5.10 Integration of cyber resilience activities with IT service continuity management

- **Manage supplier and contract performance** The performance of each individual contract, and of the supplier as a whole, is monitored on a regular basis to ensure that delivery meets expectations.
- **Contract renewal or termination** At the end of the contract period the contract should be reviewed and either renewed or terminated. Exceptionally, the contract may be terminated early if the supplier has seriously under-performed.

Cyber resilience has a slightly different perspective on suppliers from the ITSM supplier management process. To ensure cyber resilience, an organization needs to ensure that risks relating to suppliers are understood and managed, that suitable information security requirements are included in supplier contracts, and that delivery of services by suppliers is monitored to ensure that these requirements are met.

Management of risks throughout the supply chain can be a huge cyber resilience challenge. Vulnerabilities in suppliers, and in their suppliers, can be extremely hard to detect. Many reported security breaches have been enabled by vulnerabilities within the supply chain. Management of suppliers for cyber resilience cannot be done independently of the ITSM supplier management process. All negotiation and agreement with suppliers must take cyber resilience into account, and monitoring of supplier performance must include monitoring of cyber resilience expectations.

Supplier management can make significant contributions to cyber resilience by:

● Including appropriate cyber resilience requirements in evaluation criteria for suppliers and contracts
● Ensuring that all suppliers have suitable controls in place to enable them to meet the cyber resilience requirements of the organization
● Ensuring that all contracts include required cyber resilience terms
● Assisting in the selection of suppliers and specification of contracts for products and services required as part of cyber resilience (such as anti-virus controls)
● Including review of cyber resilience considerations in the regular review and monitoring of suppliers.

Cyber resilience can make a significant contribution to supplier management by:

● Defining cyber resilience requirements for suppliers and contracts
● Providing information about cyber resilience incidents for review as part of supplier and contract **performance management**.

Figure 5.11 shows the major areas of integration between cyber resilience and supplier management. Note that all steps will include cyber resilience aspects because these have been incorporated into the requirements at the beginning of the process.

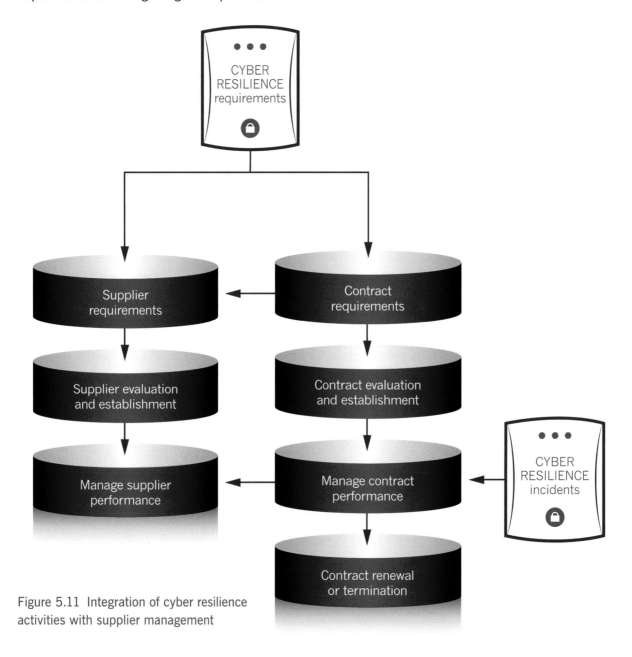

Figure 5.11 Integration of cyber resilience activities with supplier management

5.2.8 Information security management

The ITSM information security management process is considered to be part of the governance framework for IT services. It ensures that IT security is aligned with 'business security' and considers the need for confidentiality, integrity and availability of an organization's assets, information, data and IT services. The ITIL description of information security management expects there to be an overarching business security management process, outside of IT service management, which provides the context in which it operates.

Cyber resilience has a wider scope than information security management as described by ITIL. This distinction was described in Chapter 1 of this publication. Cyber resilience includes all aspects of information security management but also looks at the wider business context.

5.2.9 Aligning cyber resilience controls with IT service design

Section 5.2 of this guide has so far considered the integration of cyber resilience and IT service management by considering how each ITSM process can be integrated with cyber resilience. An alternative way to consider integration of cyber resilience and IT service management is to look at how each of the strategic cyber resilience controls described in section 5.1 can be integrated with ITSM.

5.2.9.1 Human resource security

Human resource security must be considered in the design of every ITSM process, because these processes define roles and responsibilities, and may need to provide appropriate **separation of concerns** and monitoring of activities.

The ITSM access management process must be integrated with the control for exit and termination of employees, to ensure that appropriate actions are taken to prevent continuing access to systems and information. This needs to be done as part of an overall joiners, movers and leavers (JML) process.

The ITSM access management process should also ensure that staff have appropriate training before they are granted access rights to systems or information.

Many organizations combine initial cyber resilience training and awareness for new employees with training on how to access IT resources, as part of the JML process.

5.2.9.2 System acquisition, development, architecture and design

This control contributes significantly to the design coordination process, which oversees the development of new and changed IT services. The design coordination process should help to ensure that every aspect of this control is considered when services are designed.

This control also needs to be integrated with the processes for availability management and capacity management, to ensure that new and changed systems are able to meet the availability expectations that the organization has negotiated with its customers.

5.2.9.3 Supplier and third-party security management

Many of the requirements of this control should be met by the ITSM supplier management process. A good supplier management process will ensure that all supplier contracts and agreements include suitable controls for third-party security, will monitor suppliers on a regular basis to ensure that these requirements are being met, and will ensure that interfaces with third-party suppliers are fit for purpose and encourage the required behaviours.

5.2.9.4 Endpoint security and cryptography

Endpoint security and cryptography are both very technical, and there is little interaction between these and IT service management processes.

The ITSM functions are nonetheless likely to have some responsibilities in relation to these controls. For example:

- It is important that the service desk understands how endpoint security and cryptography are used, and can advise users on their responsibilities. The service desk may also need to use mobile device management (MDM) software to erase data from lost or stolen endpoint devices, and may need to be involved in key recovery for users.

- **Technical management** staff who are responsible for creating server and client builds need to incorporate these controls and include them in standard configurations as appropriate. They also need to understand these controls to help them carry out incident and problem management.

5.2.9.5 Business continuity management

There is a strong overlap between this control and the ITSCM process, but the scope of ITSCM only includes some aspects of business continuity management (BCM), so there will be many additional aspects of business continuity management that must be implemented. This can be done by either expanding the scope of ITSCM, or by integrating cyber resilience into the wider BCM process managed outside of IT (which is also seen as the overarching process for ITSCM).

5.3 DESIGN SCENARIOS

In section 4.3 we looked at the cyber resilience strategy of our three fictitious organizations. This section considers some of the design challenges for the same organizations. As you read through these descriptions you should think about:

- Is the organization focusing on the right design challenges?
- Are the right people involved in the design work?
- Are there any other significant design controls that the organization should be considering?

Retail example: SellUGoods Ltd

Regular PCI-DSS audits at SellUGoods have verified that required controls are in place to protect payment card data. These controls include both procedural controls and technical controls such as the use of encryption. SellUGoods is confident that payment card data is well protected.

One staff member from the information security team has written a draft policy covering acquisition of new IT equipment. The draft policy has been reviewed by the risk manager and the procurement department, as well as by technical specialists from the server and network teams. It is now with the finance director who has final sign-off authority for the policy.

Another two people from the information security team have been asked to make recommendations for how security incident management could be improved. Their first recommendation is that SellUGoods should invest more in tools and processes to help detect security incidents. They have created a formal business case showing the potentially high costs of not detecting an incident, and this has been accepted by the management board. The business case focuses on the potential cost of a delay in discovering that personally identifiable data of SellUGoods' customers had been breached, but also includes a number of scenarios relating to other company assets. They are now working with the procurement department to purchase tools that could help to detect security incidents, as well as documenting a new security incident management process that will be triggered if a security incident is detected. The proposed new tools include improved server and network intrusion detection products, which will identify many different types of attack and raise alerts at the **operations bridge**. The new security incident management process will have input from a wide range of stakeholders, including:

- The owner of the ITSM event management and incident management processes, because there may be an opportunity to share resources used for monitoring and initial incident management
- The head of business continuity, who wants to make sure that business continuity plans are aligned with the new process
- The finance director, who heads up the business **crisis management** team, which will need to be involved in the event of a major security event.

Medical example: MedUServ Ltd

MedUServ needs to respond to a potential new customer who wants reassurance about the cyber resilience of their IT. Since all the IT is outsourced to a third party, the finance manager has written to the outsourcer to ask them to provide this reassurance. The outsourcer replies saying that they are compliant with ISO/IEC 27001:2013 and they have been audited and can provide certification to prove this. They say that this demonstrates the quality of their information security controls. MedUServ responds to its potential new customer with this information.

Unfortunately there is not a lot of cyber resilience expertise at MedUServ, and it accepts the outsourcer's reassurance at face value. MedUServ does not ask for a copy of the ISO/IEC 27001 certification or check the scope of the audit. The service provided to MedUServ is not actually included in the ISO/IEC 27001 certification and has not been audited. The outsourcer does use standard processes, so it is likely that they are doing a reasonable job of managing the service for MedUServ, but there is a significant risk that they may not be applying all of the required security controls. This could eventually result in MedUServ being in breach of contract with its new client for failing to ensure that its supplier meets its client's agreed requirements.

MedUServ has very good human resource security. Staff recruitment always includes checking references and academic records; all staff are regularly updated about their responsibilities, especially in relation to protecting personally identifiable information; everyone understands the importance of maintaining the ISO 9001 certification, and how their actions contribute to this.

MedUServ does not have a business continuity plan. In the event of a disaster that prevents the medical lab from operating, it will be unable to process medical samples until it has resolved the problem. MedUServ also has no plans for how to recover if the outsourcer who provides its IT services stops trading for any reason.

MedUServ relies on file protection and application-level security controls to prevent inappropriate access to the data.

Manufacturing example: MakeUGoods

MakeUGoods has a really good understanding of the need for human resource security controls. Staff are all carefully vetted before appointment, and there are regular training and awareness sessions to ensure that everyone understands the importance of protecting the organization's intellectual property.

Because many large customers are from the defence industry there is a recognition that this could lead to attacks from a number of sources, including foreign governments. This awareness has also contributed to the HR security controls, and staff are regularly warned to be wary of attacks which might try to use them to compromise security. One recent innovation has been sending emails containing tempting hyperlinks to senior management, to teach them about spear-phishing attacks. If the managers follow the links, they are taken to an internal web page with information about how to recognize future similar attacks.

The secret information about the manufacturing process is protected with very sophisticated cryptographic controls, which needs two different senior staff members to provide parts of the key. The system where this information is stored has no connection to any network.

After reading about attacks on SCADA systems, a 'SCADA-hardening project' has been initiated to ensure that controls are sufficient to protect MakeUGoods from attacks by Stuxnet and similar threats. This project identifies a number of vulnerabilities which would be very difficult to remove, including unchangeable hard-coded passwords on some devices. The cost of removing some of these vulnerabilities would be high, and a decision is taken at board level that protection of the SCADA systems must be based on protecting the existing technology, as replacing the systems would be prohibitively expensive. New controls designed by this project include:

- Improved network separation, to prevent threats from spreading across the internal MakeUGoods network
- Improved controls on removable devices (such as USB sticks), including a requirement for all media to be encrypted where possible (the SCADA systems are unable to read encrypted USB sticks), and a complete ban on sharing removable media between office systems and SCADA systems
- File integrity monitoring on all critical systems, to detect any changes to system files
- Application whitelisting to ensure that only authorized applications are allowed to run on critical systems
- Regular penetration testing of the SCADA control centre to detect vulnerabilities.

5.4 CYBER RESILIENCE DESIGN QUESTIONS

1. What is your understanding of your organization's policy on pre-employment screening of employees and contractors?

2. To what extent is employee behaviour monitored during employment?

3. To what extent does your organization provide induction training, ongoing training and awareness for cyber resilience?

4. How does your organization carry out security testing of software and infrastructure? Are issues remediated before transition into operation?

5. To what extent does your organization risk-assess its supply chain?

6. To what extent is cyber resilience design already integrated with ITSM design in your organization? Where is this integration strongest? Why? Where is this integration weakest? Why? What improvements could you suggest?

7. What are the main obstacles standing in the way of integrating cyber resilience with your ITSM design? What steps could you take to overcome them?

8. How do you know that your organization's ITSM design contributes to meeting your cyber resilience goals?

6

Cyber resilience transition

This chapter covers:

- Objectives and controls for cyber resilience transition
- Aligning with IT service transition
- Transition scenarios

6 Cyber resilience transition

Transition is the stage of the lifecycle where designs are introduced into the operational environment. An organization where nothing ever changed would be easy to manage and would rarely introduce new risks, but it would stagnate and would almost certainly not be able to survive in the long term. Whenever there is a transition there is risk, and the main purpose of the transition stage of the lifecycle is to manage these risks in a way that supports the business need for agility without compromising the business need for cyber resilience.

Cyber resilience transition has two aspects:

● It ensures that business and IT changes and transitions are managed in a way that supports the cyber resilience objectives of the organization.

● It takes the output of cyber resilience design and moves it into operational use, ensuring that risks are managed and that new or modified processes and controls deliver the expected outcomes.

When changes are made to how the business operates, new assets are introduced that need to be protected and new vulnerabilities arise which may result in increased risk. One common type of change that could impact cyber resilience is the introduction of new or changed IT services; but the scope of cyber resilience goes beyond IT, and there are many other types of business change that must be considered to ensure their impact on cyber resilience is understood. Areas of change that should be assessed for their impact on cyber resilience include:

● Changes to organization design or business processes

● Changes to IT services, including the introduction of new, modified or retired services, or transition between service providers

● Changes to IT infrastructure and applications, including upgrades to new versions, use of new technology, retirement of old technology or a change of supplier.

The organization should ensure that there are mechanisms in place to identify when any of these changes are planned, so that the change can be reviewed for its impact on cyber resilience, risk assessments can be updated, and required security controls can be designed, tested and implemented.

The other aspect of cyber resilience transition is taking the output of cyber resilience design and putting it into operational use. These outputs of cyber resilience design include:

● Design of a new or changed overall management system.

● Organization design, including roles, responsibilities and accountabilities of staff.

● New or changed processes for managing cyber resilience.

● A risk treatment plan that describes required cyber resilience controls.

Cyber resilience transition takes these designs, procures any components that are needed from external suppliers, oversees any building or integration work that is required, carries out testing to ensure that designs are able to deliver the expected outcomes, deploys the new or changed capabilities, and most importantly deals with the organizational change management aspects of introducing the new or changed capabilities. These activities are depicted in Figure 6.1. Management of organizational change is discussed in section 6.2.8.

Business and IT changes

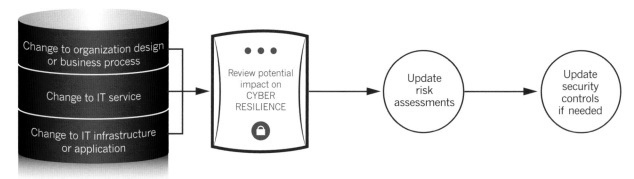

CYBER RESILIENCE changes

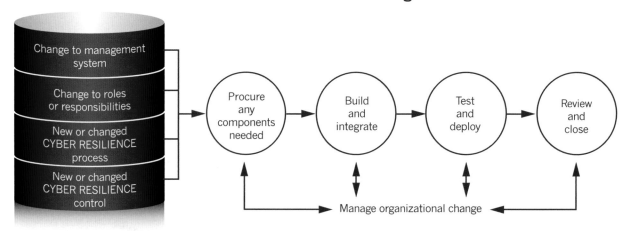

Figure 6.1 Major activities of cyber resilience transition

Organizational change management

The need for organizational change management cannot be stressed sufficiently. Every year there are large numbers of security breaches which could have been prevented if the controls the organization had designed had been effectively implemented. The most common reason for this not happening is a failure to appreciate the importance of these controls: people find them inconvenient, or they are unable to work efficiently with the controls in place, so controls are subverted.

When this happens it can be extremely difficult to remedy the situation as cyber resilience controls can be seen as conflicting with the goals of the organization. A good organizational change management programme is needed to ensure that all staff understand the need for cyber resilience controls, and the potential impact of subverting them. Management of this kind of organizational change is probably the most important aspect of cyber resilience transition.

For example, one organization installed ID card readers to control internal doors, to help prevent unauthorized people entering sensitive areas of the building. Staff members frequently allowed other people to follow them through the doors, because this was the polite thing to do, and this rendered the new control ineffective. The organization ran a campaign to inform people of the threat of unauthorized people being in the building. This included posters, emails from managers, and opportunities for staff to discuss any issues they had concerning the new card readers. As a result of this campaign the new control became much more effective.

6.1 CONTROL OBJECTIVES AND CONTROLS FOR CYBER RESILIENCE TRANSITION

The objective of asset management in cyber resilience is to ensure that critical assets are identified, classified and tracked, and that ownership of assets is assigned within an organization to ensure they are adequately protected from harm.

Sections 6.1.1–6.1.7 provide a list of best practices that organizations should follow in the use and protection of their assets.

6.1.1 Asset management and configuration management

Assets are the foundation of all cyber resilience activities because it is the assets that are being protected from harm. Without the assets, and the need to protect them, there would be no need for cyber resilience controls and all the associated activities. A full account of all critical assets is required: critical assets are the assets, be it information or infrastructure, which keep an organization afloat. Without them organizations would not be able to operate. Critical assets typically include:

- Information
- Business processes
- People
- Technology
- Physical locations.

Assets can be tangible (such as hardware and software) or intangible (such as brand image, reputation and goodwill). It is easier to catalogue tangible assets. Intangible assets are harder to define and record but they are also important to an organization and need to be protected – especially in the world of instant messaging and social media, brand and reputation can be instantly damaged.

Key message

When changing a backup schedule (for cyber resilience purposes), only the critical assets need be protected; however, in order to be able to identify critical assets, a full inventory is required. The subsequent business impact analysis will identify and rank the criticality of the assets to an organization's cyber resilience.

If an organization does not have an inventory of its assets, it will be difficult to track if an asset has been lost, stolen, modified or damaged. It may be difficult to know if an information asset has been duplicated or stolen, or if its integrity is compromised. Unlike hardcopy information, it is easier to copy and modify digital information. Furthermore, some assets have finite value and must not be overprotected whereas other assets require continual protection beyond their value to the organization.

The Queen's Birthday Honours list is a good example of an asset that needs different levels of protection at different times. When the list is provided to the media in advance of official publication, the information is highly confidential; however, once the list has been officially announced, the information is no longer confidential, is of little value and does not require the elevated protection. Organizations have all sorts of assets that are critical to their operations and resilience. Some assets are more important than others; however, all assets cost money to acquire, are valuable in some way to the organization and need to be protected from loss, damage, unauthorized modification and unavailability. Information and its supporting assets play an important part in the cyber resilience of an organization. Organizations need to record their assets so they can be managed properly.

From an IT perspective, tracking the inventory of IT hardware and software is the simplest example of asset management. Knowing what is available, where it lives, how important it is, who has or needs access to it and who is responsible for it are key steps in its protection.

From an information security perspective, tracking the inventory of information assets can help towards preserving its confidentiality, integrity and availability. An information asset is an item of value containing information. The same concepts of general asset management also apply to the management of information assets.

Key elements in asset management are:

● **Inventory of assets** What assets are available and where are they kept?

● **Responsibility and ownership** Who is responsible for each asset?

● **Value** How important is each asset in relation to the business and resilience?

● **Access control** Who has access to the asset and what level of access do they have?

● **Acceptable use** Do the users of the asset know how to securely handle and use the asset?

Inventory or asset registers record the assets, their owners, their value (impact) to the business, and any control requirements such as classification, when they were acquired, expiry dates, or even where they are used. In ITIL, the **configuration management database** (CMDB) takes this further and lists the relationships between the assets in the form of **configuration item**s (CI). Table 6.1 shows a typical asset register.

Table 6.1 A typical asset register used to record assets of an organization

Asset information								Handling and use	
Asset description	Asset identifier	Asset owner	Classification	CIA impact	Acquisition date	Retention period	Disposal requirements	Supports	Access control
CRM data on sales force	CRM-CUS001	Susan Lee	Confidential	2/3/2	10/4/2004	Retain and review	As per classification	Sales and marketing	Only to sales and marketing division

Although IT tends to primarily consider IT hardware and software as assets, in cyber resilience, assets are considered to be any item the organization needs to protect from cyber-threats and anything that it requires to support its cyber resilience. Assets are not just confined to IT hardware and software but include intangible assets such as information assets, intellectual property, software licences, R&D, patents, designs, people, processes, technology – anything that is of value to the organization and to others who may want to get hold of it.

During transition into operational service, the assets are put into use, and it is important to ensure that the transition is smooth, changes are controlled and assets are secure and are used as they were designed.

A lifecycle approach to asset management is needed to protect assets. This should include resilience consideration from the time the assets are acquired (see section 5.1.2.1, System acquisition and development), to when the assets are transitioned into operation, during improvements and maintenance, though to disposal when the asset is no longer needed. Assets that are allocated to users should be tracked and their use monitored. When a user leaves the organization, their physical assets, such as hardware and software, should be retained, and access to information and systems terminated.

6.1.1.1 Classification and handling

Classification

Classification helps to control access to and protect assets from unauthorized persons or systems. It also visually conveys the importance of an asset and the desired protection to its legitimate handlers and processors.

In the case of information assets, the classification is directly related to the level of confidentiality required. Organizations should have a classification policy that takes into consideration the confidentiality and access requirements. These will largely be driven by the business impact (value) and regulatory compliance requirements. A classification will decide how much control is afforded to the asset, and who or what can have access to it and at what level.

The classification scheme should be consistently used across the organization and conveyed to the supply chain. The classification should become the landmark and reference point for asset protection.

Hints and tips

The classification scheme and handling requirements should be communicated to all those who have access to an organization's assets, especially information assets. This includes staff, suppliers, partners, service providers etc. Include classifications in contracts so users understand exactly how information should be protected.

Asset owners are those best placed to understand how and when their information needs to be protected and who should have what access (access rights). Therefore, the classification scheme should ensure that the asset owners specify the controls that need to be applied to their assets. At the basic level, the asset owner would be the person creating a document. In larger information systems, it could be a senior manager who is accountable for the information assets processed or stored on those systems. At whatever level there needs to be ownership, accountability and responsibility for information and understanding of protection requirements within and outside the organization.

A classification scheme example

- **Public** Information for release to the public, or already available to the public.
- **Internal** Information for internal organization use only, not to be sent outside.
- **Private** Personal information, only for HR or personal use.
- **Commercial** Business-sensitive information, for example about contracts, fees, pricing etc.
- **Confidential** Highly sensitive information, sensitive personal information, earnings, financial data, valuable intellectual property, investigations, passwords, decryption keys etc.

The classification scheme should include several hierarchical classifications, commensurate with the confidentiality requirements of the assets. For example, *public*, *internal*, *private*, *commercial*, *confidential* are generally used classifications, with 'public' classification being the lowest and 'confidential' being the highest and requiring the most stringent controls. There are many others. It could be as simple as 'internal' and 'external', denoting internal information and external information, or more complex schemes that are often found in governments. Whatever scheme an organization decides on, it must use a design that is suitable for its assets. For the scheme to be successful, it must fit in with the culture of the organization balanced with the business need to protect the assets.

Hints and tips

Choose a classification scheme that is suitable and fits in with the organization's culture and keep it simple.

Implement positive classification: that is, all documents must be classified. This helps to bring cultural change to organizations.

Provide templates for all business documents so that adoption is easy and embedded within business processes.

An organization that routinely handles information from other organizations, such as customers and clients, may be obliged under contract to protect the sharing party's information. This will mean training the organization's staff in the sharing party's classifications and handling requirements. Likewise, the organization's suppliers must understand and comply with the organization's classifications. For example, an organization might encrypt its confidential information; however, its supplier might not be aware that they must also encrypt this information. Such handling requirements should be clearly communicated to suppliers through contracts and policies.

Handling

Classification conveys the confidentiality requirements, but not integrity or availability of an asset. The classification scheme should include handling instructions or a handling guide for each of the classifications so that users know when and how to handle the assets in terms of confidentiality but also integrity and availability. For example, some assets can be sent by post whereas others must only be sent by secure courier; or some assets may require encryption if emailed over a public network but can be sent unencrypted over the organization's own networks. For integrity assurance, some assets, when sent over the internet, may require some sort of integrity checking to ensure that they have not been altered in transit.

Users must be trained and educated in classifying and securely handling assets, especially information, as part of the transitioning process into the operational environment.

Classification and handling guide

A classification and handling guide explains how assets should be classified and how each classification should be handled or used. Typically, for each classification, the classification and handling guide should include the category of information and how the information is handled under each circumstance.

The instructions should include:

- The category of information for each classification
- How to decide whether the classification should be applied to a specific asset
- How it is labelled – where the classification is placed
- If it can be transmitted – emailed, faxed, posted etc
- If it can be discussed over the phone
- How it is stored – both in hardcopy and digital form
- When it needs to be encrypted
- How to share it and who it can be shared with
- How it is to be disposed of.

Information, just like other valuables, needs to be handled with care

Handling instructions help users to understand classifications (see Table 6.2).

Table 6.2 A typical classification and handling guide for commercial classification

Classification: Commercial	
Type of information	**Handling instructions**
This is generally sensitive information. If released to unauthorized persons, it could cause reputational harm, embarrassment, or financial and/or competitive harm. Examples of this type of information are: ● Contracts ● Bid/tender information ● Tender response/pricings, negotiation points etc. ● Reports/appraisals of supplier performance, market position etc. ● Generally information that is commercially sensitive	**Labelling**: Label 'Commercial' on the top and bottom of documents and on containers if possible. **Hardcopies**: Must be sent via registered post externally; do not label the envelope. Internally, use envelopes if not delivered by hand to the recipient. Envelopes should be labelled 'Commercial'. **Email**: OK to send email internally unencrypted; however, consider recipients. Encrypt attachments when sending externally via email. Include the word 'confidential' in the first line of the email. **USB drives**: Use secure USB drives for bulk data transfer. **Sharing**: Share only on a '**need to know**' basis. Only send to identified recipients who are aware of the nature of the classification and content and are able to provide the same level of protection. External recipients must be covered by a non-disclosure agreement before sharing. For regular external sharing and collaboration, use the intranet. Remove when no longer needed. **Faxing**: Can be faxed to a known fax machine, with the recipient present to receive it. The fax header should have the recipient's name on it. **Encryption**: Where files require encryption (for example email attachments) use encryption. Session-level access must be protected using SSL version 3 and above and/or TLS version 1 and above. Secure FTP (SFTP) can also be used as long as it complies with the encryption standard. **Password**: Must be as per the 'password standard' when sending over public networks. Pre-shared passwords may be used but must be changed every 30 days and sent via separate channels to the information. Passwords and/or encryption keys must not be sent over public networks, such as the internet, unencrypted. **Authentication**: Use multi-factor authentication for administrative access or mutual authentication (client and server certificates). **Storage**: Comply with the clear-desk and clear-screen policy. Lock away in a pedestal or locker when not in use. Store in secure system folders (for example, on SharePoint) with only 'need to know' access.
Disposal	**Paper (hardcopies)**: Cross-cut shred all copies, or use provided confidential disposal bins. **Magnetic storage (operational)**: Destroy data so that the data is not recoverable. Erase data using normal Windows delete on ABC encrypted laptops. **Magnetic storage (non-operational)**: Shred/crush media. **Optical storage**: Shred/crush media. **Electronic (flash) storage**: Destroy data so that data is not recoverable.

6.1.1.2 Data transportation and removable media

The greatest benefit of digitization of information is the ability to share it with others. Information is shared all the time, introducing risks. Often large amounts of information need to be transferred using portable devices such as USB drives, SD cards, CDs, DVDs and even hard drives. Email or secure file transfer methods are not well suited to transferring gigabytes of data, especially over wide area network links.

Small portable USB devices can hold tens, if not hundreds, of gigabytes of data and are ideal for transferring bulk information. As well as providing an easy means of moving large amounts of data quickly, these devices have been the cause of many data loss incidents and media headlines.

Best practice

- Keep data movement using portable devices to the minimum.
- Encrypt data by default on all portable devices.
- Audit all portable devices.
- Only permit approved devices and require authorization before data is copied on to portable devices and moved.

6.1.2 Change management

The objective of change management in cyber resilience is to manage the risks to operational services that are brought about by uncontrolled changes. Change management also ensures that changes are authorized, controlled, implemented securely and that transformation and transitions are smooth.

In cyber resilience, a proper change management regime is essential to managing risk to an operational environment and services during transition. Resilience is directly related to availability, and change control or management ensures that risk from disruption and unavailability is reduced. The scope of change management should include:

- Information assets
- All IT hardware and software
- Security policies, processes and procedures
- Architecture
- Infrastructure
- Process
- Tools
- Documentation.

Best practice

All changes in an organization should be subjected to the change management process and only be implemented on approval. Approved changes must be tested in a test environment before implementation in the operational environment.

ITIL provides a comprehensive set of well-established, tried-and-tested processes that work.

For instance, ITIL change management helps to:

- Create a culture of change management where there is zero tolerance of unauthorized change across the organization
- Align the change management process with business, project and stakeholder change management processes

- Ensure that changes create business value and that the benefits for the business created by each change are measured and reported
- Prioritize change – for example, innovation versus preventative versus detective versus corrective change
- Establish accountability and responsibilities for changes throughout the service lifecycle
- Separate duty controls
- Establish a single focal point for changes in order to minimize the likelihood of conflicting changes and potential disruption to supported environments
- Prevent people who are not authorized to make a change from having access to supported environments
- Integrate with other service management processes to establish traceability of change, detect unauthorized change and identify change-related incidents
- Establish change windows, and enforcement and authorization for exceptions
- Carry out performance and risk evaluation of all changes that impact service capability
- Carry out performance measures for the process – for example, efficiency and effectiveness.

Key message

Risks to the operational environment and services are controlled by managing changes to the environment. Planned and controlled change ensures that mistakes and errors are less likely to occur and lead to cyber resilience incidents and ultimately service outage.

All changes should be subject to a documented and approved change management process.

Change management is an important governance and control process. Without this process in place, changes would be ad hoc and uncontrolled, leading to disruption to services, introduction of vulnerabilities and risk to confidentiality, integrity and availability (CIA) – see section 1.5.5. Uncontrolled and unapproved changes could lead to:

- Errors
- Misconfiguration
- Inclusion of back-doors or unknown functions that allow unauthorized access
- Introduction of malware to destroy, damage or steal information
- Poor performance, disruption and or outage
- Data loss or corruption.

A change management process should include important operational risk management activities such as:

- Forward schedule of changes, so that changes can be planned
- Documented **request for change**
- Risk assessment of the proposed changes
- A **change advisory board** (CAB) where the proposed changes are discussed and approved by the stakeholders
- A process for review and approval of emergency changes
- Testing in a test environment
- Roll-back procedures if things go wrong.

All these activities help to reduce the risk of uncontrolled changes by protecting services from disruption, outage, poor performance, loss of service etc.

In many organizations change management is usually practised to a certain level due to the important part it plays in managing and reducing the risk from disruption, and therefore improving cyber resilience. As well as reducing the likelihood of disruption and unavailability, change management helps the organization to deliver business changes and improvements in a controlled and efficient manner. ITIL change management can provide organizations with a set of established processes and structure that can be used if they do not already have a change management process.

6.1.3 Testing

The primary control objective of testing in cyber resilience is to ensure that risks from the introduction of new products and services are reduced through thorough testing. Another aspect entails ensuring that cyber resilience controls are performing effectively. Testing can take many forms: for example technical testing (such as penetration testing of infrastructure), network, software and application testing (during and post-development), and non-technical control testing. As an organization transitions, it will need to also ensure that it has robust processes, management structures, documentation etc. However, the application and software are where the bulk of the testing is concentrated.

In **software and application testing**, the aspiration may be to identify and remove all defects before the application is released into operation. However, this objective is invariably not achievable. For the purposes of cyber resilience, the objective should be to identify and remove the security critical defects before transitioning into operation.

Testing should be based on standard testing frameworks, methodologies, tools and scripts. The tests should include assessment of the controls that were documented at the requirements capture phase.

Best practice

Always test software in a test environment: never test in the live or operational environment.

The pre-live test environment should be as similar as possible to the live or operational environment. Testing in this environment ensures that there are no unforeseen glitches when transitioning into live.

The application can undergo a number of tests during its development, including (but not limited to):

- Unit testing
- System testing
- Integration testing
- Regression testing
- User-acceptance testing (UAT)
- Penetration testing and code reviews.

For the purposes of cyber resilience, organizations should test all the security functionalities of the application such as authentication, access control, input and output validation, testing against common software vulnerabilities such as the OWASP top 10 (as shown in Table 6.3) and any other security requirements that were captured during the requirements gathering (see section 5.1.2.2).

As a minimum, the testing should include tests against the latest OWASP top 10 risks.

In transitioning and operating services from a cyber resilience perspective, organizations must ensure that they do not introduce vulnerabilities into an operation environment that can be exploited by hackers. This means testing software and applications, initially through the software-testing lifecycle, built into the software development lifecycle (SDLC), where the functional and non-functional testing takes place. At each stage of the testing, from unit testing through to user-acceptance testing, security testing should be included in order to avoid a lot of security issues being discovered just before transitioning the software into operation. Whatever development methodology an organization uses, Waterfall or Agile, whether it be scenarios, user stories or sprints, security testing can be and should be embedded throughout the development process.

Hints and tips

Do not leave the security testing until the end of the process. Include and embed security testing throughout the SDLC and the software-testing lifecycle. Testing can also be included in user scenarios and different development methodologies.

Table 6.3 2013 OWASP top 10 application security risks

Source OWASP.org

A1 – Injection	Injection flaws, such as SQL, OS and LDAP injection occur when untrusted data is sent to an interpreter as part of a command or query. The attacker's hostile data can trick the interpreter into executing unintended commands or accessing data without proper authorization.
A2 – Broken authentication and session management	Application functions related to authentication and session management are often not implemented correctly, allowing attackers to compromise passwords, keys or session tokens, or to exploit other implementation flaws to assume other users' identities.
A3 – Cross-site scripting (XSS)	XSS flaws occur whenever an application takes untrusted data and sends it to a web browser without proper validation or encoding. XSS allows attackers to execute scripts in the victim's browser which can hijack user sessions, deface websites, or redirect the user to malicious sites.
A4 – Insecure direct object references	A direct object reference occurs when a developer exposes a reference to an internal implementation object, such as a file, directory or database key. Without an access control check or other protection, attackers can manipulate these references to access unauthorized data.
A5 – Security misconfiguration	Good security requires having a secure configuration defined and deployed for the application, frameworks, application server, web server, database server and platform. Secure settings should be defined, implemented and maintained, as defaults are often insecure. Additionally, software should be kept up to date.
A6 – Sensitive data exposure	Many web applications do not properly protect sensitive data such as credit cards, tax IDs and authentication credentials. Attackers may steal or modify such weakly protected data to conduct credit card fraud, identity theft or other crimes. Sensitive data deserves extra protection such as encryption at rest or in transit, as well as special precautions when exchanged with the browser.
A7 – Missing function-level access control	Most web applications verify function-level access rights before making that functionality visible in the UI. However, applications need to perform the same access control checks on the server when each function is accessed. If requests are not verified, attackers will be able to forge requests in order to access functionality without proper authorization.
A8 – Cross-site request forgery (CSRF)	A CSRF attack forces a logged-on victim's browser to send a forged HTTP request, including the victim's session cookie and any other automatically included authentication information, to a vulnerable web application. This allows the attacker to force the victim's browser to generate requests that the vulnerable application thinks are legitimate requests from the victim.
A9 – Using components with known vulnerabilities	Components, such as libraries, frameworks and other software modules, almost always run with full privileges. If a vulnerable component is exploited, such an attack can facilitate serious data loss or server takeover. Applications using components with known vulnerabilities may undermine application defences and enable a range of possible attacks and impacts.
A10 – Unvalidated redirects and forwards	Web applications frequently redirect and forward users to other pages and websites, and use untrusted data to determine the destination pages. Without proper validation, attackers can redirect victims to phishing or malware sites, or use forwards to access unauthorized pages.

Once the software is ready to be delivered into service, ensure that the software is fully security tested; this could be in the form of automated code reviews and/or penetration testing to test risks like the OWASP top 10. However, the tests should not be limited to the OWASP top 10. These tests should be treated as the basic minimum against which an application is tested.

6.1.4 Training

When transitioning into operation, as well as ensuring that all the systems, policies, processes are in place, it is important to also ensure that users and IT staff are trained in using and administrating the system.

People who will be using and managing the system and handling the assets must be trained and ready for operation. Without training, users will not be equipped to operate the system and will cause errors, malfunction, security incidents and breaches.

Cyber resilience training should include:

● Data protection

● Secure data handling

● Secure operating procedures

● Actual training on the use of the system

● Acceptable use policy.

Some of the training may be provided as part of the user's involvement during the user-acceptance testing (UAT) of the systems, or there may be specially tailored training. Training should be designed so that it is relevant and appropriate to the users: for example, managers and administrators will require different training from the users.

6.1.5 Documentation management

Proper documentation is essential to ensure smooth transition into service and operation. Without documentation such as signed contracts and agreed service level agreements (SLAs), policies, process documentation, operating procedures, instructions and security operating procedures, it would be difficult to operate the services efficiently and securely. All documentation should be quality- and version-controlled, and reviewed and updated on a regular basis to maintain currency. Out-of-date and uncontrolled documents may actually cause operational issues and information loss or leakage. Uncontrolled documents may be copied, duplicated or lost without the knowledge of the owners. Out-of-date documents could lead to bad decisions or misconfigurations: for example, if the document was a configuration guide or if the risk treatment or remediation plan was incorrect.

Key message

Ensure that users are trained to use the system before they start using it for real to support **business operations**. Trained users are less likely to make mistakes or cause incidents.

From a cyber resilience perspective, this is especially true of documentation for critical business-supporting processes and recovery procedures such as IT service continuity management plans, cyber resilience plans, business continuity plans and incident management processes. These documents must be kept up to date and their circulations controlled, as they will contain sensitive information. Such documents should be available when required: this may mean having multiple copies, and perhaps even providing off-site or 'cloud' services where they can be made easily accessible in case the server or physical location is unavailable.

Key message

Key operating procedures and processes should be documented, communicated and kept up to date to ensure that those who need them to operate the organization's services have access to them. Additionally, it is vital to:

● Document important processes

● Classify documents

● Treat documents as assets

● Control changes to documents

● Control versions of documents

● Control circulation access to documents

● Set a review date for documents as part of the audit and review process.

Cyber resilience policies and procedures must not only be maintained but also communicated to all the relevant parties. Organizations should consider the best way to communicate these to staff. For example, not all staff may have to see the technical configuration guide, whereas all staff will need to see the acceptable use policy (AUP) to be able to comply with it.

Using the previous classifications as an example, organizations may want to consider providing staff with templates which already include classifications, headings and branding to make it easier for people to comply with business standards. Documents should be classified according to the sensitivity of the content. Configuration standards, detailed design documents, proprietary documents or documents that detail intellectual property, for example, must be kept confidential.

It is important to consider how and where to store documents. A central repository of business documents such as a document management and collaboration system will aid in this. These document management systems can control and track versions, allowing documents to be updated and shared securely and stored and communicated centrally. Documents can also be hosted internally or externally. For example, cloud-hosted systems can be accessed by external partners, such as the supply chain. This makes documents much safer to share than sending them by email or providing external users access to internal systems.

6.1.6 Information retention

Like many things in cyber resilience, information too has a lifecycle. It is created, managed, used and then disposed of when no longer required, as per Figure 6.2. How long information is retained and how it is disposed of will largely depend on specific business requirements and legal and regulatory obligations. For example, business records need to be retained for a minimum period (usually a specific number of years).

In many countries, the data protection legislation states that personal data processed for any purpose shall not be kept for longer than is necessary. This means that organizations need to understand why data was collected and the maximum period for which it can be kept. Asset registers or the retention policy should include an information schedule that contains dates for deletion of data. If information is kept beyond the stated requirement, an organization may be breaking the data protection law.

In the UK, financial data has to be retained for a minimum number of years. There is no penalty for keeping it longer, unless there is an impact on privacy in which case the information must not be retained for longer than necessary; however, it must not be disposed of earlier than the legal retention period. Therefore, organizations must ensure that data is not accidentally or deliberately disposed of. Of course the legal requirement will depend on the territorial and legal jurisdictions under which the organization is operating. Therefore, it is important for organizations to ensure that their data retention and disposal policies and processes comply with local laws.

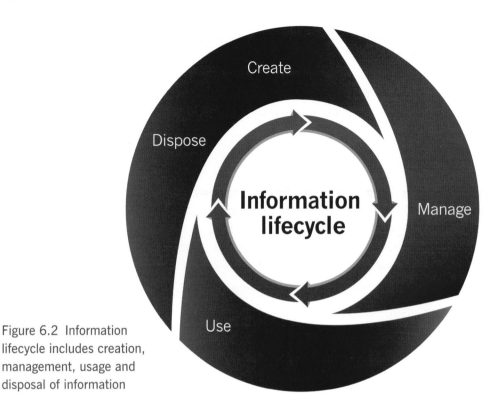

Figure 6.2 Information lifecycle includes creation, management, usage and disposal of information

A further example of the legal retention requirement is the Data Retention Directive (Directive 2006/24/EC), of the European Parliament and of the Council 2006. This directive covers the retention of data generated or processed in connection with the provision of publicly available electronic communications services or of public communications networks. According to the directive, member states will have to store citizens' telecommunications data for a minimum of 6 months and at the most 24 months.

6.1.7 Information disposal

Once information is finished with, it will need to be disposed of securely. How this is carried out will depend on the disposal policy, which should include details of how each type of information should be disposed of. The disposal policy will need to take into consideration the classification of the information to be disposed of and the type of media the information is stored on. For example, paper documents classified as 'public' could be thrown away in a normal bin; however, documents classified as 'confidential' may need to be shredded using a cross-cut shredder.

Digital information on the other hand may need special software for the deletion of confidential information so that the information cannot be recovered by unauthorized persons.

Magnetic drives such as hard drives and USB drives can be overwritten, if the drive is going to be reused, using specialized software that repeatedly overwrites areas of the disk with ones and zeros so that the information is beyond retrieval. Information stored on optical media such as CDs and DVDs is not easily erasable and the disks may need to be crushed beyond reconstitution. Organizations should have a policy on reuse of media and disposal as some media can be reused once the data is erased. Therefore, not all media needs to be destroyed. If reusing media, consider where the device will be used and what information it was previously used for.

Best practice

Disposal must ensure that data is not recoverable.

Keep records of disposal and obtain a certificate of disposal from the disposal supplier, if used.

If possible always witness the disposal of data on site.

Some countries have environmental legislation that covers disposal of hardware. For instance, in Europe the Waste Electrical and Electronic Equipment (WEEE) directive covers the disposal of electronic materials. Be sure that the disposal supplier is compliant.

If a specialist disposal company is used to dispose of assets, then ensure that it fully complies with the regulations and provides a certificate of disposal and an inventory of items disposed of. Ensure that this record of disposal is retained for audit.

6.2 ALIGNING CYBER RESILIENCE TRANSITION WITH IT SERVICE TRANSITION

IT service transition considers how an IT organization can best manage new, modified or retired IT services so that these meet the expectations of the business as documented in the service strategy and service design stages of the IT service lifecycle. Many of the activities carried out during service transition are intended to help manage the risks of transition – ensuring that everything is tested, that risks and benefits have been considered and that authorization has been granted by appropriate authorities.

During this stage of the IT service lifecycle the IT organization does everything needed to create an operational service from the service design package (SDP). Typically, this includes the following activities:

● Review the service design package created during the service design stage of the service lifecycle, and authorize the change for transition to start.
● Create a detailed transition plan, based on the contents of the SDP.
● Manage all the resources required to build, test and deploy the new or changed service.
● Obtain all the components required to build the IT service, and build the service in a non-production environment.
● Update IT service management processes and tools if required, to provide support for the new or changed service.
● Update metrics and reporting to ensure that these reflect the new or changed service.

Sensitive information should
be disposed of securely

- Carry out tests to ensure that the service is able to deliver the agreed levels of **utility** (what it does) and **warranty** (how well it does things).

- Make corrections to the design based on test results and any changes to the context in which the service will be used.

- Train IT staff so that they can support the new or changed service effectively and efficiently.

- Train users so that they can use the new or changed service effectively and efficiently.

- Capture and share knowledge about the new or changed service to make sure that this will be available to users and IT staff when and where it is needed.

- Review test results, training outcomes and other change information, and authorize the change for **deployment**.

- Deploy the service to a production environment.

- Update configuration information (at each stage during the transition), making sure that this information is available with the correct level of detail, when and where it is needed.

- Use organizational change management techniques throughout the transition to ensure that the service will be used and supported correctly and will create the value expected.

- Carry out a **post-implementation review** to ensure that the transition delivered the expected value and used the planned resources, initiating improvement plans to rectify any issues found.

Organizations that use ITIL as a basis for their IT service management systems can integrate cyber resilience transition into the service transition stage of the service lifecycle (see Figure 6.3). Organizations that are not using ITIL to manage their IT services may find it helpful to adopt some of the processes and activities described in *ITIL Service Transition* to support their cyber resilience transition.

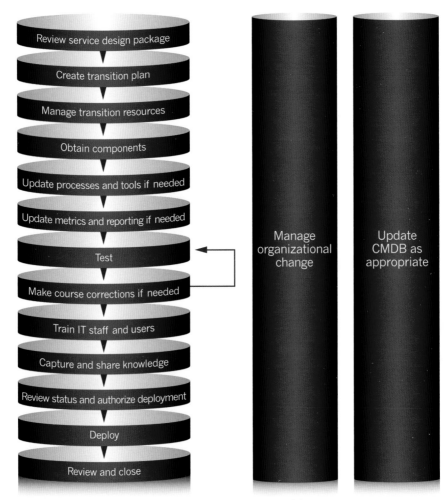

Figure 6.3 Aligning cyber resilience transition with IT service transition

ITIL Service Transition describes a number of processes that are particularly relevant to the transition stage of the service lifecycle. Every one of these processes needs to include appropriate aspects of cyber resilience. It is not possible to run cyber resilience processes that carry out similar activities to the service management processes in isolation from one another: they must be integrated or at the very least aligned to ensure that there is no conflict. Many of the controls described in section 6.1 can be implemented effectively through such integrated processes. This can enable an organization to achieve both its service transition objectives and its cyber resilience transition objectives efficiently and effectively.

Cyber resilience activities should be integrated with each of the processes described in *ITIL Service Transition*.

6.2.1 Transition planning and support

The ITSM transition planning and support process provides overall planning for service transitions and coordinates the resources they need.

Transition planning and support operates at two different levels.

- Managing the resources and capabilities needed for the overall service transition stage of the service lifecycle. This includes:
  - Understanding the business need for change, and planning to ensure that appropriate tools and funding are available to manage the expected rate of transition
  - Maintaining policies, standards and models for service transition
  - Coordinating internal resources and those managed by external suppliers
  - Coordinating service transition processes and tools to ensure that the interfaces and hand-offs between them work effectively and efficiently
  - Prioritizing conflicting requests for service transition resources.
- Planning and coordinating each service transition. This could include:
  - Implementation of new or changed IT services
  - New customers or customers leaving the service
  - Changes to management systems
  - New or changed processes
  - New or changed tools
  - New or changed standards or architectures
  - New or changed metrics or reporting.

In each case the transition planning and support process ensures that every aspect of the transition is well planned and effectively carried out; it manages any risks and issues that are identified, and it reviews the transition to ensure that it achieved the desired outcomes.

These two levels are shown in Figure 6.4.

The transition planning and support process does not provide detailed planning for individual transitions, which is done as part of other service transition processes, but it does provide the high-level coordination and planning needed to ensure that plans for specific activities fit together to deliver the required outcomes.

Transition planning and support can make a significant contribution to cyber resilience by:

- Ensuring that new or changed IT services, ITSM processes, standards, architectures, tools, processes etc. are introduced with appropriate care and attention to the risks that they could pose, including risks to cyber resilience
- Providing a mechanism for introducing new or changed cyber resilience controls to ensure that these achieve their intended purpose, and managing any conflicting resources needed, such as test systems or deployment of staff
- Sharing competence in management of organizational change to help ensure the success of cyber resilience projects.

For the overall service transition lifecycle stage

For each transition

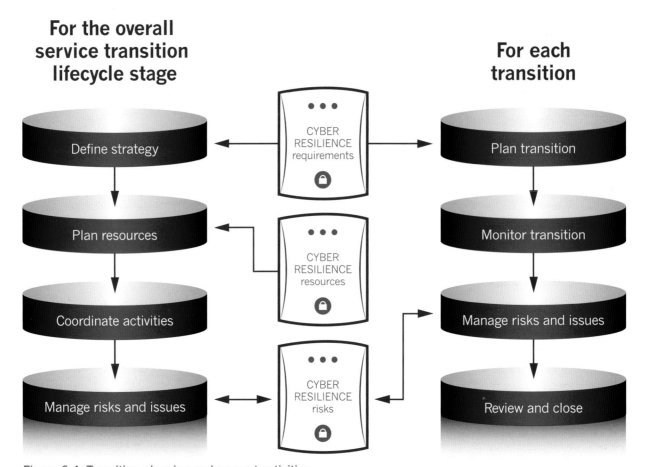

Figure 6.4 Transition planning and support activities

Cyber resilience can make a significant contribution to transition planning and support by:

● Providing guidance on what risk management activities are needed during service transition: for example by specifying required security testing of new applications.

● Identifying specific risks that must be managed during transitions: for example by specifying requirements for creation, management and deletion of test data to ensure that this does not compromise the confidentiality of any real data.

● Designing and implementing controls to help manage risks during service transition: for example by creating a penetration-testing service that can be used to test servers after deployment and before they are finally accepted in a production environment.

6.2.2 Change management

The ITSM change management process controls the lifecycle of all changes, helping to ensure that beneficial changes are made and minimizing disruption to IT services.

Change management has to balance two contradictory priorities:

● Facilitate the rate of change required by the business

● Protect the business from the negative effects of change.

ITIL describes three distinct types of change:

● **Standard changes** Predefined, low-risk changes that follow a well-established procedure. The procedure for each standard change is authorized by change management, but each instance of the standard change is usually managed by some other process such as request fulfilment or incident management.

What is a change?

ITIL defines a change as 'The addition, modification or removal of anything that could have an effect on IT services. The scope should include changes to all architectures, processes, tools, metrics and documentation, as well as changes to IT services and other configuration items.'

Examples of ITSM changes include:

- Deploying a new customer relationship management (CRM) system
- Upgrading the firmware on a disk drive.

- **Emergency changes** Changes that must be introduced as soon as possible – for example to resolve a major incident or install a security patch. These changes typically follow most steps of the normal change management process but use fast-track procedures. Emergency changes are a significant source of risk and require very careful management.

- **Normal changes** Any changes that are not standard or emergency changes. These changes are subject to the full change management process.

Change management records and evaluates changes, and if they are authorized then it ensures that they are planned, tested, implemented, documented and reviewed in a controlled manner. Much of this work is carried out by a change authority, which varies depending on the specific change. For example, major changes may be reviewed by senior management, significant changes by a change authorization board (CAB), and minor changes could be authorized by the change manager.

The main activities of change management for a normal change are shown in Figure 6.5, these activities include:

- **Create and record request for change** The change is formally requested by submitting a request for change (RFC), and a record is created to track its status.

- **Assess and evaluate change** Unsuitable or duplicate changes are filtered out. The change authority for this change is identified and they evaluate the change.

- **Authorize change build and test** The change authority authorizes the next stage, which is to build and test the change.

- **Coordinate change build and test** Work to create the change is carried out, implementation and remediation plans are created and the change is tested.

- **Authorize change deployment** The change authority authorizes the next stage, which is to deploy the change.

- **Coordinate change deployment** Work to deploy the change is carried out.

- **Review and close change** A formal review of the change is carried out to ensure that lessons are learned and improvements are planned.

Change management can make significant contributions to cyber resilience by:

- Only authorizing changes if they comply with applicable cyber resilience standards and architectures
- Reviewing changes for their potential impact on cyber resilience
- Making sure that every change is tested to ensure that it delivers the required levels of confidentiality, integrity and availability
- Reviewing and testing implementation plans to ensure that changes will be installed as designed
- Reviewing and testing remediation plans to ensure that corrective action can be taken if changes fail
- Identifying and managing change-related risks in line with the organization's risk assessment criteria and its risk acceptance criteria.

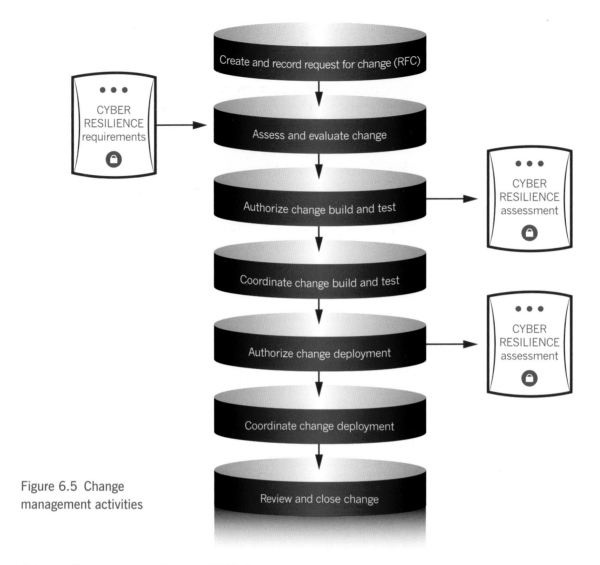

Figure 6.5 Change
management activities

Cyber resilience can contribute to ITSM change management by:

- Providing requirements and test scripts to assist in change evaluation. For example, there may be a requirement that all applications have been checked with a tool that can detect risks of buffer overflow or SQL injection threats.

- Ensuring that the CAB has representatives who understand cyber resilience and can assist with change authorization. It is important that whoever reviews changes for their cyber resilience implications has the knowledge needed to do this; just ticking a check box to say that security issues have been covered is not sufficient. Also note that only some changes will be reviewed by a CAB, depending on the design of the change management process, but all changes should be reviewed for cyber resilience risks.

- Reviewing changes to ensure that they meet cyber resilience standards and architectures. For major changes, this could be a formal review with independent security testing; for standard changes it could be a simple checklist that is completed to confirm that the appropriate checks have been made.

6.2.3 Service asset and configuration management

The ITSM service asset and configuration management (SACM) process ensures that the assets needed to deliver services are properly controlled, and that accurate and reliable information about these assets is available when and where it is needed.

Any component or service that needs to be managed is called a configuration item (CI). SACM maintains a **configuration management system** (CMS) that manages information about the configuration of CIs, and the relationships between them.

SACM also provides a mechanism for storing and protecting CIs prior to use. Hardware may be kept in a spares store and software in a definitive media library (DML). In each case this ensures that assets required for deployment are maintained in a protected environment with control over their integrity.

It is important to plan SACM carefully. Storing and managing too much information about CIs can be very expensive with little return on investment, while storing and managing insufficient information can result in a process that provides little value. Achieving the correct balance requires a good understanding of how the IT organization operates and therefore of who needs what information, and when and where it is needed.

The main activities of SACM are shown in Figure 6.6; these include:

- **Management and planning** Deciding what CIs should be recorded, with how much detail, and creating a plan to do this.
- **Configuration control** Ensuring that CIs are properly controlled, collecting and maintaining the required data, and recording changes to configurations and relationships of CIs.
- **Status reporting** Tracking the status of CIs throughout their lifecycle and producing relevant reports: for example a list of all PCs that have a particular software package/version installed, or a count of how many of a particular server model are available for deployment.
- **Verification and audit** Ensuring that all CIs are recorded in the CMS and comparing the physical CIs to the recorded information.

Figure 6.6 Service asset and configuration management activities

SACM can make significant contributions to cyber resilience by:

● Working with change management to help prevent unauthorized changes to CIs

● Detecting and reporting unauthorized changes to CIs

● Providing information about numbers, types and configuration of CIs to assist with cyber resilience planning

● Maintaining definitive, controlled hardware and software assets for deployment into production environments

● Maintaining information about the correct configuration and relationships of CIs that can be used during **diagnosis** and recovery from cyber-incidents.

Change management and SACM reduce risk from unauthorized changes

If change management and SACM are working together effectively, they help to protect assets by making unauthorized changes more difficult; they also assist recovery by making it easier to detect unauthorized changes and recover to the correct state.

A classification and handling guide (see section 6.1.1.1) explains how assets should be classified and how each classification should be handled or used. Typically, for each classification, the classification and handling guide should include the category of information and how the information is handled under each circumstance.

The instructions should include:

● The category of information for each classification

● How to decide whether the classification should be applied to a specific asset

● How it is labelled – where the classification is placed

● If it can be transmitted – emailed, faxed, posted etc

● If it can be discussed over the phone

● How it is stored – both in hardcopy and digital form

● When it needs to be encrypted

● How to share it and who it can be shared with

● How it is to be disposed of.

Cyber resilience can contribute to SACM by:

● Helping to protect the confidentiality, integrity and availability of the CMS: for example, by providing a standard server build that ensures the system complies with agreed standards, by carrying out security testing at regular intervals and by providing information classification that can be used to identify appropriate controls for information in the CMS.

● Providing mechanisms to help prevent unauthorized changes, such as physical protection of a critical server or logical protection of a critical file. For example, cyber resilience should provide a mechanism for identifying and authenticating users, providing them with different levels of access to data and information depending on their needs.

● Helping to identify unauthorized changes to critical components: for example, by comparing encrypted checksums of software modules with previously stored values.

6.2.4 Release and deployment management

Key definition

A release is a change (or changes) to an IT service that is built, tested and deployed at a specified time. A single release may include changes to hardware, software, documentation, processes and other components.

Examples of releases include:

● An updated desktop PC build that includes new hardware, operating system and standard applications

● An updated version of a customer relationship management (CRM) system that includes a number of new software modules.

The ITSM release and deployment management process plans, schedules and controls the build, test and deployment of releases. It delivers new functionality required by the business while protecting the integrity of existing services.

Release and deployment management is tightly integrated with change management and SACM. Change management reviews risks and benefits, and provides authorization to start each stage of the work; release and deployment management builds, tests and deploys new and changed IT services and components; SACM records the configuration and status of services and components at each stage.

Release and deployment management has four main activities, which are shown in Figure 6.7. Change management authorization is typically required at the start and end of each of these activities. Release and deployment management oversees all of these activities, but the actual work will often be done as part of other processes and functions, such as service validation and testing (see section 6.2.5) or **application management** (see section 7.2.8). The four main activities are as follows:

● **Release and deployment planning** Creates a plan for how the release will be built, tested and deployed

● **Release build and test** Builds the **release package**, tests it, and checks it into a definitive media library (DML) ready for deployment. Release build and test only happens once for each release

● **Deployment** Deploys the release from the DML into the production environment. There could be many deployments of a single release. In an extreme case there could be a single release that is deployed thousands of times to many different PCs, under the control of the end users

● **Review and close** Like all other ITSM activities, it is essential to learn and improve. A formal review of the release is carried out to ensure that lessons are learned and improvements are planned.

Release and deployment management can make significant contributions to cyber resilience by:

● Ensuring that all services and components are built correctly with no unauthorized code being added

● Improving integrity by using a DML to ensure that all software deployed to production environments is version-controlled, tested and free of alterations

● Carrying out security tests on new or changed services to ensure that these meet required standards before they are deployed

● Providing knowledge transfer to ensure that users and IT staff are aware of any cyber resilience responsibilities for new or changed IT services.

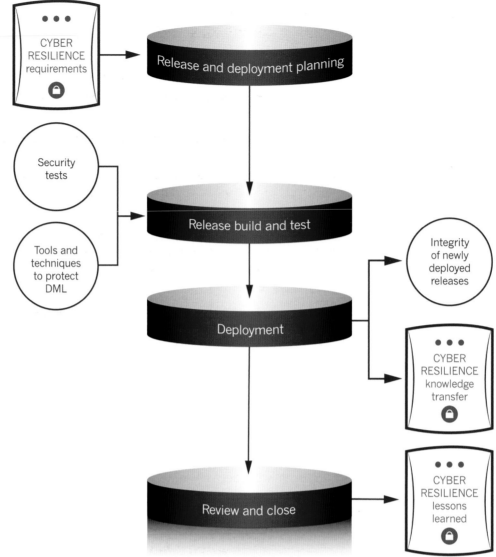

Figure 6.7 Release and deployment management activities

Cyber resilience can contribute to release and deployment by:

- Defining cyber resilience requirements to assist with release and deployment planning. For example, there may be a requirement for all software to be scanned for viruses, or other threats, before it can be stored in the DML; there may be a requirement for all servers to be created from a standard build with a predefined configuration; or there may be a requirement for all newly deployed servers to undergo a vulnerability scan or penetration test before they are made available for production use.

- Providing tools and mechanisms to protect the integrity and availability of the DML: for example, tools for user identification and authentication that can help to prevent unauthorized modifications, tools to scan for viruses or other threats, or tools to create cryptographic signatures which can reveal unauthorized changes.

- Defining and automating security tests for use during release build and test activities.

6.2.5 Service validation and testing

The ITSM service validation and testing process ensures that new or changed IT services match their design specifications and will meet the needs of the business. Service validation and testing is not just for in-house-developed software – all new or changed services should be tested regardless of the sourcing model in use. The actual testing required may be different for in-house development, outsourced development, commercial off-the-shelf (COTS) packages or cloud services, but each of these needs to be subject to appropriate testing.

Service validation and testing ensures that the new or changed service will be fit for purpose (does what the business needs) and fit for use (meets the business requirements for availability, performance/capacity, service continuity, security etc.).

Activities in service validation and testing are shown in Figure 6.8. These include:

- **Plan and design tests** Define the tests to be carried out and the resources needed. Create an overall plan to deliver the tests.
- **Verify test plan and design** Check that the test scope and coverage is appropriate and that test scripts are accurate and complete.
- **Prepare test environment** Testing needs to be carried out in a suitable test environment, which should include not only the right hardware and software but also test data that is a close copy of that used in the actual production environment.
- **Perform tests** Ideally, tests will be automated as much as possible, but some manual testing is acceptable so long as the tests are properly documented and test results are reproducible. If a test fails then the issue should be resolved if possible: in any event the remaining tests should be run even after one test has failed (unless they can no longer be run due to the failure).
- **Evaluate exit criteria and report** Actual test results are compared with expected results and with exit criteria, and a report is created. An example exit criterion might be that a service meets a specific quality requirement such as 'no more than four medium-impact errors'.

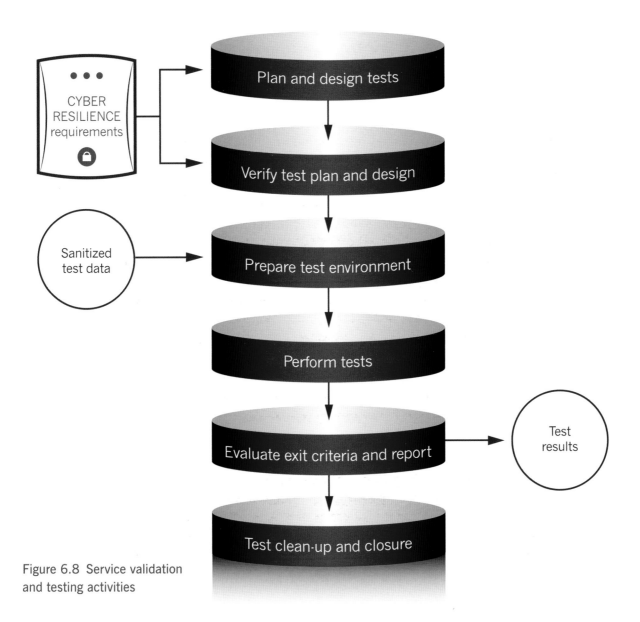

Figure 6.8 Service validation and testing activities

- **Test clean-up and closure** After testing is complete, sensitive data may need to be removed from the test environment, or the environment may need to be restored to a known baseline configuration. Lessons should be drawn from any test failures or difficulties encountered during testing.

Service validation and testing can make significant contributions to cyber resilience by:

- Testing the ability of services and components to resist specific threats
- Testing the ability of services and components to recover from specific failure scenarios
- Providing assurance that the new or changed service will deliver expected levels of confidentiality, integrity and availability.

Cyber resilience can contribute to service testing and validation by:

- Providing cyber resilience requirements to support test planning and design. Typically, this might include different tests for systems that hold data with different requirements. For example, all servers may require vulnerability scanning, external-facing servers may require penetration tests, and customer-facing web servers may require a very extensive penetration test carried out by independent testers. In any case this requires a classification system that identifies which cyber resilience tests are required for which systems.

- Creating automated tests or test scripts to test cyber resilience aspects of new or changed services: for example standard vulnerability scans for servers, or application test tools for identifying vulnerabilities in in-house applications.

- Helping to create sanitized data for use in test environments, or providing standards and mechanisms for creating appropriate test data. In many organizations test data can have extremely high requirements for confidentiality. For example, there may be a need for valid payment card details to test an online shopping service, and tests of a medical records system may require genuine patient data (or patient data that has been sanitized but could be de-anonymized and used to identify patients).

6.2.6 Change evaluation

The ITSM change evaluation process provides a mechanism for formally evaluating a change, looking at the likely impacts on business outcomes. The actual business performance of the change is compared with the predicted performance, and risks and issues relating to the change are identified and managed.

Every change will be evaluated at multiple points in its lifecycle. The change evaluation process describes a formal process that is suitable for evaluation of significant changes. Each organization should decide when formal evaluation is needed based on its approach to risk management and its risk appetite.

Activities in change evaluation are shown in Figure 6.9; these include:

- **Plan the evaluation** Creating a plan to ensure that the evaluation considers the different perspectives required to ensure that potential unintended consequences of the change will be identified, as well as the intended effects.

- **Evaluate predicted performance** Carrying out an evaluation to compare the predicted business performance of the change with the customer requirements. This evaluation is usually carried out quite early in the change lifecycle, based on design documents or behaviour of the change in test environments. This evaluation may be repeated at multiple points in the change lifecycle.

- **Evaluate actual performance** This evaluation compares the actual performance of the changed IT service with the customer requirements and recommends whether to proceed with the change, and whether any remediation is required. The extent to which the actual business performance of the change can be evaluated depends on how far through the change lifecycle evaluation is carried out. This assessment may also be carried out more than once in the lifecycle of the change.

- **Create evaluation report** An evaluation report documents the results of change evaluation. Typically, this includes the risk profile, any deviations between predicted and actual performance, and a recommendation stating whether or not the change should be accepted. If appropriate for the context then the report may also contain one or both of:

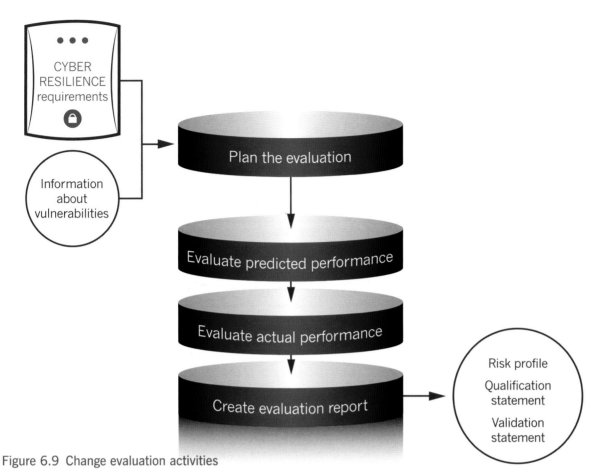

Figure 6.9 Change evaluation activities

- A qualification statement, formally stating whether the IT infrastructure is appropriate and correctly configured
- A validation statement, formally stating whether the new or changed service meets a documented set of requirements.

Change evaluation can make significant contributions to cyber resilience by:

- Assessing both intended and unintended effects of changes on the confidentiality, integrity and availability of the new or changed IT service, and on other IT services
- Providing a risk profile for the new or changed service which may be required for ongoing cyber resilience risk management for the service
- Providing formal qualification statements and validation statements that may be required to meet cyber resilience standards.

Cyber resilience can contribute to change evaluation by:

- Providing cyber resilience requirements for the new or changed IT service. Typically, these would be similar requirements to those used to evaluate any change – see section 6.2.2.
- Providing information about common vulnerabilities that may be relevant to the evaluation. This can be particularly problematic, since the list of common vulnerabilities needs constant maintenance as new threats are discovered. It is rare that an older vulnerability can be removed from the list because these can still be exploited by current threats, but if the list is not updated it will not be fit for purpose.

6.2.7 Knowledge management

The ITSM knowledge management process ensures that perspectives, ideas, experiences and information are shared, and made available in the right place and at the right time to enable informed decision-making, and to improve efficiency by reducing the need for people to rediscover knowledge.

Although knowledge management is described in *ITIL Service Transition*, it is relevant to all stages of the service lifecycle. Many ITSM processes are active across more than one stage of the service lifecycle, but this is particularly the case for knowledge management.

Knowledge management in ITSM is no different from knowledge management in any other area of the business, and can often be usefully integrated with management of knowledge for other business units.

Knowledge management defines a hierarchy that shows how value is added along the path described by Data-to-Information-to-Knowledge-to-Wisdom (DIKW):

● **Data** Discrete facts – for example, the time at which incident 2014536 was logged
● **Information** The result of providing context to data – for example, the average time to resolve Priority 1 incidents
● **Knowledge** The result of applying insight, values and judgement to information – for example, the average time to resolve Priority 1 incidents has increased by 15% since a new version of an IT service was released
● **Wisdom** This makes use of knowledge to create value through decisions. For example, it is recognized that the reason for the increase in resolution time for Priority 1 incidents is the poor quality of technical documentation, so a decision is taken to invest in improved documentation.

Knowledge management maintains a **service knowledge management system** (SKMS), which is used to manage knowledge, information and data. This is not usually a single repository but a logical entity, which may consist of multiple tools and databases. The SKMS has four architectural layers:

● **Data layer** Including tools and processes for discovery, collection and audit of the data
● **Information integration layer** Including tools and processes for metadata management, reconciliation, extraction, transformation and mining of information
● **Knowledge-processing layer** Including tools and processes for query, analysis, reporting, modelling, monitoring and alerting
● **Presentation layer** Including tools and processes for retrieving, updating, publishing, subscribing and collaborating, and management of different views for different stakeholders.

Knowledge management can make significant contributions to cyber resilience by:

● Ensuring that knowledge, information and data are categorized according to cyber resilience requirements
● Applying agreed cyber resilience controls to help ensure the confidentiality, integrity and availability of shared knowledge, information and data
● Maintaining and sharing knowledge, information and data needed for management of cyber resilience, such as security policies, technology standards and audit reports.

Cyber resilience can contribute to knowledge management by:

● Defining a categorization system that can be used to help knowledge management apply appropriate protection. For example, information may be marked 'internal use only', 'confidential' or 'restricted distribution' – each of these will have a definition of the classification and an explanation of how material with that marking should be treated. This does not just apply to information held on IT systems: it is equally applicable to printed or handwritten documents, photographs or any other type of information.
● Defining requirements for the confidentiality, integrity and availability of knowledge, information and data. This will typically be defined differently for different categories of data. Requirements may include for example:
  ○ This data may not be stored on removable media.
  ○ This data must always be encrypted.
  ○ This data must be deleted after it has been used for a specific purpose.
  ○ This data must be backed up and the backup retained for seven years.

- Providing tools, standards and processes to help manage the confidentiality, integrity and availability of knowledge, information and data. For example:
  - A mechanism for identifying and authenticating users to enable allocation of different access rights to different roles or people
  - Encryption to help protect the confidentiality and integrity of knowledge, information and data.

6.2.8 Management of organizational change

Managing organizational change is an essential aspect of managing any transition. *ITIL Service Transition* does not describe management of organizational change as a process, but it does include a chapter on 'Managing people through service transitions'. This describes two activities that it says are important to service transition:

- **Communication** To deliver prompt understanding of the implications, benefits and usage of new or changed IT services.
- **Organizational and stakeholder change** To support organization changes needed to enable people to make best use of new and changed services.

These activities are not specific to ITSM changes: changes required for implementing a cyber resilience project need to take the same approach.

6.2.8.1 Communication

Communication is not just about telling people things. All communication must work in two directions – speaking and listening, writing and reading. To obtain buy-in from stakeholders it is important to understand their current attitudes, opinions and level of commitment to the change before deciding how to communicate with them.

A triage approach to communication can be very helpful, dividing up the stakeholders into those who are already committed to the change, those who will oppose the change whatever is done, and those who are open to the idea but are not yet convinced. Communication to each of these groups needs to be appropriate to their needs.

A communication plan should identify:

- The objective and desired outcomes of each communication
- What information will be delivered, who to, and when
- How the information will be delivered
- The tone of each communication
- Which groups or people will be involved in cascading or distributing each communication
- How the success of each communication will be measured.

There are many different methods of communication that can be used. A good communication plan should include multiple methods, as appropriate for the particular communication. Some methods that can be used are:

- Workshops
- Newsletters
- Training
- Team meetings
- Meetings of the whole organization
- One-to-one meetings
- Q&A feedback or FAQs, posted to public forums or mailboxes
- Corporate intranet
- Simulation games
- Posters.

6.2.8.2 Organizational and stakeholder change

Managing organizational change is the responsibility of the managers and executives involved in each change. Clear strategic vision from senior management is essential, as is active management of the change.

For change to be successful it is important that it fits with the organization's culture and values. Understanding these is therefore an important step in managing the change. This understanding needs to cover many areas including:

● Is change seen as normal and good, or are people generally resistant to change?

● What types of communication do people prefer?

● How is knowledge shared?

● Are there clear communities and community leaders who need to be engaged?

● How effectively are meetings managed? Are they seen as effective?

● How are people rewarded or recognized for their contributions?

One helpful approach for managing organizational change is J. P. Kotter's eight steps for leading change:

1. **Establish a sense of urgency** This gets people into a frame of mind where they are ready to accept change.

2. **Create a guiding coalition** This puts the right people in place to oversee and drive the change.

3. **Develop a vision and strategy** The guiding team creates this to guide action in the remaining stages.

4. **Communicate the change vision (and communicate it over and over again)** This gets as many people as possible acting to make the vision a reality.

5. **Empower broad-based action** Remove obstacles and make people feel able to act.

6. **Create short-term wins** Enough short-term wins, created quickly, help to build momentum and convert people who were doubtful.

7. **Consolidate gains and produce more change** Continue making changes without stopping until the vision becomes a reality.

8. **Anchor new approaches in the culture** Create supporting structures that provide support for the new way of working.

6.2.9 Aligning cyber resilience controls with IT service transition

This section has so far considered the integration of cyber resilience and IT service management by considering how each ITSM process can be integrated with cyber resilience. An alternative way to consider integration of cyber resilience and IT service management is to look at how each of the strategic cyber resilience controls described in section 6.1 can be integrated with ITSM.

6.2.9.1 Asset management and configuration management

This control contributes significantly to the ITSM service asset and configuration management process. When considering how these can work together it is important to understand the differences as well as the similarities. It is likely that the cyber resilience control will have a wider scope than the ITSM SACM process, and that the two processes will have different definitions of what an asset is.

The list of assets maintained by the ITSM SACM process is an important input to the cyber resilience process, but because of the difference in scope it is likely that the cyber resilience control will need to maintain a separate list of assets.

6.2.9.2 Change management

This control overlaps considerably with the ITSM change management process, but again it is important to understand the differences between them. The scope of cyber resilience change management is very wide compared with the scope of ITSM change management, and the objectives are also different.

The ITSM change management process can provide the cyber resilience control with information about changes to IT services, but the cyber resilience control will need other sources of information to find out about non-IT-related business changes. For example, if the business process for storing and archiving confidential paper-based information changes, this would not be identified by ITSM change management.

6.2.9.3 Testing

This control can work very effectively with the service validation and testing process. Some cyber resilience testing would be outside the scope of the ITSM process (for example testing that a business process control is effective), and some ITSM testing would be outside the scope of the cyber resilience control (for example verifying that a new service meets its agreed functional requirements). Nonetheless, there are many areas where the two can work very effectively together.

6.2.9.4 Training

There is no ITSM process that aligns well with the cyber resilience training control. The release and deployment management process should ensure that users and IT staff have received appropriate training for each new or changed service, and this should certainly include aspects of cyber resilience. Also there will be a need for technical management and application management staff to receive suitable training in cyber resilience aspects of the technology domains for which they are responsible. Technical management and application management are discussed in sections 7.2.7 and 7.2.8.

6.2.9.5 Documentation management

Cyber resilience documentation management should be supported by the ITSM knowledge management process. It is very important that the cyber resilience requirements for management of documents are included in policies and objectives for knowledge management, as this process should provide a mechanism for implementing these requirements.

6.2.9.6 Information retention and disposal

The ITSM knowledge management process will support many aspects of information retention and disposal. Requirements for retention and disposal of knowledge should be included in knowledge management policies and objectives, and knowledge management should provide a mechanism for implementing these.

The ITSM service asset and configuration management process will also provide support for retention and disposal of information assets. This may include processes for secure erasure and disposal of media, as well as logging and tracking the status and location of media.

6.3 TRANSITION SCENARIOS

This section looks at some aspects of transition for the three fictitious organizations. Each of these organizations is undergoing some kind of transition, based on the strategy and design efforts described in previous sections. As you read through these descriptions you should think about:

● How well are changes managed? Is it likely that a change could introduce new security vulnerabilities?

● Does the organization understand the assets that they need to protect? How likely is it that some assets could be missed?

● What cyber resilience testing is carried out? Is this sufficient or what additional testing might be needed?

Retail example: SellUGoods Ltd

The new tools and processes for detecting and managing security incidents are now being tested. The tools include both server and network intrusion detection products, which will generate alerts at the operations bridge in each data centre. Operations personnel are being trained in how to respond to the various alerts that might be generated by the tools. When the testing is complete the tools will be deployed to all servers and firewalls. The ITSM configuration management system will be used to record the deployments and ensure that no servers or firewalls are omitted.

The new security incident management process has been approved. To help the people involved understand and adopt the new process, the project team are running a series of tests. These will include a number of scenario tests where the staff members involved in the new process will be presented with information as though a security incident is taking place, and they will have to respond appropriately. This testing will include personnel from the ITSM operations management team, the ITSM incident management team, the information security team, the network and server teams, the business continuity team and the crisis management team. This testing will take place on a Sunday when the factories are shut down, to ensure that it does not disrupt production. The testing will be quite expensive, but the finance director has approved the budget for this because it is really important that the new process works effectively. After the testing is complete there will probably be some improvement suggestions for the new process.

One of the requirements for PCI-DSS certification is that SellUGoods conducts an annual penetration test. Planning for the next annual test is currently under way. To contain the cost as much as possible the scope of the penetration testing will be limited to just those systems which are involved in the processing of payment cards. The first time a penetration test was run, a number of vulnerabilities were discovered, but since then these annual tests have not identified any new issues.

Medical example: MedUServ Ltd

MedUServ has a very stable environment with a low rate of change. The business is growing at a slow rate, and this is not sufficient to require significant changes in IT, or in cyber resilience. There is very little transition activity, either in relation to IT or cyber resilience. The increased cyber resilience requirements of the potential new customer contract may require significant transition effort, but MedUServ has not yet realized this.

Contract negotiations with the new customer are going well, and it is likely that this contract will be signed in the next few weeks. This will involve some increase in lab staff, so the project team are now considering possible changes to the lab layout to support the additional staff. The process for taking on new staff is quite robust, and all new staff will receive training in handling personally identifiable information as part of the onboarding process.

Although all IT at MedUServ has been outsourced, there are some computers on site at the lab. Most of the onsite IT comprises computers that are used to process medical samples and to manage lab equipment. There are also a few laptops that are used by management and sales staff. The IT outsourcer maintains all of these onsite computers, ensuring that they have appropriate anti-virus software installed and receive regular security updates as needed. MedUServ does not invest more than it absolutely has to in IT: the computers and laptops are quite old, but they function perfectly well and there are no plans for upgrades.

Protection of personally identifiable information is taken very seriously at MedUServ, and all staff have regular update training on their responsibilities. MedUServ is starting to plan for changes that might be needed to support the new European General Data Protection Regulation (GDPR), which is expected to come into force soon. This may require some changes to the IT outsourcing contract, so discussions with the supplier will be needed. Changes to the IT outsourcing contract can be quite expensive, and there is not a lot of money available to support this.

Manufacturing example: MakeUGoods

The SCADA-hardening project is now ready to deploy the new cyber resilience controls that it designed. These have already been deployed to a test environment and no issues were noted, so now it is time to deploy them more widely. The project will be rolled out in a number of stages:

- Changes to the SCADA servers to implement file integrity monitoring and application whitelisting is seen as the most urgent control, and this will be deployed first. The SCADA environment is very well documented and the project team have complete details on every server where this is to be deployed. The testing has ensured that the deployment process works well, and that the backout is effective if it should be needed. Because the SCADA systems are so critical to production a lot of effort has been put in to designing and testing backout plans; this ensures that if anything unexpected happens during the deployment, the risk to production can be minimized.

- Changes to other critical servers to implement file integrity monitoring will be next, but application whitelisting has been postponed for these servers due to some issues found during testing. A number of applications that are used at MakeUGoods were incompatible with the application whitelisting software, and they could not run when this was installed.

- The need for improved network separation has resulted in a design for additional segregated networks. This could be quite disruptive so it has been decided to deploy these changes next December when the factory is shut down for the long holiday. This will allow plenty of time for extended testing, and for the changes to be backed out if any issues are noted.

- Improved controls on removable devices will be brought in gradually. The initial step will be for a separate design of USB stick to be purchased for use on SCADA systems only. This will help to ensure that these USB sticks are never inserted in any other system. There will be extensive awareness training to ensure that all staff understand the importance of this. Controls to enforce encryption of data on all removable media will be rolled out to general office computers over the next few months.

- The scope for penetration testing of the SCADA control centre has been defined, and a selection process is under way to select a vendor to carry out this testing.

6.4 CYBER RESILIENCE TRANSITION QUESTIONS

1. How does your organization manage service transition risks that could impact IT services? What steps could you take to improve risk management during service transition? How could you do this without having a negative impact on business agility?

2. How well is cyber resilience integrated with ITSM change management and SACM in your organization? How could this be improved? How could you measure the impact of any changes?

3. What are the strengths of your organization's approach for managing knowledge, information and data? What are the weaknesses? How could you improve this? How is responsibility for knowledge management assigned in your organization? What changes in responsibilities or processes would improve this?

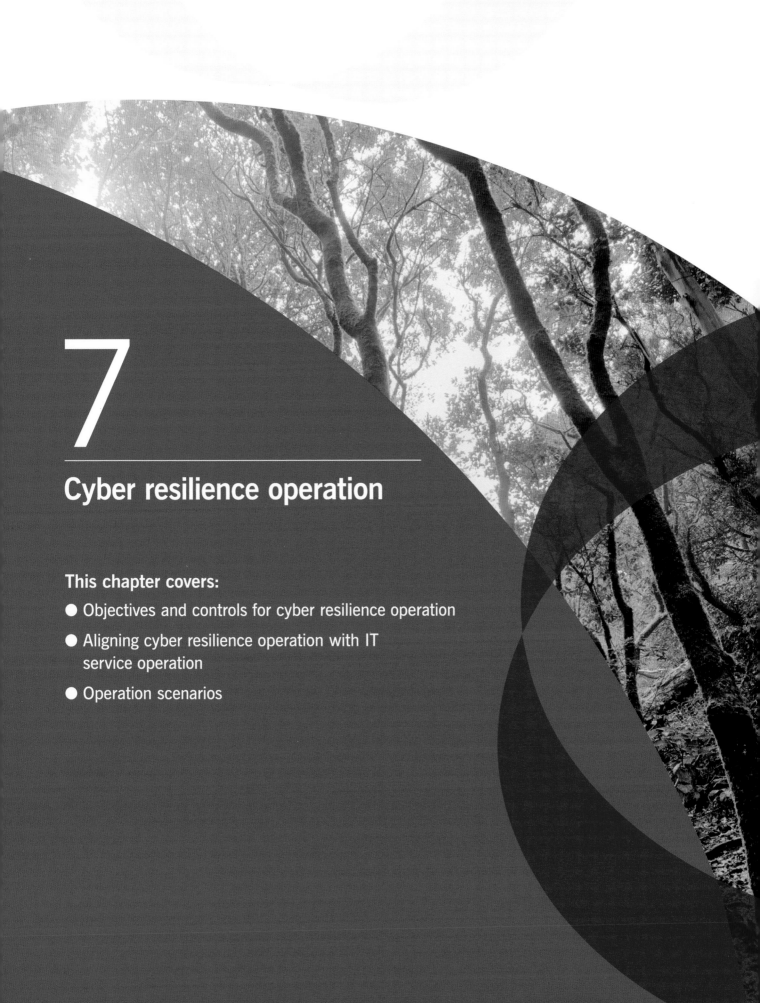

7

Cyber resilience operation

This chapter covers:

- Objectives and controls for cyber resilience operation
- Aligning cyber resilience operation with IT service operation
- Operation scenarios

7 Cyber resilience operation

Cyber resilience operation is the part of the lifecycle where the controls that have been put in place to protect the organization's assets actually have an effect. Everything done in strategy, design and transition is put to use in preventing, detecting and resolving cyber-incidents that could otherwise have a significant impact on the business. Figure 7.1 shows the lifecycle stages with the size of each area indicating how much time is spent in that lifecycle stage. As can be seen, the vast majority of the time is spent in operation – the stage of the lifecycle where controls have been deployed and are available to enhance the cyber resilience of the organization's assets.

> ## Operation without strategy, design or transition
>
> A newly formed small business purchases a laptop for use by a manager. Even though the business has no formal cyber resilience strategy, the manager takes the reasonable steps of installing anti-virus software on the laptop and making sure it is never left unattended in a public place.

Even organizations that do not have formal strategy, design and transition still have cyber resilience controls that they operate, and this chapter of the guide will be relevant to those organizations too. Many organizations start their cyber resilience by implementing and operating some controls, and later go on to develop strategy and design to improve their cyber resilience. Organizations that are just starting to formalize their approach to cyber resilience may find the UK Cyber Essentials scheme to be a good starting approach (www.gov.uk/government/publications/cyber-essentials-scheme-overview).

Cyber resilience controls must be integrated with all aspects of running the business, so that they can provide the protection that is required while having the smallest possible negative impact on the efficiency and effectiveness of normal business operations.

If the strategy, design and transition stages have delivered the right balance, there should be many different types of control active during the operation stage. To ensure a good balance, it is helpful to categorize controls as:

● **Preventative controls** These are intended to prevent threats from succeeding. They should be monitored and audited during operation to ensure that they remain effective, and that they have been applied to all assets where they might be needed.

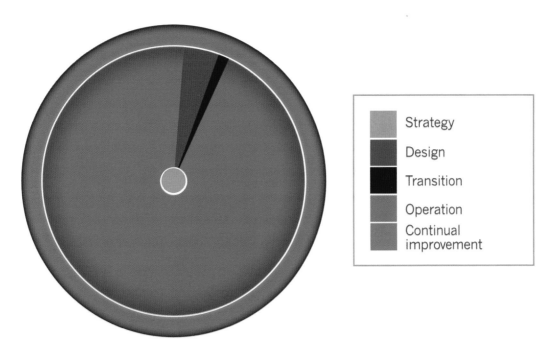

Figure 7.1 Time spent in each lifecycle stage

- **Detective controls** These are intended to identify when a threat has succeeded, so that the organization can respond appropriately. It is important to test detective controls on a regular basis to ensure that they are working correctly. These tests should include not only the technical aspects of the control, but also the human aspects – do the correct people with the right knowledge and skills respond in the right way, in an acceptable time?

- **Corrective controls** These are intended to correct the situation after a security incident has been detected. There are many different types of corrective controls, including for example restoring backups, invoking business continuity plans, engaging crisis management teams, or simply running manual anti-virus tools to remove an infection from a single PC. These controls should also be regularly tested during the operation stage – ideally as part of holistic integrated testing that includes a range of scenarios and covers the whole lifecycle of one or more security incidents (scenario testing).

It is very important to have a good balance between preventative, detective and corrective controls. Some implementations of information security management tend to focus too much on preventative controls: one of the important principles of cyber resilience is that it is not feasible to prevent every possible threat from succeeding, so organizations must plan the actions they will take to minimize the harm caused by any threat that does succeed. This is achieved by using detective controls to notify the organization when a security incident has occurred and invoking corrective controls to recover from the situation.

Some authorities define additional types of control: for example, the SANS Institute defines compensatory controls and the International Information Systems Security Certification Consortium (ISC²) defines deterrent controls as described in the following list. These additional types of control can usually be described as preventative, detective or corrective, but some of the additional terms may be useful to help think about more specific types of control that could be implemented:

- **Deterrent controls** These are a type of preventative control; they work by discouraging people from launching attacks against an organization's assets. For example, a sign reading 'beware of the dog' may deter a thief, or the expectation of being caught by routine audits may deter staff from committing fraud. Most deterrent controls cannot be tested easily, but they should be monitored to ensure that they are in place as designed.

- **Reductive controls** These are things done before there has been an attack, which will help to improve the effectiveness of recovery or reduce the potential damage – for example, creating a backup, or testing a recovery plan. These are effectively the proactive part of corrective controls. Reductive controls should be tested as part of scenario testing; they should also be subject to audits to ensure that they are taking place as planned.

- **Repressive controls** These are controls that prevent a successful attack from progressing further. Repressive controls usually involve automating a combination of a detective control and a preventative control. For example, an **intrusion prevention system** may detect a port scan from a particular IP address and invoke a firewall rule to block any further access from that IP address. Repressive controls should be tested as part of scenario testing, and audits should be carried out to ensure they have been applied to all assets where they are appropriate.

- **Compensatory controls** These are additional controls that provide some level of protection when another control is not effective. They can help to provide defence-in-depth, because even if a preventative, detective or corrective control is not effective, the compensatory control may still prevent the threat from succeeding. Examples of compensatory controls might be use of a backup generator when the primary and secondary electricity supplies fail, or invocation of IT service continuity plans when the primary site has been infected with a computer virus. Compensatory controls should be tested as part of scenario testing.

Table 7.1 Examples of controls by category

Preventative	Users are required to log in before they can see or change data.
	All input data on a web form is validated before being used, to prevent exploits such as buffer overflow or SQL injection.
	Doors and windows are locked to prevent unauthorized entry.
	File access permissions are used to ensure that people who only need to see some data are unable to modify it.
Detective	Network logs are reviewed daily to detect unusual patterns of activity.
	Financial audits are carried out to detect unauthorized spending.
	Encrypted checksums are used to verify that critical system files have not been changed.
	Doors and windows are fitted with alarms to notify security guards when they are opened.
Corrective	Backups are restored to ensure complete removal of unauthorized software.
	A disk RAID set still delivers the correct data after one disk has failed, by applying recovery algorithms to data on the remaining disks.
	A crisis management team meets to manage stakeholder communication after a major security breach.
	All users are forced to change their passwords after a suspected breach of login data.
Deterrent	Contracts of employment say that employees can be dismissed for violating acceptable use policies, and this is reinforced with regular awareness training.
	Regular audits are carried out to detect unauthorized devices on the network and staff know they will be disciplined if any are discovered.
	Contracts with third parties include large penalties for disclosing confidential information.
Reductive	Backups are carried out so that data can be restored if necessary.
	Continuity plans are created and tested to ensure that they will work when needed.
	Crisis management teams have regular rehearsals, using scenarios based on events that have happened at other organizations, to help them respond appropriately in an emergency.
	A configuration management system is maintained so that the correct configuration of hardware and software can be recovered when needed.
Repressive	An intrusion prevention system disables all access to the network from a particular IP address when a firewall detects a port scan from that address.
	An ATM retains a user's card after three incorrect attempts to enter the PIN.
	A user is prevented from logging in for five minutes after three incorrect login attempts.
Compensatory	A recovery site can be used to deliver an IT service that has been compromised on the main site.
	A standby generator can provide power if the main and backup power supplies both fail.
	A critical business process can be run as a manual process if the IT service completely fails.

Table 7.1 lists some examples of controls that match each of the foregoing control categories.

Section 7.1 describes controls that are required to support cyber resilience operation, and section 7.2 discusses how these controls could be integrated into an overall IT service management system design.

7.1 CONTROL OBJECTIVES AND CONTROLS FOR CYBER RESILIENCE OPERATION

The control objective of cyber resilience in operation is to ensure that risks to the disruption of operational services are managed.

7.1.1 Access control

The control objective for access control is to ensure that only authorized entities have access to the assets, and that the access granted is appropriate, within the principles of '**least privilege**' and 'need to know' (see section 7.1.1.3).

7.1.1.1 Logical access control

Access control is the primary means for protecting information from unauthorized access. **Logical access control**, as opposed to physical access control, is the technique for controlling access via digital means to information, information systems and networks. However, physical access cannot be considered as being separate from logical access, as they both provide layers of access control security that complement each other. For example, many organizations have electronic access controls to their buildings and office areas based on the security of the areas and the assets contained within and depend on the physical access control to provide the initial layer of protection.

The reason for access control is to ensure that the minimum level of access rights is granted to legitimate users or systems and to completely stop access from unauthorized users or systems. Without access control, confidentiality, integrity and availability of sensitive and valuable information cannot be assured. Organizations store and process many types of important information that are not only valuable organizational assets but are also covered by law in terms of the requirement to preserve confidentiality. Personal data, financial data, medical records, criminal records intellectual property, research and development, business strategy and risk registers are examples of sensitive information. An organization will not want everyone in the organization to have unlimited access, let alone entities outside the organization.

Disclosure of personal data can cause reputational damage and attract financial penalty. Disclosure of intellectual property could cause financial loss. Loss of confidentiality or integrity of an industrial control system (ICS) could have severe implications for national infrastructure. Organizations subject to data breaches lose the trust of their customers and the confidence of shareholders and the markets, resulting in huge financial losses. If it is a governmental organization, loss of personal data could lead to loss of public confidence with regard to sharing people's information, thus affecting the organization's ability to provide public services.

7.1.1.2 Business requirements and access policy

All access control should be aligned with the organization's access control policy, which should set out the principles by which access control may be granted. The policy should specify the roles and responsibilities for authorization, the process for verification of a subject's identity, the minimum access rights and review of access, certification of accounts, the level of auditing and compliance required etc.

7.1.1.3 Authorization, registration and provisioning

All access should be authorized. The persons responsible for the asset should authorize the access: in the case of information or data, the responsible person is usually the owner. Depending on the size of the organization, the responsibility may be delegated down the chain of authority; however, accountability for authorization should remain at the asset ownership level. Some organizations have the concept of application owners or system owners; however, ultimately these systems are protecting the information (or data) that are stored or processed in them. Whatever the position, it should be a senior person who has the required authority. In larger organizations the authorization process may be automated through an access control system. The authorization process should ensure that users' access rights are allocated on the basis of '**least privilege**' – limited to those rights required to carry out their role. The access rights or privileges could be based on user roles rather than on each individual user. This is known as '**role-based access control**' (RBAC). This makes provisioning and managing access for a large user base easier. Access rights allocation should take into account the organization's information classification policy and ensure that entities are only allocated access on a '**need to know**' basis. Role-based access again can help support this principle.

Best practice

Follow the principles 'least privilege' and 'need to know' when allocating access rights.

Reference all access back to the information classification policy and the entity's role. Ensure that they are commensurate.

7.1.1.4 Identity verification

Identity verification is the processes of verifying an entity's claim to their identity. In the case of access control, it is ensuring that the (user or system) identity of the claimant is verified against some form of official record such as a photo-ID, or an employee code, that has been previously allocated.

Access should only be authorized after verifying the identity of the entity requesting access. If identities are not checked then impersonators could gain access to systems through a weak verification process. How this is done is not material: what is important is that it is done and in a secure way. For example, the authorization identity verification processes could be integrated into the outcome of the HR identity verification process, which would usually allocate a unique identifier for each employee.

7.1.1.5 Secure use of systems

Systems often have acceptable use policies or operating procedures which users have to comply with. Before users start using the system, they should be trained on its use and how to report any weaknesses. Users should require registration and provisioning on the system, be provided with a unique identity, and not be reallocated pre-existing accounts or share accounts with other users. Users should be made aware of their security obligations such as keeping passwords and PINs secret.

7.1.1.6 Authentication and credentials management

Access management policy should include authentication for users and systems, where system-to-system access is required. Authentication is the process of a user proving their claimed identity. Authentication can be as simple as user-ID with a password, but may include stronger multi-factor authentication, biometric and/or digital certificates. The most common authentication method is still a user-ID and a password. This is a single-factor authentication because only the password is secret. More secure systems or remote access may require two-factor authentication (2FA). Two-factor authentication is based on something the user knows (the password) and something the user has in their possession (usually a token) or, in the case of biometrics, some physical attribute of the user. This provides an extra level of security; for example, a token may generate a one-time **personal identification number** (PIN) to use as a password.

Access control is the means of protecting assets through stopping illegitimate entry and limiting legitimate access

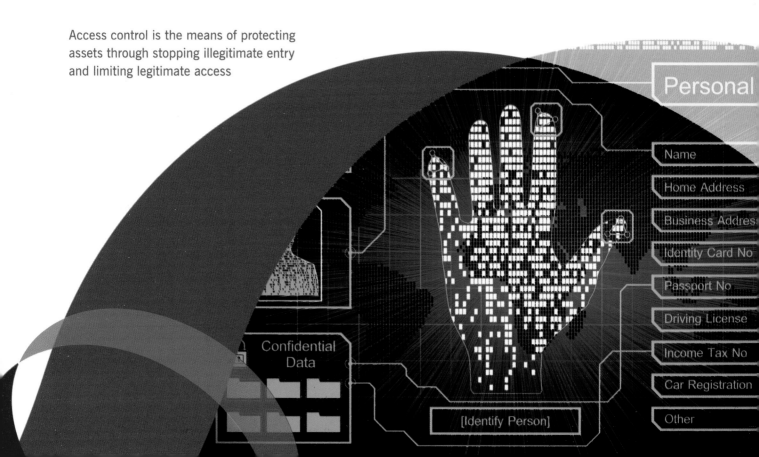

Note that the 'tokens' can be hardware, software or smartcards containing digital certificates. Biometric authentication is becoming more affordable and efficient, with better algorithms easing the enrolment issues and false error rates. More and more devices are being shipped with built-in biometric scanners.

Other forms of authentication are one-time passwords, digital certificates and tokenization. The PIN generated by a token is an example of a one-time-password.

Best practice

- Keep authentication credentials secure. Encrypt if sending over insecure networks.
- Do not write down passwords. Use passphrases instead of passwords – phrases are easier to remember.
- Use multi-factor or biometrics for accessing secure or sensitive information or secure areas.
- Enforce the organization's password policy.
- Large organizations should implement **single-sign-on** (SSO) or tools for managing passwords.

It all very good designing a secure system; however, the users (often cited as the weakest link in cyber resilience) also need to be trained to keep their authentication credentials secret. This means they should be trained to not write down passwords or share their accounts with others, and to not send passwords in a format that can be easily intercepted in transit.

On a system level, systems should be designed to encrypt credentials in transit and in storage, enforce strong and complex password selection and force periodic changes based on the password management policy of the organization. More secure systems can be designed to not send the passwords across the network but a hash of the passwords, which can be used to derive the password at the receiving end. This way the password never leaves the endpoint.

Self-enrolling and self-service systems save organizations time and resources by providing the user with the ability to enrol and manage their own credentials. This still requires authorization and authentication. The self-service is based on pre-registered secrets, which the user inputs to reset or recover their lost passwords. Unfortunately, self-service secret questions often use predictable questions and answers which are easily guessable such as 'mother's maiden name?' Questions should be designed not to be guessable.

Larger organizations should consider single-sign-on or password management systems to aid users in secure use and handling of the ever-expanding lists of credentials they have to manage.

7.1.1.7 Joiners movers and leavers process and access management

An organization's joiners movers and leavers (JML) process plays an important part in access control and access rights allocation. An effective JML process (covered in sections 5.1.1.4 and 8.1.3.3) can ensure that access rights are managed effectively when employees join the organization and are provisioned on the system. Line management duties are incorporated into the JML process so that any changes in employee (or contractor) roles can be reflected in their access rights. HR is usually the first organizational function that is aware of changes to employee status or roles. HR processes are therefore integral to the success of the JML process. Ensure that HR is integrated into the JML and is an active participant in the design and planning of the JML process. Indeed, it is preferable for HR to own the JML process.

Employee engagement, development and welfare should be a part of cyber resilience managerial controls. Line managers should monitor and review employee behaviour and access rights as part of their line management duties (see section 7.1.1.8). When people leave the organization, line managers should be responsible for instigating termination of access and recovering any assets, computers, smartphones and even data on BYOD devices, and updating the relevant registers and records.

7.1.1.8 Access monitoring, review, certification and compliance

Once the access rights are granted this is not the end of the process: user activities need to be monitored and logged for audit purposes and to detect misuse and abuse of privileges. Users should be told that their activities may be monitored for business and security purposes so that they do not assume that they have privacy. Legal and HR advice should be sought to ensure that laws are not violated by monitoring user activities. The monitoring warning can either be executed through an acceptable use policy, or pop-up warning message on logon. At the minimum the following access activities should be monitored:

- Successful logons
- Failed logons
- Locked accounts
- Privilege changes (changes in access rights)
- Source IP address
- User IDs
- Time and date.

Over time, access requirements and rights change as people change jobs and move around in the organization. As a consequence, they may accumulate privileges or simply gain rights that they are not supposed to have – by misconfiguration, mismanagement or simply because of a broken JML process. Regardless of how they occur, excess privileges are a vulnerability to organizations as these can be used by insiders to exfiltrate data out of the organizations, or to damage the integrity or affect the availability of data and systems. Furthermore, with privileged access rights people can hide malicious activities. An additional threat to these privileged (super-user) accounts is that they are usually the target of hackers due to their all-powerful nature. As well as regular monitoring of networks, servers and access rights, the super-user accounts should be audited frequently and recertified by the information, data or system owners. If this role is not defined, it should be carried out at senior-manager level in the organization. However, the actual certification activity may be delegated to more appropriate roles, where needed. At the minimum an account audit and recertification should be carried out annually.

7.1.1.9 Types of access control

Role-based access control is covered elsewhere in this guide (see sections 5.1.1.3 and 8.1.3.3); however, there are other types of access control in use that support RBAC. These are:

- **Discretionary access control (DAC)** A traditional access control that is used to control access from a subject to an object based on group membership or the identity of the subject. This is still a common access control used in many systems, especially stand-alone systems. In DAC, the owner of the system has the discretion to grant access rights to the entity or the subject.

- **Mandatory access control (MAC)** Access control attributes are mandated by the system, usually based on the subject's and the object's attributes – for example the classification of the information and the clearance of the subject wanting access; access to the classified information may or may not be granted to the subject based on their clearance.

The above access control methods can be accommodated into role-based access control, making role-based access control a flexible method for organizations to consider.

7.1.1.10 Network access control

Just like access control to applications and operating systems, controlled access to networks provides another layer of protection to organizations. Technical hacks, including insider and external attacks, rely on the connected network to gain access to servers. Unless the attacker has direct physical access to the server containing the data, the attacker has to reach it over the network, whether it's the organization's LAN or WAN or the internet connection to cloud-hosted information. Access to networks therefore should be challenged, verified and authenticated. This includes remote connections as well as local connections.

Organizations often allow uncontrolled connections to their networks, for example by means of open ports on switches. Unused network ports should be disabled and locked down so that unauthorized devices cannot be connected to gain access to the network. If network ports are open, then devices should be challenged to authenticate themselves before being authorized to access network resources. This can be done via the network access control (NAC) protocol to ensure that security controls on the device meet the organization's policy and standards. The NAC protocol can provide extensive control over connecting devices by checking minimum build standards, and operating system and application patches. It can restrict access to certain zones or part of the network, or only allow access to certain services. The port-based NAC (PNAC) is defined in the 802.1x standard. An 802.1x-based NAC can support higher levels of authentication, including support for multi-factor authentication and digital certificates. NAC is used mainly to secure endpoint devices connecting to networks by ensuring they meet the organization's security policy and standards. The policies can be enforced before and after connection to the network. For example, the device once authenticated could be allowed onto a 'dirty network' where it could update missing critical patches from a server before being allowed access to the rest of the network.

The ITIL access management process provides a comprehensive set of end-to-end access management guidance that organizations can adopt or adapt to their cyber resilience requirements (see section 7.2.5).

Key message

- Access control is the primary means for protecting the confidentiality, integrity and availability of systems and therefore should be judiciously controlled to protect the resilience of systems. Access control may be principally about protecting confidentiality of information; however, controlled access can ensure that entities with limited access cannot tamper with systems or controls designed to ensure resiliency.

- Access control is not limited to just systems and applications but also includes physical and network access and system-to-system access, as many systems are now interconnected in trust models and can provide an attack vector if not managed cautiously.

- Allocated access rights may change over time and must be regularly reviewed to ensure that they continue to remain appropriate to the entity's role. Allow the minimum access rights required to discharge the entity's (user's or system's) duties.

7.1.2 Network security management

The objective of network security management is to ensure that the organization's internal infrastructure networks, LANs and WANs, are protected from access by unauthorized entities.

Best practice

- Design access controls based on the minimum access, least privilege and need-to-know principles.
- Use information classification as a reference to regulate access to information.
- Consider the minimum access rights required for the role of the entity (user or system).
- Implement a JML process.
- Enforce a strong password policy – use passphrases instead of passwords.
- Use multi-factor authentication for more sensitive system information.
- All user activities should be monitored, especially logon and authentication: repeated failed logins may point to hacking attempts.
- Control access to the network – use authentication and screen devices before allowing access.
- Access rights and accounts should be audited, and all logons and access rights reviewed for appropriateness against access requirements and users' roles, and recertified.

The protection of networks is essential to ensure that the organization's assets are protected from unauthorized access from external (and internal) threats. The network boundary, usually controlled by a firewall, acts as a border between the organization's trusted zones and the external untrusted networks and threats. Even though the boundary is becoming more and more porous or elasticized in this connected information-sharing and collaborative era with cloud computing presenting new challenges, internal assets still need to be protected.

7.1.2.1 Network design for resilience

Internal networks include local area networks (LANs), in the form of physical switches or virtual LANs within those switches. Larger organizations may have their own organization-wide, wide area networks (WANs). These networks are either managed by third-party service providers or by the organizations themselves. The LANs and WANs may be under the control of the same entity or distributed across the organization in a federated governance structure. The network architecture could be flat or hierarchical, segmented into secure zones or domains. Either way the cyber resilience consideration should be inherent in the network design, including ensuring that the network is resilient to routeing failures through use of fast adaptive and established routeing protocols such as **'open shortest path first'** (OSPF) and **'border gateway protocol'** (BGP). The network devices should be selected for their resilience, proven by their **mean time between failures** (MTBF) and **failure mode and effects analysis** (FMEA). Resilience by design ensures that components such as routers, switches, firewalls, load-balancers etc. are built to withstand failures, with no single point of failure, and to be resilient to attacks. This may mean using clustering, virtualization technologies or alternative and diverse routeing to ensure that the network can adapt rapidly to failures. Select hardware products for the network that are easily replaced, or software that can be easily replicated or 'spun up', if using virtualization technology.

The network should be designed in a hierarchical segmented model, with security domains or zones, so that failures or breaches can be contained within affected zones. Segmented networks provide a better level of security and resilience by restricting traffic and connectivity to segments of the network, thus providing additional control over the data and data flows. From a cyber resilience perspective, if one section of the network is compromised or fails, the other segments are likely to remain secure or resilient. For example, if hackers penetrate one domain, they will then have to hack into another domain to get to the valuable assets. N-Tier web network architecture design is a good example of this: application, logic and data layers are separated by firewalls and different security policies and trusts, separating traffic at each layer and not allowing direct connection to the data layer where the data ('valuable assets') is stored. This is a form of defence-in-depth security layering.

7.1.2.2 Segmenting networks with firewalls

Firewalls act as traffic-filtering gateways in TCP/IP networks, generally controlling access based on source and destination of the TCP/IP address or the TCP/IP ports. They can also translate or hide internal network addressing and route all communication through an externally advertised TCP/IP address, so that internal addresses are obscure to outsiders – a sort of 'security by obscurity'.

Newer firewalls can operate at the application level and are able to make filtering (access control) decisions on multiple levels, including the higher-level protocols in the TCP/IP suite of protocols such as FTP, DNS, HTTP, SSL/TLS and the content of the messages in these protocols. These firewalls can understand and inspect application-level attacks and are generally known as 'applications' or the more intelligent **'web application firewalls'** (WAFs). WAFs are much more sophisticated than the traditional packet-filtering or even stateful inspection firewalls. WAFs can filter against web-borne attacks that are disguised as legitimate traffic through permitted protocols such as HTTP, which firewalls are configured to allow. Firewalls can be embedded in all sorts of devices, including in network switches as software modules. Firewalls can also be virtual or software as a service (SaaS) provided in the cloud.

Firewalls are also a useful tool for segmenting networks, providing layers of defence and segregation of traffic and user connection in a flat network. They can be used to segregate and separate network-traffic-based rules and preconfigured rules on internal networks, and control access to internal networks for untrusted networks such as the internet. The rules can be configured to filter at the network level or at the application level. Internally, firewalls can regulate traffic at each security domain, providing a point to inspect the traffic – another opportunity to detect and stop malicious traffic or activity. Where segmentation is not desired or not implementable, compensating controls such as rigorous monitoring of traffic using IDS/IPS (see section 7.1.2.4) and **security information and event management** (SIEM) should be employed to detect anomalies.

7.1.2.3 Network switch and logical segmentation

Network switches were designed to provide high-speed traffic switching between computers on the same networks, but they have now developed into highly sophisticated devices that can logically separate physical networks based on hardware ports, TCP/IP addresses and even services, into virtual LANs or VLANs. The latest powerful switches can also route traffic and provide firewall services as described above. Switches are ideal for segregating local traffic, based on classification and impact of data. VLANs can be a cheap way of segmenting traffic and creating multiple local networks in a single switch. For example, organizations could separate their data and voice traffic using VLANs.

7.1.2.4 Detecting and preventing intrusions using IDS/IPS

As mentioned in sections 7.1.2.1 and 7.1.2.2, in both hierarchical and flat networks, intrusion detection systems and intrusion prevention systems (IDS/IPS) can be used to monitor traffic. Use of IDS/IPS is invaluable in flat networks, which provide little protection against insider attacks and successful external infiltration. Carefully placed sensors in the network can be used to detect anomalies in network traffic behaviour or patterns and can raise alerts or shut down services and block sources of attacks. The downside of using IDS is the many false alarms it can raise if not tuned properly, and IPS can even effect a denial of service by stopping legitimate connections. The other limitation of IDS/IPS is their inability to inspect encrypted data. IDS/IPS nevertheless are valuable tools against insider attacks and can complement firewalls and other network security tools.

7.1.2.5 Monitoring and logging

It is important to monitor and log activities in the network. High-speed switched networks are difficult to monitor: it is necessary to place sensors at key points or create a security domain within the flat network to house the organization's high-value servers. IDS/IPS and security event monitoring using SIEMs can be used to protect high-value servers.

Best practice

Design networks with cyber resilience in mind so that they are robust, durable and resilient to attacks.

Segment networks so that they provide a layer of protection, performance and availability.

Use monitoring tools such as IDS/IPS and SIEMs to monitor network traffic, especially in flat networks

7.1.2.6 External network connections

Organizations are no longer islands of mainframe computers and local area networks. Many are now connected to the internet and to partner and supplier networks. The ability to connect externally to share and communicate, or procure and sell, has provided organizations with immense opportunities; however, these opportunities have also come with corresponding risks. The risks include the loss of confidentiality of valuable intellectual property, loss of personal data and damage to assets and systems leading to lost production and sales. There is also the threat to national security from attacks on critical national infrastructure such as electricity, water and transport networks and their control systems through externally connected networks.

External connections therefore need to be secure, terminating at a point outside the internal network, known as the **demilitarized zone** (DMZ). A DMZ is a part of the network where insecure connections are terminated and then routed (or reverse-proxied) through the firewall into the internal network (see Figure 7.2). The DMZ is usually a LAN on a network interface on the external firewall that provides an extra layer of protection for the internal networks from external connections. Organizations can and should design networks to terminate partner or supplier connections in a DMZ and then screen and filter traffic before forwarding the connections. Any external-facing servers can be placed in the DMZ so that the external connections do not have to traverse the firewall into the internal networks. Mailserver, DNS and public FTP servers and remote access VPNs are usually hosted in the DMZ.

Best practice

Terminate external connections outside the network in a DMZ.

Authenticate all connections and screen all data originating from outside the network for malware, content payloads etc.

Place all external-facing services in the DMZ and not in internal networks.

7.1.2.7 Firewall management

Firewalls are the traffic police of an organization's network, which filter and regulate access between networks based on preconfigured firewall rules or policy. These policing functions have to be carefully designed, maintained and reviewed. Regular review of rules is required to ensure that unwanted services are not being allowed through the firewall. Firewall rules should be as strict and granular as possible and on a 'deny-by-default' and explicit 'deny all' principle.

Firewalls should be managed by trained people, and any changes to the firewall must be under strict change control. The management connections to the firewall should be over trusted networks, on a dedicated management interface: if not, then the connections should be encrypted and authenticated using multi-factor authentication.

7.1.2.8 Remote maintenance

Remote maintenance is sometimes used to enable support personnel to access users' devices: this could be from the service desk located locally or from another country. These connections are usually all-powerful and have administrative privileges. They should only be allowed with strong authentication, and their connections should be protected over insecure networks using encryption. As a further control against rogue remote access, connection to a user's desktop should require permission from the user.

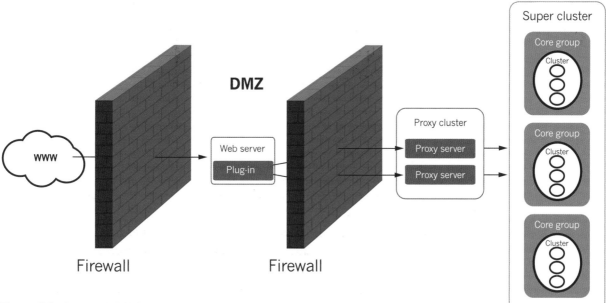

Figure 7.2 A typical DMZ firewall design

7.1.2.9 Wireless access

Wireless (or WiFi) networks are ubiquitous. They are available on trains, hotels, taxis and cafes and even in underground metro stations. Wireless networks provide organizations with a cheap, clean and quick way to connect devices. However, wireless networks, like any other, need to be designed, configured and used correctly to avoid breaches. WiFi access is very convenient but, unlike physical network cables and links, WiFi signals cannot be easily controlled. The signals can be emitted outside the physical boundaries of an organization and be accessed by external unauthorized persons. WiFi broadcasts the **service set identifier** (SSID) as the identifier for wireless endpoints to connect to. Many of these are set as default by the WiFi equipment vendors with a default password which is generally known or can be worked out even by a lay person. Once the device is turned on the SSID is broadcast and used by endpoints to connect to the WiFi; SSID is used by users to identify the WiFi access point they need to connect to. The SSID can be cloaked or not broadcast, permitting only those who know the SSID to type it in manually and connect to the device.

The signal emission is very difficult to control; therefore, other protective measures must be taken such as use of strong encryption and authentication combined with endpoint security measures. Rudimentary measures such as hiding or 'cloaking' the SSID may only provide limited protection against a determined attacker but can be used as a protection against casual attacks.

Best practice

- WiFi connections should be secured using strong passwords and encryption.
- **Wired equivalent privacy** (WEP) encryption should be avoided, as it is no longer secure.
- Use **WiFi Protected Access 2** (WPA2) with AES encryption.
- Use WiFi-certified products.
- Authenticate all wireless connections: they should be integrated with external authentication services such as RADIUS using 802.1x/ extensible authentication protocol (EAP).
- Although it is not as secure as EAP, smaller organizations may want to consider MAC address-based authentication.
- Wireless network connections should be segregated from a physical network and treated as a separate network behind a firewall.
- Default settings should be removed, as wireless products come with known passwords and service set identifier (SSID) settings, making it easy for attackers to guess passwords. Select a SSID name so it cannot be easily ascribed to the organization.
- Have a policy on public WiFi use for the organization, as many attackers set up rogue hotspots to capture organizations' credentials.
- Use a separate WiFi network for guest access.

7.1.2.10 Security of voice over IP networks

Voice over IP (VoIP) allows organizations to leverage their existing network infrastructure and the **internet protocol** (IP) for cheap voice services. This is highly attractive to organizations under budgetary pressure. However, from a cyber resilience perspective, this is a single point of failure for two important services because if the data network goes down, both the organization's data network and its telephony will be unavailable. Furthermore, VoIP connections, to be able to communicate to the outside world, will at some point have to connect to a **private automatic branch exchange** (PABX) or the internet. PABX exchanges are not usually secured behind a firewall and may connect directly to the telecommunications provider, or even the internet, and (even worse) may have other remote access connections for maintenance etc. An unsecured PABX may open up several vulnerabilities for threats to exploit if not secured properly. Where an organization has voice and data running over the same network, with no physical or logical separation, compromise of the PABX could let intruders into the organization's internal network. Other issues with VoIP are that the inherent protocols which VoIP relies on, such as session initiation protocols (SIP), bootstrap protocol (BootP) and trivial file transfer protocol (TFTP), were not designed to be secure; there is no authentication support in these protocols. Therefore, the VoIP infrastructure, the servers that contain the configuration for the handsets, and the handsets themselves need to be secure.

As VoIP runs on the same network infrastructure as other data, it has the same frailty as normal data traffic and needs to be protected in the same way, including ensuring that unnecessary services are not enabled and ensuring default configurations are reset before transitioning into service.

Best practice

● Keep voice and data traffic logically if not physically separate using VLANs, or use VPNs to separate them.

● Like data servers, VoIP servers and endpoints must be kept up to date with patches. Ensure that firewalls are VoIP traffic-aware and do not drop packets.

● VoIP traffic traversing data networks is also susceptible to the same vulnerabilities and threats as normal data traffic, so ensure that the network is secure.

● Practise strict access control for management and maintenance access, and implement wireless security where traffic is routed over wireless networks.

7.1.2.11 Protecting networks from distributed denial of service attacks

Distributed denial of service (DDoS) attacks originate from hundreds (sometimes thousands or even millions) of computers under the control of an attacker, which send targeted host packets disguised as legitimate requests. Another type of DDoS attack is to send large numbers of data packets to a single target with the objective of either taking the computer down completely or exhausting its services to the point that it cannot service legitimate requests, therefore causing a denial of service. This is an easy attack to mount and is often used by 'hacktivists' to protest or make a point. The attack may be simple to effect but is difficult to protect against. It is not possible to simply filter millions of TCP/IP source addresses on an organization's firewall. The application-based attacks are near impossible to defend against as they impersonate legitimate services, which cannot be stopped without impacting legitimate traffic.

This has spawned an industry of service providers that offer anti-DDoS solutions. They usually redirect the traffic, stop the traffic near the originating sources, increase the bandwidth on networks or disconnect networks that have become saturated. Organizations that are likely to become targets of DDoS should consider:

● Procuring anti-DDoS services from specialist service providers.

● Procuring infrastructure to 'scrub' and 'clean' the illegitimate DDoS traffic from the legitimate traffic and redirect legitimate traffic to the organization's servers. This scrub-and-clean service separates the DDoS traffic from the normal traffic and the DDoS traffic is discarded. The normal traffic is forwarded on to the destination.

7.1.2.12 Network management

Network management includes the ability to monitor the network, and reconfigure it when needed. This is usually carried out remotely from network management or operation centres. The connections to the supported network should be designed to be secure, over encrypted connections, if not via a dedicated point-to-point link. Management tools such as **simple network management protocol** (SNMP) network system managers should be located in physically secure buildings in a protected area such as a network or security operations centre. For SNMP-based management, the default SNMP community strings that are configured by the vendors should be changed and configured so that only authorized and authenticated network management systems are allowed to connect to manage the network. An SNMP community string is a simple method for network devices to authenticate network management systems that are used to monitor and configure the network devices. Often the community string is set to 'public' or 'private' by the vendors. The string should be set to something confidential.

Access to these tools by network management and support staff should be controlled so that unauthorized changes to the network configuration are avoided.

Best practice

- Harden all network devices – disable all services that are not essential.
- Use application-aware firewalls to protect the boundaries of the organization, or a combination of filtering and application firewalls. Consider using WAFs for protecting against the OWASP top 10.
- Monitor the network for anomalies and suspicious activities using IDS/IPS and SIEMs; review firewall rules and IDS/IPS polices regularly.
- Use NAC to authenticate devices before they connect to the network. This includes wireless connections as well as physical connections.
- Segment networks into security domains of zones, place high-impacting services in the core of the network, with public-facing services in the outer, less secure domains such as DMZs.
- Segregate internal traffic such as data, VoIP and management. Management traffic should preferably be out of band so that it is not a single point of failure.
- Control all external network connections into the network. Terminate them in a DMZ for screening before proxying them into the internal network. Do not allow direct access to internal networks.
- Encrypted traffic into the internal network should only be from a secured endpoint. Otherwise, terminate encrypted connections (in a DMZ) for screening and inspection of the traffic before forwarding.
- Secure the endpoints (see section 7.1.5).

7.1.3 Physical security

The objective of physical security is to ensure that an organization's buildings, offices and data centres etc. are secure from physical infiltration by unauthorized persons.

7.1.3.1 Physical access control

Physical access control is important to cyber resilience as it complements logical access control by providing an additional layer of protection from physical intrusion, infiltration, physical tampering, damage and even theft of critical assets by physical means. Unlike logical security, physical security is visible and is a good deterrence for malicious persons.

To be able to gain the most from physical access control, organizations at the very outset should carefully consider the siting of their buildings to ensure they are in a safe and secure location, situated in a low-crime area, with easy access to emergency services etc.

Within the building, access to secure and sensitive areas such as the computer, communications cabinet or wiring closet should be controlled to prevent access by unauthorized persons. Certain offices, especially shared offices, must be secured through physical access control measures. Door locks, proximity passes etc. are good ways to do this.

7.1.3.2 Perimeter security

Perimeter security should include fences and barriers for data centres or offices in remote areas. These should provide separation between public roads and the buildings. Barriers should be designed so that they are high enough to prevent intruders climbing over them. Consider using anti-climb paint on walls, fences and gates as additional measures.

Using security guards, perimeter patrols, lighting and CCTV cameras to monitor perimeters, exits and entrances of areas that need to be secure will help to deter and detect intrusions. Loading bays where goods are delivered should be set away from the main entrance and separated if possible. Access to loading bays and secure areas should be specifically monitored. Delivery should be by appointment only so that hazardous materials or theft of equipment can be detected.

Data centres should be designed and built to specific data centre standards covering security of data halls, plants, fuel supplies and resilient routeing of communication and power. Data centre standards include:

- ANSI/TIA-942 – telecommunications standard for data centres
- ISO/IEC 24762 – IT disaster recovery
- ISO 27001 – information security management
- ISO 9001 – quality management
- ISO 14001 – environment management
- OHSAS 18001 – occupational health and safety management
- ISO 22301 – business continuity management (BCM)
- ISO 50001 – energy management
- PCI-DSS – cardholder data security.

7.1.3.3 Visitor management

Visitors should be required to visit by appointment only and should report to the reception for registration and identity verification before accessing more secure sites. The building should be designed so that visitors cannot bypass the reception area. In larger, more populated buildings it may be easier to install turnstiles. A log of all visitors should be kept for a minimum period as per the organization's retention policy. Visitors should be required to sign in and sign out, not only for security reasons but also for health and safety purposes – for example, if the building needs to be vacated a register of users can be used to ensure that the building has been fully evacuated. From a security point of view, signing in and out ensures that there's a record of who entered the building, who they visited and (more importantly) that they have actually left.

Visitors should be allocated temporary passes, be required to wear them at all times and return them when leaving the premises. This ensures that visitors are easily identifiable and prevents them from loitering or venturing into sensitive areas. An audit of passes should be made at the end of the day to ensure all passes have been returned. Any missing passes should be investigated and the visitors' register audit can help to identify if the passes were handed in by the visitor. In secure locations, such as in government or military facilities, visitors may be allocated separate car parking areas from staff and require photo-ID to register.

Visitors should always be escorted and not left on their own. The host should ensure that visitors do not wander about, as in many organizations open-plan offices provide little privacy or confidentiality: visitors may easily view or hear sensitive information. A clear-desk and clear-screen policy will help to ensure that desks are clear and free of sensitive documents and screens are locked when people are away from their desks.

Key message

Physical access control includes internal as well as external controls – managing staff as well as visitors, maintenance personnel, cleaners etc.

Access to secure areas should be limited.

7.1.3.4 Identity badges and passes

In smaller locations (of 50 or fewer people) it may be realistic for everyone to know each other; however, in larger buildings where hundreds or thousands of people work it will be impossible to remember everyone. Organizations should implement a mandatory photo-ID-wearing policy for all.

7.1.3.5 Equipment siting, cabling and labelling

Within the building, computer equipment should be sited and located away from generally accessible areas such as reception, restaurants and visitors' waiting rooms so that sensitive information on computer screens cannot be visible to unauthorized persons, and equipment cannot be tampered with or **key loggers** inserted. Cables should be routed away from visitors' areas and hidden in cabling trays or ducts, colour-coded and labelled for easy identification. Where cabling is exposed in public areas, armoured cables should be used so that they are protected from accidental damage and deliberate tampering.

Office areas should be designed so that meeting rooms and communal areas (such as kitchens, restaurants, meeting and conference rooms etc.) are separated. Access to offices should be controlled either by lock and key, swipe cards, biometric controls or a combination thereof as appropriate.

All IT equipment, whether in data centres or in general office space, should be labelled. In shared environments, the ownership should be clearly identifiable if items are not labelled for confidentiality reasons. Cages or secure rooms in shared data centres should be considered as an extra measure for cyber resilience and security.

7.1.3.6 Protection of supporting utilities

Many organizations rely on supporting utilities for power, telecommunications and water etc., and fuel for generators for resilient operation of data centres and other important buildings. These supporting utilities provide backup for the main operation of buildings in case of failures. Supporting utilities should form part of the supply chain risk management and BCM planning of an organization, to ensure that they do not become single points of failure when they are put into action. Their design should ensure that there is capacity and sufficient supply. For example, ensure that fuel for generators is available at short notice in case generators are required to run for a prolonged period during a disaster. There should be sufficient capacity in the uninterruptible power supply (UPS) before generators initiate and take over.

Best practice

- Telecommunication links should have diverse routeing and providers, preferably from Tier 1 suppliers.
- Routeing of network cabling should be separate from power cables.
- Telecoms termination points should be protected and not exposed to the public or the weather.
- Plant and machinery should be kept secure from tampering or damage.
- Supporting utilities should be regularly tested – at least monthly for data centres and perhaps quarterly for other locations.

7.1.3.7 Security of unattended equipment

Mobile workforce, support and maintenance people often travel off site with equipment in cars and on public transport, which can expose the equipment and information contained within to risk from theft, loss or damage. To ensure that the risk is minimized, employees should:

- Use full disk encryption
- Use tamper-proof seals

- Ensure that equipment is with the person or in sight when on public transport
- Ensure that equipment is stored away in the boot of the car when driving, or at least discretely covered so that it is not visible to passers-by.

When staying in hotels people should not assume that the hotel room is secure, as cleaning and other hotel staff may have access to the room when it's empty. The 'evil-maid attack' is a threat that is specific to guests' unattended computers in hotels. Other typical places where computers are used in public are exhibitions and conferences: often thousands of people are in attendance, providing opportunities for malicious theft of unattended equipment and information. Computer equipment in such situations should be tethered using security locks, and screen privacy filters should be considered for protecting information on screens from prying eyes.

The rules around unattended equipment also apply to unattended equipment left out of hours in the normal office environment. Where cleaners and maintenance people are likely to be in attendance out of office hours, the computers should be shut down rather than left logged on. Mobile devices should be locked away in secure storage.

Best practice

- Protect equipment outside the organization's secure premises. Do not leave equipment unattended and out of sight, without appropriate protections.
- Be aware of bystanders overlooking information on screens; use privacy screen filters to prevent casual overlooking by bystanders.
- Do not leave equipment on car seats; lock items away in the car boot if available.
- Use security leashes to tether mobile equipment in public areas.
- Use hotel safes if available to store computer equipment.

7.1.4 Operations security

The objective of operations security is to ensure the secure and resilient operation of information and communication technology, including services in cyberspace, to minimize disruption to operational services.

Operations security ensures that the organization's operational environment, including its IT infrastructure, is operated and maintained so that it is stable and resilient to support business activities. Operations security also ensures that any changes are controlled and managed to prevent risks being introduced to the operational environment.

Key message

Operations security management should ensure that risks to the operational environment are managed, that the environment is kept safe from hardware and software vulnerabilities and that changes when required are implemented under control.

7.1.4.1 Documentation

To be able to operate effectively, documented security policies, standards and procedures, work instructions etc. are needed. This may also include security and operating procedures for:

- The network
- Servers
- Routers
- Switches

- Firewalls
- Desktops
- Virtual environments and management tools
- Cloud-based services.

This will include procedures and instructions for:

- Incident management
- Change, capacity, performance and demand management, acceptance into service
- Logging and monitoring
- Backup and restore schedules
- Testing, system restarts and recovery and roll-back processes
- Compliance monitoring
- Controlling access to operational environments.

These written procedures and instructions will be required by the operations staff and should be made available in an easily accessible format.

7.1.4.2 Operational activities

Operational environments must be as stable and reliable as possible; however, at some point, changes and enhancements will be required to the services, such as vulnerability patches, software updates and hardware maintenance. Operations staff – be it network, data centre or even the cloud service provider – will schedule these changes through a change management process. Operations staff will need to:

- Implement changes that have been approved to the operational environments.
- Monitor the operational environment for alerts from the event managers such as the SIEM and ensure that they are dealt with or escalated as required.
- Check IDS/IPS, firewall alerts and logs for unusual activities.
- Investigate events such as failed logons, privilege use and escalations, performance degradation, software and hardware failures.
- Ensure that malware and software patches are up to date and that critical and emergency patches are tested and implemented as soon as possible.
- Ensure that uncontrolled and unplanned changes are not introduced by controlling new release of software and enhancements or products into operations.
- Schedule maintenance and arrange visits by support and maintenance persons; host and chaperone them.

7.1.5 Cyber resilience incident management

The objective of security incident management in cyber resilience is: to be able to respond effectively to cyber resilience incidents; to detect, contain, investigate, eradicate and recover from a major incident with the minimum of disruption to the organization; and to learn lessons from incidents in order to improve.

One objective of cyber resilience is to prevent incidents, if possible. However, this is not always feasible; therefore, organizations should be prepared for the certainty that they will at some point be attacked and lose information through insider threats or accidental disclosure of information by poorly trained employees. Many organizations are targets of **advanced persistent threat**s (APTs) which try to steal their valuable intellectual property, or attacks on industrial control systems aiming to disrupt or damage critical infrastructure. These attacks may be carried out by well-motivated and skilled state actors as well as by criminal organizations.

Organizations cannot afford to be unprepared for the eventuality of incidents. The incident could be internal or external, and external threats may come from the supply chain as well as from third parties. Preparation starts with planning; threats and vulnerabilities should be assessed and risk assessments carried out, ensuring that if a risk is realized, organizations have a contingency plan.

Key message

Cyber resilience incidents hit the headlines all the time causing disruption to business, reputational damage and financial loss. Widely publicized attacks include:

- **UK's HMRC department child benefit CDs** Loss of CDs containing personal information of approximately 25 million citizens in 2007.

- **Heartland Payment Systems** Breach of over 100 million credit card details in 2008.

- **Edward Snowden incident** Insider threat that crystallized in the form of exfiltration of sensitive government information, which was leaked extensively to the press in 2013.

- **Target** Hack exploited supplier's systems to attack Target, resulting in exposure of about 40 million payment cards; this had a massive impact on Target's reputation and profits in late 2013.

- **Home Depot** Attack reportedly lasted five months and exposed 56 million cards using an unknown malware in September 2014.

The above incidents show that it is not good enough for organizations to only have preventative security arrangements. Security arrangements need to deal with incidents in an effective and timely manner when they occur. The difference between a proactive response and a reactive response could decide whether an organization survives or goes under, whether careers are destroyed and whether millions of dollars are lost.

Incident management requires the ability to detect and respond to incidents, and to recover from them, while all the time communicating internally and externally with stakeholders and other interested parties such as regulators, the media and law enforcement agencies.

ITIL incident management provides a set of best-practice processes to manage incidents (see section 7.2.2).

7.1.5.1 Cyber resilience incident planning

Incident planning is part of the preparation phase, which documents how an organization will manage different types of incidents, including:

- Defining whether a formal response team will be required
- Identifying the skills and training that people in the response team will need
- Identifying the tools and methods required
- Identifying the escalation points, and how and where incidents will be logged, classified, prioritized and coordinated
- Defining who the stakeholders are, and how and when they will need to be informed
- Deciding whether external specialist help will be required with investigations and forensic analysis.

A communication plan will be required covering who will handle press and media enquiries and how. A cyber-incident response plan should at the minimum include:

- **Roles and responsibilities** Who does what in an incident response.
- **Reporting and escalation** How incidents are detected, reported, logged, assessed and escalated. Be prepared for incidents to be reported by various sources and methods.
- **Incident triage** How incidents are initially assessed and prioritized.
- **Response** When and how incidents will be responded to.
- **Investigation and evidence collection** Whether incidents will be investigated and if evidence needs to be collected for further action.
- **Post-incident review** Learning from incidents.

7.1.5.2 Incident reporting, logging and initial assessment

Once an incident has been detected, it should be reported to a central point and logged. Organizations need to ensure there is a central or single point where all cybersecurity incidents are recorded. This could be the ITIL service desk or simply the helpdesk, which can be the coordination point. Once the incident is logged, a triage or initial assessment of the incident will need to be carried out to ensure that incident response is not triggered for non-cyber resilience events. The service desk can also check whether this is a known issue and, if so, hand it over to the problem management team to resolve. Not all incidents require the activation of an incident response team as some may be able to be managed within the organization's normal business processes. The first responders will have to be trained to identify and rank incidents and decide whether the incident response team activation is required.

Key message

Organizations should plan and prepare for incident response and management. It is no longer a matter of *whether it will happen* but *when*, and *how much impact* it will have on the organization.

A prepared organization, with a tried-and-tested incident management plan and a process, with trained and skilled people, will be in a better position to detect, respond and recover from cybersecurity incidents and improve its resilience in the face of future incidents.

7.1.5.3 Responding to the incident – response team and escalation

To minimize the fallout from incidents, they must be responded to rapidly once the incidents have been identified. Leaving an incident to spread uncontrolled will mean a bigger impact on the organization and higher costs to recover. This requires incident responders to be able to work effectively and efficiently under pressure. A balanced mixture of technical, analytical and leadership skills is vital.

The incident response team can be a virtual team of specialists, resolvers or simply the subject matter experts from across the organization. In small organizations, however, this may not be possible and it may be the security manager or the 'IT guy' who has to deal with the situation. In such cases, organizations should seek external specialist help. Many countries and industries, and even some large organizations, have central **computer emergency response team**s (CERTs) who will be able to assist and advise, and this should be part of the organization's incident response plan.

Where there are formal incident response teams, they should have their roles and responsibilities defined, with an incident response manager responsible as the single point of coordination and leadership. In larger organizations, there may be multiple teams in dispersed locations or one virtual team. Whatever the construction of the team, it should be designed and trained to be able to respond effectively in order to contain, eradicate and recover from the incident with minimum impact to the organization.

For escalation, senior managers should be available to make quick decisions or empower the response team to make their own decisions in responding to usually fluid incident situations. For example, to contain an active attack it may be necessary to disconnect networks or isolate live servers. If servers have been infected with malware, it may be necessary to disconnect them from the network. These decisions need to be taken instantly to limit the damage that can be caused by attacks. These are big decisions that can affect the bottom line or reputation of the organization.

7.1.5.4 Cyber forensics evidence collection and chain of custody

There may be times when an organization will want to carry out forensic analysis and collect evidence to pursue the perpetrator(s) of an incident. This may, however, delay recovery and involve collecting evidence and preserving the chain of custody of evidence so that it can be presented in a court of law. Legal and specialist advice should be sought, as contaminated evidence will not be admissible in court.

7.1.5.5 Containing the incident, eradicating and recovering

The initial objective of the response team should be to contain the incident so that further damage is not caused. Once the incident has been contained, a decision needs to be made as to whether an attempt at recovery will be carried out, or the cause investigated and preventative measures taken, or if evidence needs to be collected. Recovering a system without eradicating the cause of the incident may result in recurrence and further damage.

7.1.5.6 Learning lessons from the incident and improving

Once a recovery has been made, understanding of the incident should be used to learn lessons and make improvements. A **root cause** analysis of the incident will help to identify the cause of the problem, and if the root cause is fixed it could prevent the issue reoccurring. Improvements identified as a result could feed into the organization's continual improvement process. Organizations may not want to review all incidents and may wish to review only high-impacting ones, but all incidents nevertheless should be considered for review.

Key message

All actions taken should be logged, date- and time-stamped so that the rationale and audit of actions can be traced in post-incident reviews.

Incident response should be tested with scenario-based tests, which include the key suppliers and stakeholders.

Incidents may not always be technical; the problem could be as simple as the loss of a sensitive document. However, a similar process would apply, as there is still a need for detection, containment and recovery.

Incident responders should be trained and equipped to handle a cyber-incident. Tools may include access to computers and specialist software for taking images of hard disks, recovery toolkits and replacement hardware, notepads for recording actions etc.

Best practice

● Train employees to detect and report any weaknesses and threats such as phishing, spear-phishing and social-engineering attacks.

● Test incident management plans, based on scenarios.

● Include recent incidents in tests.

● Learn from incidents and improve planning, incident response, controls and training.

7.2 ALIGNING CYBER RESILIENCE OPERATION WITH IT SERVICE OPERATION

IT service operation considers how an IT service provider can deliver agreed levels of service to users and customers, and manage the applications and technology that support delivery of the IT services. The objectives of this stage of the IT service lifecycle are to:

● Maintain user and customer satisfaction by delivering agreed levels of service

● Minimize the impact of incidents and problems on customers' business activities

● Ensure that access to IT services is available to authorized people, and not to others.

During the service operation stage of the IT service lifecycle, the service provider:

● Helps to ensure that the business meets the objectives that the IT services are intended to facilitate

● Carries out processes that optimize the cost and quality of the IT services

- Carries out operational control activities needed to manage and deliver the IT services
- Monitors and maintains the technology and application components that are required to support the IT services.

Organizations that use ITIL as a basis for their IT service management system can integrate cyber resilience operation into the service operation stage of the service lifecycle. Organizations that are not using ITIL to manage their IT services may find it helpful to adopt some of the processes and activities described in *ITIL Service Operation* to support their cyber resilience operation. For example, the ITSM event management and incident management processes could provide a framework for managing detective and corrective controls. Further suggestions for how cyber resilience and ITSM could be integrated are included in the descriptions of each ITSM process in this section.

ITIL Service Operation describes a number of processes that are particularly relevant to the operation stage of the service lifecycle. Every one of these processes needs to include appropriate aspects of cyber resilience; it is not possible to run cyber resilience processes that carry out similar activities to the service management processes in isolation from one another. They must be integrated or at the very least aligned to ensure that there is no conflict. Many of the controls described in section 7.1 can be implemented effectively through such integrated processes. This can enable an organization to achieve both its service operation objectives and its cyber resilience operation objectives efficiently and effectively. Cyber resilience activities should be integrated with these processes as described in sections 7.2.1 to 7.2.5.

What is a function?

ITIL defines a function as 'a group of people and the tools or other resources they use to carry out one or more processes or activities'.

There is no simple relationship between processes and functions: parts of a single process may be carried out by multiple functions, and each function may carry out parts of many processes.

Many organizations have an information security management function or risk management function that carries out many of the cyber resilience activities described in this publication.

ITIL Service Operation also describes four functions:

- Service desk
- Technical management
- Application management
- **IT operations management**.

Each of these functions can make significant contributions to cyber resilience operation. It may be appropriate to integrate some (or all) of these functions so that they carry out both IT service management and cyber resilience activities. Integration of cyber resilience with service operation functions is described in sections 7.2.6 to 7.2.9.

7.2.1 Event management

The ITSM event management process detects events, makes sense of them and takes the appropriate action to ensure that the events are properly managed. Events are typically initiated by a notification created by an IT service, another configuration item (CI) such as an application, or a monitoring tool.

Event management can apply to a wide range of things that need to be monitored, for example:

- Environmental systems such as power, cooling or fire detection
- Servers and storage, both physical and virtual

- Network hardware and software
- Applications, including software licence monitoring
- Service management tools
- Interfaces with third parties.

What is an event?

ITIL defines an event as 'a change of state that has significance for the management of an IT service or other configuration item'.

Events that are of interest to cyber resilience might include the following:

- A user logs in to a sensitive account.
- A firewall detects a port scan from a remote IP address.

Event management can be used to identify changes of state that are not desired: for example a hardware failure or a performance threshold being breached. It can also be used to identify when a desired change of state does not occur: for example a backup does not complete.

Events are categorized according to the three types listed in Table 7.2.

Table 7.2 Event types used in the event management process

Category	Description	Cyber resilience example
Informational events	These are typically just logged and no further action is taken. For example, an authorized user may have logged on to a critical service or a backup may have completed as expected.	A user has logged on to an application.
Warning events	These are indications of a non-standard situation which should be monitored but does not usually require immediate action. For example, transaction performance is slower than normal but still within the agreed target.	A user has entered the wrong password three times in a row.
Exception events	These require action to be taken. This may be an automated response or it may result in the logging of an incident, a problem or a change. For example, a server has crashed, or a backup has failed to complete.	Many user accounts have had repeated incorrect password attempts in a short period of time.

The main activities for event management are shown in Figure 7.3. These activities include:

- **Event occurs** This event may not be detected, depending on the effectiveness of the tools and process.
- **Event notification, detection and logging** The event is discovered and logged.
- **First-level correlation and filtering** Duplicate events are merged and related events are associated with one another.
- **Significance** The event is categorized as an informational, warning or exception event.
- **Second-level correlation and filtering** The event (or set of events) is compared with business rules to set priority and decide what further action is needed.
- **Response selection** An appropriate response is selected. This may be a manual or automated action, and it may result in the logging of an incident, problem or change.
- **Review and close** Only significant events are reviewed, as there could be many thousands of minor events logged each day. This review results in lessons being learned and improvements being planned.

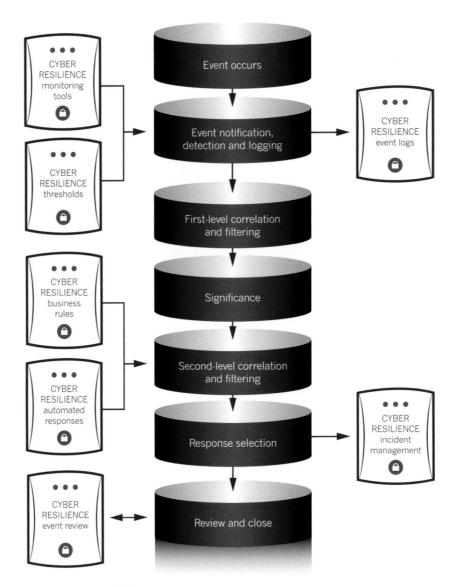

Figure 7.3 Event management activities

Event management can make significant contributions to cyber resilience by:

● Providing a framework for detection of cyber resilience events and notifying them to appropriate personnel

● Monitoring assets to detect changes in state that may be significant for cyber resilience

● Detecting unusual patterns of behaviour in people, processes or technology that may indicate a potential attack

● Creating and maintaining event logs that may be required for later analysis of cyber resilience incidents

● Escalating relevant events to personnel with appropriate cyber resilience knowledge and skills when appropriate.

Cyber resilience can contribute to ITSM event management by:

● Defining thresholds to be monitored to detect events that are relevant to cyber resilience: for example, the number of failed attempts to log in to a privileged account, or the number of failed attempts to access a protected file

● Selecting and configuring tools to monitor and report events that are relevant to cyber resilience. This could range from sophisticated intrusion detection tools running on servers or firewalls to simple scripts that monitor attempts to carry out unauthorized activities and raise an alert

- Selecting and configuring tools that can take automated action in response to some cyber resilience events, for example an intrusion prevention system (IPS) which can respond to port scans on a firewall
- Contributing to the review of events that are relevant to cyber resilience.

Example of a cyber resilience event

- **Event occurs** A hacker tries breaking into the company website using scripts that exploit common vulnerabilities.
- **Event notification, detection and logging** Network intrusion detection software running on a firewall detects the known pattern of behaviour and raises an alert. This is displayed on a console in the operations room, and automatically generates a log entry in the operations event log.
- **First-level correlation and filtering** The operations management software identifies that this is part of a sequence of events and associates them with one another.
- **Significance** The event is automatically categorized as a warning, and set to the appropriate colour and font on the display.
- **Second-level correlation and filtering** The rules for this kind of event require someone from the information security team to review the firewall logs, in case there are any other previously unknown attacks taking place.
- **Response selection** An alert message is sent to the information security team, who acknowledge it.
- **Review and close** This is not seen as a significant event, and it is **closed** without further review.

This sequence of actions results in someone in the information security team taking an action to review firewall logs. Depending on the outcome of this review they may then log an incident, or make recommendations for improvements to monitoring. These activities would not form part of the event management process.

7.2.2 Incident management

The ITSM incident management process restores service as quickly as possible, and minimizes the adverse impact on business operations.

Incidents may be initiated by event management, or by users contacting the service desk, or by technical staff. The exact mechanisms used to trigger event management will be determined by the organization as part of the process design. Whatever the trigger, all incidents will be handled in a similar way by the incident management process.

What is an incident?

ITIL defines an incident as 'An unplanned interruption to an IT service or reduction in the quality of an IT service. Failure of a configuration item that has not yet affected service is also an incident – for example, failure of one disk from a mirror set.'

Examples of incidents that are relevant to cyber resilience could be:

- Somebody breaks into the office and steals a laptop.
- A distributed denial of service (DDoS) attack against the organization's customer-facing website is detected.

It is important to distinguish incidents from events. Some events may lead to incidents, but many events are informational or related to routine operational activities. Some incidents may be logged as a result of events, but most incidents are logged as a result of users contacting the service desk.

Incidents are prioritized, based on the impact to the business and the urgency. Targets for incident resolution are usually based on this priority. Incidents are also categorized to help identify which team should resolve the incident, and to assist in reporting and trend analysis.

Incident management often involves many different teams working together. The service desk usually logs and manages incidents (see section 7.2.6), but escalates them to other teams if they are unable to resolve the incidents themselves. These other teams are typically technical or application management (see sections 7.2.7 and 7.2.8) or third parties with whom the organization has **underpinning contract**s. There are two distinct types of escalation depending on the circumstances – either or both may be called into play in relation to an incident:

- **Functional escalation** The incident is escalated to a support group with different skills or tools, or with more time. There may be multiple levels of functional escalation used for very complex incidents.
- **Hierarchical escalation** More senior management are engaged to assist with resource allocation and communication. There may be multiple levels of hierarchical escalation for incidents with significant business impact, especially when resolution targets are missed.

The main activities for incident management are shown in Figure 7.4. These activities include:

- **Incident identification** Many incidents are logged directly by the users but, ideally, as many incidents as possible should be detected by the IT organization using event management before they impact users.
- **Logging, categorization and prioritization** Every incident must be logged, categorized and prioritized. The **incident record** is maintained through the lifecycle of the incident. There may be special considerations when logging security incidents, due to the need for confidentiality of the information. The incident management process should identify these requirements and ensure that confidential information about security breaches is not logged in a way that exposes it unnecessarily.

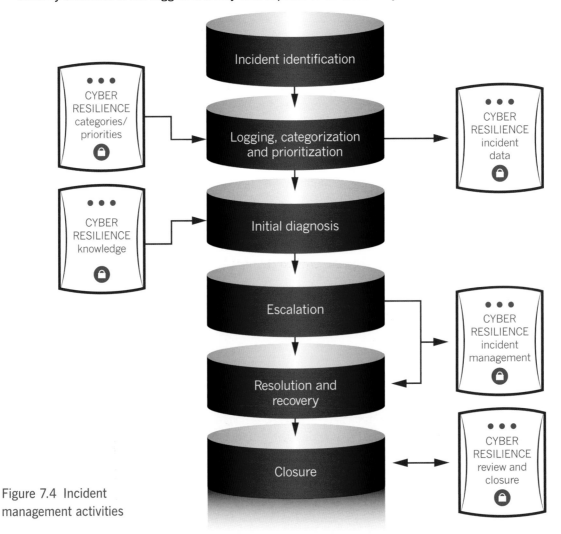

Figure 7.4 Incident management activities

Example of a cyber resilience incident

- **Incident identification** Somebody notices that the corporate website has been hacked, and an inappropriate graphic is being displayed.

- **Logging, categorization and prioritization** The service desk is contacted. They categorize this as a security incident, with high business impact and high urgency. It therefore has high priority.

- **Initial diagnosis** The service desk has a knowledge base article that tells them how to respond to this kind of event. Following instructions in that article they immediately close external access to the corporate website so that it can no longer be seen by external customers.

- **Escalation** The service desk contacts the computer emergency response team (CERT) with information about the incident, including a description of the action they have taken so far. They also contact the IT **business relationship manager** (BRM) with information about the incident, so that they can brief the appropriate customer managers.

- **Resolution and recovery** CERT takes a backup of the hacked server, and then restores the previous day's backup and brings the web server back online. They verify that the server is now working properly. They then log a problem to ensure that the underlying cause of the incident will be investigated.

- **Closure** The incident is returned to the service desk, who ensure that the problem has been correctly categorized and prioritized, and ask the BRM if the customer agrees for the incident to be closed. When they get agreement via the BRM they close the incident and update the person who initially reported this incident.

After the incident has been closed, CERT continues to investigate the underlying problem. This will enable them to understand the cause of the incident and take corrective action to prevent a repetition.

- **Initial diagnosis** An incident-matching procedure should be used to match incidents to a **knowledge base**, and if possible the service desk should diagnose and resolve the incident during the initial customer contact. This initial diagnosis should have specific triggers for identifying and managing security incidents. There may also be a requirement to maintain evidence for use in later forensic analysis, and a proper verifiable chain of custody may need to be established for this.

- **Escalation** The service desk retains ownership of the incident at all times, but escalates it to appropriate management and technical teams to engage the resources needed to resolve the incident. Most organizations have specific incident management activities that must be followed when handling security incidents, including specific escalation procedures.

- **Resolution and recovery** The resolving group identifies and applies a resolution to the incident, and tests it to ensure that normal service operation has been restored.

- **Closure** All incidents should be passed back to the service desk for closure. During closure the incident record is checked and updated to ensure that all required data has been captured; a problem may be logged if the root cause of the incident has not been identified; the user is contacted to ensure they agree that the incident can be closed; and a satisfaction survey is carried out for an agreed percentage of incidents.

There should be a separate procedure with shorter timescales and greater urgency for managing major incidents.

Major incident management

An example of a major incident that is relevant to cyber resilience is a breach of security which reveals data to an attacker about thousands of customers.

How long would you expect to wait before someone has started investigating this and provided an initial update to senior management?

If this happened in your organization, who would be involved in the investigation and communication?

Incident management can make significant contributions to cyber resilience by:

- Providing a process for users to report cyber resilience incidents. There will often be a specific set of actions that are taken when a security incident is logged, which are different from those used for other incidents. For example, the details may be recorded in a different place so that they are not available for as many people to read.

- Identifying cyber resilience incidents and categorizing and prioritizing them appropriately. This requires the service desk to have appropriate categories, which should be defined during the design of the cyber resilience incident management process.

- Resolving routine cyber resilience incidents by matching them to entries in a knowledge base and carrying out agreed activities. For example, there should be an article explaining what to do if a user laptop is infected with a virus, or if a user's mobile phone is stolen.

- Capturing data about cyber resilience incidents for use in trend analysis and problem identification. This may be captured on the standard incident management tool, but in some organizations information about these incidents is maintained in a separate tool to provide a higher level of confidentiality and prevent other people copying an attack.

- Escalating cyber resilience incidents to the appropriate resolution team within agreed times. It is often important to escalate these incidents very fast, so that people with appropriate expertise can capture data that may be needed in an investigation or prosecution, and so that they can take action to prevent the incident from getting worse.

- Ensuring that users are satisfied with the resolution of cyber resilience incidents.

- Contributing to the review and closure of cyber resilience incidents.

Cyber resilience can contribute to ITSM incident management by:

- Helping to define categories and priorities for cyber resilience incidents. In some organizations there may be a single 'security' category, but in others there may be separate categories for 'virus', 'unauthorized access', 'DDoS attack' etc. Each organization decides what categories it needs based on how it intends to report and analyse the incidents later.

- Providing scripts and knowledge base articles to assist in initial diagnosis of cyber resilience incidents: for example, how to recover a laptop that has been infected with a virus, or what action to take if a user's phone is stolen.

- Accepting escalated cyber resilience incidents and resolving them within agreed times.

- Contributing to the review and closure of cyber resilience incidents.

7.2.3 Request fulfilment

The ITSM request fulfilment process manages all **service request**s from users.

Request fulfilment aims to:

- Provide a channel for users to request and receive standard services
- Provide information about the availability of services and the procedure for obtaining them
- Source and deliver components of requested standard services (such as software licences)
- Assist with requests for information, complaints and comments.

In some organizations, request fulfilment is part of the incident management process and service requests are treated as a type of incident. It is nevertheless important to manage service requests and incidents in different ways and to report them separately. For example, each service request should have a predefined set of steps to fulfil the specific request, whereas each incident should be investigated to understand how service can be restored for the user. If these are reported together then rapid solving of simple service requests can distort incident management statistics, making it appear that user incidents are being resolved quickly.

What is a service request?

ITIL defines a service request as 'a formal request from a user for something to be provided – for example, a request for information or advice; to reset a password; or to install a workstation for a new user'.

Service requests that are relevant to cyber resilience might include:

● A request for a firewall rule to be added for use by a new supplier.

● A request from a user for their password to be reset.

Many service requests are implemented as standard changes (see section 6.2.2), but some may require a normal **change request** and others may not be changes at all. Where possible, request fulfilment should be automated, with a web-based front end for users to log requests and automation to fulfil them; but this should only be done where it is cost-effective, and it must include all aspects of funding and authorization that are appropriate for each particular request.

Table 7.3 summarizes the differences between incidents, service requests and changes.

Table 7.3 Distinguishing incidents, service requests and changes

Incident	Something is not working correctly.
Service request	Someone wants an additional pre-agreed, standard offering.
Change	Someone wants something new that has not been pre-agreed.

Examples of service requests

A user logs in to the organization's intranet and fills in a form to request a standard PC application. The server automatically downloads the software to the user's laptop, and assigns a licence. The request is completed in just a few minutes.

A software developer contacts the Windows server team to ask for a new virtual server for testing some software. The server team logs this as a service request on the ITSM tool, obtains email approval from the development team leader, creates the virtual server with the correct version of the operating system and hands it over to the development team. They notify the financial controller, who adds the cost of this virtual server to the development team's IT costs. They then notify the service desk, who close the request and conduct a user satisfaction survey.

The main activities for request fulfilment are shown in Figure 7.5; these activities include:

● **Receive request** Work on fulfilling a service request should not start until it has been formally requested by the user.

● **Logging and validation** All service requests must be logged, regardless of how they are received. The request record should include all information needed to manage the request. Validation ensures that the request is within the scope of the services offered and that the requester is entitled to submit this request.

● **Categorization and prioritization** Service requests should be categorized to assist with management of the request, and with trend analysis and reporting. They should be prioritized based on impact and urgency. Even though this sounds very similar to incident prioritization it is likely that there will be different categories and targets.

● **Authorization** Some requests may be authorized by the service desk based on agreed rules. Other requests may require management approval to ensure that the approver is entitled to the specific service they have requested, or to authorize the budget required. Pre-authorized requests may be completely automated, but even requests that require management approval can be automated via a workflow management system.

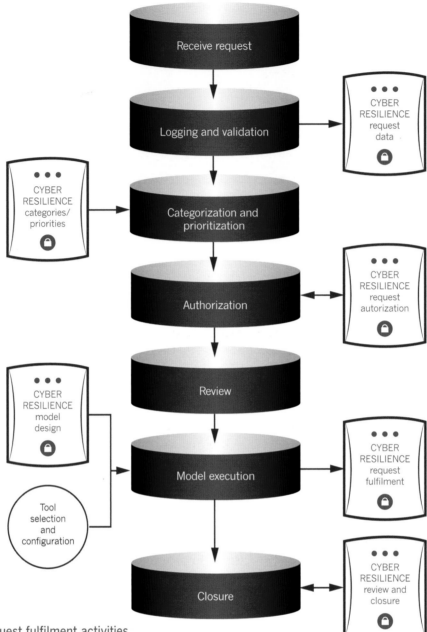

Figure 7.5 Request fulfilment activities

- **Review** The request is reviewed to identify how it will be fulfilled, and whether it needs escalation to obtain the required resources.
- **Model execution** Each valid service request should have a model that defines the steps taken to fulfil it.
- **Closure** All service requests should be passed back to the service desk for closure. During closure the request record is checked and updated to ensure that all required data has been captured; financial information is updated to ensure that charging takes place if appropriate; the user is contacted to ensure they agree that the request can be closed; and a satisfaction survey is carried out for an agreed percentage of service requests. Like all other steps of request fulfilment, closure should be automated when this is practical.

Request fulfilment can make significant contributions to cyber resilience by:

- Providing an auditable process for users to request access to IT services and other resources. This can supply information needed after a security incident to understand who requested access to a particular service, who authorized it and when it was granted. This can make analysis of the incident much easier than if these activities were not logged.

> ### Example of a request fulfilment process for password reset on a sensitive system
>
> - User contacts their manager to explain that they need a password reset; user confirms the phone number on which they can be contacted.
> - User phones the service desk to log the request.
> - User provides their manager's name and phone number for authorization (model shows the exact fields that the service desk should enter on its tool).
> - Service desk checks the organization directory to validate the manager's name and phone number, then phones the manager to get agreement for a password change.
> - Service desk resets the password and sets a flag to enforce a password change on next login.
> - Service desk phones the user on the number provided by the manager to give them the new password.

- Providing an auditable process for resetting user passwords and other access credentials. Poorly managed user password resets can be a significant vulnerability for many organizations. If an attacker is able to impersonate a user and obtain a newly reset password for their account, this could enable them to log on to the organization's network to mount further attacks on more sensitive assets. Cyber resilience can define strong controls to ensure that password resets are handled correctly, and these can then be implemented as part of the request fulfilment process (see example above).

- Providing an auditable process for users and IT staff to request changes to system and network parameters that are relevant to cyber resilience, such as firewall rules or file protections. Changes to system and network parameters can result in vulnerabilities, so they must be carefully managed. It might be possible for all of these to be treated as normal change requests, with review by a change advisory board (CAB) and formal approval before they are implemented, but in many organizations this would not be appropriate due to the need for greater agility and a faster response. In these circumstances the controls can be built into a request model, so that they are reliably executed as part of the request fulfilment process.

- Providing reports on service requests that are relevant to cyber resilience. Reports on the number and frequency of service requests such as password resets and firewall rule changes can provide significant input to improvement of cyber resilience controls.

Cyber resilience can contribute to ITSM request fulfilment by:

- Creating request models for fulfilment of service requests that are relevant to cyber resilience – for example password resets. This enables the required cyber resilience controls to be built into the request model, so that user requests can be fulfilled quickly while managing the risks involved. All security involves a balance between reduction of risk and facilitation of business agility, and request models like this help to manage this balance.

- Selecting and configuring tools to carry out service requests such as password resets, including full automation where practical.

- Helping to define categories and prioritization for service requests that are relevant to cyber resilience.

- Defining steps required to carry out service requests related to cyber resilience: for example, how to reset a user password or how to open a firewall port for an application.

- Accepting and responding to authorization requests as appropriate: for example requests for changes to firewall rules on networks that support critical infrastructure.

- Accepting escalations and managing service requests that require specialist cyber resilience skills: for example, reviewing requests for creation of privileged accounts on a server.

7.2.4 Problem management

The ITSM problem management process manages all problems, from when they are initially identified through investigation, documentation, **workaround** and eventual removal.

What is a problem?

ITIL defines a problem as 'A cause of one or more incidents. The cause is not usually known at the time a problem record is created, and the problem management process is responsible for further investigation.'

Examples of problems that are relevant to cyber resilience could be:

● Many staff have had laptops stolen, and it is not known whether this has led to any data being breached.

● There have been repeated DDoS attacks, each of which has had a significant business impact.

Problem management aims to:

● Prevent problems and the resulting incidents from happening.

● Eliminate recurring incidents.

● Minimize the impact of incidents that cannot be prevented.

Problem management has both reactive and proactive activities. Table 7.4 shows the difference between these.

Table 7.4 Proactive and reactive problem management

	Proactive problem management	Reactive problem management
Purpose	To identify problems that have not yet been noticed	To resolve problems that have already been identified
Trigger	Periodic scheduled review of incident records or events	A problem has been identified
Typical activities	Analysis of incident records to identify trends	Root cause analysis of a problem
	Creation of monthly 'Top 5 incident' reports to identify incidents causing most business impact	Documenting a workaround
	Logging new problems	Submitting a change request to remove a problem
		Updating the business with problem status

As well as diagnosing the root cause of problems, and planning changes to resolve them, problem management also maintains workarounds for problems that have not yet been resolved. These workarounds are documented in **known error** records and made available to the service desk to assist in incident management. A workaround documents what should be done when a problem occurs again; it includes information needed to identify the specific problem, and recovery actions to be taken to resolve new incidents. Workarounds do not eliminate problems, but they do reduce the impact of the associated incidents. A good workaround may be so effective that the business is prepared to live with the problem indefinitely rather than invest in the change needed to resolve it.

The main activities for problem management are shown in Figure 7.6; these activities include:

● **Problem detection and logging** Problems may be detected by proactive problem management, or by incident management, or by people engaged in other IT activities. Regardless of the source they must all be logged with links to relevant incident records.

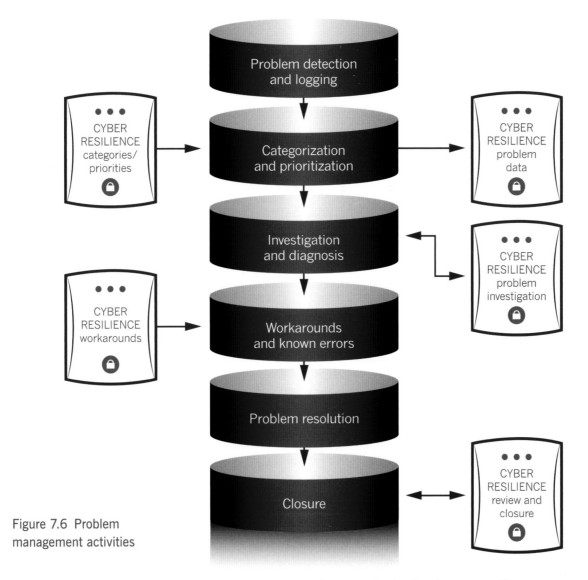

Figure 7.6 Problem management activities

● **Categorization and prioritization** Problems are usually categorized using the same coding system as incidents. Problem prioritization adopts a different approach based on frequency and impact of related incidents as well as other factors such as cost to diagnose or resolve (if known).

● **Investigation and diagnosis** Many different techniques can be used to identify the root cause of a problem. Commonly used approaches include chronological analysis, pain value analysis, Kepner-Tregoe problem-solving, **brainstorming** and Ishikawa diagrams. Problem investigation and diagnosis may involve contributions from multiple different groups, and may require escalation to engage the correct managerial and technical resources (see section 7.2.2 for information about escalation).

● **Workarounds and known errors** Whenever possible a workaround should be documented for use until the problem can be resolved. Workarounds are published in known error records and made available to the service desk so that future incidents can be resolved with minimum business impact.

● **Problem resolution** When the root cause of a problem is understood a decision should be made on whether to resolve the problem. Depending on the business impact of the problem and the cost to resolve it, it may be appropriate for a workaround to remain in place indefinitely. If a change is needed to resolve the problem, a formal request for change should be submitted.

● **Closure** When the problem has been resolved, related incident records and known error records should be reviewed and updated or closed as appropriate.

Example of a cyber resilience problem

- **Problem detection and logging** The service desk is told that a server has been infected with a virus. This has happened before so they log a problem. The server management team resolves the incident by restoring the previous day's backup and running a virus scan to ensure that the server is now clean.

- **Categorization and prioritization** The organization has a standard incident category for a virus infection, so this category is applied to the new problem. Because the virus was on a critical server and this has happened before, the problem priority is set to high.

- **Investigation and diagnosis** Investigation shows that the virus was introduced by a system administrator reading email on the server and opening an infected attachment.

- **Workarounds and known errors** A new policy is implemented to ban everyone from reading emails on servers. This is communicated to all system administrators. The cyber resilience team confirms that restoring the previous day's backup is the right recovery action if this happens again.

- **Problem resolution** The administrator involved is required to retake the security awareness training that includes guidance about opening email attachments. There is an ongoing discussion on whether to install anti-virus software on servers. This will not be decided in the short term, but may happen after extensive testing. The problem is left open with a status of known error while the discussion continues.

Problem management can make significant contributions to cyber resilience by:

- Providing a framework for identifying and managing cyber resilience problems. This will help to ensure that repeated cyber resilience incidents are correctly prioritized and managed.

- Identifying cyber resilience problems using proactive problem management.

- Providing data on frequency and impact of cyber resilience problems. This data can help to identify areas where additional investment is needed in cyber resilience controls.

- Facilitating use of techniques such as Kepner-Tregoe problem analysis or Ishikawa diagrams in diagnosis of cyber resilience problems. There are many problem management techniques that can help in the investigation and diagnosis of cyber resilience problems. A good problem management process will be designed to assist technical teams in learning about these techniques and applying them when appropriate.

- Maintaining known error records that describe workarounds for cyber resilience problems, to ensure that the service desk takes the best action when dealing with these. One of the biggest issues faced by cyber resilience is communication – a good knowledge base can help to ensure that service desk personnel take the best possible action when faced with a cyber resilience incident. This knowledge base can also be extended for use by users as a self-help tool.

Cyber resilience can contribute to ITSM request fulfilment by:

- Helping to define categories and priorities for cyber resilience problems. These can help to ensure that problems are properly managed and that appropriate levels of resource are applied.

- Accepting escalated cyber resilience problems and carrying out investigation and diagnosis of these. Most cyber resilience incidents require specialized handling by an expert team of security specialists. This team should work with problem management to ensure that they accept and manage cyber resilience problems when needed.

- Contributing to multi-disciplinary teams that may be set up to investigate complex problems. It can be very difficult to identify which team should be investigating a complex problem, and it is often necessary to pull together a team with skills across a range of different areas, including people who understand servers, networks, applications, suppliers and cyber resilience. Members of these teams must work constructively together with a shared focus on understanding the problem.

● Documenting workarounds for cyber resilience problems for use in known error records. For example, there may be a set of instructions for how to respond when an individual PC has been infected with a virus, or when a web server is subjected to a distributed denial of service attack.

● Contributing to the review and closure of cyber resilience problems.

7.2.5 Access management

The ITSM access management process provides users with the right to use services, or groups of services. Access management ensures that authorized users are able to access the appropriate resources, and that unauthorized users are not able to access resources which they should not be able to use. This process may be called 'identity management' or 'rights management' in some organizations.

The access management process does not make decisions about who should be allowed to access what resource, but grants and revokes access permissions based on policy and rules set by others. These rules are typically set by human resources (HR) staff or senior management, but they take into account the cyber resilience policies and other controls that are in place to protect the organization and its assets.

Access management also maintains logs of access rights, indicating who has been granted access to which resources, when they have logged in to each service, and what failed login attempts have occurred.

The main activities for access management are shown in Figure 7.7 – these activities include:

● **Request access** Many access requests are submitted as service requests via the request fulfilment process. They may also come from automated or manual triggers in HR systems, as requests for change, or from a pre-authorized script (e.g. when an application is downloaded to a system).

● **Verification** There are two distinct aspects to verification:

  ○ Is the user who is requesting access actually who they claim to be? Verification in this case might be based on credentials provided by HR such as an identity tag, by requiring the user to submit the request online so that their login credentials can be verified, or by confirming the user's identity via their manager (assuming that managers are known to the service desk).

  ○ Does the user have a legitimate requirement for the access requested? The access management team need well-documented rules telling them who is entitled to what level of access. For example, it may require a request from HR to create a new-user account, but a request from the finance director to create a new account on the financial management system. It is important to ensure that the requested access is appropriate for the user's requirements. There should be a suitable granularity of access controls, such that each user has the minimum level of access needed to perform their role. For example, someone who only needs to access information in a database should not be able to modify the data. Special care is needed for administrative access rights (or 'super-user' rights), which may enable a user to access and modify all data within a service, and to modify access rights for other users.

● **Provide rights** Access rights are granted based on the policies and rules, and the outcome of the verification.

● **Check and monitor identity status** When users leave the organization or change roles, access management should modify or remove their access rights. This may require tools and integration with HR systems.

● **Log and track access** Monitor services and resources to identify and log access requests as appropriate. The access logs should be suitably protected and made available when needed to investigate security incidents.

Every access management activity makes a contribution to cyber resilience, since the granting and management of access rights is a significant factor in cyber resilience controls. Significant contributions include:

● Providing an auditable process for granting and revoking access rights to users. This is very important since it also provides the data needed to review access rights and ensure that they have been set correctly. If access rights are only recorded in the database that controls the access, there is no way to audit all accounts to see if they should be there.

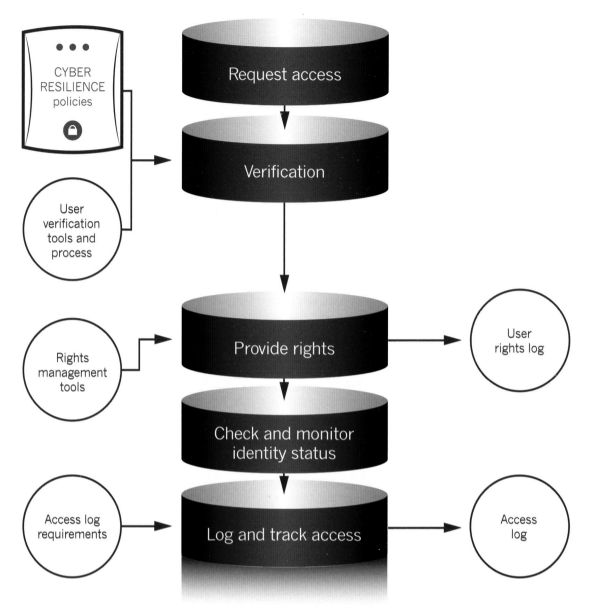

Figure 7.7 Access management activities

- Maintaining audit logs of user logins and access to critical resources and making these available when needed. For example, if there is a suspicion that there may have been a financial fraud, it may be essential to know the exact times at which staff logged on or off the financial management system, and what device they logged in from.

- Maintaining interfaces with HR to ensure that changes in roles and job status result in modification to access rights. This area is poorly managed in many organizations, with large numbers of user accounts that should have been disabled. This can provide a great opportunity for an attacker as there could be many accounts to try to breach, and the real users of these accounts will not notice messages about failed logins.

- Executing access management policies defined by cyber resilience. Access management does not decide what account access should be granted: it simply executes rules that have been defined by HR and senior management in line with cyber resilience policies and controls.

Cyber resilience can contribute to ITSM access management by:

- Defining policies for granting and removal of access rights. Typically, these policies will be formally approved by HR and/or senior management, but cyber resilience experts are often very good at identifying the requirements.

Example of access management activities

A new employee joins the organization. They will be working in the finance department as a financial controller. The manager agrees on a start date with HR.

- **Request access** HR submits a standard 'new-user' service request, so that the appropriate user accounts will be created. The manager submits a service request asking for accounts to be created so that the new financial controller can access the finance systems.

- **Verification** There are two aspects of verification:

  - The access management team verifies the identity of the HR person and confirms that they are allowed to request standard user accounts be created. HR provides the access management team with the full name and company ID of the new employee.

  - The access management team verifies the identity of the manager and checks that they are on their list of people allowed to request access to financial management systems.

- **Provide rights** The access management team creates the requested accounts. They print access information for the new accounts and provide this to the manager in a sealed envelope, to be handed to the new employee.

- **Check and monitor identity status** Some time later the employee changes jobs, moving to a role where they no longer need access to the financial management system. The HR department notifies the access management team who revoke the user's rights to access financial management systems.

- **Log and track access** Every time the user logs in or out of the financial management system a record is created. These records are made available to the financial auditors when they are investigating suspected fraudulent activities.

- Providing tools and processes to enable verification of user identities (for example usernames and passwords, identity cards, or public key infrastructure (PKI) tokens). There are many different tools that can be used to support access management. Selection and configuration of these tools requires specialist cyber resilience knowledge.

- Selection and configuration of tools to manage access rights. This includes tools such as Windows Active Directory, or Kerberos, which store information about users and their access rights, as well as integrated identity management systems and single sign-on (SSO) solutions that combine management of identity with management of access rights.

- Definition of rules for granting and removal of access rights when users change roles or leave the organization. These will normally be negotiated and agreed with the HR department.

- Providing requirements for logging and tracking access, so that the required audit logs will be available when needed for investigation of cyber resilience incidents.

7.2.6 Service desk

ITIL Service Operation describes four functions: these are the service desk, technical management, application management and IT operations management.

A service desk is a **single point of contact** between the service provider and the users of the services. A typical service desk is responsible for:

- Logging incidents and service requests, and assigning categories and priorities to them
- Managing the full lifecycle of all incidents and service requests
- First-line investigation and diagnosis of incidents
- Authorizing, reviewing or fulfilling service requests where the request model makes this a service desk task
- Resolving incidents and service requests during initial contact where this is possible
- Escalating incidents and service requests to appropriate technical or managerial staff where this is required

- Communicating with users to ensure that they understand the status of their incidents and service requests, and to maximize user satisfaction
- Updating configuration management data where appropriate
- Closing all incidents and service requests
- Conducting user surveys on an agreed percentage of incidents and service requests.

ITIL describes a number of different service desk organizational structures:

- **Local service desk** This is physically close to the users. A local service desk can often provide high levels of service due to good communication channels to the users but may be expensive to run, especially if there are many user locations, a need for 24-hour service, or specialized groups of users who are distributed throughout the organization (see Figure 7.8).

- **Centralized service desk** This provides a single service desk that supports many locations. It can be more cost-effective, allowing fewer IT staff to support more users, but may require some local staff for physical support requirements and may have difficulties supporting large numbers of languages (see Figure 7.9).

- **Virtual service desk** This provides the appearance of a centralized service desk, but uses technology to allow the service desk agents to be remotely located. This can allow for offshoring and use of groups in specific countries where needed, but it requires safeguards to ensure that the distributed personnel follow the specified process consistently (see Figure 7.10).

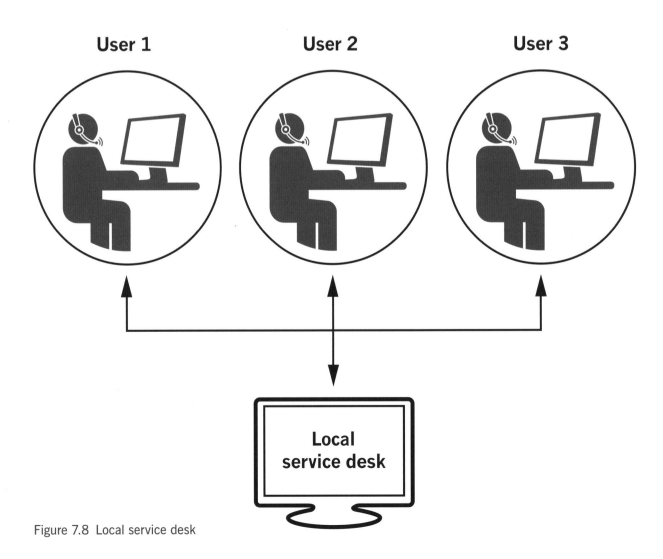

Figure 7.8 Local service desk

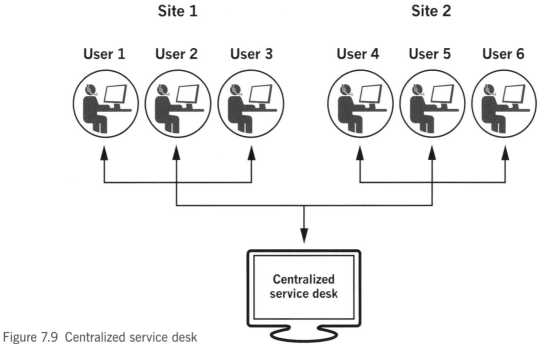

Figure 7.9 Centralized service desk

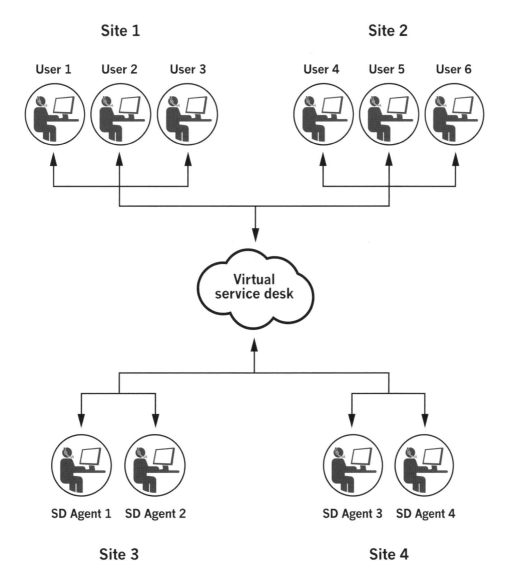

Figure 7.10 Virtual service desk

- **Follow the sun** This involves the use of a small number of geographically dispersed service desks, where each service desk works during daytime hours in a different time zone, and hands open calls to a different service desk when they go home at night.

A service desk usually needs a range of specialized tools, including:

- **Telephony** Most service desks use automatic call distribution (ACD) systems to distribute calls to suitable service agents. Many also use interactive voice response (IVR) to allow the user to provide information used in call routeing.

- **ITSM tools** The service desk needs a suitable tool for logging and managing incidents and service requests. Most organizations use an integrated ITSM toolset that also supports problem management, change management, configuration management and possibly other ITSM processes.

- **Known error database** This is often part of a more extensive knowledge base, where information required by the service desk can be easily located. Ideally this will be integrated into a comprehensive ITSM toolset. A known error database enables the service desk to find out about workarounds for problems that have already been investigated, providing a faster and better service for the users. A wider knowledge base can also provide access to lots of other helpful information that can enable the service desk to provide a better service to the users: for example, instructions for carrying out common tasks that users may have difficulty with.

- **Self-help web interface** It is often cost-effective to provide a web interface to allow users to log incidents and service requests, and resolve these for themselves where possible.

- **Remote control** These tools allow the service desk to take control of end-user PCs to investigate incidents.

The service desk can make significant contributions to cyber resilience by:

- Providing a single point of contact for users to report cyber resilience incidents and requests. Since users know that the service desk is the single point of contact for reporting all IT issues it makes sense to use the same service desk for reporting cyber resilience issues, even those that are not related to IT.

- Providing a channel for communicating cyber resilience messages to users. For example, if the cyber resilience team learn of a new phishing attack that has affected other organizations, the service desk could send a message to users warning them to be wary.

- Helping to foster a culture of cyber resilience awareness in the way people deal with user incidents and service requests: for example, by never asking users to supply their passwords, by checking that user PCs have appropriate encryption and anti-virus measures, or by sending out security tips as part of incident closure.

Why shouldn't a service desk ask users for their passwords?

If a service desk asks users for their passwords when trying to resolve incidents, this can create a number of vulnerabilities:

- Users may divulge their passwords to attackers if the attacker can convince them that they are talking to the service desk.

- If users are regularly required to share their passwords with the service desk, this makes it more likely that they will agree to share their password under other circumstances.

- Service desk staff may be able to use the user's credentials to access or modify assets that they would not normally have access to.

Cyber resilience can contribute to the service desk by:

- Helping to ensure that tools used by the service desk are secure and fit for use: for example, by carrying out vulnerability scans of the service desk software or auditing the security features of the telephone system

● Providing cyber resilience training and fostering awareness to ensure that service desk personnel understand their role in helping to protect the organization

● Providing messages that the service desk can communicate to users during major cyber resilience incidents or as part of overall user communication: for example, providing status updates advising users on actions to take when there has been a virus outbreak, or creating text for an article that the service desk can send to users advising them how to safely use removable media.

7.2.7 Technical management

Technical management comprises all the groups, departments or teams that provide technical expertise to manage the IT infrastructure and support the delivery of services. Technical management is responsible for planning, implementing and maintaining a reliable IT infrastructure to support the organization's business processes. Technical management has two roles:

● It is the custodian of technical knowledge needed to manage the IT infrastructure, making sure that this is available to all personnel when and where needed.

● It provides people with technical expertise who are needed throughout the entire service lifecycle. Technical management personnel are not just involved in the service operation stage of the service lifecycle: they are involved in the design, build, transition, operation and improvement of IT infrastructure.

Note that technical management is responsible for the IT infrastructure, but not for the applications that run on this infrastructure (see section 7.2.8 for information on application management).

Technical management personnel are involved in the execution of many service management processes across the entire service lifecycle. For example, they may act as second- or third-line support for incident management or problem management, they may review changes to ensure that the impact on the infrastructure is understood, and they may design infrastructure solutions to meet availability or capacity requirements.

Technical management is not usually a single monolithic team of people. It is typically organized as a number of distinct teams, each with a focus on a different technology domain. For example, there may be a server team, a UNIX team, a Windows team, a storage team, a network team etc.

Retail example: SellUGoods

The overall requirements for cyber resilience at SellUGoods are defined by the information security team in the risk management department. This information security team does not have the people or time to manage all aspects of infrastructure security, so they delegate tasks such as creating secure builds for servers and PCs and defining firewall rules to various infrastructure teams.

The server team creates secure server builds, the network team defines firewall rules and the PC build team creates and manages environments for desktop PCs and laptops. Each of these infrastructure teams has the appropriate knowledge and skills to carry out these specific aspects of security management, but they do so under the guidance of the information security team, and following agreed cyber resilience policies. These infrastructure teams are effectively part of technical management, although SellUGoods does not use this term.

Technical management can make significant contributions to cyber resilience by:

● Providing personnel with technical expertise to assist in the design and implementation of cyber resilience controls related to IT infrastructure: for example by helping them to create a secure process for updating firmware on servers and network switches

● Ensuring that all IT infrastructure designs meet cyber resilience standards and implement agreed cyber resilience controls: for example by using standard builds, and completing checklists during deployment

- Carrying out audits to ensure that cyber resilience controls have been correctly and fully implemented on all IT infrastructure assets
- Providing knowledge of IT infrastructure to cyber resilience personnel as needed.

Cyber resilience can contribute to technical management by:

- Defining standards and other controls to ensure that the design and implementation of IT infrastructure meets the organization's need for cyber resilience
- Providing cyber resilience training, and fostering awareness to ensure that technical management personnel understand their role in helping to protect the organization
- Providing knowledge of cyber resilience to technical management personnel as needed: for example by providing training and information on how to configure firewalls or deploy encryption tools.

7.2.8 Application management

Application management comprises all the groups, departments or teams that provide expertise to manage applications and support the delivery of services. Application management is responsible for managing applications throughout their lifecycle to support the organization's business processes.

Application management should be distinguished from application development. Application management provides ongoing management of applications, while application development is mainly concerned with project-based activities for requirements, design and build of applications. Application management may also be involved in requirements, design and build activities, but usually this would be to ensure that the new or changed application is maintainable, rather than to design the basic functionality. Table 7.5 shows the major differences between application development and application management.

Table 7.5 Comparison of application development and application management

	Application development	Application management
Type of work	One-off activities to design and build applications	Ongoing activities to oversee and manage applications
Type of application	Mainly development of in-house software	Management of all applications, whether in-house or purchased
Primary focus	Mainly application functionality required by the customer	Both application functionality and service warranty aspects such as stability, performance, continuity and security
Type of management	Most work is part of a project	Most work is part of repeatable processes

Like technical management, application management has two roles:

- It is the custodian of technical knowledge needed to manage applications, making sure that this is available to all personnel when and where needed.
- It provides people with technical expertise, who are needed throughout the entire service lifecycle. Application management personnel are not just involved in the service operation stage of the service lifecycle: they are involved in the design, build, transition, operation and improvement of applications.

Application management personnel are involved in the execution of many service management processes across the entire service lifecycle. For example, they may act as second- or third-line support for incident management or problem management, they may review changes to ensure that the impact on applications is understood, and they may help with the design of applications to ensure that availability or capacity requirements are met. Figure 7.11 shows some typical activities that are carried out by application management and technical management.

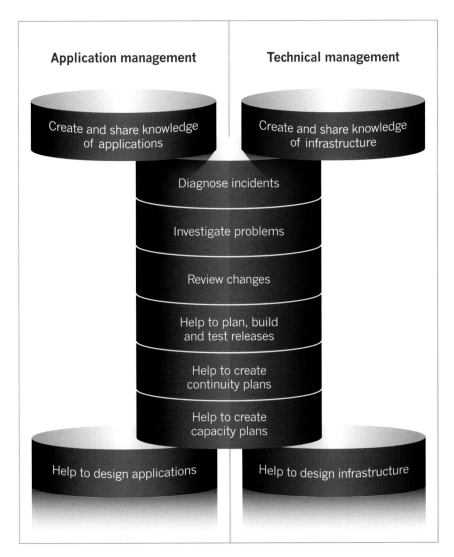

Figure 7.11 Typical activities carried out by application management and technical management

Application management can make significant contributions to cyber resilience by:

● Providing personnel with technical expertise to assist in the design and implementation of cyber resilience controls related to applications. This is especially important if specialist knowledge of the application is needed to understand the different sorts of control that might be appropriate.

● Ensuring that all application designs meet cyber resilience standards and implement agreed cyber resilience controls. For example, there may be a requirement to validate all user-supplied data before it is used, to prevent buffer overflow and SQL injection attacks.

● Carrying out audits to ensure that cyber resilience controls have been correctly and fully implemented in all applications. An audit could be in the form of a code review or a formal response from a third-party software developer in reply to a request.

● Providing knowledge of applications to cyber resilience personnel as needed. For example, the cyber resilience team may need to understand the architecture of an application so that they can determine the correct firewall configuration to support it.

Cyber resilience can contribute to technical management by:

● Defining standards and other controls to ensure that the design and implementation of applications meets the organization's need for cyber resilience

● Providing cyber resilience training and fostering awareness to ensure that application management personnel understand their role in helping to protect the organization

- Providing knowledge of cyber resilience to application management personnel as needed. For example, it might be appropriate to train application management staff on how to safely configure common applications, or ensure that they understand the best way to implement password management for an application.

7.2.9 IT operations management

IT operations management carries out the routine activities needed to monitor, manage and maintain IT infrastructure, applications and services on a daily basis. This function comprises two distinct sub-functions:

- **IT operations control** Oversees the operation and monitors activities and events. This typically includes:
  - Managing an operations bridge where events are monitored
  - Backing up and restoring data as needed
  - Managing batch and print operations where appropriate
  - Providing routine server, mainframe and network management such as system start-up and shut-down.
- **Facilities management** Provides management of the physical IT environment (data centres, computer rooms etc.) and the supporting facilities such as power and cooling.

There is some potential overlap between IT operations management, technical management and application management. Each organization should define the exact roles based on their needs and assign work to teams as appropriate.

Manufacturing example: MakeUGoods

Technical management at MakeUGoods is carried out by a single IT infrastructure team. This team includes people with server, network and storage skills. There is a separate PC team responsible for client builds. There is also a single application management team responsible for all applications.

Routine operational activity at MakeUGoods is carried out by the IT infrastructure team, which also monitors the infrastructure during the daytime.

MakeUGoods has just one data centre, which is co-located with the main manufacturing site. **Facilities management** and out-of-hours monitoring of IT infrastructure are carried out by the manufacturing operations team – this is not an IT team, but they monitor IT events and contact a duty IT infrastructure management person if they are needed at night.

Retail example: SellUGoods

Technical management at SellUGoods is carried out by teams for server management, client PC builds, storage management and network management. Application management is the responsibility of three business-focused application teams: retail application support, financial application support and general business systems support. These are all global teams that have worldwide responsibilities.

SellUGoods has three data centres – one in the UK, one in the USA and one in India. Each data centre has an operations bridge and a separate facilities department. Staff on the operations bridge are responsible for monitoring servers and carrying out routine activities such as server reboots. Infrastructure changes, such as firmware updates for servers, are designed by the global teams but they are implemented by staff from the operations bridge.

IT operations management can make significant contributions to cyber resilience by:

- Operating all IT infrastructure and applications in line with agreed cyber resilience standards and controls.
- Reporting unusual activities or cyber resilience-relevant events to cyber resilience personnel – for example if a backup job suddenly starts to take much longer because there is twice as much data as there used to

be, or if users are logging in to critical servers at unusual times of day, or the usage of a network link to a supplier suddenly increases.

Cyber resilience can contribute to IT operations management by:

● Defining standards and controls to ensure that routine operational activities such as backup or server management support the cyber resilience needs of the business. For example, this could include requirements to log what was done and who by, to have multiple people involved to check one another's actions, or to ensure that backup media are stored in secure locations.

● Providing cyber resilience training and fostering awareness to ensure that IT operations management personnel understand their role in helping to protect the organization.

● Providing knowledge of cyber resilience to IT operations management personnel as needed: for example guidance on how to properly secure backup media, or how to escalate a security incident out of hours.

7.2.10 Aligning cyber resilience controls with IT service operation

Section 7.2 has so far addressed the integration of cyber resilience and IT service management by considering how each ITSM process can be integrated with cyber resilience. An alternative way to consider integration of cyber resilience and IT service management is to look at how each of the strategic cyber resilience controls described in section 7.1 can be integrated with ITSM.

7.2.10.1 Access control

The access management process can help to implement many operational requirements of access control. Technical management and application management personnel may help with the design of the controls required for identifying and authenticating users, and granting access to services.

7.2.10.2 Network security management

The event management process provides monitoring of networks as well as other infrastructure. This activity may be carried out by IT operations management personnel. Technical management personnel are often involved in both the design and operation of network security management controls.

7.2.10.3 Physical security management

Most activities required for physical security management control will be carried out by facilities management. This function is typically not part of IT, but it provides services to support IT as well as cyber resilience and all other business functions.

7.2.10.4 Operations security

Operations security covers a number of areas within ITSM. The main support for this control will come from IT operations management, but both technical management and application management will create documented operating procedures which contribute to operations security. Operations security also includes aspects of change management and capacity management, which are usually treated as separate processes in ITSM.

7.2.10.5 Cyber resilience incident management

There is a lot of overlap between the ITSM incident management process and cyber resilience incident management. It is essential that these two processes have well-integrated linkages to ensure that cyber resilience incidents which arrive at the service desk are correctly managed, and that appropriate escalation takes place.

Some organizations run a single incident management process that meets the needs of both cyber resilience and IT service management. Other organizations have separate processes with formal handovers to ensure that incidents are handled by appropriate people following the correct process.

7.3 OPERATION SCENARIOS

This section looks at some aspects of operation for the three fictitious organizations. As you read through these descriptions you should think about:

● How well did their controls protect them from the incident in this scenario?

● Do they have the right balance of preventative, detective and corrective controls?

● What should they have done differently before or during the incident?

Retail example: SellUGoods Ltd

The testing of the new security incident management process went very well, and people at SellUGoods seem confident that they know what to do if there is a real security incident. Everyone agrees that this testing is an important aspect of maintaining good security defences, and the finance director has added the cost of an annual test to the budget.

As the new intrusion detection tools are deployed to additional servers and firewalls, the operations bridge gets a small number of false alarms. These trigger the incident management process, but in each case a quick assessment identifies a reason why the intrusion detection triggered an alert and the thresholds are modified to be slightly less sensitive.

Another security incident was raised this morning. The intrusion detection software has just been installed on a server in the finance department and it reports that this server is sending credit card numbers to the internet. Nobody is too worried about this, as that server does not store payment card data, but someone in the information security team is reviewing the network logs to make sure that there is not a problem. After a brief investigation they discover that this could potentially be a real issue, and they escalate the security incident. Within a few minutes it has been agreed to disconnect this server from the internet to prevent any further data leaks while the investigation continues.

As the investigation progresses it is discovered that this server appears to have a malware infection. A decision is made to disconnect the internal network from the internet while a scan is conducted to check for any other infected servers. This does not immediately affect customers, as there is very good network isolation between these internal systems and all customer-facing servers.

Meanwhile, the investigation on the original server turns up some very bad news. A file has been discovered that contains five-year-old payment card data from before the organization had its PCI-DSS certification. This data should have been deleted, but nobody realized it was there. The crisis management team is now asking for details of the numbers and types of data that might have been compromised so that they can plan their communication strategy.

Further investigation reveals that the server had information about 75,000 payment cards. Fortunately these are all old cards, with expiry dates that have passed, so the breach is not as bad as it might have been, but the data does include names and addresses of the cardholders so this will require careful management.

It is now one hour since the event was detected, and the security incident management process appears to be working well. The scale of the problem has been understood and information is flowing to the people who need it. The problem has been contained and the investigation is reviewing other servers to see what other data might have been compromised.

By the end of the day SellUGoods has identified a number of other infected servers and has removed the malware from all of them. The authorities have been notified of the breach and customer communication has started. Because the crisis management team had the information they needed they have been able to start the customer communication with a very positive message about the level of risk and the measures that are being taken to contain this. There were some negative comments on social media, but the company responded well, giving clear and helpful information about what had happened and how customers should contact them if they are worried.

During this initial stage of the incident nobody identified how the event had started, but now that things have been contained there is a team investigating how the malware got onto the server. This problem management activity is very important, but it has not been allowed to distract people from the initial urgent work to identify the scale of the breach, get the communication right, and remove the malware. The investigation shows that someone working in the finance department had opened an email from a friend that contained a malware link, and this had resulted in their laptop being infected. This infection then spread to the servers in the finance department where they had administrator privileges. Clearly improvements are going to be needed to prevent this from happening again, and these will be discussed in the continual improvement section.

Medical example: MedUServ Ltd

The MedUServ **account manager** for a large hospital has been contacted by a hospital manager, who says that there is a problem with the results they received this morning. The results do not make sense and the hospital suspects that MedUServ may have mixed up some samples in the lab. The account manager is sure that this cannot have happened because the process for handling samples is well designed to prevent samples being mixed up and the people are very good at following this process. He asks for more information about the problem results and says he will get back to the hospital.

The account manager goes to see the technical director to discuss the results, and they log on to the lab computer to see if they can find the problem. As expected, the information on the lab computer matches what the hospital says it received. The technical director then reviews the paper forms from the tests they are discussing and she discovers, to her horror, that these show completely different results. This has never happened before, and she does not know what could have caused the error. She contacts the IT service desk and explains the problem, and the service desk says this must have been a data entry error made at MedUServ, as there is no way that an IT failure could have swapped results round. The technical director interviews the technician who carried out the tests, but he says that everything was perfectly normal, and the results were entered in the usual way.

To make sure that this is just an isolated issue the technical director asks one of the lab supervisors to carry out an audit of results from the previous week, comparing the online results to the results on the paper forms. Much to everyone's shock it seems that every result from the past week has been entered incorrectly. She immediately speaks to the managing director, and then the directors and account managers contact all of their customers to notify them of the problem and to promise to make copies of the paper forms and send these to the hospitals and clinics so that they have the correct results. They contact a local agency to recruit extra staff to enable them to do this work. Understandably many of the customers are very angry and demand to know how this has happened.

The managing director of MedUServ contacts a senior manager at the outsourcing company which carries out the data entry and asks him to investigate what has happened. In the meantime MedUServ arranges for someone to log in each evening and verify that the day's results have all been recorded correctly.

After three days the outsourcing company contacts MedUServ to explain that their investigation is now complete. They have found out that one of their staff members was angry over not being promoted, and they think he may have intentionally corrupted the databases of some customers in revenge before leaving the company with no notice. MedUServ asks if this employee had been vetted before being employed, and the outsourcer gives a vague answer. Lawyers on both sides are instructed and tasked with apportioning blame for the incident.

Unfortunately, this incident receives wide media coverage and the desirable new customer that MedUServ has been in negotiations with drops MedUServ from its shortlist. Some other customers threaten to move their business elsewhere. This will have a significant impact on next year's revenue.

Manufacturing example: MakeUGoods

Application whitelisting and file integrity monitoring are now in place on the SCADA servers. Testing of file integrity monitoring on the remaining critical systems at MakeUGoods is still ongoing.

Company-branded USB sticks have been ordered for use on the SCADA systems. These will have the company logo and the word SCADA printed on them. After these have been introduced no other USB sticks will be allowed to be inserted into these systems. Staff training has ensured that everyone understands this is a very serious matter and failure to comply would lead to disciplinary action. Software is being tested that would ensure that user PCs, laptops and non-SCADA servers will only allow the use of encrypted media. This should be deployed within a few weeks. Since the SCADA systems are unable to read the encrypted media, this will ensure a complete separation of removable media between the two environments.

The IT infrastructure team have just received an alert from the application whitelisting software, saying that an unauthorized application attempted to run on one of the SCADA control systems. On investigation it appears that someone was installing a firmware upgrade on the server, and it is initially assumed that this was a false alarm due to the upgrade process. Further analysis shows that something strange has been happening. It looks as if the USB stick containing the new firmware may have contained some kind of malware. MakeUGoods has a support contract with the supplier of the new security software that implements file integrity checking and application whitelisting, so MakeUGoods contacts the supplier to ask for advice. In the meantime the firmware update is postponed until more information is available. The supplier confirms MakeUGoods' belief that this is not normal behaviour for the upgrade that was being implemented and that the USB stick must have introduced malware onto the SCADA system.

Investigation of the USB stick shows that it is indeed infected with malware that could have caused serious damage to the SCADA environment. Fortunately, the new controls have prevented this from happening. The infection has come from the laptop of the engineer who was performing the update. It is not entirely clear how the laptop was infected, but no other computers seem to have this malware so it was probably infected quite recently. An investigation is initiated to discover how this laptop became infected.

Everyone is very glad that the new controls have been so effective and that the additional controls on removable media will provide an extra layer of defence against this kind of threat in future.

7.4 CYBER RESILIENCE OPERATION QUESTIONS

1. How effective is the monitoring in your organization? Are there cyber-attacks that you might not detect? What improvements could you make in this area of event monitoring?

2. Does your process for managing cybersecurity incidents work effectively? How do you know? Is it regularly tested? How could you ensure that future cybersecurity incidents are handled faster and more effectively?

3. What is the procedure for resetting user passwords in your organization? Is it sufficiently quick, efficient and effective? How easily could this procedure be used to hack into someone's account? How could this be improved?

4. How well is the access management process in your organization integrated with your HR procedures? How confident are you that the right actions are taken when people leave the organization or change roles? What could you do to improve this?

5. How well do the cyber resilience people in your organization work with the people responsible for managing infrastructure and applications? Does this relationship help to foster good cyber resilience? How could this be improved?

8

Cyber resilience
continual improvement

This chapter covers:

- Objectives and controls for cyber resilience continual improvement

- Aligning with IT continual service improvement

- Using the ITIL CSI approach to plan cyber resilience improvements

- Using MSP to plan and manage cyber resilience improvements

- Maturity models

- Continual improvement scenarios

8 Cyber resilience continual improvement

Continual or continuous?

Continual improvement never ends. There are always opportunities to improve, and an organization that does not improve will gradually fall behind.

Continuous improvement would require people to be actively making improvements all the time, even at night!

Continual improvement is not so much a stage in the lifecycle of cyber resilience as a set of attitudes, behaviours and culture that helps to ensure that cyber resilience continues to provide the protection needed in a constantly changing environment.

If an organization could design and implement perfect cyber resilience controls that deliver everything it needs as efficiently as possible, it would still need continual improvement to ensure that its controls remain appropriate and effective in the face of:

- **A continually changing threat environment** Controls that were previously perfect may no longer be good enough because of the new threats and new vulnerabilities being developed by people working to undermine cyber resilience. This means that an organization must constantly be monitoring what is happening and trying to understand whether it could be vulnerable to attacks that have affected other organizations. For example, in 2010 it was discovered that industrial control systems based on SCADA were vulnerable to attacks from a cyber-threat called 'Stuxnet', even if they were completely isolated from the internet. This required every organization with a SCADA system to review and update their process for managing updates (see section 4.3 for a brief description of SCADA).

- **A continually changing business environment** The risk analysis previously carried out may no longer be appropriate for the business needs because of new customer expectations, new business opportunities, new laws and regulations, and new competitive pressures which require ever-higher levels of confidentiality, integrity and availability.

- **A continually changing technology environment** Controls that worked previously may no longer be effective because of new infrastructure, new applications and new services that require updated, expanded or completely redesigned controls to achieve the same effect. For example, a user authentication scheme based on locally managed usernames and passwords, which was ideal for a single-server environment, may not provide the appropriate level of protection in a new cloud environment where software is supplied as a service by a third party.

Business environment changes

Many businesses are gaining competitive advantage by converting physical activities into virtual activities on the internet: for example moving a store from bricks and mortar to a website.

These changes require significant investment in cyber resilience controls, as virtual activities are critically dependent on the confidentiality, integrity and availability of information.

For example, an organization may have had sufficient controls to protect its website when it was only used for sharing information with customers, but if it adds internet shopping capability to this website then it may need to invest in significant hardening of the server due to the increased exposure. Alternatively, it could outsource the internet shopping capability to a third party, but this would require investment in increased capability to manage cyber resilience risk from suppliers.

Continual improvement is not just about things that are currently in operation. Everything that the organization does should be subjected to a process of understanding and improvement. This is why the ITIL lifecycle is depicted with design, transition and operation as a cycle, with strategy at the centre informing everything that happens and continual improvement round the outside ensuring that everything is efficient, effective and relevant (see Figure 3.4).

Continual improvement of how an organization designs and transitions cyber resilience controls is just as important as continual improvement of the controls themselves and how they are operated. Similarly, an organization should continually improve its strategy and how it manages continual improvement itself. This process of continual feedback from each stage of the lifecycle to other stages is shown graphically in Figure 8.1. This constant monitoring, reviewing and feeding back provides the organization with the ability to learn and improve, to avoid making the same mistakes over and over again, and to continually improve the effectiveness of cyber resilience. To achieve this requires a combination of metrics, reporting and processes, many of which are described in this chapter, but more importantly it needs the right attitudes, behaviour and culture. An organization where mistakes are seen as opportunities to learn and honest feedback is valued will be able to improve much more effectively than one where mistakes are punished and feedback is resented.

8.1 CONTROL OBJECTIVES AND CONTROLS FOR CYBER RESILIENCE CONTINUAL IMPROVEMENT

The objective of continual improvement in cyber resilience is to ensure that the controls or protections that were designed and implemented in the design and planning phase continue to remain effective over time and provide the desired protection, and that they are continually improved to protect against new threats.

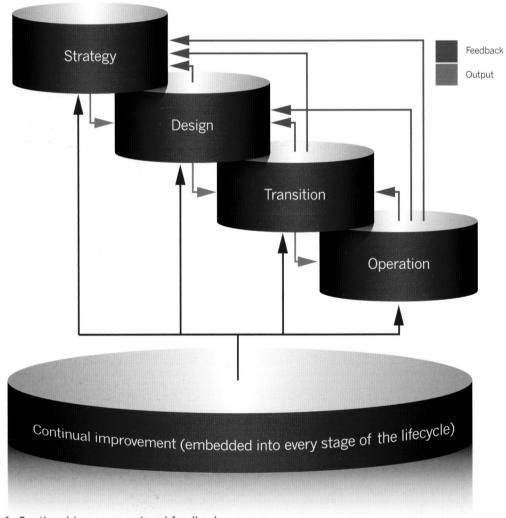

Figure 8.1 Continual improvement and feedback

8.1.1 Cyber resilience audit and review

The primary objective of cyber resilience audit and review from a continual improvement perspective is to help an organization identify where it is in the continual improvement process. The improvement made as a result of the findings can help an organization to plan to get to where it wants to be – that is, help to improve cyber resilience controls.

The cyber risk landscape is ever evolving and changing. Every day hundreds of new vulnerabilities are discovered: some are known and others are so new that they have not yet been noticed – so-called zero-day vulnerabilities can be exploited by new and old threats. A recent globally impacting example is the Heartbleed (OpenSSL) flaw, which exposed millions of websites and products to threats. Therefore, it is no longer enough to just rely on the designed and implemented controls: it is essential that organizations also continue to evolve and improve their cyber resilience controls.

The audit may be internal or external but should be independent and objective, and although not strictly necessary, it should ideally be carried out by persons outside the area being audited to avoid conflicts of interest and to provide objectivity. Security standards such as the ISO/IEC 27001 for instance require internal and external audits for certification of the information security management system (ISMS).

If an organization operates in a compliance-driven industry such as finance, it will already require auditing and review of its controls. Industry compliance standards such as the PCI-DSS and SAE 16 (Statement on Standards for Attestation Engagements (SSAE) No. 16) require regular review and compliance audits. Audit and review of an organization as part of its existing compliance framework is also a good opportunity to re-validate existing cyber resilience controls, test assumptions, plug gaps and more importantly improve controls. However, cyber resilience is wider than just compliance with industry standards. Whilst these have limited scope (for example the PCI-DSS only applies to the security of the cardholder environment), cyber resilience is about the entire organization.

Audit and review is one way to get a comprehensive view of security arrangements. Good cyber controls become ineffective over time or do not remain as optimal as when they were designed. They may have been designed for managing risks that have changed or threats that have become more motivated or more competent. Some threats may have ceased, so the controls are no longer required or can be relaxed since the threats are not as effective as initially envisaged. Therefore, it is important to continually review and assess the effectiveness of existing controls with a view to improving them, replacing them if they are no longer needed, or removing them completely if they cause significant business impact and the threat they were designed to defeat no longer exists.

Technical continual improvement

A good example of technical continual improvement would be a traditional firewall that was effective when it was installed several years ago but is no longer an optimal control (see Figure 8.2). This could be due to a change in business operation or changes in the technical environment. Examples of these changes might be the launch of a new product or deployment of a new e-commerce application using web services. The traditional firewall may now need to be replaced with a web application firewall (WAF) that is able to handle more sophisticated application-borne attacks.

An example of an improvement of a non-technical control may be to review the firewall logs more often and retrain people to recognize and respond to new types of attack. This is just one example of good cyber resilience best practice and how and why it should be reviewed. It also illustrates that controls are not always technical and could be procedural or managerial.

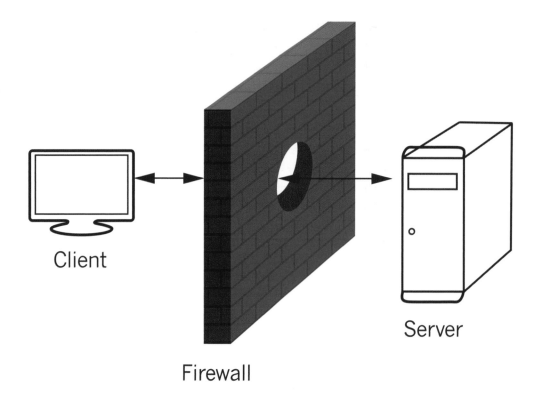

Client

Firewall

Server

Figure 8.2 A traditional firewall that is no longer effective

8.1.1.1 Technology review and audit

Every organization should carry out a regular technology review and audit to ensure that technical controls are performing as designed. These reviews can be carried out by the organization's internal experts or independent specialists from outside the organization to provide technical assurance for the organization. Technology review and audit can be in the form of either internal or external assessment using automated vulnerability scanning tools and penetration testing.

The scanning and testing can be carried out either across the entire technical infrastructure or target specific risks or compliance requirements such as PCI-DSS. This type of assurance review and audit is mostly driven by compliance requirements and usually carried out annually. However, from a cyber resilience perspective organizations must not wait until the annual assessments dictated by compliance. Compliance-driven security is no longer sufficient in the dynamic evolving world of cyber-threats. To provide continual assurance there needs be the sort of continual compliance regime seen in other industry sectors.

Technology review should assess not only the controls but also the hardware and software being used. Some vulnerability may be introduced naturally as technologies come to the end of their life and are no longer supported by their vendors, with the result that patches and updates become unavailable.

Audit and review should also consider **digital obsolescence**, where information stored in legacy technology or media cannot be accessed. This presents a threat to integrity and availability and therefore poses a cyber resilience risk to organizations reliant on unsupported systems and software or archived historical data. Improvements should consider transferring the data to new media, updating legacy hardware and software or buying extended support and/or training in-house support personnel.

8.1.1.2 Control performance evaluation

Before an organization can look at how to improve, it is important for the organization to understand where it is in the continual improvement cycle: i.e. how well or poorly existing controls are performing. It is important to understand what needs to be improved, if anything. The performance evaluation, generated by an organization's audit and review process, would provide the answer.

Best practice

The audit and review process should not be limited to just technical controls but also include the physical, procedural and managerial controls and the supporting cyber resilience policies, standards, procedures and processes.

For the purposes of cyber resilience, performance evaluation would fall into the Check-Act phase of the Deming PDCA continuous improvement model and steps 5, 6 and 7 of the continual service improvement (CSI) seven-step improvement process model (see sections 8.2.1 and 8.2.3 for further detail on these). The 'check' is where the effectiveness of the controls is audited and reviewed, The objective is to assess the controls to see if they are performing as they were designed to. If they are, then they do not need to be changed. However, if they are found to be ineffective or not as optimal as they were perceived to be then the audit and review provide an opportunity to fix or improve them.

To be able to evaluate the performance of the controls, an organization needs to be able to monitor and benchmark them against its control objectives or best practice. A good framework for auditing is using a checklist of compliance against the set of controls provided by the ISO/IEC 27001 standard. Whilst ISO/IEC 27001 takes a systemic approach to managing information security, it can still be used as a guide even if an organization does not have a fully compliant information security management system (ISMS). However, it should be noted that it is not a panacea for security protection: an organization should build its own auditing tools based on the business, organization and risk context, but ISO/IEC 27001 is a good starting point.

8.1.2 Control assessment

The technical control performance assessment includes reviewing the configuration of an organization's infrastructure, software and hardware builds as well as penetration testing of systems and networks using external experts such as ethical hackers. This will test the effectiveness of the organization's technical controls such as firewall rules against the firewall policy. It will also compare the controls to best-practice configuration and application security, and identify any new vulnerabilities that have been re-introduced through uncontrolled changes. For example, if the change management process has not been adhered to or is non-existent, changes to the operation environment won't have been documented or tested for effectiveness. For an application security review this could be specialized code reviews using one of the many automated tools based on best practice such as the OWASP (open web application security project) framework or vendor-specific tools based on vendors' secure coding standards.

A more regular form of continual improvement can be implemented through automated vulnerability scans. A good example of this is the PCI-DSS quarterly scans required of merchants that process or store credit cardholder data. Vulnerability scans can find missing system and application patches and provide a generic vulnerability and/or risk score against lists of common vulnerabilities – an organization will still have to contextualize the risk to its technical and business environment.

In terms of the assessment of non-technical controls, these can be manually tested through a combination of procedural review and testing. Physical security of secure locations can be evaluated using measures such as:

● Site security assessments
● Walk-through checks
● Review of site logs and procedures
● CCTV footage
● Attempts at accessing the site to test physical security controls.

8.1.3 Key performance indicators, key risk indicators and benchmarking

Security metrics such as key performance indicators (KPIs) can be used to assess how well controls are performing. If these have already been set in the design phase, they can be assessed as part of the audit and review.

Hints and tips
Tie the KPIs to control objectives and the benefits to be derived. Set these at the beginning in the 'plan' phase of the PDCA model, and as improvements are made fine-tune these KPIs or add new KPIs at the next iteration of the cycle.

During this review process, management should consider other findings, including historical evidence of vulnerability. This can be collated from incident reports, security metrics (KPIs and key risk indicators) internal and external audits, input from non-conformity reports from ISO/IEC 27001, or from other compliance audits. Input from real incidents and reports helps to ensure that the findings and improvements to be made reflect real risks and are not purely subjective; this will help to secure funding and balance the costs of improvements against the benefits to be achieved. If there has been under- or over-performance against KPIs for instance, management should consider whether the KPI metrics were set to high or too low.

In such cases it may be necessary to redefine or refine the KPIs for the next iteration of the improvement cycle.

Cyber resilience incidents provide a good opportunity for setting KPIs for measuring maturity. Some examples of KPIs to measure incident management are provided in Tables 8.1 and 8.2. An organization can produce its own measures and modify them as the organization's cyber resilience matures.

Table 8.1 KPIs can be constructed around incidents and subcategories

Number of cyber resilience incidents logged
Number of incidents per priority, impact, urgency
Number of incidents per type and category (e.g. user error, phishing, information loss, hacks, DDoS etc.)
Number of incidents per asset
Number of incidents per service
Number of incidents per business/organizational area
Number of internal vs external incidents (supply chain incidents)
Number of incidents reported by internal users

Table 8.2 KPIs can measure how well an organization has responded to incidents

Average time to discover an incident
Time taken to triage (initial assessment)
Number of known problems (recurrence)
Number of cases in each priority (1, 2, 3, 4)
Number of incidents that required activation of a cyber resilience response team vs those dealt by with by the business-as-usual team
Number of incidents that required escalation to senior management
Number of incidents that resulted in service outages
Number of incidents that breached SLA targets
Number of incidents that involved disclosure of personal information

Whilst KPIs measure control performance and maturity, key risk indicators (KRIs) point to potential risk areas. As an organization's risk management activities mature, it should be possible to set KRIs to forecast risks and be able to deal with them before they become incidents or issues. An example of a risk indicator could be the continual or increasing number of incidents against an asset. This could indicate that either the asset is not sufficiently protected or it is a particular target of a threat.

Key message

Assess KPIs to identify that the controls are working effectively; refine or even redefine KPIs as required.

KRIs can be used to point to potential risks.

Furthermore, KPIs and KRIs can be used together to complement one another. If KPIs are being met then KRIs should reduce. Equally, KRIs may point to deficiencies or areas for improvement. KPIs can be designed to measure those risk areas.

8.1.3.1 What should be audited?

The audit and review should include all areas of the control objectives, concentrating on the areas of risks from previous audits, incidents etc. The following sections (8.1.3.2 to 8.1.3.5) provide some examples of areas that are perceived to be the most effective for cyber resilience improvement.

8.1.3.2 Policy review

Any audit and review should ensure that compliance with the policies is included. The continual improvement review will validate the effectiveness of controls to ensure that they still meet the objectives set out in the cyber resilience policy, and conversely that the policy is still relevant to the risks being faced by the organization. The policy should reflect the control objectives to manage the risks. The policies over time can also become misaligned with the risks being faced and therefore should be reviewed and realigned with the business objectives and risk if necessary. An example of where a policy may become misaligned is where changes in regulatory or contractual requirements occur. Changes in the policy should automatically trigger a review of the policy framework, including the low-level technical standards and processes.

Key risk indicators can point to future risks

8.1.3.3 Review of access rights

One of the most important areas of control, and one that has the most return on investment, is the review of access rights. Access control is the primary means of stopping intruders and allowing the right people access to the appropriate areas. Access rights are planned in the design phase and when developing or acquiring systems, through authorizing access by information owners in operation. These access rights should be designed with the principles of '**least privilege**' and '**need to know**' to allow employees the minimum access rights required to carry out their duties and only allow access to the information they require. Situations and circumstances change over time (roles alter, people change jobs, people get promoted or demoted) and employees' access rights should also be updated accordingly.

HR policy should include a process for keeping the users' roles and their access rights up to date. This is usually managed by HR through the **joiners, movers and leavers** (JML) process. When roles change, access rights should be re-evaluated and amended accordingly based on the new roles and the access required. However, this rarely happens; even if it does happen, it rarely does so successfully. There is invariably a break in this process, and many organizations do not have the people or the end-to-end controls in place for an effective JML process. Any misaligned access rights to roles would indicate failure in the JML process and the need to review and improve the JML.

Best practice

Review access rights frequently: quarterly and annually. Have the asset owners certify access rights to their assets on an annual basis at the minimum.

If a JML process does not currently exist, implement one by working closely with the HR department. If a JML process is in place, check that it is functioning effectively. It should be an end-to-end process.

Organizations with poor or ineffective JML processes will have access control issues. As people change jobs within an organization, they often amass access rights that are not appropriate to their roles. Their access rights can snowball and have undesired consequences if the access is abused or misused. By not monitoring JML, it is possible that an organization may have more accounts than people, or dormant accounts that use up licences or are open to abuse by others. This is especially risky for privileged accounts. The audit and review should include review of all access rights to an organization's systems, buildings and information. At the minimum, all privileged access must be reviewed and accounted for. Any failing process that has led to **account sprawl**, elevated privileges and dormant accounts must be improved. Manual access control is resource intensive and burdensome for organizations; however, automation and profiling improves this in some way. **Role-based access control (RBAC)** and single sign-on are the other ways to improve the administration overhead.

The access tied to user roles is known as RBAC and can be used to improve and automate user access administration in an automated access control system, as access can be automated using policy rules. Access is granted or revoked dynamically based on predefined roles. A well-designed RBAC system can remove a lot of overheads associated with access management (see Figure 8.3 for an example of an RBAC system).

Single sign-on (SSO) removes the burden of administration and credential management from users by allowing access to many systems using a single credential. This is a complex topic and cannot be covered in detail here.

8.1.3.4 Review of administrator and operator logs

Administrators have privileged access to systems by virtue of their roles. As these are powerful roles, their misuse can cause enormous damage to organizations. Administrator logs should be reviewed for suspicious activities so that abuse of access rights can be identified. Review user activity logs regularly, especially administrator activity. The following should be logged and reviewed on a regular basis:

- Logon accounts or user IDs
- Successful and unsuccessful logons

- Date and time of activity
- IP addresses of source computers
- IP address of destination networks.

Some high-security and regulated organizations will require all activities to be logged and retained for a certain time to aid retrospective investigation. An organization may need to make an informed and balanced decision based on its business requirements and the risk it needs to manage in order to decide on how much logging needs to be done. If a large number of events are logged, it will be difficult to keep up with logs or review them often and in real time. Improvements may include implementation of automated log filtering and parsing technology. Many organizations use security information and event management (SIEM) tools, which can monitor and report in real time, correlate activities, filter and spot anomalies based on configured policies and provide analysis on retained logs.

Logs should be kept separately and secured so that staff whose activity is being monitored do not have access to the logs. The logs should be stored on a centralized server with strict access control and access permitted only for those who need to review the logs. In some environments the integrity of these logs may be further protected by using message digests, or by writing the logs to read-only media.

8.1.3.5 Monitor, review and audit of third parties and suppliers

An audit and review process should also review the supply chain to ensure that it is intact and stable, and that risks have not been introduced. Audits should be extended to the key suppliers and their sub-contractors. Larger organizations with long supply chains may consider risk-based audits. The findings of the audit should be used to improve supply chain resilience through review and enforcement of contracts.

Target, a large US retailer, was allegedly hacked through one of its smaller suppliers, compromising some 40 million customer credit cards, leading to tremendous adverse publicity, reputational damage, the threat of legal action and loss of market value. Cyber-criminals are increasingly turning their attention to smaller suppliers in order to compromise their ultimate targets. A supply chain is as strong as the weakest link in the chain; many organizations have been hacked through their suppliers' systems which are connected to their system or have had their information compromised by their suppliers.

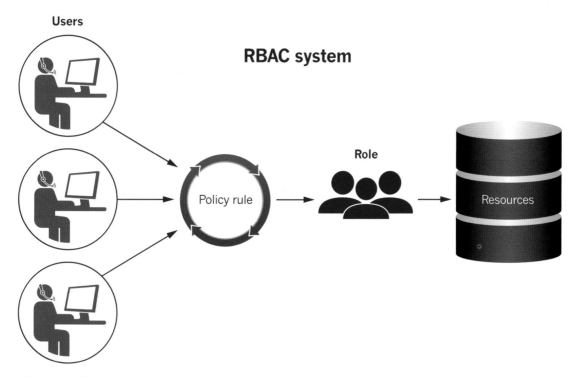

Figure 8.3 Role-based access control (RBAC) reflects a user's role and duties

Key message

The cost of the attack on the retailer Target in 2013:

- 40 million credit card numbers affected
- $350 million costs
- 46% drop in profit (4th quarter)
- 1–3 million cards sold on black market
- Resignation of CEO.

Many organizations falsely believe that by outsourcing they have also relinquished their responsibility and accountability to their suppliers: this is not the case, and many are living with unquantified risks. Having assessed suppliers and selected them as partners, an organization must continue to ensure that it manages the risk from suppliers through ongoing audits and spot checks. To be effective an organization must understand its supply chain and the risk of each supplier to the organization's cyber resilience. Security requirements should be included in the contract with the supplier, and also the right to audit and spot check them. For large supply chains, there needs to be an agreed audit plan and a schedule of audits, which must include the critical suppliers. An organization should not rely on the assurance of the supplier but also assess the cyber resilience of their sub-contractors where possible. Often primary suppliers use smaller suppliers to service contracts. These smaller suppliers may not be as resilient themselves, or they may have weaknesses in their security controls that could compromise an organization's cyber resilience.

Review the contracts that suppliers have with their sub-contractors to ensure security requirements flow down the supply chain. Ensure that the primary supplier is not taking undue risks and is also continually assessing its risks from its own supply chain, including reporting incidents and breaches. Spot checks should be used to ensure that assumptions are correct.

Key message

Do not rely on the contracts. Ensure that suppliers understand the security requirements and comply with them. Audit the supply chain. Be aware of the weakest point in the supply chain and ensure that it is strengthened. Ensure the supplier is also managing the risk from their supply chain.

Trust but verify!

8.1.4 Business continuity improvements

Many organizations have business continuity plans but have never tested them, and their plans are often out of date. This presents a major risk to the organizations. They may be making certain assumptions or may not be aware of changed risks. Untested plans are likely to fail because, when it comes to an actual event and these plans need to be activated, organizations may find that the information they depend on is out of date, response team members or suppliers they were relying on for recovery do not exist or their contact details have changed and they cannot be contacted.

IT service continuity management (ITSCM) provides not only a way to manage IT disaster recovery but also includes service continuity and recovery planning, taking into account the other organizational business continuity requirements and planning efforts.

Continual improvement should involve regular monitoring and reporting from the supply chain, through security reporting, attending security working groups, information security and business resilience forums. Plans and contact details should be kept up to date and business impact analyses should be reviewed to ensure that they are still correct and include current products and services so that new critical business systems and processes are not left out. Build resilience controls into projects and programmes, with the end goal of cyber resilience as the outcome.

Key message

Test business resilience plans at least annually. Include critical business processes and critical suppliers in the test.

Keep plans up to date and ensure that key suppliers are doing the same.

Test continuity plans regularly, in the form of desktop or table-top exercises, and include suppliers in business resilience planning and testing. Scenarios should be used based on risk assessments. Each scenario should be tested in rotation, if not at once. As a minimum, carry out a real test once a year. The results of the tests should be fed back into the ITSCM and business resilience planning to drive further improvements.

If complete plans cannot be tested, start with the most critical ones first. These are the business processes that keep an organization in business – usually the money-making ones if it is a commercial organization, and critical-service-supporting ones if it is in the public sector. Progressively complete a full cycle of the business resilience plan.

Hints and tips

If it is difficult to test a complete resilience plan in one go, test parts of it at a time. Start with the most critical business-sustaining processes in the resilience plan.

Use the outcome of the tests to fine-tune plans. Lessons learned should drive improvement in response and recovery times. Setting KPIs here may help to measure how well an organization is performing.

8.1.4.1 Learning from information security incidents

Throughout the cyber resilience lifecycle there will be plenty of opportunities for improvement of controls. Cyber resilience incidents usually occur as a result of missing or ineffective controls. The post-incident analysis or review phase of the incident management process should provide an opportunity for improvements to be made after incidents. Every incident should be seen as an opportunity for improvement and a chance to reduce the likelihood of recurrence.

Every incident should be reviewed, including both near misses and actual breaches, with a view to learning and improving controls. The post-incident review should include root cause analysis to understand why the incident occurred in the first place. Root cause analysis is significant because if the root cause can be fixed, it will stop the incident recurring. Once the cause of the incident has been identified, action can be taken to prevent it recurring. Even if a review cannot prevent it from recurring, a review can at least still help to improve other areas of incident management, such as the processes for monitoring and early identification, responding to incidents, logging, reporting and communication. Any new training requirement for the response team and general staff can also be identified. For example, if an incident involving a virus outbreak was not spotted and reported within the time required in the incident management process, and as a consequence the recovery time was delayed due to the spread of the virus impacting the service level agreement, the post-incident review could help to identify the need to update the anti-virus policy and related software and train staff to report infections sooner. It could also help to identify recurring incidents that need to be managed within the ITIL problem management process (rather than the incident management process).

Key message

- To learn lessons from incidents, ensure that all cyber-incidents are considered for post-incident review or a lessons-learned exercise. Use this to improve cyber resilience, to prevent recurrence, and to update policies, processes and training of staff and the incident response team.
- Do not wait for the annual audit and review to improve.
- Include and integrate the incident management process with supplier's processes; ensure that they are reporting incidents in a timely manner.

8.1.4.2 Training and awareness

Improvement should not be limited to just the technical and physical elements of the cyber resilience armour. Improvements will naturally include changes to technology, policies, processes, working practices, roles and responsibilities of employees. Staff will need to be aligned with the improved ways of working: employees' skills should be reviewed to ensure that people can manage the improvements, and where required appropriate training should be provided.

Hints and tips

Continually assess training needs, especially after incidents and breaches or major changes to security polices and processes.

Identify interesting and innovative ways of delivering the training.

Test staff's understanding of policies and processes using tests, quizzes and surveys.

Refresh training: make training topical – use recent news items or breaches to illustrate the points.

Serious gaming is a new concept in cyber resilience training

At the minimum staff should be provided with induction training, which should include training in cyber resilience policies, standards and processes supplemented by annual cyber resilience refresher training. Improved training could be tailored to an organization's risks and culture.

For the training to remain interesting and more importantly effective, it should be relevant, topical and engaging. This is why there should be a continual improvement process for reviewing and updating cyber resilience training. Use historical incidents to build scenario-based training: perhaps the outcome of a post-incident review of a real incident. Consider current training and communication methods and identify new, innovative and durable delivery methods such as gamification, role playing and scenario-based training on the changing risk landscape.

Threat and vulnerability assessments

Threats change and new vulnerabilities are discovered all the time. Organizations should understand the threats they face and their vulnerabilities that can be exploited by those threats. Threats and vulnerabilities are fed into risk assessments; however, there should be continual assessment of threats and vulnerabilities so that organizations are not caught out between risk assessments, as risk assessments are usually carried out annually and/or when there is a significant change. For example, if an organization is operating in a territory or sector that is particularly volatile, the threat in respect of that sector or territory must be assessed.

Hints and tips

Verizon's annual 'Data Breach Investigations Report' and the Ponemon Institute's 'Cost of Data Breach Study' are global security reports which are published annually and provide insights into threats and vulnerabilities by sector, along with the costs of breaches.

Governments also carry out their own threat assessments, which are usually made available to commercial organizations.

Carry out research or use the numerous reports and surveys that commercial and defence organizations commission and publish annually. Some are subscription-based and others are free. Review the threat reports when they are published, and feed the findings into risk assessments. Carry out a new risk assessment if the threat landscape changes, and improve controls. Do not wait for the annual risk assessment before assessing risks!

8.1.5 Process improvement

Processes are the bedrock of an organization's cyber resilience toolbox: policies without processes invariably fail. As polices are high-level principles which set out management intentions and objectives, they are usually not too prescriptive – they set out why something should be done but not how. This is why supporting processes are needed to support the policies.

For example, an organization may have a cybersecurity incident management policy, which states why it should manage incidents, what should be managed and even perhaps who should manage it. However, without a supporting incident management process explaining how, what and when, it is highly likely to fail, not be repeatable, not be consistent etc.

Key message

Ensure that policies are supported by processes. Review and improve processes, especially the business-critical and business resilience processes, and those that manage the risks to the operational environment.

Change management is another good example of a process that is essential to managing risks. In cyber resilience, risks to an operational IT infrastructure are managed through controlled changes. This requires a fit-for-purpose change management process. Without this, changes would be ad hoc and uncontrolled leading to disruption to services, the introduction of vulnerabilities, and the exposure of confidentiality, integrity and availability to risk. If a review finds that operational environments have changed and that changes are not documented, this could indicate an ineffective change control process; in this case it would be important to consider reviewing and improving the change management process.

In fact, when policies change or new ways of working are introduced, the supporting processes should also be reviewed and updated. An organization's audit and review should incorporate an assessment of supporting processes with a view to enhancing and improving them. At the minimum, the critical business processes should be included in any review.

8.1.6 Remediation and improvement planning

The findings of the audit should be presented to senior management so that they can review all findings with the relevant experts, agree on improvements and direct the relevant teams to take action.

The findings of the audit and review should be recorded in a suitable manner for the target audience. For presentation to senior management, it is best expressed in a non-technical manner or framed in business language. Findings could be presented in the form of a risk report or a register such as the CSI register in service improvement. In information security, this may be known as a corrective action plan or a remediation plan.

Hints and tips

Although we are slightly conflating the two here, it should be noted that an audit finding is usually an issue and not a risk, and therefore it needs immediate corrective action or improvement. On the other hand a risk is an exposure to a threat, with a likelihood of becoming an issue. A risk allows time for management to make risk decisions to assess the best course of action to mitigate the risk before it becomes an issue.

Risk and issues are different – issues may be risks that have already crystallized. What it is called is not important here: the emphasis is on the clear communication of content and the actions to be taken.

8.1.6.1 The remediation plan

The remediation plan should at the minimum list:

- The issue number
- The issue that has been identified
- A description of the issue
- Recommendation of action to be taken
- The action owner
- The date for completion
- The current status.

Table 8.3 shows a typical remediation plan, where some columns have been removed for the sake of brevity. As the remediation progresses, additional columns may be added to document these. Residual or remaining risks could then be included in the risk register for management to review and make risk decisions.

Table 8.3 An example of a remediation or corrective action plan

Code	Issue title	Risk	CVSS score	Description	Affected hosts	Recommendations	Remediation	Owner	Status
BPG01	Missing Microsoft patches	M	H	Some critical security patches are missing. Patch.......	XX.XX. XX.XX	Apply patches asap	Patches applied as emergency change on 18/04/2014. See CR number CR324.2014	M U	Closed
BPG02	Load balancer flawed SSL	H	H	Load balancer 003, using old SSL version 2	xx.xx. xx.xx.	Patch load balancer, upgrade to SSL3.0 or TLS 1.0 or above	Load balancer forced to use SSL3 and TLS1.0. Support for older SSL disabled	SL	To be tested

8.1.6.2 Implementing improvements

This section covers how identified improvements should be implemented. This is the 'act' in the PDCA cycle.

Risk decision example

Although it is up to management to decide what improvements they will approve for implementation, some controls are too risky not to implement.

Management have finite resources, which they need to spend where there is most return. However, there are some good practices that do not require a formal risk assessment. For example, for an organization that has access to the internet and valuable assets to protect on its servers, it is too risky for it not to have a firewall or anti-malware protection. It is generally not an option for management to decide that it is too expensive to install a firewall. If they did decide to forgo a firewall, there would have to be an extremely strong justification.

Prior to the implementation of the remediation or improvements that have been identified during an organization's audit and review process, the senior management must review and approve implementation of the recommended controls. At this stage cost benefit analysis, economies of scale against identified risks and objectives should be re-assessed.

There should be clear justification for the improvement, and senior management should ask the following questions before making any decisions:

● Why are we making the improvement?
● How much will it cost?
● What benefits will we derive from it?
● How will we measure it?
● What will a successful change look like?
● How will we monitor progress?
● What resources will be required?
● Who will be responsible for the improvement?
● When will it be implemented?

A risk-based decision to make improvements must be taken because not all controls can be implemented at the same time, in one attempt or within the limited resource usually available for cyber resilience. There should be a short-term, medium-term and long-term improvement plan.

Senior management may decide that some improvements may not provide the return on investment (cost versus benefit) and therefore they should not be implemented. However, some simple enhancement or tweaking of existing controls may bring greater rewards, and they may opt for these as quick wins and decide that these should be implemented first.

The control that will provide the most improvement with the least cost and least impact to the business environment should be implemented first, but there is always a trade-off between what is wanted and what can be achieved.

By looking across the organization, management might notice a pattern that can be addressed by other controls or risk decisions. For example, senior management might modify their risk appetite or extend their tolerance of the risk or simply accept it. Some risks may not be remediable, and management will have to make decisions as how to manage those risks.

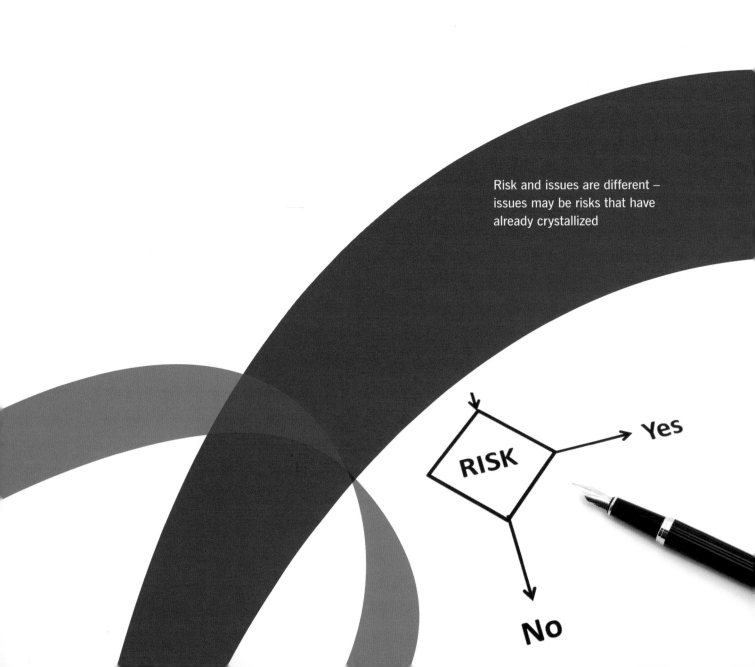

Risk and issues are different – issues may be risks that have already crystallized

RISK

Yes

NO

8.2 ALIGNING CYBER RESILIENCE CONTINUAL IMPROVEMENT WITH IT CONTINUAL SERVICE IMPROVEMENT

IT continual service improvement considers how a service provider can create and maintain value for its customers by continually improving IT services, and all aspects of the IT service management system that supports these IT services. For instance:

● Improving services might include providing increased capacity or availability, or providing additional features with a new release.

● Improving IT service management might include improving the ability to respond to user requests or correct problems.

The objectives of continual improvement are to continually:

● Align IT services with evolving business needs by identifying and implementing improvements to IT services that support business processes.

● Improve the quality of IT services, and the customer experience of these services.

● Improve all aspects of each stage of the IT service management lifecycle: strategy, design, transition, operation and continual improvement.

● Improve the efficiency, effectiveness and **cost effectiveness** of IT service management processes.

● Improve the knowledge and competence of people in the IT organization.

These objectives are not alternatives: they are all part of the same thing. Each one of these contributes to the ability to achieve the others. For example, improved knowledge may result in improved effectiveness of a process, or improved alignment of a service with business needs might result in improved customer experience.

The techniques that can be used to achieve this continual improvement are described throughout this section, but in summary they include:

● Monitoring and measuring the things that matter

● Analysing data and information to develop knowledge and wisdom

● Providing opportunities for reflection and feedback

● Identifying, prioritizing, selecting and managing opportunities for improvement.

There is a common misunderstanding that ITIL continual service improvement is only about improving processes, with an internal focus on how IT works. This could not be further from the truth. Figure 8.4 shows some of the things that continual improvement should be considering. As Figure 8.4 makes clear, the scope of continual improvement should include not only IT services and the ITSM processes, but also relationships with customers, the overall service portfolio, the skills and competence of the people, the design of the organization, contracts and relationships with suppliers, and the tools and technology that support all of these.

ITIL Continual Service Improvement describes many useful techniques and also includes one process – the seven-step improvement process (see section 8.2.3). This process is just as relevant to cyber resilience as it is to IT service management. Organizations that use ITIL as a basis for their IT service management system can integrate cyber resilience continual improvement into their continual service improvement. Organizations that are not using ITIL to manage their IT services may find it helpful to adopt the seven-step improvement process to support their continual improvement of cyber resilience.

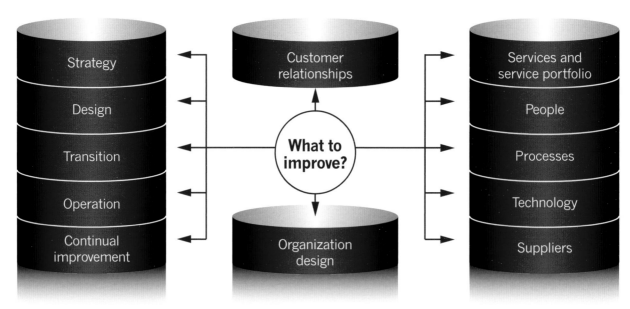

Figure 8.4 What to improve?

8.2.1 Plan-Do-Check-Act

One approach to managing and improving services is named after its four stages Plan-Do-Check-Act (PDCA). This simple lifecycle is recommended as a management system approach in ISO/IEC 20000, as well as in ITIL and many other sources of best practice. PDCA is sometimes called the **Deming Cycle** after W. Edwards Deming who proposed this model (see Figure 8.5).

PDCA is a continual lifecycle approach, with each Plan-Do-Check-Act cycle leading to some improvement and being followed by another PDCA cycle. PDCA can be applied to a small project, to the entire management system used within a large organization, or to any other situation where delivery of a high-quality outcome is required. It can be used as a framework for implementing or improving cyber resilience, as well as for implementing or improving IT service management.

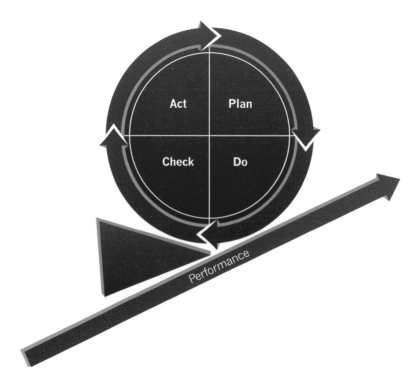

Figure 8.5 Plan-Do-Check-Act

The four stages of PDCA can be summarized as:

- **Plan** Establish objectives and processes needed to deliver results that meet customer requirements and the organization's policies. For a project this will result in a project plan; for a management system this may result in a number of plans for different aspects; for continual improvement this may be a single improvement plan or a set of related improvement plans.

- **Do** Implement the processes or project established in the plan. This is the stage where most of the work and investment are required.

- **Check** Monitor progress, measure results and compare actual outcomes with objectives and expected outcomes.

- **Act** Take action based on the results of the check, to improve performance of the process, project, management system or improvement plan.

After 'act' there is usually a period of consolidation, to embed the new behaviour into the culture of the organization and ensure that improvements are not lost. This is represented by the wedge in Figure 8.5. The four stages of PDCA are shown as a wheel or cycle because of the need for continual improvement. Each period of consolidation is followed by another PDCA cycle to ensure that the performance of the organization continues to improve.

An example of Plan-Do-Check-Act

An organization decides to improve how it identifies and authenticates users logging in to its IT systems. They have heard of another organization that had a failure of a similar project because the people who implemented it only considered the technology. They use PDCA to ensure that their project delivers value:

- **Plan** They establish the project requirements, review tools and processes in use at other organizations, select a preferred solution, document a business case and get business approval to proceed. The business case includes measurable benefits that they expect to achieve. They then create detailed plans to implement the new single sign-on process and tool. These plans include technology implementation; training for users, for the service desk and for **technical support** teams; and KPIs and reporting to monitor the effectiveness of the new solution.

- **Do** They implement the new single sign-on technology that they have chosen. This includes procuring and installing a vendor-supplied solution, integrating this with their existing services, training technical support teams in how the new solution works, training the service desk in how to support the users, and training users in how to use the new process and tool. The tool is deployed in a pilot and improvements are made to the process before it is deployed to the rest of the staff.

- **Check** They review the project achievements against the measurable benefits in the business case. They also review the cost and time of the overall project, and identify a number of areas where things could have been done better.

- **Act** Improvement recommendations for the project management process are added to a risk register for evaluation by the risk manager. Suggested improvements to the new single sign-on service are added to the CSI register (see section 8.2.2).

- **Consolidation** New people joining the organization are trained in the new single sign-on process. Service desk staff regularly review and update a document and a video that are available on the in-house knowledge system to assist users. Incidents relating to the new single sign-on are reviewed every month to see if there are further lessons to learn. Regular reports are reviewed to ensure that the solution continues to deliver the expected value.

8.2.2 The CSI register

ITIL Continual Service Improvement describes a CSI register, which is used to record and manage improvement opportunities. By recording all improvement opportunities in one place the organization is able to compare and prioritize them, so that limited funds and resources are invested in the most appropriate way. Table 8.4 shows an example of a simple CSI register.

Table 8.4 Example of a simple CSI register

ID	Description	Benefits	Urgency	Time	Cost	Owner	Date submitted	Status	Percent complete
CSI001	Install card key access system for computer room doors	Prevent unauthorized access to computers. Reduce chances of someone installing a key-logger or stealing a disk drive	Medium. We currently have a security guard stationed at the computer room door 24 hours a day, but this is expensive	3 months	Medium	J Brown	02-Oct-2014	Approved	0%
CSI002	Install anti-virus software on all Windows servers	Reduce the risk of malware being installed on a server	High. We have already had one incident due to an administrator reading email on a server	6 months	Medium	R Jones	14-Nov-2014	Under review	0%
CSI003	Update firmware on all firewalls	Prevent known remote attack, which could compromise all firewalls	High. This vulnerability has been widely published	3 days	Low	C Smith	16-Nov-2014	Complete	100%
CSI004	Deliver updated security awareness training to all staff	Increase understanding of cyber resilience, increase compliance to controls and reduce incidents	Medium. Most staff have completed the previous awareness training, but this version has many new features	1 year	Low	J Tree	17-Nov-2014	Ongoing	15%
CSI005	Insource all external-facing web servers	Remove the risk from third parties managing critical resources	Low. There have been no incidents	6 months	High	L James	21-Nov-2014	Rejected	0%

The entry in the CSI register for each improvement opportunity will typically include information about:

● Cost or resources required to design and implement the improvement. It is usually sufficient to use a simple small/medium/large category. Eventually there may be a need for a detailed plan, but that plan would not appear in the CSI register

● Time required to make the improvement. For the purpose of prioritization a simple scale of quick/medium-term/long-term may be sufficient

● Benefits that the improvement will create

● Urgency for implementing the improvement (typically based on when the business requires the expected benefits)

- People involved in the improvement (submitter, owner)
- Timestamps (when submitted, when planned for execution, when completed).

The CSI register can be used for a number of related purposes:

- To prioritize improvement opportunities, and select those that will be funded based on the resources they require, the benefits they will create, and the urgency with which they are needed
- To ensure that improvement ideas are not lost when an organization decides not to fund an improvement, since the suggestion may remain on the register for reconsideration at a more appropriate time
- To oversee improvements that have been selected for implementation to ensure that they are making progress
- To re-prioritize improvement opportunities whenever there is a relevant change, such as completion of an improvement project or a change in the needs of the business
- To provide data for reporting on the overall cost and benefit of continual improvement, which can be used to justify further investments in improvement and to identify opportunities to improve CSI itself.

The CSI register can be thought of as a subset of the risks and issues register, as each improvement opportunity is typically intended to address a risk or issue. An organization could create a CSI register for cyber resilience in addition to an existing CSI register for IT services. It would be unusual to combine these, as the scope of cyber resilience is usually much broader than the scope of IT service management. In some organizations each team maintains a CSI register, which includes opportunities that are within its own control. This could result in an entire hierarchy of CSI registers, with higher levels in the organization maintaining CSI registers for more significant improvements. In other organizations there is just one CSI register owned by a central quality management team. There is no simple one-size-fits-all solution to who should own the CSI register or how many an organization should have. Definition of how this is done should be considered as part of organization governance.

8.2.3 The seven-step improvement process

The seven-step improvement process is usually depicted as a cycle, as shown in Figure 8.6.

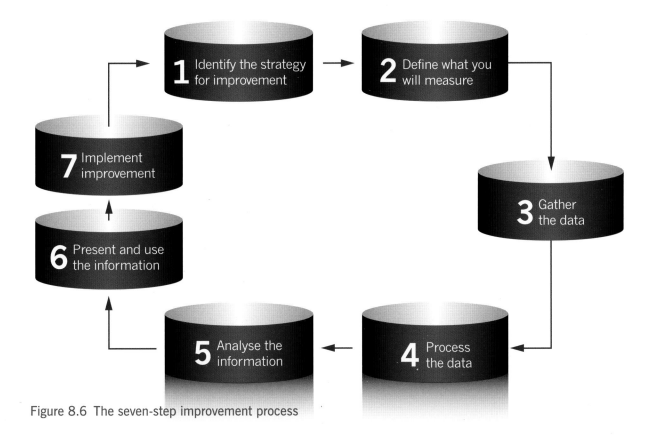

Figure 8.6 The seven-step improvement process

The seven-step improvement process collects and analyses data, which it uses to identify and then implement improvements that are needed. It can be used to analyse the performance and capabilities of services, processes, people, functions, suppliers or anything else involved in providing IT services to customers. Many of the steps in this process are about measurement and analysis, because it is only through measurement and analysis that we can really understand what is happening, and this understanding is needed to identify the improvements we need to make.

Every aspect of this seven-step improvement process applies just as much to cyber resilience as to IT service management and could usefully be adopted into a cyber resilience programme to help ensure an organization measures and improves all aspects of cyber resilience. However, it is unlikely that an organization would want to integrate a seven-step improvement process for ITSM with a similar process for cyber resilience, because the two areas have very different scope and management responsibility. On the other hand, teams responsible for each might well benefit from working together in those areas where common data collection and analysis make sense.

Although the seven-step improvement process is an excellent fit for managing continual improvement of cyber resilience, there will be small differences in focus and implementation when the process is to be used in a cyber resilience context. The following description of the seven-step improvement process includes some indication of these differences.

The steps of the seven-step improvement process are:

- **Step 1 – Identify the strategy for improvement** To plan and implement effective improvements it is important to understand the context. The first step of the process is therefore to understand the vision, mission, goals and objectives of the business, and the current and future business plans intended to deliver these. It is also important to understand how IT services contribute to the business, and how improvements in IT could contribute to improved business success.

Step 1: Cyber resilience focus and implementation…

Both an ITSM and a cyber resilience programme will need to identify the strategy for improvement, and in both cases the strategy will be based on understanding the business vision, mission, goals and objectives. The difference is that a cyber resilience programme will need to focus on how cyber resilience contributes to the business and how it could contribute to improved business success.

For example, a retailer may need improved integrity and availability of a customer-facing website to ensure that it supports the brand image which the business relies on; or a medical practice may need improved confidentiality of patient records to enable the organization to be certified to an external standard.

- **Step 2 – Define what will be measured** Start by identifying what should be measured, making sure to include measurement of services, processes, people, technology and suppliers. Then define what actually can be measured and create a **gap analysis**. Based on this, decide what to actually measure. Like all other steps of the seven-step improvement process this is an iterative activity: there should be regular checks to ensure that the right data is still being collected and analysed, and that effort is not being wasted collecting data that is not needed.

Step 2: Cyber resilience focus and implementation…

When defining what to measure for cyber resilience, an organization needs to be sure that it collects data to help it understand whether risk analysis has been carried out and suitable risk treatments have been selected. It must measure the effectiveness, efficiency and cost effectiveness of a wide range of controls to ensure that these provide the business value that is needed.

This requires many different types of measurement, including audits, reviews, data from tools and processes, financial data, customer satisfaction data and more. There may be some overlap of data collection with the ITSM seven-step improvement process, but much of this data will be specific to the needs of cyber resilience.

- **Step 3 – Gather the data** Where possible, data should be gathered using tools and automation, but some data can only be collected manually. Ideally the data collection requirements will be included in the design of services, processes and technology, so that the required data can be collected easily and efficiently.

Manual data collection

An IT organization wanted to understand how much time technical staff spent working on projects, and how much time was spent on operational activities.

To collect this data in a simple way, each staff member completed a spreadsheet showing how many hours they spent on each project. Whilst the data was not 100% accurate, it was sufficient to provide insights into the cost of each project, which resulted in an improvement to the way future projects were funded.

Step 3: Cyber resilience focus and implementation...

Because of the need for confidentiality, integrity and availability, there may be special considerations as to how some data is gathered for cyber resilience. For example, if an organization is collecting data about the effectiveness of anti-virus measures, it needs to be sure that a virus cannot tamper with the data; or if the data is about the effectiveness of anti-fraud controls then an organization needs to be sure that someone committing a fraud cannot delete the data. This is especially important where the data may include evidence of staff attempting to breach controls. The required levels of integrity and availability could be achieved by use of encrypted checksums and by storing data on read-only media.

The data may also need to be carefully protected to prevent breaches of confidentiality, as cyber resilience data may provide information that would be useful to an attacker or embarrassing to the organization if it were leaked. The controls required to protect the data depend on its sensitivity and the organization's attitude towards risk. In some organizations simple file protections may be sufficient; in others it may be necessary to encrypt the data, or to store it on a physically isolated server.

- **Step 4 – Process the data** In this step the data is converted into the right format for the intended audience. The data collected in Step 3 is converted into information, which has more value (see section 6.2.7 for an explanation of data, information, knowledge and wisdom). For example, metrics may be converted into KPIs and critical success factors (CSFs); information about end-to-end services may be created from data about individual activities. Spreadsheets and report-generating tools are often used during this step.

Step 4: Cyber resilience focus and implementation...

Cyber resilience will need to ensure that the information generated at this stage is robustly protected. Spreadsheets and reports containing data about the efficiency, effectiveness and cost effectiveness of cyber resilience are likely to be extremely confidential. Their exposure could facilitate a security breach, completely defeating the purpose for which we have cyber resilience in the first place.

Similarly, if the data may later be needed for forensic analysis or to support a prosecution then care must be taken to preserve the chain of evidence and protect the integrity of the collected data.

- **Step 5 – Analyse the information** Analysis of the data produces trends, and knowledge of what is good or bad about the things being measured. This enables an organization to understand whether goals are being met, and whether its services and processes are improving or getting worse. This knowledge of trends may allow an organization to intervene during subsequent steps to ensure that goals are met. For example, if the average time required to resolve incidents has consistently reduced over a period of time, this good trend suggests that improvements to the incident management process have been effective. Equally, if the number of high-priority incidents increases every time there is a new release of the customer relationship management (CRM) software, this bad trend suggests that there is a need to improve the service transition processes.

Step 5: Cyber resilience focus and implementation...

This step in the process is no different for cyber resilience than it is for IT service management. It is equally important to understand trends, and to interpret the information and data to identify both good and bad things that are happening.

● **Step 6 – Present and use the information** The knowledge can now be presented to management in a clear and helpful format, to help them make decisions. Often this will be in the form of a report with a management summary, graphs and charts to show data and trends, and clear recommendations based on the data. It is important to present the right level of detail to each specific audience, with a focus on how it will help to inform decisions. Audiences for the reports should include customers, senior IT management, internal IT staff, and suppliers. Reporting should not just be about issues and exceptions, but should also show what is working well, and what trends are improving. One of the best ways to get funding for continual improvement is to report the good results of previous improvement investments.

Step 6: Cyber resilience focus and implementation...

The audience for cyber resilience reports and presentations is likely to be very different from that for IT service management. Audiences for cyber resilience reports should include organizational governance officers (executive board), internal audit and risk management, and IT management. Some summary reporting may also be required for all staff or for suppliers.

● **Step 7 – Implement improvement** The knowledge that has been assembled in the earlier steps is combined with previous experience to help decide what improvements are needed. Many possible improvement opportunities may be identified, and these should be added to a CSI register so they can be prioritized, and decisions can be made about which improvements to invest in.

Step 7: Cyber resilience focus and implementation...

Cyber resilience should maintain its own CSI register. It is unlikely that an organization will want to combine this with the CSI register for IT services because the scope of cyber resilience is much wider than just IT services.

The seven-step process then loops back to the beginning, continuing to understand the business; to decide what to measure; to gather and process data; to analyse and present information; and to implement further improvements.

8.3 USING THE ITIL CSI APPROACH TO PLAN CYBER RESILIENCE IMPROVEMENTS

ITIL describes a continual service improvement approach for structuring IT service improvement projects, and this approach is summarized in Figure 8.7. This is quite different from the seven-step improvement process as it serves a different need:

● The seven-step improvement process is intended to run continually – measuring, processing, analysing and reporting so that improvements can be identified and implemented.

● The CSI approach is intended to structure a major improvement project. It typically has well-defined start and endpoints, and a specific scope and set of deliverables.

Every organization has some aspects of cyber resilience in place, and it is important to recognize this in a project to implement cyber resilience. It would be very rare for an organization to implement a completely new management system for cyber resilience: it is much more common to look for ways to improve the existing management system and controls.

8.3.1 The vision

Before starting to plan and implement cyber resilience it is important to understand the high-level vision, mission, goals and objectives of the project and of the organization as a whole. Cyber resilience should be designed to support and complement these, and that means that they must be fully understood and communicated to the project team.

It may be necessary to extend and supplement the vision of the organization to include aspects of cyber resilience, and this is something that should be discussed with the stakeholders at the very start of the project. It will also be necessary to establish a mission and vision for the cyber resilience project.

This essential step is often not taken at the beginning of major projects, resulting in a situation where different stakeholders have different ideas about why they are implementing a cyber resilience project. This can lead to many conflicts and differences later in the project when specific decisions must be made without real agreement on the outcomes that are needed.

The outcome of this first step should be clear and well-documented vision, mission, goals and objectives for the cyber resilience improvement project.

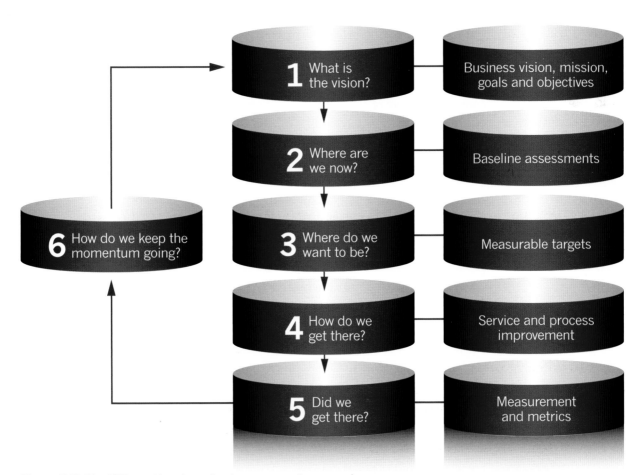

Figure 8.7 The ITIL continual service improvement approach

8.3.2 The current position

Every organization has some cyber resilience in place, and a project to implement cyber resilience needs to understand the current situation before it can begin to plan improvements. The cyber resilience project should define a journey from the current situation to a new improved situation, and this can only be done with a good understanding of the organization's current position.

This step usually involves carrying out some form of assessment. This assessment can be undertaken by external consultants or by in-house staff, depending on availability of skills. It is often a good idea for the assessment to be conducted by someone independent of the group(s) being assessed, as it can be hard to identify issues. An assessment carried out at this stage of an improvement project is called a 'baseline assessment' because it provides a baseline against which we can measure future improvements.

The scope of the assessment needs to be defined in terms of which business units and other assets should be included. It is also important to decide what assessment criteria to use. For example, an organization could carry out an assessment against the requirements of ISO/IEC 27001 or the NIST cybersecurity framework.

When planning the assessment, an organization should agree what output it needs. The assessment output could include:

- A gap analysis comparing controls to a standard list such as ISO/IEC 27002:2013
- A process assessment, identifying good and poor practice for a range of processes
- A maturity assessment, including process maturity, organizational maturity etc. (see section 8.5 for more information on maturity models)
- Outcome metrics, showing achievements against current goals. For example, number and severity of security incidents logged, percentage of staff who have completed security awareness training, number of applications with known security weaknesses.

8.3.3 The desired position

The vision that was identified in section 8.3.1 may take a long time to achieve. At this point in the project an organization should define measurable success criteria for the next stage of the project. This will typically include specific improvements that will be made, the outcomes expected as a result of those improvements, and the date by which each improvement will be complete. It could also include targets for results of a future assessment, such as a maturity target, a set of controls that should be in place, or a set of KPI targets that should be achieved.

It is important that the success criteria defined in this stage are **SMART** – specific, measurable, achievable, relevant and time-based (see Table 8.5). This ensures that they can be used later in the project to answer the question 'Did we get there?'

Table 8.5 Why do success criteria need to be SMART?

Specific	So that people will agree what the criteria mean
Measurable	So that people can provide evidence that they have met the criteria
Achievable	Otherwise, nothing people do will enable them to meet the criteria
Relevant	So that achieving the criteria means people have moved towards their real goals
Time-based	So that people cannot keep claiming that the criteria will be met soon

8.3.4 How to get to the desired position

At this point a detailed plan for one or more improvements is created. In an Agile environment this means actually running the first sprint; in a more traditional environment, it would be appropriate to create and execute a plan to deliver the SMART results identified in the previous activity.

Using an Agile approach to implement CSI

Many organizations use an Agile approach to implement continual service improvement. Agile and CSI fit together very well, as the Agile approach can result in rapid iterative improvements.

Agile is a way of managing IT development teams and projects, based on an 'Agile manifesto'. It commonly uses a methodology called 'scrum', which is a framework for completing complex projects. These projects include:

- A product backlog, which is a prioritized list of possible things to develop
- A series of 'sprints', which are short, timed activities each of which develops one item from the backlog
- A review or retrospective at the end of each sprint.

For these organizations, the first sprint would be defined at the 'Where do we want to be?' stage.

It is very important that every improvement is designed and implemented in a way that embeds it into the organization. Improving cyber resilience is not just about creating and deploying technical controls: it is about getting the right balance of people, process and technology to achieve cyber resilience needs. The best technical controls will have very little effect if people do not make proper use of them. This means that every planned cyber resilience improvement, however small, must include an understanding of how people are going to interact with the assets, and it must incorporate aspects of organizational change management as part of the plan.

8.3.5 The results

Regular progress meetings should be conducted to ensure that each cyber resilience improvement is making progress. This could involve daily scrum meetings for an Agile implementation or weekly project meetings for a more traditional approach.

As each improvement is completed, the agreed SMART targets should be measured to ensure that it has delivered the expected results, and the CSI register updated to show the new status.

After completing each improvement, it is important to carry out a review to see what lessons can be learned to help with future cyber resilience improvement projects. For an Agile approach this is where the retrospective takes place.

8.3.6 How to keep the momentum going

There are two aspects to keeping the momentum going.

Firstly, ensure that improvements have been embedded into the organization, as described in the PDCA model in section 8.2.1. For example, update any ongoing measurements and reports to ensure that new controls are included in regular monitoring of cyber resilience, and update any regular audit activity to include an audit of the new controls.

Secondly, monitor and report progress on the overall cyber resilience project. The SMART targets that were defined in section 8.3.3 can be used to demonstrate the improvements that have been achieved so far, so that management continues to support the ongoing improvement of cyber resilience. Keep monitoring for changes in the threat environment, the business environment and the technology environment, to ensure that the overall cyber resilience programme remains relevant.

8.4 USING MSP TO PLAN AND MANAGE CYBER RESILIENCE IMPROVEMENTS

Managing Successful Programmes (MSP®) is a best-practice approach for achieving successful outcomes from transformational change. It describes how to:

- Create a vision and blueprint for transformational change
- Design a programme to deliver the blueprint
- Identify the right outcomes and benefits, and plan for their delivery
- Deliver on time and on budget
- Break down initiatives into clearly defined projects and offer a framework for handling them
- Define responsibilities and lines of communication
- Involve interested stakeholders
- Manage risk and ensure that the programme responds to change
- Audit and maintain quality.

The MSP vision sets out the future state, the blueprint describes the elements of the future state and drives a coherent solution, and the programme plan creates projects to deliver outputs that move the organization towards the future state.

A programme is able to respond mid-delivery to changing external factors in a way that a single monolithic project is rarely able to achieve, which for the changing world of cyber resilience is a valuable attribute. This also benefits organizations, as it prevents a mindset that cyber resilience is 'done' when the project is closed.

Typically, a programme comprises a number of discrete projects with less-complex deliverables, smaller project budgets and consequently lower levels of project risk. The cancellation or failure of a single project within a programme is unlikely to place the whole programme at significant risk.

As an example of using MSP concepts for a cyber resilience programme:

- The vision of the future state could be that the organization delivers cyber resilience to a standard acceptable to the board.
- A highly simplified cyber resilience blueprint, detailing the elements that will deliver the vision for an organization, might be:
  - We will identify and classify all data we hold.
  - We will apply suitable processes to satisfy the organizational control areas of ISO/IEC 27002:2013.
  - IT systems will be technically secured to relevant standards.
  - Staff will be trained and resourced to contribute to cyber resilience.
- A gap analysis will determine the current state and desired future state.
- The programme plan might create a number of discrete projects to move towards the state described by this blueprint. There may be few or many projects identified, depending on the outcome of the gap analysis exercise.
- Should the organization's vision change (for example as a result of a decision to outsource IT), the cyber resilience blueprint would be reviewed. Projects within the programme can then be re-assessed for their continued viability without jeopardizing the viability of the overall programme. Some projects may be cancelled, some may continue to completion, and new projects may be created to respond to the changing business needs.

A link to more information about MSP can be found in the 'Further research' section of this publication.

8.5 MATURITY MODELS

Maturity models can be used to help assess and define the status of cyber resilience within an organization. They can be particularly useful when trying to define a target state for the 'Where do we want to be?' stage of the CSI approach described in section 8.3.

An assessment against a maturity model will not give a detailed gap analysis, but it can be very helpful to give a high-level summary of current status or target requirements.

Two maturity models that should be considered when planning a cyber resilience project are the ITIL process maturity framework and the NIST cybersecurity framework. The NIST cybersecurity framework says that its tiers 'do not represent **maturity level**s', but they can be used in a very similar way, as described in section 8.5.2.

Other sections have already shown how ITIL can be used as a best-practice approach for implementation of cyber resilience. The NIST cybersecurity framework can also be used to help define the current state and desired future state, and to create a detailed gap analysis. Organizations in the UK may also wish to consider using HMG Information Assurance Maturity Model (IAMM): see 'Further research' for details.

8.5.1 ITIL process maturity framework

ITIL Service Design describes a service management process maturity framework. This framework is aligned with the Software Engineering Institute Capability Maturity Model® Integrations (SEI CMMI), and it can be used either to measure the maturity of individual processes or to measure the maturity of service management as a whole.

An assessment against the framework can be used to establish 'Where are we now?' and the framework can also be used to identify a target maturity level to help define 'Where do we want to be?'

The framework identifies five distinct areas that should be assessed:

● Vision and steering

● Process

● People

● Technology

● Culture.

All five of these areas are considered during each assessment, whether it is an assessment of a single process, multiple processes or the whole of IT service management. The framework describes five different maturity levels, each of which describes a balance of features across the five areas (listed in Tables 8.6 to 8.10). Each level assumes that the requirements of the previous level have also been met.

What should the target maturity level be?

Many organizations make the mistake of thinking that higher levels of maturity are always better, and they should have a target of the highest possible level of maturity for every process. This would almost certainly lead to a very expensive management system that is not well focused on the real needs of the business.

The best way to use a maturity model is to understand the current maturity level and the differences between the various levels, and then decide on an appropriate level of maturity based on what is trying to be achieved. Based on this, it is possible to identify the areas where development is needed.

If the desired maturity level is significantly above the actual level then it is likely to require a long time to develop all the required capabilities, and each maturity level will need to be achieved on the way: it is not possible to jump from one maturity level to another much higher level without going through the intermediate levels.

Table 8.6 ITIL maturity level 1: initial

This initial level is sometimes described as ad hoc or chaotic.

Framework area	Characteristics
Vision and steering	Minimal resources
	Temporary results
	Sporadic reports
Process	Loosely defined
	Totally reactive
	Irregular unplanned activities
People	Loosely defined roles and responsibilities
Technology	Manual processes or a few discrete tools
Culture	Technology-based
	Activity-focused

Table 8.7 ITIL maturity level 2: repeatable

At this level, irregular activities are generally directed towards process effectiveness.

Framework area	Characteristics
Vision and steering	Objectives unclear
	Resources available
	Irregular reports
Process	Defined processes
	Largely reactive
	Irregular unplanned activities
People	Self-contained roles and responsibilities
Technology	Many discrete tools
	No overall control or data consolidation
Culture	Product- and service-based

Table 8.8 ITIL maturity level 3: defined

Activities are directed towards efficiency and effectiveness, with formal ownership and targets.

Framework area	Characteristics
Vision and steering	Formal objectives and plans
	Well-funded
	Formal reporting
Process	Processes well defined and communicated
	Regular planned activities
	Some proactive activities
People	Defined and agreed roles and responsibilities
	Formal objectives
	Formal training plans
Technology	Continuous data collection with thresholds and alarms
	Consolidated data used for planning
Culture	Service- and customer-oriented
	Formal approach

Table 8.9 ITIL maturity level 4: managed

Service is focused, with targets based on business goals.

Framework area	Characteristics
Vision and steering	Clear direction based on business goals
	Effective reporting
	Integrated plans linked to business
	Regular planned improvement
Process	Well-defined processes
	Clear interfaces
	Integrated ITSM and system development
	Mainly proactive
People	Inter- and intra-process team working
	Responsibilities defined in all job descriptions
Technology	Continuous monitoring, measurement, reporting and alerting
	Centralized tools, databases and processes
Culture	Business-focused

Table 8.10 ITIL maturity level 5: optimized

Strategic goals based on business goals, with continual improvement.

Framework area	Characteristics
Vision and steering	Strategic plans integrated with strategic business plans
	Continual monitoring and review linked to continual improvement
Process	Well-defined proactive and pre-emptive processes are part of culture
People	Formal business-aligned objectives are routinely monitored
	Roles and responsibilities are part of overall culture
Technology	Well-documented overall architecture
	Complete integration of people, processes and technology
Culture	Continual improvement attitude with strategic business focus
	Understanding of how IT creates value for the business

8.5.2 NIST cybersecurity framework

Cyber resilience or cybersecurity?

This section uses the term 'cybersecurity' when referring to the NIST cybersecurity framework, as this is the term that NIST uses. The meaning in this context is the same as cyber resilience as described in Chapter 1.

The *Framework for Improving Critical Infrastructure Cybersecurity* was published by the US National Institute of Standards and Technology (NIST) in February 2014. Although this is a US publication, many of its recommendations are appropriate for organizations worldwide. The framework is intended for organizations that are responsible for critical infrastructure, defined as 'systems and assets, whether physical or virtual, so vital to the United States that the incapacity or destruction of such systems and assets would have a debilitating impact on security, national economic security, national public health or safety...'. Many of the recommendations are appropriate for any organization that wishes to provide a resilient approach to cybersecurity.

What is critical infrastructure?

Different jurisdictions have slightly different views of what constitutes critical infrastructure, but typically it includes essential things that need to be protected such as:

- Supply of energy such as electricity, gas or fuel for vehicles
- Transport systems such as airports, railway stations or traffic control centres
- Communications infrastructure such as mobile phone networks, TV and radio stations, and major internet switches.

The NIST framework defines a framework core, framework implementation tiers and framework profiles. These are briefly described in Table 8.11 and then more fully in the remainder of this section.

Table 8.11 Components of the NIST cybersecurity framework

Component	Description
Framework core	Cybersecurity controls described in a formal structured hierarchy
Framework implementation tiers	A four-layer model describing levels of alignment to the framework
Framework profiles	A selection of controls from the core that is appropriate for a particular organization or context

8.5.2.1 Framework core

The NIST framework core describes five functions – identify, protect, detect, respond and recover. These represent a lifecycle view of cybersecurity risk management. Within each function the framework describes categories and subcategories which are mapped to existing standards, guidelines and practices. The categories and subcategories of the NIST framework core are very similar to the controls described in other publications (such as Annex A of ISO/IEC 27001).

For example, the identify function includes a category of 'asset management', which has six subcategories. One of these subcategories is 'Physical devices and systems within the organization are inventoried.' This subcategory is mapped to a number of references including COBIT 5 and ISO/IEC 27001. The structure of the NIST framework core is shown in Table 8.12.

Table 8.12 The NIST framework core

Function	Category	Subcategory	Informative references
Identify (ID)	Asset management (ID.AM) The data, personnel, devices, systems and facilities that enable the organization to achieve business purposes are identified and managed according to their relative importance to business objectives and the organization's risk strategy	ID.AM-1 Physical devices and systems within the organization are inventoried	References from COBIT, NIST, ISO/IEC 27000, ISA 62443, SANS Institute, critical security controls etc.
		ID.AM-2 Software platforms and applications...	References from other sources
		ID.AM-3...	etc...
		etc...	
	Business environment (ID.BE) ...	ID.BE-1	
		ID.BE-2	
	etc...	etc...	

The framework core can be thought of as a structured list of controls that an organization may choose to implement. At the very least the organization should ensure that it understands each component of the core and makes a clear decision as to whether it is relevant to its needs or not. This decision should be documented in one or more framework profiles, which are discussed in section 8.5.2.3.

8.5.2.2 Framework implementation tiers

The NIST framework implementation tiers describe the degree to which an organization's cybersecurity risk management practices exhibit the characteristics defined in the framework. The framework states that 'tiers do not represent maturity levels', but nevertheless they can be used in a very similar way to maturity levels. Each organization should determine its desired tier based on the threat environment, legal and regulatory requirements, business/mission objectives and organizational constraints. It can also determine its current tier level, and use this to identify the progression that is appropriate for its needs.

Implementation of the framework is not judged based on the tier level achieved, but on achieving the outcomes described in the organization's target profile(s).

Table 8.13 shows a summary of the four tiers.

Table 8.13 Summary of NIST framework tiers

	Risk management process	Integrated risk management programme	External participation
Tier 1: Partial	Informal processes, ad hoc and sometimes reactive. Prioritization not linked to organizational risk objectives, threat environment or business requirements.	Limited organizational risk awareness. Irregular case-by-case risk management, no effective processes for sharing cybersecurity information.	May not have processes for collaborating with other entities.
Tier 2: Risk-informed	Risk management practices approved by management but no organization-wide policy. Prioritization based on organizational risk objectives, threat or business requirements.	Organizational awareness of risk, but no organization-wide approach to risk management. Processes and procedures in place with adequate resources. Information informally shared within the organization.	Role in relation to other organizations understood but no formal capability to share information externally.
Tier 3: Repeatable	Organization-wide formal practices expressed as policy, and regularly updated based on risk management understanding of business requirements, threats and technology.	Consistent processes and methods are in place and reviewed. People have the knowledge and skills they need.	Information sharing with other organizations to enable collaboration and risk-based decision-making.
Tier 4: Adaptive	Practices based on lessons learned and predictive indicators. Continuous improvement with advanced technology and practices responding to evolving threats.	Risk management is part of organizational culture, with shared information and continuous awareness of system and network activity.	Information is actively shared with partners and improves cybersecurity before events occur.

8.5.2.3 Framework profiles

The NIST framework core defines a large number of functions, categories and subcategories which an organization could implement. Each organization needs to document which of these it has implemented, and which it plans to implement in the future. A selection of functions, categories and subcategories from the framework core is known as a framework profile.

A framework profile can describe the current state or the desired target state of specific cybersecurity activities, and it can be used to document a gap analysis between the current and desired state.

An organization may define many different framework profiles, based on a need for different controls for different assets, or different parts of the organization.

The NIST document does not define profiles, as this must be done by the organization using the framework.

An example of a framework profile in use

One subfunction from the framework core relates to managing remote access:

- Function: Protect
- Category: Access control (PR.AC)
- Subcategory: PR.AC-3 Remote access is managed
- References: ISO/IEC 27001:2013 A.6.2.2, A13.1.1, A13.2.1 etc.

Within an organization there may be one department where remote access is needed, and others where it is not. It may be appropriate for the organization to have two distinct framework profiles: one of which requires this subcategory, and the other does not.

To create a real framework profile it would be necessary to review every function, category and subcategory and define which are required in the profile. Each profile also needs to specify the scope to which it should be applied (for example the whole organization, or just one particular department or IT service).

When carrying out audits or planning improvements, the organization can then compare what is currently in place with the appropriate framework profile to determine what gaps are present.

8.6 CONTINUAL IMPROVEMENT SCENARIOS

This section looks at some aspects of continual improvement for the three fictitious organizations. As you read through these descriptions you should think about:

- Is the organization learning from what has happened and making the necessary improvements to ensure their future cyber resilience?
- What is the most important thing the organization should do to improve its cyber resilience?
- How well does the culture of the organization support continual improvement?

Retail example: SellUGoods Ltd

The new security incident management process includes a post-incident review, and one of these took place after the recent security breach. This review looked at everything that had happened so that lessons could be learned. Everyone was encouraged to share their observations and insights into what had happened, and people understood that the purpose of the review was to identify improvement opportunities, not to assign blame.

Some of the things that were identified during the review were:

- Overall, the planning and design for detecting and responding to security incidents has worked well. This incident has confirmed SellUGoods' belief that a balanced approach is needed between preventative, detective and corrective controls.
- The intrusion detection software did a good job of identifying unusual network traffic and flagging up the incident. There are still some servers and firewalls that do not have these tools installed, and that might mean SellUGoods is at risk of other undetected breaches. The deployment of these tools should be completed as quickly as possible.
- The number of false alarms created by the intrusion detection software could result in a real incident being ignored. Everyone thinks that this is just a temporary issue which will resolve itself after the initial installations, but this must be monitored and managed carefully to ensure that the rate of false alarms is acceptable.

- The security incident management process worked well. Everyone had the information they needed and decisions were made quickly. When SellUGoods needed to disconnect servers from the internet, experts had to make quick decisions about exactly how to do this. The company did get this right, but it would have been better if there was a tested procedure for this that could be followed, to prevent mistakes and speed up the process.

- Data on most servers has not been classified. If all data had been reviewed and classified appropriately then maybe the old credit card data would have been noticed and dealt with appropriately.

- The laptop where the infection originated was running the approved anti-virus software. It had been updated regularly but it still missed this malware. There should be an investigation to understand why this happened, and whether the anti-virus software that SellUGoods is using is good enough.

- Staff had been repeatedly warned about following links in emails, but this exploit still tricked one of SellUGoods' staff. SellUGoods needs to review this training and make sure that people understand the risks, and know what they should do to protect the company. SellUGoods understand that anti-virus controls can only protect them from a limited range of threats, and that a more comprehensive approach will be required to provide comprehensive end-user device security. In addition, everyone must take responsibility for avoiding potential threats, and this message needs to be reinforced.

- If staff need administrator privileges on servers, the accounts they use for this should have complete isolation from their normal user accounts, and they should connect to the server using a secure workstation, not a normal user laptop.

- The way SellUGoods communicated with its customers and the wider public over the incident was very effective. The speed and transparency of the company's communications really helped to contain the incident and protect its reputation. SellUGoods should follow this up by letting people know the measures that it is putting in place to make sure a similar incident will not happen again.

The head of risk management is now sponsoring a project to design and implement improvements based on these findings. She has also allocated funding for a formal assessment of information security at SellUGoods to be carried out by a third party, to see if there are any other areas that could be improved.

SellUGoods has been very lucky; the company suffered a significant security breach but good incident management mitigated the impact and ensured that the company could learn from the events and move forward with greater confidence.

Medical example: MedUServ Ltd

It is quite difficult for MedUServ to get the information it wants about exactly how the data corruption occurred, because the lawyers on both sides are trying to make sure that their organization does not take the blame for this incident.

MedUServ has now seen the ISO/IEC 27001 certificate from the outsourcer, and this clearly shows that the scope of the certification includes services delivered to a specific set of customers, which does not include MedUServ.

MedUServ has reviewed the contract with the outsourcer and this has very few requirements for security. There is nothing in the contract about staff vetting, or about limiting the ability of the outsourcer's staff to access and modify MedUServ's data. This contract still has four years to run before it is due for renewal, and early termination of the contract would incur a significant penalty. The lawyers think it might be possible to get out of the contract if they can show negligence on the part of the outsourcer.

If MedUServ had had a business continuity plan that included failure of this strategic supplier, this might have helped to prevent the incident, but the main failing was a lack of supplier controls and a failure to understand how the supply chain is a critical part of cyber resilience.

Example continues

Medical example *continued*

In the meantime, MedUServ has been keeping in close contact with its customers. MedUServ has pointed out how its quality management system meant that the paper records of each test had been archived and were available to support recovery of the data. It looks as if MedUServ should be able to retain about 85% of its customers, but unfortunately the others are no longer prepared to trust the company and are moving their business to competitors. MedUServ is not a large company and this loss of customers will have a huge impact on its business.

Manufacturing example: MakeUGoods

Although the latest attack did not have any impact, it did provide everyone with a bit of a scare. If it had not been for the newly installed application whitelisting, the consequences could have been severe. Not only would there have been disruption of production with consequent loss of revenue, but the attack could even have resulted in physical damage to the production facilities and a potential health and safety issue.

There has been extensive investigation to find out how the infection got onto the engineer's laptop. The engineer had connected this laptop to a public WiFi network, and it is probable that this infection was introduced at that time. This has resulted in MakeUGoods introducing new controls to ensure that equipment that has been connected to public WiFi networks is never used to handle critical production data.

The information security manager understands that they need defence-in-depth, so that they are not dependent on just one control to protect the company from an attack, and this incident has made everyone realize just how vulnerable they could be.

The project team for the SCADA-hardening project is asked to review the latest incident to see if there are any improvements they could make in the controls they are planning, to ensure that there are at least two different ways in which each likely threat could be defeated. This review does not identify any new technical controls, as they have already done a pretty good job of analysing SCADA vulnerabilities, but the SCADA-hardening project team does make a number of recommendations:

● Accelerate the deployment of removable media controls, including increased training of staff to ensure that they understand the risks.

● Provide additional testing resources to enable the file integrity checking to be tested on more critical servers, so that it can be deployed sooner than originally planned.

● Work with the vendors of applications that caused problems with application whitelisting on some critical servers to see if these can be resolved. Alternatively, consider whether to migrate to applications that will work with this control in place.

● Increase the scope of penetration testing to cover all servers at MakeUGoods, not just the SCADA control centre, and consider increasing the frequency from once a year.

The project team also made some more general recommendations that they think will help to improve security defences in the long term:

● Carry out regular formal assessments of all security controls against a standard such as ISO/IEC 27001:2013 or the NIST cybersecurity framework. Ideally, this should include an external assessment of how effectively MakeUGoods has applied these standards.

● Create a continual improvement register for cyber resilience and encourage all staff to contribute improvement suggestions.

● Make the staff security awareness training more effective by using scenarios and simulations, rather than the current rather dry offering.

8.7 CYBER RESILIENCE CONTINUAL IMPROVEMENT QUESTIONS

1. How do you measure the effectiveness of your controls?

2. What have you done to ensure that your controls are working as designed, and how do you go about improving the controls?

3. How do you assess what and where your supply chain risks are, and how do you mitigate these risks?

4. How do you manage risks from third parties connecting to your systems, and what measures do you take to mitigate the risk of sharing information with third parties?

5. How is a culture of continual improvement encouraged in your organization? What changes might help to improve this culture?

6. Who makes improvement suggestions in your organization? How are the people who actually do the work involved? Who else should be making improvement suggestions, and how could you encourage them?

7. How do you ensure that your measurement and reporting provides the information you need to understand your cyber resilience and plan improvements? How do you identify and reduce unnecessary metrics and reports? What changes in measurement and reporting are needed to facilitate continual improvement?

8. How do you manage, prioritize and track improvement suggestions? How could this be improved?

9. How does your organization (or your part of the organization) fund continual improvement? How do you think it should be funded? If there is limited funding for continual improvement then what could you do within your existing budget?

10. What is the scope of continual improvement in your organization? To what extent does it cover governance, management, people, processes, technology and suppliers? How could this be improved?

11. What maturity level do you think is appropriate for your cyber resilience? Why is this the correct level? Do you know your current maturity level? Which areas of cyber resilience are most urgently in need of improvement?

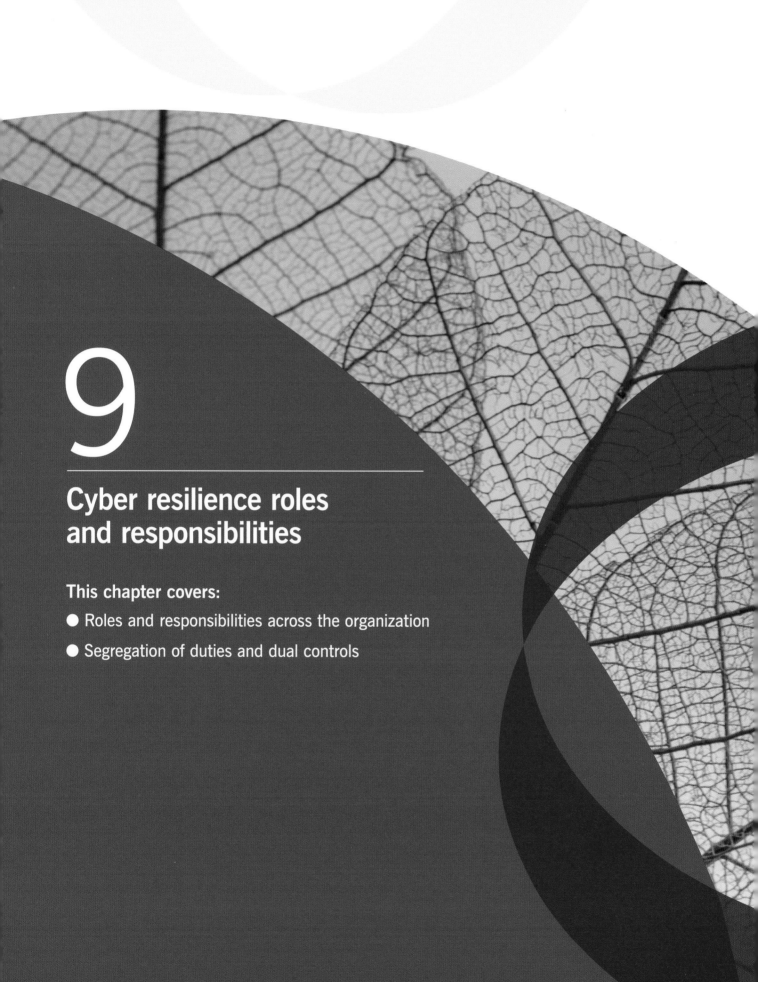

9

Cyber resilience roles and responsibilities

This chapter covers:

- Roles and responsibilities across the organization
- Segregation of duties and dual controls

Cyber Resilience Best Practices

9 Cyber resilience roles and responsibilities

9.1 ROLES AND RESPONSIBILITIES ACROSS THE ORGANIZATION

Being sufficiently cyber resilient involves staff from across the organization, its suppliers and partners. Cyber resilience relies upon the trustworthiness of the data that is processed by the IT systems, under the direction of the people, according to the organization's processes. Therefore, while the IT systems form the trusted infrastructure on which vital information is processed, it is just as much the trusted people and trusted processes that are instrumental in achieving adequate resilience for the organization. Consequently, the roles and responsibilities for cyber resilience described in this section will extend well beyond the IT department, the help desk and other roles conventionally associated with IT delivery, to include areas such as HR and project management.

Key message
Data ownership is a critical foundation for cyber resilience risk management.

The assignment of ownership of data is also a critical foundation for effective cyber resilience risk management. In order to achieve a proportionate balance between the cost and inconvenience of controls on the one hand and the residual cyber resilience risk on the other, the ownership of data should be vested in those best able to make those choices. For example, the sales director could be the data owner for all client data, setting the cyber resilience policies concerning the handling of client data, both internally and when shared with partners and suppliers. Some of those policies will require technical controls that will be implemented by the IT department. Some policies will require different behaviours from employees and this should be reflected in employee contracts, standing instructions, disciplinary procedures etc. Some policies and controls will apply outside the organization and these must be passed to relevant suppliers by the contracts team. Critically, the assessment of cost benefit over the choice of technical controls used within an organization is a business matter and not the sole responsibility of the IT department; however, the IT department may have considerable influence in explaining the impact that different controls would have on a range of factors, including employee productivity and operating costs, to help the business make the best choices.

Medical example: MedUServ

In light of the major incident at MedUServ caused by outsourcing problems and its dependency on a critical supplier, the company has re-evaluated is supplier management and there will soon be a new contract with a new supplier, which will have cyber resilience is at its heart.

It is now apparent that cyber resilience requirements are vital to the MedUServ operation, particularly in respect of the integrity of data. In this small and specialized company, the managing director is now taking a personal interest in how the medical data is processed, to put cyber resilience at the heart of MedUServ's strategy and operation.

Many organizations will have data ownership that coincides almost perfectly with the IT system that processes the data. For example, the head of finance owns all the data in the finance system, and the head of HR owns all the data in the HR system. Consequently, the head of finance might feel a strong sense of ownership for the finance system and its cyber resilience controls. This elegant simplicity may have worked well in the past but in the more connected world, with systems that integrate data types, this approach is less successful. For example, an **enterprise resource-planning** (ERP) system will contain HR, finance and quite possibly project **management information**, yet frequently no senior manager will have the same sense of ownership of the whole ERP system. This situation demands a more sophisticated relationship between those who run such systems and the data owners. Figure 9.1 shows an example of how sensitive information can be shared across the supply chain.

As businesses place greater reliance on outsourced functions, such as customer-facing help desks and billing services, those systems may be in the hands of suppliers. Data owners, for example head of finance and head of HR, will require their outsourced suppliers to implement cyber resilience controls. Many organizations are heavily dependent on their supply chain in other ways, with ever-closer relationships with both suppliers and clients – for example, where suppliers are made responsible for actively managing the stock levels of components used on their clients' production lines.

Retail example: SellUGoods

As a result of its new detection and incident management processes, SellUGoods has discovered and dealt with the loss of sensitive information from its data centre. The lessons from this incident include improving the SellUGoods approach to data ownership so that in future the storage and handling of all sensitive data is actively managed. The data owner will determine which controls must be put in place in order to balance the risks against the costs of the controls, while meeting the business needs to use the data efficiently and conveniently.

This close relationship between organizations and their suppliers necessitates the sharing of highly sensitive information of which the confidentiality, integrity and availability can variously be business-critical: if a manufacturing plant's supplier-managed inventory control system suffers a loss of availability or integrity, the manufacturing production line could be interrupted.

Cyber resilience has frequently been undermined by an organization's suppliers because suppliers have not protected information with sufficient diligence. This can arise because an organization does not realize what information is being shared, or because cyber resilience requirements are not placed on the supplier. Even when those requirements form part of the contract, the supplier may not be monitored and audited in a meaningful way, and cyber resilience controls may be ineffective. Achieving cyber resilience in the supply chain requires information owners to understand where their information is processed and to work with the contract management and supplier management teams. This discussion may not involve the IT teams at all.

Introducing new systems presents an opportunity to implement cyber resilience from the outset. This is cheaper, more efficient and more likely to deliver an enduring solution than applying cyber resilience controls to an operational system retrospectively. Project and programme management therefore play an important role in delivering adequate cyber resilience for individual systems being introduced, and in continuing cyber resilience of the entire enterprise of the organization.

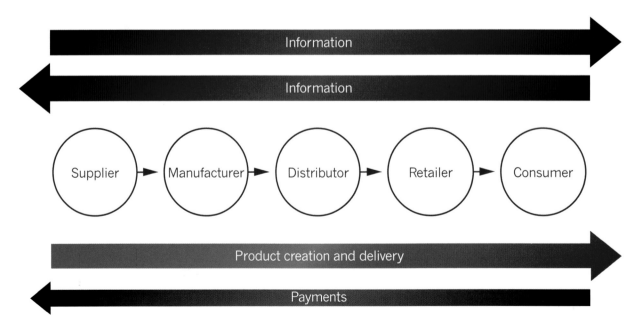

Figure 9.1 Sensitive information is shared up and down the supply chain

Leadership and governance create the environment for cyber resilience to enjoy the right priority – neither too little nor too much – in order to maintain the residual cyber resilience risks at an acceptable level. Leadership is important to set the direction, the tone and the risk appetite to decide what should be done. Governance arrangements see that the organization is managing risks and opportunities so as to meet stakeholders' expectations, and that the leadership team are implementing these policies to deliver the desired outcomes. This includes management as described in Chapter 3.

Key message

As the digital age brings IT centre stage for most organizations, cyber resilience must be put centre stage for their leadership and governance activities.

There is no simple cut-and-paste approach to introducing the necessary roles and responsibilities for cyber resilience into an existing organization. Table 9.1 is a composite from the roles implicit in ITIL, PRINCE2 and MSP. It also includes the concept of information and knowledge ownership. Note that this is a simplified illustration and some organizations may use different titles and lines of reporting.

Manufacturers' suppliers are actively managing stock levels of clients' production lines

Table 9.1 Typical activities and job titles of those involved in cyber resilience

Category	Activity	Examples of job titles of those involved in cyber resilience (also as featured in the scenarios)
Governance	External governance	Full board with non-executive directors, external audit, regulators and legal officers
	Internal governance	Executive board covering internal audit and risk, knowledge owners and information/data owners, company secretary
Leadership and management	Managing projects, programmes and portfolios	Chief information officer (CIO), project managers, programme managers, business change managers (see MSP) responsible for introducing new services
	Leadership and management of cyber resilience	Chief information security officer (CISO), cyber governance steering committee, or information security steering committee
	Managing strategy and portfolio of services	CIO and other managers responsible for delivering the portfolio of IT services
	Supporting management activities	Finance functions at various levels, resource managers and supplier management teams
		HR functions at various levels
		Business relationship managers responsible for internal and external stakeholder engagement
		Risk managers and quality managers. Business continuity manager, health and safety manager
		Knowledge and information/data managers
Delivery	Services	**Service owner**s and managers
	Underlying processes	**Process owner**s and managers
	Relationships with customers	Business relationship managers and service level managers

Services will often be something the internal or external customer will recognize, such as the corporate email service. Services in turn depend on processes. ITIL has common management processes that support services (see Table 9.2). Processes have been grouped to show where their most important contribution to cyber resilience occurs in the ITIL lifecycle.

Chapters 4 to 8 described how cyber resilience can be delivered through service management processes, using ITIL terminology to illustrate this. These processes are listed in Table 9.2. It should be noted that individuals rarely have a job title that corresponds precisely and uniquely to the processes listed in Table 9.2. ITIL does not define many of the more familiar job titles shown in the final column of the table, so the associations shown are not definitive. Nevertheless, Table 9.2 serves to illustrate how cyber resilience will affect the jobs of those engaged in service management.

Table 9.2 ITIL processes and job titles of staff contributing to cyber resilience across the ITIL lifecycle

ITIL process	Where each process is most important for cyber resilience	ITIL lifecycle	Familiar job titles
Service level management	The service level management process negotiates, agrees, measures, reports and improves all the services.	Throughout	Head of IT, responsible for day-to-day delivery, service level manager, client manager
Demand management	Collectively, these are important during service strategy and service design, but they all have operational aspects too. The requirement for cyber resilience will be delivered through detailed requirements across all these processes, including the design of proportionate and effective controls. The supply chain and its controls will form a vital part of overall cyber resilience.	ITIL service strategy and design	Capacity planning team
Availability management			
Capacity management			
IT service continuity management			Business continuity team
Information security management			Information security team
Supplier management			Information security and procurement
			Technical teams such as server management, storage management, network management etc.
Change management	Collectively, these processes are important during initial service transition and during changes to the configuration of the systems and processes, to ensure that cyber resilience is not unintentionally reduced.	ITIL service transition	Change manager, change advisory board (CAB), test team, release team, configuration control team
Service asset and configuration management			
Service validation and testing			
Release and deployment management			
Event management	Collectively, these processes are important to detect, remediate and recover from any incident and ensure that problem management addresses cyber resilience issues alongside user and other business issues.	ITIL service operation	Service desk team, incident manager, problem manager, operations bridge, network operations centre
Incident management			
Problem management			
Access management	Control of user access is a foundation of assuring confidentiality, integrity and availability.		

Manufacturing example: MakeUGoods

At the MakeUGoods data centre, late one night the out-of-hours team had an unusual series of requests for system accounts to be reset after being locked out. The requests were legitimate and the immediate remedy was to unlock the accounts promptly so that the plant did not initiate a shut-down procedure.

The story could have stopped there but further investigation by the curious operator, at the expense of some less urgent tasks, led to the discovery the following day of malicious code on an infected desktop that was password-guessing across the network. MakeUGoods had long recognized the potential value of vigilant and enquiring staff in their operations centre as a key part of their cyber resilience front line, and the operator was duly rewarded for her initiative.

Individuals who are tasked with new objectives for cyber resilience may find these in conflict with their existing objectives, and further policy guidance will be necessary. This is a good outcome because it shows the priorities of the organization changing to reflect a different posture towards cyber resilience. For example, the service desk team is likely to be rewarded for getting calls closed to the satisfaction of users as quickly as possible, and there may be tangible incentives driven by monthly statistics or more immediately by a wall-mounted display showing call waiting times. The service desk operators should also be the front line in detecting certain kinds of anomalous activities that could be the first indication of hostile activity against the organization. They also need to be rewarded for:

● Taking a moment

● Delaying a user by asking some further questions

● Looking for certain patterns of activity

● Alerting management to unusual activity.

Vigilant service desk staff form part of an organization's cyber resilience front line

9.2 SEGREGATION OF DUTIES AND DUAL CONTROLS

The objective of **segregation of duties** (SoD) in cyber resilience is to ensure that privileges and roles are separated so that they cannot be used commit fraud or carry out and hide malicious activities.

9.2.1 What is meant by 'segregation of duties'?

Segregation of duties (SoD), also known as separation of duties, is the concept of separating what is known as a toxic combination of roles and privileges so that they cannot be used to cause and hide malicious activities and errors. The simplest example of a toxic combination would be the ability for a person to apply for a loan while also being the person responsible for approving that loan.

The concept of SoD has its origin in accounting, finance and other regulated industries; it is used to provide internal control, and to prevent fraud and unintentional errors. The Sarbanes-Oxley Act is a good example of a regulation that places great importance on SoD for internal control. Many of these regulations depend on IT for providing these segregation controls.

Toxic combinations of roles and privileges present cyber resilience risks to organizations, as these roles can have powerful privileges – often gained through combinations of roles that have accumulated over time.

The principle behind SoD is that roles should be separated to make it difficult to commit a malicious act. SoD does not totally prevent this but makes it harder. To commit a malicious act in a segregated environment, two or more parties would be required to collude. The idea is that collusion is difficult because colluders have to find like-minded people to collude with. The colluders then have to plan and discuss the malicious activity and they are more likely to be discovered in the act.

Key message

Segregate powerful roles and avoid toxic combinations that can be used to circumvent controls.

It should be noted that SoD is an administrative overhead and should be designed so it makes the best use of resources and does not negatively impact on business processes.

9.2.1.1 Segregation of duties: development and operations

As well as playing an important part in IT operation, SoD also has a significant role in system development. The SoD concept is used to ensure that development and operation activities are separated. For example, traditionally a developer who is responsible for writing codes would not have access to the operational IT environment. However, with the inception of DevOps, where the developers are also the operators and need access to the development and operational environments, this demarcation is becoming tenuous. Even so, it is still an important control that should be considered and applied. For example, developers are expected to do a certain amount of testing as they develop the code, but security and user-acceptance testing should not be carried out by the developers. The responsibility for final testing should be separated from those who are developing. Developer access to the operational environment, if required, should be managed and controlled.

9.2.1.2 Roles and responsibilities, and separation of controls

Roles such as network and database administrator or any other administrative or support roles (the super users) will have powerful privileges and will need to be monitored. However, if these roles are combined into one person, they become toxic in the sense that they can be used to reconfigure the network and remove network controls to allow access to the database, enabling the person to use their database role to copy and exfiltrate the data from the organization. This is a simple illustration using two powerful roles; however, imagine if the same person was also the firewall administrator, and the network and firewall log reviewer. They would have all-pervasive control over the organization's IT and network to do as they wished. Organizations should plan and design their privileges, roles and profiles carefully so as to avoid these toxic combinations. Table 9.3 shows a simple illustration of a SoD matrix with roles that generally should be segregated.

Table 9.3 A simplified segregation-of-duties matrix

Activities	Security manager	Database admin	Network admin	Developer	Solutions architect
Network administration	–	–	X	–	–
Database administration	–	X	–	–	–
Access authorization	X	–	–	–	–
Audit and review	X	–	–	–	–
Security management	X	–	–	–	–
Programming	–	–	–	X	X

Organizations should identify all their roles (especially the privileged ones), map them to processes and document them in a SoD matrix. They can then work out which roles need to be segregated from one another. This matrix can also be used to design access privileges and access controls.

9.2.2 What is meant by 'dual control'?

It may not always be possible to segregate all roles in an organization. This is especially true for a smaller organization where they may be relying on a small number of people for important activities. In such cases, additional controls will be required to manage the risk. Dual control is a method used to control abuse of privileges. Dual control requires that two or more persons are required to complete a task or a procedure. Where roles cannot be fully segregated, additional controls such as dual control, monitoring and audit should be used to mitigate risks from the lack of segregation. This of course means that the monitoring and auditing roles must be separate from those being monitored and audited.

The simplest dual control is a managerial or supervisory control. For example, a clerk may be allowed to run small transactions but a larger transaction will require approval by their manager. This prevents the clerk from carrying out high-value transactions, either maliciously or in error. This sort of control could be required to stop fraud or to stop the clerk making mistakes involving large amounts of money. Another example, from cyber resilience, could be the encrypting of information using two separate encryption keys, each key belonging to a different person to protect the information from being accessed by just one of the key owners.

9.2.2.1 Segregation of duties and cyber resilience

In cyber resilience, SoD is one of the principal security controls against insider threats and errors. Regulations such as Sarbanes-Oxley depend on it. For cyber resilience, SoD should be designed and implemented to ensure that no single person or entity is able to circumvent, modify, degrade or abuse any of the security controls to affect the confidentiality, integrity and/or availability of information. If they manage to do so, it should be possible to detect it. This means that all-powerful super users and conflicting roles are separated. Conflicting roles include those who can influence decisions and carry out the work. For example, the people auditor should not also be implementing the controls.

Some systems rely heavily on roles and profiles to implement access controls and authorization. They combine roles, and also profiles, and in the process some of these roles and profiles can become very powerful.

SoD should be the foundation of access control through the implementation of the 'least privilege' principle. The roles should be segregated so that they have minimum privileges. Uncontrolled privileges and powerful roles can be used to either deliberately or unintentionally cause harm to the system, and thus could violate any, or all, of the security attributes of confidentiality, integrity and availability. Furthermore, as most regulated environments depend on IT for their internal controls, it makes having proper control over IT roles that much more important.

Best practice

- Concentrate on the most risky roles or toxic combinations and separate these first.
- Identify conflicting roles such as those who can execute tasks and also approve them: for example a person implementing the controls and also auditing them.
- Take a risk-based approach – look at risk to sensitive data.
- Use matrices provided by regulatory bodies to design and build a SoD matrix.
- SoD should be reviewed as part of the access rights review and annual certification of accounts.

9.3 CYBER RESILIENCE ROLES AND RESPONSIBILITIES QUESTIONS

1. Who sets the policy on the handling of sensitive and valuable information? If it is the IT department, from whom do they get endorsement and support for the cost and inconvenience caused by the imposition of controls?

2. Do the HR department, the contract/supplier management team and the project management office recognize their central role in delivering cyber resilience? How would you go about explaining this to them?

3. Construct a quick list, based on Table 9.1, of all the areas of your organization you need to call upon to improve cyber resilience, and add an assessment of their readiness to play their part.

4. Delivering improved cyber resilience includes a large degree of change management. To what extent do you have the necessary leadership support of people who recognizes that cyber resilience requires more than technical controls delivered by the IT department?

5. To what extent do you have the environment for a staff member to acquire too many access privileges through operating in a lax governance regime?

Further research

PUBLICATIONS

Cabinet Office (2011). *ITIL Continual Service Improvement*. The Stationery Office, London.

Cabinet Office (2011). *ITIL Service Design*. The Stationery Office, London.

Cabinet Office (2011). *ITIL Service Operation*. The Stationery Office, London.

Cabinet Office (2011). *ITIL Service Strategy*. The Stationery Office, London.

Cabinet Office (2011). *ITIL Service Transition*. The Stationery Office, London.

Cabinet Office (2011). *Managing Successful Programmes* (MSP). The Stationery Office, London.

CESG (2009). *HMG Information Assurance Standard No. 1 Technical Risk Assessment*

Information Security Forum (2013). *The 2013 Standard of Good Practice for Information Security.*

ISO 27001:2013 Information technology – Security techniques – Information security management systems – Requirements.

Kotter, J. P. and Schlesinger, L. A. (2008). Choosing strategies for change. *Harvard Business Review, 86* (7/8), 130

Office of Government Commerce (2009). *An Introduction to PRINCE2: Managing and Directing Successful Projects*. The Stationery Office, London.

Office of Government Commerce (2010). *Management of Risk* (M_o_R): *Guidance for Practitioners,* 3rd Edition. The Stationery Office, London.

Office of Government Commerce (2010). *Management of Value* (MoV®). The Stationery Office, London.

Statement on Standards for Attestation Engagements (SSAE) No. 16. AICPA (2010).

WEBSITES

HMG Information Assurance Maturity Model (IAMM): www.cesg.gov.uk/publications/Pages/categorylist.aspx?cat=HMG+IA+Maturity+Model

Insider Threat: see the CPNI advice pages at www.cpni.gov.uk

Management of Risk (M_o_R): https://www.axelos.com/mor

Management of Value (MoV): https://www.axelos.com/mov

Managing Successful Programmes (MSP): https://www.axelos.com/msp

NIST Framework for Improving Critical Infrastructure Cybersecurity: www.nist.gov/cyberframework

PRojects IN Controlled Environments (PRINCE2): https://www.axelos.com/prince2

UK Cyber Essentials Scheme: www.gov.uk/government/publications/cyber-essentials-scheme-overview

OTHER RESOURCES

Information about COBIT 5 is available from ISACA, www.isaca.org. Members of ISACA can download the key COBIT 5 publications, as well as attend local ISACA events for presentations on COBIT and related topics.

Ponemon Institute publishes an annual Cost of Data Breach Study. Visit www.ponemon.org for more information.

Verizon publishes an annual Data Breach Investigations Report. Visit www.verizonenterprise.com/DBIR/ for more information.

Copies of all **ISO** standards can be purchased from the International Standards Organization, www.iso.org, or from the standards organization in your local country.

ITIL publications are available from AXELOS, www.axelos.com, or from many bookshops. Learn about ITIL by studying an ITIL Foundation training course. Presentations and other opportunities to learn about ITIL are also available from many local chapters of the **IT Service Management Forum** (*it*SMF). Find links to all *it*SMF chapters at the *it*SMF International website, www.itsmfi.org.

A list of accredited training organizations (ATOs) can be found at https://www.axelos.com/find-a-training-provider. A list of examining institutes (EIs) can be found at www.axelos.com/examination-institutes

Abbreviations and glossary

ABBREVIATIONS

2FA	two-factor authentication
ACD	automatic call distribution
ADM	Architecture Development Method
AES	advance encryption standard
ALE	annualized loss expectancy
APT	advanced persistent threat
ARO	annual rate of occurrence
ATM	automated teller machine
BCM	business continuity management
BCP	business continuity plan
BGP	border gateway protocol
BIA	business impact analysis
BRM	business relationship manager
BSI	British Standards Institute
BYOD	bring your own device
CA	certification authority
CAB	change advisory board
CERT	computer emergency response team
CI	configuration item
CIA	confidentiality, integrity and availability
CIO	chief information officer
CISO	chief information security officer
CMDB	configuration management database
CMMI	Capability Maturity Model Integration
CMS	configuration management system
CoCo	code of connection
COTS	commercial off the shelf
CRM	customer relationship management
CSA	Cloud Security Alliance
CSF	critical success factor
CSI	continual service improvement
DDoS	distributed denial of service
DIKW	Data-to-Information-to-Knowledge-to-Wisdom
DML	definitive media library
DMZ	demilitarized zone
DSA	digital signature algorithm
EAP	extensible authentication protocol
ERP	enterprise resource planning
FAQ	frequently asked question
FMEA	failure mode and effects analysis
GDPR	General Data Protection Regulation
HIPAA	Health Insurance Portability and Accountability Act

HMG	Her Majesty's Government
HR	human resources
HVAC	heating, ventilation and air conditioning
IAAM	Information Assurance Maturity Model
IaaS	IT infrastructure as a service
ICS	industrial control system
IDS	intrusion detection system
IEC	International Electrotechnical Commission
IP	internet protocol
IPS	intrusion prevention system
IPSec	Internet Protocol Security
ISG	IT steering group
ISO	International Organization for Standardization
IT	information technology
ITSCM	IT service continuity management
ITSM	IT service management
itSMF	IT Service Management Forum
JML	joiners, movers and leavers
KPI	key performance indicator
KRI	key risk indicator
LAN	local area network
M_o_R	management of risk
MDM	mobile device management
MSP	Managing Successful Programmes
MTBF	mean time between failures
MTBSI	mean time between service incidents
MTRS	mean time to restore service
NAC	network access control
NIST	National Institute of Standards Technology
OLA	operational level agreement
OSI	open systems interconnection
OSPF	open shortest path first
OWASP	Open Web Application Security Project
PABX	private automatic branch exchange
PCI-DSS	payment card industry data security standard
PDCA	Plan-Do-Check-Act
PIN	personal information number
PKE	public key encryption
PKI	public key infrastructure
RAID	redundant array of independent disks
RBAC	role-based access control
RCA	root cause analysis
RFC	request for change

ROI	return on investment
SaaS	software as a service
SACM	service asset and configuration management
SCADA	supervisory control and data acquisition
SDP	service design package
SIEM	security information and event management
SKMS	service knowledge management system
SLA	service level agreement
SLE	single loss expectancy
SLM	service level management
SLR	service level requirement
SMART	specific, measurable, achievable, relevant and time-bound
SME	small or medium enterprise
SNMP	simple network management protocol
SoD	segregation of duties
SQL	structured query language
SSL	secure sockets layer
SSO	single-sign-on
TLS	transport layer security
USB	universal serial bus
VLAN	virtual local area networks
VoIP	voice over IP
VPN	virtual private network
WAF	web application firewall
WAN	wide area network
WEP	wired equivalent privacy
WPA	WiFi Protected Access
WPA2	WiFi Protected Access 2

GLOSSARY

The **Best Management Practice** portfolio is owned by AXELOS which is jointly owned by the Cabinet Office, part of HM Government, and Capita. Formerly owned by CCTA and then OGC, the Best Management Practice functions moved to the Cabinet Office in June 2010. In July 2013 the Cabinet Office formed a joint venture with Capita called AXELOS. AXELOS now owns and manages the Best Management Practice portfolio which includes guidance on IT service management, project, programme, risk, portfolio and value management, and cyber resilience. There is also a management maturity model as well as related glossaries of terms.

acceptance

Formal agreement that an IT service, process, plan or other deliverable is complete, accurate, reliable and meets its specified requirements. Acceptance is usually preceded by change evaluation or testing and is often required before proceeding to the next stage of a project or process.

access management

The ITSM process responsible for allowing users to make use of IT services, data or other assets. Access management helps to protect the confidentiality, integrity and availability of assets by ensuring that only authorized users are able to access or modify them. Access management implements the policies of information security management and is sometimes referred to as rights management or identity management.

account manager

A role that is very similar to that of the business relationship manager, but includes more commercial aspects. Most commonly used by external service providers.

account sprawl

A situation where the number of users or privileged accounts has become unmanageable, often due to uncontrolled creation of accounts.

accounting

The process responsible for identifying the actual costs of delivering IT services, comparing these with budgeted costs, and managing variance from the budget.

accredited

Officially authorized to carry out a role. For example, an accredited body may be authorized to provide training or to conduct audits.

activity

A set of actions designed to achieve a particular result. Activities are usually defined as part of processes or plans, and are documented in procedures.

advanced encryption standard (AES)

A symmetric key encryption standard that was approved by NIST for encrypting information.

advanced persistent threat (APT)

A persistent attack targeted at organizations using generally available or specially developed malware designed to steal valuable information. The attack is stealthy and takes place over a long period of time.

agreement

A document that describes a formal understanding between two or more parties. An agreement is not legally binding, unless it forms part of a contract. See also operational level agreement; service level agreement.

alert

A notification that a threshold has been reached, something has changed, or a failure has occurred. Alerts are often created and managed by system management tools and are managed by the event management process.

annual rate of occurrence (ARO)

The probability that a specific risk will occur in a single year.

annualized loss expectancy (ALE)

The expected financial loss due to a risk, averaged over a one-year period. ALE is calculated by multiplying the single loss expectancy (SLE) by the annual rate of occurrence (ARO).

application

Software that provides functions which are required by an IT service. Each application may be part of more than one IT service. An application runs on one or more servers or clients. See also application management.

application management

The ITSM function responsible for managing applications throughout their lifecycle.

Architecture Development Method (ADM)

A method for enterprise architecture development defined in TOGAF, which takes an iterative lifecycle approach to architecture development.

architecture

The structure of a system or IT service, including the relationships of components to each other and to the environment they are in. Architecture also includes the standards and guidelines that guide the design and evolution of the system.

assessment

Inspection and analysis to check whether a standard or set of guidelines is being followed, that records are accurate, or that efficiency and effectiveness targets are being met. *See also* audit.

asset

Anything that has value to an organization. Assets can be physical things such as servers and buildings or intangible things such as a company's reputation.

asset management

A generic activity or process responsible for tracking and reporting the value and ownership of assets throughout their lifecycle. *See also* service asset and configuration management.

asset owners

The persons or roles accountable for the assets in an organization. There may be one or many asset owners, depending on the size and nature of the organization. Responsibility for the assets may be delegated to others as appropriate.

asset register

A list of assets and the information required to manage them. For information security management this could be a list of information and related assets with owners, value to the business, classification and applicable security controls. For financial management this could be a list of fixed assets with owners, financial value and information about deprecation.

asymmetric key pair

A pair of related encryption keys. Data that is encrypted by one key in the pair can only be decrypted by using the other key. *See also* public key; private key.

attribute

A piece of information about a configuration item (CI). Examples are name, location, version number and cost. Attributes of CIs are recorded in a configuration management database (CMDB) and maintained as part of a configuration management system (CMS). *See also* relationship; configuration management system.

audit

Formal inspection and verification to check whether a standard or set of guidelines is being followed, that records are accurate, or that efficiency and effectiveness targets are being met. An audit may be carried out by internal or external groups. *See also* assessment; certification.

authentication

Verification that a characteristic or attribute that appears to be true or is claimed to be true is in fact true: for example, that a specific user is who they claim to be.

availability

A characteristic of information that ensures it is able to be used when needed. Confidentiality, integrity and availability are the three core characteristics which confer requirements on information security systems and processes.

availability management (AM)

The ITSM process responsible for ensuring that IT services meet the current and future availability needs of the business in a cost-effective and timely manner. Availability management defines, analyses, plans, measures and improves all aspects of the availability of IT services, and ensures that all IT infrastructures, processes, tools, roles etc. are appropriate for the agreed service level targets for availability.

backup

Copying data to protect against loss of integrity or availability of the original.

Best Management Practice

The Best Management Practice portfolio is jointly owned by the Cabinet Office, part of HM Government, and Capita. Formerly owned by CCTA and then OGC, the Best Management Practice functions moved to the Cabinet Office in June 2010. In July 2013 the Cabinet Office formed a joint venture with Capita called AXELOS. AXELOS now manages the Best Management Practice portfolio which includes guidance on IT service management, project, programme, risk, portfolio and value management, and cyber resilience. There is also a management maturity model as well as related glossaries of terms.

best practice

Proven activities or processes that have been successfully used by multiple organizations. *Cyber Resilience Best Practices* is an example of best practice.

border gateway protocol (BGP)

A routeing protocol used for routeing data between autonomous areas in a network.

brainstorming

A technique that helps a team to generate ideas. Ideas are not reviewed during the brainstorming session, but at a later stage. Brainstorming is often used by problem management to identify possible causes.

breach

An intentional or unintentional incident that results in the loss of confidentiality, integrity or availability of information.

British Standards Institution (BSI)

The UK national standards body, responsible for creating and maintaining British standards. See www. bsi-global.com for more information. *See also* International Organization for Standardization.

budget

A list of all the money an organization or business unit plans to receive, and plans to pay out, over a specified period of time. *See also* budgeting.

budgeting

The activity of predicting and controlling the spending of money. Budgeting consists of a periodic negotiation cycle to set future budgets (usually annual) and the routine monitoring and adjusting of current budgets.

build

The activity of assembling a number of configuration items to create part of an IT service. The term is also used to refer to a release that is authorized for distribution – for example, server build or laptop build.

business capacity management

The sub-process of capacity management responsible for understanding future business requirements for use in the capacity plan. *See also* service capacity management.

business continuity management (BCM)

The business process responsible for managing risks that could seriously affect the business. Business continuity management safeguards the interests of key stakeholders, reputation, brand and value-creating activities. The process involves reducing risks to an acceptable level and planning for the recovery of business processes should a disruption to the business occur. Business continuity management sets the objectives, scope and requirements for IT service continuity management.

business impact analysis (BIA)

The activity in business continuity management that identifies vital business functions and their dependencies. These dependencies may include suppliers, people, other business processes, IT services etc. Business impact analysis defines the recovery requirements for IT services. These requirements include recovery time objectives, recovery point objectives and minimum service level targets for each IT service.

business objective

The objective of a business process, or of the business as a whole. Business objectives support the business vision, provide guidance for the IT strategy, and are often supported by IT services.

business operations

The routine execution, monitoring and management of business processes.

business relationship manager (BRM)

A role responsible for maintaining the relationship with one or more customers. This role is often combined with the service level manager role.

business unit

A segment of the business that has its own plans, metrics, income and costs. Each business unit owns assets and uses these to create value for customers in the form of goods and services.

capability

The ability of an organization, person, process, application, IT service or other configuration item to carry out an activity. Capabilities are intangible assets of an organization. *See also* resource.

Capability Maturity Model Integration (CMMI)

A process improvement approach developed by the Software Engineering Institute (SEI) of Carnegie Mellon University, USA. CMMI provides organizations with the essential elements of effective processes. It can be used to guide process improvement across a project, a division or an entire organization. CMMI helps to integrate traditionally separate organizational functions, set process improvement goals and priorities, provide guidance for quality processes, and provide a point of reference for appraising current processes. See www. sei.cmu.edu/cmmi for more information. *See also* maturity.

capacity

The maximum throughput that a configuration item or IT service can deliver. For some types of CI, capacity may be the size or volume – for example, a disk drive.

capacity management

The ITSM process responsible for ensuring that the capacity of IT services and the IT infrastructure are able to meet agreed capacity – and performance-related requirements in a cost-effective and timely manner. Capacity management considers all resources required to deliver an IT service, and is concerned with meeting the current and future capacity needs along with the performance requirements of the business. Capacity management includes three sub-processes: business capacity management, service capacity management and component capacity management.

certification

Issuing a certificate to confirm compliance to a standard. Certification includes a formal audit by an independent and accredited body. The term is also used to mean awarding a certificate to provide evidence that a person has achieved a qualification.

change

The addition, modification or removal of anything that could have an effect on IT services. The scope should include changes to all architectures, processes, tools, metrics and documentation, as well as changes to IT services and other configuration items.

change advisory board (CAB)

A group of people who support the assessment, prioritization, authorization and scheduling of changes. A change advisory board is usually made up of representatives from all areas within the IT service provider; the business; and third parties such as suppliers.

change evaluation

The ITSM process responsible for formal assessment of a new or changed IT service to ensure that risks have been managed and to help determine whether to authorize the change.

change management

The ITSM process responsible for controlling the lifecycle of all changes, enabling beneficial changes to be made with minimum disruption to IT services.

change proposal

A document that includes a high-level description of a potential service introduction or significant change, along with a corresponding business case and an expected implementation schedule. Change proposals are normally created by the service portfolio management process and are passed to change management for authorization. Change management will review the potential impact on other services, on shared resources, and on the overall change schedule. Once the change proposal has been authorized, service portfolio management will charter the service.

change request

See request for change.

charter

A document that contains details of a new service, a significant change or other significant project. Charters are typically authorized by service portfolio management or by a project management office. The term charter is also used to describe the act of authorizing the work required to complete a service change or project.

cipher-text

The resultant output from an encryption of plain text.

classification

The act of assigning a category to something. Classification is used to ensure consistent management and reporting. Configuration items, incidents, problems, changes etc. are usually classified.

client

A generic term that means a customer, the business or a business customer. For example, client manager may be used as a synonym for business relationship manager. The term is also used to mean:

● A computer that is used directly by a user – for example, a PC, a handheld computer or a work station.

● The part of a client server application that the user directly interfaces with – for example, an email client.

closed

The final status in the lifecycle of an incident, problem, change etc. When the status is closed, no further action is taken.

Cloud Security Alliance (CSA)

An organization that defines a set of security practices, principally in the form of the cloud control matrix (CCM). See https://cloudsecurityalliance.org/

COBIT

A business framework for the governance and management of enterprise IT. COBIT is published by ISACA. See www.isaca.org for more information.

code of connection (CoCo)

An agreement between parties to obey a set of rules as a condition for connecting the parties' networks.

commercial off the shelf (COTS)

Pre-existing application software or middleware that can be purchased from a third party.

compliance

Ensuring that a standard or set of guidelines is followed, or that proper, consistent accounting or other practices are being employed.

component

A general term that is used to mean one part of something more complex. For example, a computer system may be a component of an IT service; an application may be a component of a release unit. Components that need to be managed should be configuration items.

computer emergency response team (CERT)

A group of security incident response experts who respond to security incidents and advise an organization on handling of security incidents.

confidentiality

A characteristic of information that ensures it is not made available or disclosed to unauthorized entities. Confidentiality, integrity and availability are the three core characteristics which confer requirements on information security systems and processes.

configuration

A generic term used to describe a group of configuration items that work together to deliver an IT service, or a recognizable part of an IT service. Configuration is also used to describe the parameter settings for one or more configuration items.

configuration item (CI)

Any component or other service asset that needs to be managed in order to deliver an IT service. Information about each configuration item is recorded in a configuration record within the configuration management system and is maintained throughout its lifecycle by service asset and configuration management. Configuration items are under the control of change management. They typically include IT services, hardware, software, buildings, people and formal documentation such as process documentation and service level agreements.

configuration management database (CMDB)

A database used to store configuration records throughout their lifecycle. The configuration management system (CMS) maintains one or more configuration management databases (CMDBs), and each database stores attributes of configuration items, and relationships with other configuration items.

configuration management system (CMS)

A set of tools, data and information that is used to support service asset and configuration management. The CMS is part of an overall service knowledge management system and includes tools for collecting, storing, managing, updating, analysing and presenting data about all configuration items and their relationships. The CMS may also include information about incidents, problems, known errors, changes and releases. The CMS is maintained by service asset and configuration management and is used by all IT service management processes.

continual service improvement (CSI)

A stage in the lifecycle of a service. Continual service improvement ensures that services are aligned with changing business needs by identifying and implementing improvements to IT services that support business processes. The performance of the IT service provider is continually measured, and improvements are made to processes, IT services and IT infrastructure in order to increase efficiency, effectiveness and cost effectiveness. Continual service improvement includes the seven-step improvement process. Although this process is associated with continual service improvement, most processes have activities that take place across multiple stages of the service lifecycle. *See also* Plan-Do-Check-Act.

continual service improvement (CSI) register

A database or structured document used to record and manage improvement opportunities throughout the lifecycle.

contract

A legally binding agreement between two or more parties.

control

A means of managing a risk, ensuring that a business objective is achieved or that a process is followed. Examples of controls include policies, procedures, roles, RAID, door locks etc. A control is sometimes called a countermeasure or safeguard. Control also means to manage the utilization or behaviour of a configuration item, system or IT service.

corrective control

A control that is intended to correct the situation after an incident has been detected.

cost

The amount of money spent on a specific activity, IT service or business unit. Costs consist of real cost (money), notional cost (such as people's time) and depreciation.

cost benefit analysis

An activity that analyses and compares the costs and the benefits involved in one or more alternative courses of action.

cost centre

A business unit or project to which costs are assigned. A cost centre does not charge for services provided. An IT service provider can be run as a cost centre or a profit centre.

cost effectiveness

A measure of the balance between the effectiveness and cost of a service, process or activity. A cost-effective process is one that achieves its objectives at minimum cost.

countermeasure

Can be used to refer to any type of control. The term is most often used when referring to measures that increase resilience, fault tolerance or reliability of an IT service.

course corrections

Changes made to a plan or activity which has already started to ensure that it will meet its objectives. Course corrections are made as a result of monitoring progress.

crisis management

Crisis management is the process responsible for managing the wider implications of business continuity. A crisis management team is responsible for strategic issues such as managing media relations and shareholder confidence, and deciding when to invoke business continuity plans.

critical success factor (CSF)

Something that must happen if an IT service, process, plan, project or other activity is to succeed. Key performance indicators are used to measure the achievement of each critical success factor. For example, a critical success factor of 'protect IT services when making changes' could be measured by key performance indicators such as 'percentage reduction of unsuccessful changes', 'percentage reduction in changes causing incidents' etc.

culture

A set of values that is shared by a group of people, including expectations about how people should behave, their ideas, beliefs and practices.

customer

Someone who buys goods or services. The customer of an IT service provider is the person or group who defines and agrees the service level targets. The term is also sometimes used informally to mean user – for example, 'This is a customer-focused organization.'

cyber resilience

The ability to prevent, detect and correct any impact that incidents have on the information required to do business.

data

A collection of characters, signs and symbols that has to be processed to have relevance, context or value. Data is the lowest level in a hierarchy of increasing value from Data-to-Information-to-Knowledge-to-Wisdom.

data-at-rest

Data stored on disk, in memory or being processed as opposed to being in transit or in motion.

data-in-transit

Data that is being moved from one place to another, usually across a network.

defence-in-depth

Using multiple independent security controls to provide redundancy. If one control fails or a vulnerability is exploited, assets will be protected by alternative controls.

demand management

The ITSM process responsible for understanding, anticipating and influencing customer demand for services. Demand management works with capacity management to ensure that the service provider has sufficient capacity to meet the required demand. At a strategic level, demand management can involve analysis of patterns of business activity and user profiles, while at a tactical level, it can involve the use of differential charging to encourage customers to use IT services at less busy times, or require short-term activities to respond to unexpected demand or the failure of a configuration item.

demilitarized zone (DMZ)

An area of a network that sits outside the firewall. A DMZ is semi-trusted and is used for hosting services that are accessible from outside the organization.

Deming Cycle

See Plan-Do-Check-Act.

deployment

The activity responsible for movement of new or changed hardware, software, documentation, process etc. to the live environment. Deployment is part of the ITSM release and deployment management process.

design

An activity or process that identifies requirements and then defines a solution that is able to meet these requirements.

design coordination

The ITSM process responsible for coordinating all service design activities, processes and resources. Design coordination ensures the consistent and effective design of new or changed IT services, service management information systems, architectures, technology, processes, information and metrics.

detection

A stage in the lifecycle of an incident. Detection results in the incident becoming known to the service provider. Detection can be automatic or the result of a user logging an incident.

detective control

A control that is intended to identify when a threat has succeeded, so that the organization can respond appropriately.

diagnosis

A stage in the incident and problem lifecycles. The purpose of diagnosis is to identify a workaround for an incident or establish the root cause of a problem.

digital obsolescence

A situation where information stored in legacy technology, or media cannot be accessed because the required infrastructure is no longer available.

digital signature

The product of using the private key of an asymmetric key pair and a hashing algorithm to encrypt information that can act as an electronic signature. Digital signatures can be used to vouch for the authenticity of activities of the private key owner, such as their documents and software.

document

Information in readable form. A document may be paper or electronic – for example, a policy statement, service level agreement, incident record or diagram of a computer room layout. *See also* record.

effectiveness

A measure of whether the objectives of a process, service or activity have been achieved. An effective process or activity is one that achieves its agreed objectives. *See also* key performance indicator.

efficiency

A measure of whether the right amount of resource has been used to deliver a process, service or activity. An efficient process achieves its objectives with the minimum amount of time, money, people or other resources. *See also* key performance indicator.

endpoint

A device that can send and receive data on a network: for example a server, a laptop, a PC, a mobile phone or a tablet.

enterprise financial management

The function and processes responsible for managing the overall organization's budgeting, accounting and charging requirements. Enterprise financial management is sometimes referred to as the 'corporate' financial department. *See also* financial management for IT services.

enterprise resource planning (ERP)

An enterprise planning tool that comprises a modular suite of applications. Organizations can use ERP for each of their business functions such as accounting, invoicing, production and manufacturing.

environment

A subset of the IT infrastructure that is used for a particular purpose – for example, live environment, test environment, build environment. Also used in the term 'physical environment' to mean the accommodation, air conditioning, power system etc. Environment is used as a generic term to mean the external conditions that influence or affect something.

error

A design flaw or malfunction that causes a failure of one or more IT services or other configuration items. A mistake made by a person or a faulty process that impacts a configuration item is also an error.

escalation

An activity that obtains additional resources when these are needed to meet service level targets or customer expectations. Escalation may be needed within any process, but is most commonly associated with incident management, problem management and the management of customer complaints. There are two types of escalation: functional escalation and hierarchic escalation.

event

A change of state that has significance for the management of an IT service or other configuration item. The term is also used to mean an alert or notification created by any IT service, configuration item or monitoring tool. Events typically require IT operations personnel to take action, and often lead to incidents being logged.

event management

The ITSM process responsible for managing events throughout their lifecycle. Event management is one of the main activities of IT operations.

external service provider

An IT service provider that is part of a different organization from its customer. An IT service provider may have both internal and external customers. *See also* outsourcing.

facilities management

The function responsible for managing the physical environment where the IT infrastructure is located. Facilities management includes all aspects of managing the physical environment – for example, power and cooling, building access management, and environmental monitoring.

failure

Loss of ability to operate to specification, or to deliver the required output. The term may be used when referring to IT services, processes, activities, configuration items etc. A failure often causes an incident.

failure mode and effects analysis (FMEA)

A method for analysing possible failures in products, processes or services and the consequences of failures.

financial management

A generic term used to describe the function and processes responsible for managing an organization's budgeting, accounting and charging requirements. Enterprise financial management is the specific term used to describe the function and processes from the perspective of the overall organization. Financial management for IT services is the specific term used to describe the function and processes from the perspective of the IT service provider.

financial management for IT services

The ITSM function and processes responsible for managing an IT service provider's budgeting, accounting and charging requirements. Financial management for IT services secures an appropriate level of funding to design, develop and deliver services that meet the strategy of the organization in a cost-effective manner. *See also* enterprise financial management.

fit for purpose

The ability to meet an agreed level of utility. Fit for purpose is also used informally to describe a process, configuration item, IT service etc. that is capable of meeting its objectives or service levels. Being fit for purpose requires suitable design, implementation, control and maintenance.

fit for use

The ability to meet an agreed level of warranty. Being fit for use requires suitable design, implementation, control and maintenance.

fixed asset

A tangible business asset that has a long-term useful life (for example, a building, a piece of land, a server or a software licence). *See also* service asset; configuration item.

fulfilment

Performing activities to meet a need or requirement – for example, by providing a new IT service, or meeting a service request.

function

A team or group of people and the tools or other resources they use to carry out one or more processes or activities – for example the service desk.

The term also has two other meanings. Firstly, an intended purpose of a configuration item, person, team, process or IT service: for example, one function of an email service may be to store and forward outgoing mails, while the function of a business process may be to despatch goods to customers. The second meaning is to perform the intended purpose correctly, as in 'The computer is functioning.'

gap analysis

An activity that compares two sets of data and identifies the differences. Gap analysis is commonly used to compare a set of requirements with actual delivery.

governance

Ensuring that an organization meets the expectations of its stakeholders. These stakeholders may include legal and regulatory authorities as well as shareholders or citizens. Governance includes defining what management should do and ensuring that this is carried out as intended.

guideline

A document describing best practice, which recommends what should be done. Compliance with a guideline is not normally enforced.

identity

A unique name that is used to identify a user, person or role. The identity is used to grant rights to that user, person or role. Example identities might be the username 'SmithJ' or the role 'change manager'.

impact

A measure of the effect of an incident, problem or change on business processes. Impact is often based on how service levels will be affected. Impact and urgency are used to assign priority.

incident

An unplanned interruption to an IT service or reduction in the quality of an IT service. Any breach of confidentiality, integrity or availability should be treated as an information security incident.

incident management

The process responsible for managing the lifecycle of all incidents. Incident management ensures that normal service operation is restored as quickly as possible and the business impact is minimized.

incident record

A record containing the details of an incident. Each incident record documents the lifecycle of a single incident.

information

Structured data that is meaningful, relevant and useful and has value in context. Information is the second level in a hierarchy of increasing value from Data-to-Information-to-Knowledge-to-Wisdom.

information security management

The process responsible for ensuring that the confidentiality, integrity and availability of an organization's assets, information, data and IT services match the agreed needs of the business. Note that the information security objectives will now need to deliver cyber resilience, which is a development on past definitions of information security, reflecting the changing nature of the networked environment and the threats that this brings. Information security management supports business security and has a wider scope than that of the IT service provider, including handling of paper, building access, phone calls etc. for the entire organization.

information security management system (ISMS)

The framework of policy, processes, functions, standards, guidelines and tools that ensures an organization can achieve its information security management objectives. Note that the nature of an ISMS depends upon the breadth of security objectives and, for this publication, the ISMS will need to deliver cyber resilience, which is a development on past definitions of information security, reflecting the changing nature of the networked environment and the threats that this brings.

information system

See management information system.

information technology (IT)

The use of technology for the storage, communication or processing of information. The technology typically includes computers, telecommunications, applications and other software. The information may include business data, voice, images, video etc. Information technology is often used to support business processes through IT services.

integrity

A characteristic of information that ensures it is only modified by authorized personnel and activities. Confidentiality, integrity and availability are the three core characteristics which confer requirements on information security systems and processes.

internal service provider

An IT service provider that is part of the same organization as its customer. An IT service provider may have both internal and external customers.

International Organization for Standardization (ISO)

The International Organization for Standardization (ISO) is the world's largest developer of standards. ISO is a non-governmental organization that is a network of the national standards institutes of 156 countries. See www.iso.org for further information about ISO.

International Standards Organization

See International Organization for Standardization.

internet protocol (IP)

One of the protocols in the TCP/IP suite that is used for communicating between networked devices and routeing data over networks.

internet service provider (ISP)

An external service provider that provides access to the internet. Most ISPs also provide other IT services such as web hosting.

intrusion detection system/intrusion prevention system (IDS/IPS)

Network devices used for detecting and preventing intrusions in networks. IDS/IPS sensors are placed at strategic points in the network or on devices to detect malicious activities and to alert or prevent attacks. The IDS detects and raises alerts whereas the IPS tries to prevent attacks.

ISO 9000

A generic term that refers to a number of international standards and guidelines for quality management systems. See www.iso.org for more information. *See also* International Organization for Standardization.

ISO 9001

An international standard for quality management systems. *See also* ISO 9000.

ISO/IEC 20000

An international standard for IT service management.

ISO/IEC 27001

An international specification for information security management. The corresponding code of practice is ISO/IEC 27002.

IT infrastructure

All of the hardware, software, networks, facilities etc. that are required to develop, test, deliver, monitor, control or support applications and IT services. The term includes all of the information technology but not the associated people, processes and documentation.

IT operations

Activities carried out by IT operations control, including console management/operations bridge, job scheduling, backup and restore, and print and output management. IT operations is also used as a synonym for service operation.

IT operations control

The ITSM function responsible for monitoring and control of the IT services and IT infrastructure. *See also* operations bridge.

IT operations management

The ITSM function within an IT service provider that performs the daily activities needed to manage IT services and the supporting IT infrastructure. IT operations management includes IT operations control and facilities management.

IT service

A service provided by an IT service provider. An IT service is made up of a combination of information technology, people and processes. A customer-facing IT service directly supports the business processes of one or more customers, and its service level targets should be defined in a service level agreement. Other IT services, called supporting services, are not directly used by the business but are required by the service provider to deliver customer-facing services.

IT service continuity management (ITSCM)

The process responsible for managing risks that could seriously affect IT services. IT service continuity management ensures that the IT service provider can always provide minimum agreed service levels, by reducing the risk to an acceptable level and planning for the recovery of IT services. IT service continuity management supports business continuity management.

IT service management (ITSM)

The implementation and management of quality IT services that meet the needs of the business. IT service management is performed by IT service providers through an appropriate mix of people, process and information technology. *See also* service management.

IT Service Management Forum (*it*SMF)

An independent organization dedicated to promoting a professional approach to IT service management. The *it*SMF is a not-for-profit membership organization with representation in many countries around the world (*it*SMF chapters). The *it*SMF and its membership contribute to the development of ITIL and associated IT service management standards. See www.itsmfi.org for more information.

IT service provider

A service provider that provides IT services to internal or external customers.

IT steering group (ISG)

A formal group that is responsible for ensuring that business and IT service provider strategies and plans are closely aligned. An IT steering group includes senior representatives from the business and the IT service provider. Also known as IT strategy group or IT steering committee.

ITIL

A set of best-practice publications for IT service management. Owned by AXELOS, ITIL gives guidance on the provision of quality IT services and the processes, functions and other capabilities needed to support them. The ITIL framework is based on a service lifecycle and consists of five lifecycle stages (service strategy, service design, service transition, service operation and continual service improvement), each of which has its own supporting publication. There is also a set of complementary ITIL publications providing guidance specific to industry sectors, organization types, operating models and technology architectures. See https://www.axelos.com/itil for more information.

job description

A document that defines the roles, responsibilities, skills and knowledge required by a particular person. One job description can include multiple roles – for example, the roles of configuration manager and change manager may be carried out by one person.

joiners, movers and leavers (JML)

A process that includes pre-employment screening, recruitment, onboarding and line management during employment, and exit management of employees. JML is usually managed by an HR organization and it should be closely tied with access management.

key loggers

Hardware or software that can be used to monitor and capture keystrokes on a keyboard with the purpose of capturing sensitive information such as account information and passwords. Key loggers are sometimes called key stroke loggers.

key performance indicator (KPI)

A metric that is used to help manage an IT service, process, plan, project or other activity. Key performance indicators are used to measure the achievement of critical success factors. Many metrics may be measured, but only the most important of these are defined as key performance indicators and used to actively manage and report on the process, IT service or activity. They should be selected to ensure that efficiency, effectiveness and cost effectiveness are all managed.

knowledge base

A logical database containing data and information used by the service knowledge management system.

knowledge management

The ITSM process responsible for sharing perspectives, ideas, experience and information, and for ensuring that these are available in the right place and at the right time. The knowledge management process enables informed decisions, and improves efficiency by reducing the need to rediscover knowledge. *See also* service knowledge management system.

known error

A problem that has a documented root cause and a workaround. Known errors are created and managed throughout their lifecycle by problem management. Known errors may also be identified by development staff or suppliers.

least privilege

The principle of access control whereby entities are only allocated the minimum access rights or privileges needed to carry out their duties.

lifecycle

The various stages in the life of an IT service, configuration item, incident, problem, change etc. The lifecycle defines the categories for status and the status transitions that are permitted. For example, the lifecycle of an application includes requirements, design, build, deploy, operate, optimize. The expanded incident lifecycle includes detection, diagnosis, repair, recovery and restoration. The lifecycle of a server may include: ordered, received, in test, live, disposed of etc.

live

Refers to an IT service or other configuration item that is being used to deliver a service to a customer.

live environment

A controlled environment containing live configuration items used to deliver IT services to customers.

logical access

Interaction with hardware or software via a remote connection. This can be contrasted with physical access where the user needs to be in the same physical environment as the component they are interacting with.

maintainability

A measure of how quickly and effectively an IT service or other configuration item can be restored to normal working after a failure. Maintainability is often measured and reported as MTRS. Maintainability is also used in the context of software or IT service development to mean ability to be changed or repaired easily.

major incident

The highest category of impact for an incident. A major incident results in significant disruption to the business.

manageability

An informal measure of how easily and effectively an IT service or other component can be managed.

management information

Information that is used to support decision-making by managers. Management information is often generated automatically by tools supporting the various IT service management processes. Management information often includes the values of key performance indicators, such as 'percentage of changes leading to incidents' or 'first-time fix rate'.

management information system (MIS)

A set of tools, data and information that is used to support a process or function. Examples include the availability management information system and the supplier and contract management information system. *See also* service knowledge management system.

Management of Risk (M_o_R)

Systemic application of policies, procedures, methods and practices to the tasks of identifying and assessing risks, and then planning and implementing risk responses. This provides a disciplined environment for a proactive decision-making management system.

The framework of policy, processes, functions, standards, guidelines and tools that ensures an organization or part of an organization can achieve its objectives. This term is also used with a smaller scope to support a specific process or activity – for example, an event management system or risk management system. *See also* system.

maturity

A measure of the reliability, efficiency and effectiveness of a process, function, organization etc. The most mature processes and functions are formally aligned with business objectives and strategy, and are supported by a framework for continual improvement.

maturity level

A named level in a maturity model, such as the Carnegie Mellon Capability Maturity Model Integration (CMMI).

mean time between failures (MTBF)

A metric for measuring and reporting reliability. MTBF is the average time that a service, system or component can perform its agreed function without interruption. This is measured from when the service, system or component starts working, until it next fails.

mean time to restore service (MTRS)

The average time taken to restore an IT service or other configuration item after a failure. MTRS is measured from when the configuration item fails until it is fully restored and delivering its normal functionality.

metric

Something that is measured and reported to help manage a process, IT service or activity. *See also* key performance indicator.

mission

A short but complete description of the overall purpose and intentions of an organization. It states what is to be achieved, but not how this should be done.

mobile device management (MDM)

Remote management of mobile devices such as tablets, smartphones and laptops. MDM can be used to apply and enforce security policies, and to update, lock and wipe mobile devices.

model

A representation of a system, process, IT service, configuration item etc. that is used to help understand or predict future behaviour.

modelling

A technique that is used to predict the future behaviour of a system, process, IT service, configuration item etc. Modelling is commonly used in financial management, capacity management and availability management.

monitoring

Repeated observation of a configuration item, IT service or process to detect events and to ensure that the current status is known.

multi-factor authentication

The use of more than one form of authentication information required to verify the identity of an entity. The authentication information is usually something one knows (for example, a password) something one possesses (for example, a token) or something one is (a biometric).

need to know

A principle of confidentiality that requires information to be shared with only those who need to know the information to carry out their duties.

network access control (NAC)

A way to control access to networks from endpoints by ensuring that the endpoint devices meet the minimum or baseline configuration requirements, including in the areas of anti-virus software, patches etc. before they are allowed to connect to the network.

non-repudiation

Providing undeniable proof that an alleged event actually happened or an alleged action was actually carried out, and that these events and actions were carried out by a particular entity.

objective

The outcomes required from a process, activity or organization in order to ensure that its purpose will be fulfilled. Objectives are usually expressed as measurable targets. The term is also informally used to mean a requirement.

off the shelf

See commercial off the shelf.

open shortest path first (OSPF)

A dynamic IP-based routeing protocol that routers use to work out the shortest path to the target destination network.

Open Web Application Security Project (OWASP)

An online non-profit community dedicated to web application security. The OWASP community includes organizations and individuals from across the globe that publishes articles, provides documentation, tools and technologies for application security.

operate

To perform as expected. A process or configuration item is said to operate if it is delivering the required outputs. Operate also means to perform one or more operations. For example, to operate a computer is to do the day-to-day operations needed for it to perform as expected.

operation

Routine management of an IT service, system or other configuration item. Operation is also used to mean any predefined activity or transaction – for example, accepting money at a point of sale, or reading data from a disk drive.

operational

The lowest of three levels of planning and delivery (strategic, tactical, operational). Operational activities include the day-to-day or short-term planning or delivery of a business process or IT service management process. The term is also a synonym for live.

operational level agreement (OLA)

An agreement between an IT service provider and another part of the same organization. It supports the IT service provider's delivery of IT services to customers and defines the goods or services to be provided and the responsibilities of both parties. For example, there could be an operational level agreement:

● Between the IT service provider and a procurement department to obtain hardware in agreed times

● Between the service desk and a support group to provide incident resolution in agreed times.

See also service level agreement.

operations bridge

A physical location where IT services and IT infrastructure are monitored and managed.

operations control

See IT operations control.

operations management

See IT operations management.

optimize

Review, plan and request changes, in order to obtain the maximum efficiency and effectiveness from a process, configuration item, application etc.

organization

A company, legal entity or other institution. The term is sometimes used to refer to any entity that has people, resources and budgets – for example, a project or business unit.

outcome

The result of carrying out an activity, following a process, or delivering an IT service etc. The term is used to refer to intended results as well as to actual results. See also objective.

outsourcing

Using an external service provider to manage IT services.

patching

Installing vendor updates to operating systems, applications or firmware, usually in response to vulnerabilities, to correct errors or to support new hardware.

performance

A measure of what is achieved or delivered by a system, person, team, process or IT service.

performance management

Activities to ensure that something achieves its expected outcomes in an efficient and consistent manner.

personal identification number (PIN)

A numeric password that can be used in authentication.

plain text

Readable information before it is subjected to encryption. See cipher-text.

plan

A detailed proposal that describes the activities and resources needed to achieve an objective – for example, a risk treatment plan.

Plan-Do-Check-Act (PDCA)

A four-stage cycle for process management, attributed to Edward Deming. Plan-Do-Check-Act is also called the Deming Cycle. It comprises:

- **Plan** Design or revise processes to deliver desired outcomes.
- **Do** Implement the plan and manage the processes.
- **Check** Measure the processes and the outcomes, compare with objectives and produce reports.
- **Act** Plan and implement changes to improve the processes.

policy

Formally documented management expectations and intentions. Policies are used to direct decisions, and to ensure consistent and appropriate development and implementation of processes, standards, roles, activities, IT infrastructure etc.

post-implementation review (PIR)

A review that takes place after a change or a project has been implemented. It determines if the change or project was successful, and identifies opportunities for improvement.

practice

A way of working, or a way in which work must be done. Practices can include activities, processes, functions, standards and guidelines. *See also* best practice.

preventative control

A control that is intended to prevent a threat from succeeding.

PRINCE2

See PRojects IN Controlled Environments.

priority

A category used to identify the relative importance of an incident, problem or change. Priority is based on impact and urgency, and is used to identify required times for actions to be taken. For example, the service level agreement may state that Priority 2 incidents must be resolved within 12 hours.

private automatic branch exchange (PABX)

An automatic telephone switch that emulates an internal telephone network and can also act as the gateway to external networks for outgoing calls.

private key

A portion of an asymmetric key pair that is kept confidential or private. A private key can be used to decrypt information that has been encrypted with the corresponding public key. It can also be used to encrypt a message hash to be used as a digital signature.

problem

A cause of one or more incidents. The cause is not usually known at the time a problem record is created, and the problem management process is responsible for further investigation.

problem management

The process responsible for managing the lifecycle of all problems. Problem management proactively prevents incidents from happening and minimizes the impact of incidents that cannot be prevented.

procedure

The steps that specify how to achieve an activity. Procedures are defined as part of processes.

process

A structured set of activities designed to accomplish a specific objective. A process takes one or more defined inputs and turns them into defined outputs. It may include any of the roles, responsibilities, tools and management controls required to reliably deliver the outputs. A process may define policies, standards, guidelines, activities and work instructions if they are needed.

process control

The activity of planning and regulating a process, with the objective of performing the process in an effective, efficient and consistent manner.

process owner

The person who is held accountable for ensuring that a process is fit for purpose. The process owner's responsibilities include sponsorship, design, change management and continual improvement of the process and its metrics. This role can be assigned to the same person who carries out the process manager role, but the two roles may be separate in larger organizations.

production environment

See live environment.

programme

A number of projects and activities that are planned and managed together to achieve an overall set of related objectives and other outcomes.

project

A temporary organization, with people and other assets, that is required to achieve an objective or other outcome. Each project has a lifecycle that typically includes initiation, planning, execution and closure. Projects are usually managed using a formal methodology such as PRojects IN Controlled Environments (PRINCE2) or the Project Management Body of Knowledge (PMBOK®).

Project Management Body of Knowledge (PMBOK)

A project management standard maintained and published by the Project Management Institute. See www. pmi.org for more information. *See also* PRojects IN Controlled Environments (PRINCE2).

PRojects IN Controlled Environments (PRINCE2)

The standard UK government methodology for project management. See https://www.axelos.com/prince2 for more information. *See also* Project Management Body of Knowledge (PMBOK).

public key

A portion of an asymmetric key pair that is generally made available and is used to encrypt data which only the corresponding private key can decrypt. A public key can also be used to decrypt a message hash to verify a digital signature.

public key encryption (PKE)

An encryption system that uses asymmetric key pairs (public and private) to encrypt and decrypt information.

public key infrastructure (PKI)

Infrastructure required to manage digital certificates. PKI provides the ability to create, distribute, use and revoke digital certificates to support authentication and non-repudiation.

qualification

An activity that ensures that the IT infrastructure is appropriate and correctly configured to support an application or IT service. *See also* validation.

quality

The ability of a product, service or process to provide the intended value. For example, a hardware component can be considered to be of high quality if it performs as expected and delivers the required reliability. Process quality also requires an ability to monitor effectiveness and efficiency, and to improve them if necessary. *See also* quality management system.

quality management system (QMS)

The framework of policy, processes, functions, standards, guidelines and tools that ensures an organization is of a suitable quality to reliably meet business objectives or service levels. *See also* ISO 9000.

RACI

A model used to help define roles and responsibilities. RACI stands for responsible, accountable, consulted and informed.

record

A document containing the results or other output from a process or activity. Records are evidence of the fact that an activity took place, and they may be paper or electronic – for example, an audit report, an incident record or the minutes of a meeting.

recovery

Returning a configuration item or an IT service to a working state. Recovery of an IT service often includes recovering data to a known consistent state. After recovery, further steps may be needed before the IT service can be made available to the users (restoration). Recovery may also include working with regulators, customers or other external stakeholders to remediate the impact of a security incident.

redundancy

Use of one or more additional configuration items to provide fault tolerance. The term also has a generic meaning of obsolescence, or no longer being needed. *See also* defence-in-depth.

relationship

A connection or interaction between two people or things. In business relationship management, it is the interaction between the IT service provider and the business. In service asset and configuration management, it is a link between two configuration items that identifies a dependency or connection between them. For example, applications may be linked to the servers they run on, and IT services have many links to all the configuration items that contribute to that IT service.

release

One or more changes to an IT service that are built, tested and deployed together. A single release may include changes to hardware, software, documentation, processes and other components.

release and deployment management

The ITSM process responsible for planning, scheduling and controlling the build, test and deployment of releases, and for delivering new functionality required by the business while protecting the integrity of existing services.

release package

A set of configuration items that will be built, tested and deployed together as a single release. Each release package will usually include one or more release units.

reliability

A measure of how long an IT service or other configuration item can perform its agreed function without interruption. Usually measured as MTBF or MTBSI. The term can also be used to state how likely it is that a process, function etc. will deliver its required outputs. See also availability.

remediation

The act of correcting vulnerabilities, deficiencies, faults or failed changes. This could be by installing a patch, adjusting configuration settings, or installing or uninstalling software applications including undoing changes.

repair

The replacement or correction of a failed configuration item.

request for change (RFC)

A formal proposal for a change to be made. It includes details of the proposed change, and may be recorded on paper or electronically. The term is often misused to mean a change record, or the change itself.

request fulfilment

The ITSM process responsible for managing the lifecycle of all service requests.

requirement

A formal statement of what is needed – for example, a legal requirement, a service level requirement, a project requirement or the required deliverables for a process.

RESILIA

A set of best-practice publications in cyber resilience. Owned by AXELOS (a joint venture between the Cabinet Office (part of HM Government) and Capita), RESILIA gives guidance on the deployment and management of cyber resilience, including the processes, functions and other capabilities needed to support them. The RESILIA framework is based on a service lifecycle and consists of five lifecycle stages (strategy, design, transition, operation and continual improvement). See https://www.axelos.com/resilia for more information.

resilience

The ability of a system or component to resist an unplanned disturbance or failure, and the ability to recover in a timely manner following any unplanned disturbance or failure. For example, an armoured cable will resist failure when put under stress and therefore demonstrates resilience.

resolution

Action taken to repair the root cause of an incident or problem, or to implement a workaround. In ISO/IEC 20000, 'resolution processes' is the process group that includes incident and problem management.

resource

A generic term that includes IT infrastructure, people, money or anything else that might help to deliver an IT service. Resources are considered to be assets of an organization. *See also* capability; service asset.

restore

Taking action to return an IT service to the users after repair and recovery from an incident. Restoration is the primary objective of incident management.

retire

Permanently remove an IT service, or other configuration item, from the live environment. Being retired is a stage in the lifecycle of many configuration items.

review

An evaluation of a change, problem, process, project etc. Reviews are typically carried out at predefined points in the lifecycle, and especially after closure. The purpose of a review is to ensure that all deliverables have been provided, and to identify opportunities for improvement. *See also* change evaluation; post-implementation review.

rights

Entitlements, or permissions, granted to a user or role – for example, the right to modify particular data, or to authorize a change.

risk

A possible event that could cause harm or loss, or affect the ability to achieve objectives. A risk is measured by the probability of a threat, the vulnerability of the asset to that threat, and the impact it would have if it occurred. Risk can also be defined as uncertainty of outcome, and can be used in the context of measuring the probability of positive outcomes as well as negative outcomes.

risk assessment

The initial steps of risk management: analysing the value of assets to the business, identifying threats to those assets, and evaluating how vulnerable each asset is to those threats. Risk assessment can be quantitative (based on numerical data) or qualitative.

risk management

The process responsible for identifying, assessing and controlling risks. Risk management is also sometimes used to refer to the second part of the overall process after risks have been identified and assessed, as in 'risk assessment and management'. *See also* risk assessment.

role

A set of responsibilities, activities and authorities assigned to a person or team. A role is defined in a process or function. One person or team may have multiple roles – for example, the roles of configuration manager and change manager may be carried out by a single person. Role is also used to describe the purpose of something or what it is used for.

role-based access control (RBAC)

A method of access control that bases access rights on the role of the user.

root cause

The underlying or original cause of an incident or problem.

Sarbanes-Oxley Act

A US federal law for internal control that governs all publicly listed companies. The Sarbanes-Oxley Act requires an organization's board to certify its company's financial records.

scalability

The ability of an IT service, process, configuration item etc. to continue to perform its agreed function when the workload or scope changes.

scope

The boundary or extent to which a process, procedure, certification, contract etc. applies. For example, the scope of change management may include all live IT services and related configuration items; the scope of an ISO/IEC 27001 certificate may include all IT services delivered out of a named data centre.

secure sockets layer (SSL)

A session-based encryption methodology that is used to protect internet connections between two points. *See also* transport layer security.

security information and event management (SIEM)

An application that monitors and collates information and provides real-time analysis of the security alerts generated by hardware and software.

segregation of duties

An internal control principle of separating roles and privileges to ensure that one entity cannot have enough privileges to abuse its role.

separation of concerns (SoC)

An approach to designing a solution or IT service that divides the problem into parts that can be solved independently. This approach separates what is to be done from how it is to be done.

server

A computer that is connected to a network and provides software functions that are used by other computers.

service

A means of delivering value to customers by facilitating outcomes that customers want to achieve without the ownership of specific costs and risks.

service asset

Any resource or capability of a service provider. *See also* asset.

service asset and configuration management (SACM)

The ITSM process responsible for ensuring that the assets required to deliver services are properly controlled, and that accurate and reliable information about those assets is available when and where it is needed. This information includes details of how the assets have been configured and the relationships between assets. *See also* configuration management system.

service capacity management

The sub-process of capacity management responsible for understanding the performance and capacity of IT services. Information on the resources used by each IT service and the pattern of usage over time are collected, recorded and analysed for use in the capacity plan. *See also* business capacity management; component capacity management.

service catalogue

A database or structured document with information about all live IT services, including those available for deployment. The service catalogue is part of the service portfolio and contains information about two types of IT service: customer-facing services that are visible to the business, and supporting services required by the service provider to deliver customer-facing services.

service catalogue management

The ITSM process responsible for providing and maintaining the service catalogue and for ensuring that it is available to those who are authorized to access it.

service design

A stage in the lifecycle of a service. Service design includes the design of the services, governing practices, processes and policies required to realize the service provider's strategy and to facilitate the introduction of services into supported environments. Service design includes the following processes: design coordination, service catalogue management, service level management, availability management, capacity management, IT service continuity management, information security management and supplier management. Although these processes are associated with service design, most processes have activities that take place across multiple stages of the service lifecycle. *See also* design.

service design package (SDP)

Document(s) defining all aspects of an IT service and its requirements through each stage of its lifecycle. A service design package is produced for each new IT service, major change or IT service retirement.

service desk

The single point of contact between the service provider and the users. A typical service desk manages incidents and service requests, and also handles communication with the users.

service knowledge management system (SKMS)

A set of tools and databases that is used to manage knowledge, information and data. The service knowledge management system includes the configuration management system, as well as other databases and information systems. The service knowledge management system includes tools for collecting, storing, managing, updating, analysing and presenting all the knowledge, information and data that an IT service provider will need to manage the full lifecycle of IT services. *See also* knowledge management.

service level agreement (SLA)

An agreement between an IT service provider and a customer. A service level agreement describes the IT service, documents service level targets, and specifies the responsibilities of the IT service provider and the customer. A single agreement may cover multiple IT services or multiple customers. See also operational level agreement.

service level management (SLM)

The ITSM process responsible for negotiating achievable service level agreements and ensuring that these are met. It is responsible for ensuring that all IT service management processes, operational level agreements and underpinning contracts are appropriate for the agreed service level targets. Service level management monitors and reports on service levels, holds regular service reviews with customers, and identifies required improvements.

service level requirement (SLR)

A customer requirement for an aspect of an IT service. Service level requirements are based on business objectives and used to negotiate agreed service level targets.

service level target

A commitment that is documented in a service level agreement. Service level targets are based on service level requirements, and are needed to ensure that the IT service is able to meet business objectives. They should be SMART, and are usually based on key performance indicators.

service lifecycle

An approach to IT service management that emphasizes the importance of coordination and control across the various functions, processes and systems necessary to manage the full lifecycle of IT services. The service lifecycle approach considers the strategy, design, transition, operation and continual improvement of IT services. Also known as service management lifecycle.

service management

A set of specialized organizational capabilities for providing value to customers in the form of services.

service operation

A stage in the lifecycle of a service. Service operation coordinates and carries out the activities and processes required to deliver and manage services at agreed levels to business users and customers. Service operation also manages the technology that is used to deliver and support services. Service operation includes the following processes: event management, incident management, request fulfilment, problem management and access management. Service operation also includes the following functions: service desk, technical management, IT operations management and application management. Although these processes and functions are associated with service operation, most processes and functions have activities that take place across multiple stages of the service lifecycle.

service owner

A role responsible for managing one or more services throughout their entire lifecycle. Service owners are instrumental in the development of service strategy and are responsible for the content of the service portfolio.

service pipeline

A database or structured document listing all IT services that are under consideration or development, but are not yet available to customers. The service pipeline provides a business view of possible future IT services and is part of the service portfolio that is not normally published to customers.

service portfolio

The complete set of services that is managed by a service provider. The service portfolio is used to manage the entire lifecycle of all services, and includes three categories: service pipeline (proposed or in development), service catalogue (live or available for deployment), and retired services. *See also* service portfolio management.

service portfolio management

The process responsible for managing the service portfolio. Service portfolio management ensures that the service provider has the right mix of services to meet required business outcomes at an appropriate level of investment. Service portfolio management considers services in terms of the business value that they provide.

service provider

An organization supplying services to one or more internal customers or external customers. Service provider is often used as an abbreviation for IT service provider.

service request

A formal request from a user for something to be provided – for example, a request for information or advice, to reset a password, or to install a workstation for a new user. Service requests are managed by the request fulfilment process, usually in conjunction with the service desk. Service requests may be linked to a request for change as part of fulfilling the request.

service set identifier (SSID)

The name of a wireless network that is broadcast to enable endpoints to connect. Wireless endpoints connect to the SSID to form a wireless local area network.

service strategy

A stage in the lifecycle of a service. Service strategy defines the perspective, position, plans and patterns that a service provider needs to execute to meet an organization's business outcomes. Service strategy includes the following processes: strategy management for IT services, service portfolio management, financial management for IT services, demand management and business relationship management. Although these processes are associated with service strategy, most processes have activities that take place across multiple stages of the service lifecycle.

service transition

A stage in the lifecycle of a service. Service transition ensures that new, modified or retired services meet the expectations of the business as documented in the service strategy and service design stages of the lifecycle. Service transition includes the following processes: transition planning and support, change management, service asset and configuration management, release and deployment management, service validation and testing, change evaluation and knowledge management. Although these processes are associated with service transition, most processes have activities that take place across multiple stages of the service lifecycle. *See also* transition.

service validation and testing

The ITSM process responsible for validation and testing of a new or changed IT service. Service validation and testing ensures that the IT service matches its design specification and will meet the needs of the business.

serviceability

The ability of a third-party supplier to meet the terms of its contract. This contract will include agreed levels of reliability, maintainability and availability for a configuration item.

seven-step improvement process

The ITSM process responsible for defining and managing the steps needed to identify, define, gather, process, analyse, present and implement improvements. The performance of the IT service provider is continually measured by this process, and improvements are made to processes, IT services and IT infrastructure in order to increase efficiency, effectiveness and cost effectiveness. Opportunities for improvement are recorded and managed in the CSI register.

simple network management protocol (SNMP)

A protocol from the TCP/IP suite of protocols that is used to monitor, configure and manage network devices.

single loss expectancy (SLE)

The expected financial loss due to a risk, each time that risk occurs.

single point of contact

Providing a single consistent way to communicate with an organization or business unit. For example, a single point of contact for an IT service provider is usually called a service desk.

single-sign-on (SSO)

An authentication method that uses the same logon credentials across multiple systems, so that the user is only required to log on once to be able to access multiple systems.

SMART

An acronym for helping to remember that targets in service level agreements and project plans should be specific, measurable, achievable, relevant and time-bound.

software as a service (SaaS)

A model for delivery of software, and software licensing, in which the software is hosted by a service provider, which provides access to the software on a subscription basis.

specification

A formal definition of requirements. A specification may be used to define technical or operational requirements, and may be internal or external. Many public standards consist of a code of practice and a specification. The specification defines the standard against which an organization can be audited.

stakeholder

A person who has an interest in an organization, project, IT service etc. Stakeholders may be interested in the activities, targets, resources or deliverables. Stakeholders may include customers, partners, employees, shareholders, owners etc. *See also* RACI.

standard

A mandatory requirement. Examples include ISO/IEC 27001 (an international standard), an internal security standard for UNIX configuration, or a government standard setting out how financial records should be maintained. The term is also used to refer to a code of practice or specification published by a standards organization such as ISO or BSI. *See also* guideline.

standard change

A pre-authorized change that is low risk, relatively common and follows a procedure or work instruction – for example, a password reset or provision of standard equipment to a new employee. Requests for change are not required to implement a standard change, and they are logged and tracked using a different mechanism, such as a service request.

status

The name of a required field in many types of record. It shows the current stage in the lifecycle of the associated configuration item, incident, problem etc.

strategic

The highest of three levels of planning and delivery (strategic, tactical, operational). Strategic activities include objective-setting and long-term planning to achieve the overall vision.

strategy

A strategic plan designed to achieve defined objectives.

strategy management for IT services

The ITSM process responsible for defining and maintaining an organization's perspective, position, plans and patterns with regard to its services and the management of those services. Once the strategy has been defined, strategy management for IT services is also responsible for ensuring that it achieves its intended business outcomes.

supplier

A third party responsible for supplying goods or services that are required to manage cyber resilience or to deliver IT services. Examples of suppliers include commodity hardware and software vendors, network and telecom providers, and outsourcing organizations. *See also* supply chain; underpinning contract.

supplier management

The process responsible for obtaining value for money from suppliers, ensuring that all contracts and agreements with suppliers support the needs of the business, and that all suppliers meet their contractual commitments.

supply chain

The activities in a value chain carried out by suppliers. A supply chain typically involves multiple suppliers, each adding value to the product or service. *See also* value network.

symmetric key

An encryption key used to encrypt and also decrypt information. A symmetric key is sometimes called a secret key.

system

A number of related things that work together to achieve an overall objective. For example:

- A computer system including hardware, software and applications
- A management system, including the framework of policy, processes, functions, standards, guidelines and tools that are planned and managed together – for example, a quality management system
- A database management system or operating system that includes many software modules which are designed to perform a set of related functions.

tactical

The middle of three levels of planning and delivery (strategic, tactical, operational). Tactical activities include the medium-term plans required to achieve specific objectives, typically over a period of weeks to months.

technical management

The ITSM function responsible for providing technical skills in support of IT services and management of the IT infrastructure. Technical management defines the roles of support groups, as well as the tools, processes and procedures required.

technical support

See technical management.

terms of reference

A document specifying the requirements, scope, deliverables, resources and schedule for a project or activity.

test

An activity that verifies that a cyber resilience control, configuration item, IT service, process etc. meets its specification or agreed requirements. *See also* acceptance; service validation and testing.

TOGAF

An enterprise architecture methodology and framework, owned and maintained by The Open Group.

third party

A person, organization or other entity that is not one of the two primarily concerned. In information security this could be an external entity (who is not the organization that owns the information or an internal user). In IT service management it could be a supplier (who is not the IT service provider or their customer).

threat

Anything that might exploit a vulnerability. Any potential cause of an incident can be considered a threat. For example, a fire is a threat that could exploit the vulnerability of flammable floor coverings.

threshold

The value of a metric that should cause an alert to be generated or management action to be taken. For example, 'Priority 1 incident not solved within four hours', 'More than five soft disk errors in an hour', or 'More than 10 failed changes in a month'.

throughput

A measure of the number of transactions or other operations performed in a fixed time – for example, 5,000 emails sent per hour, or 200 disk I/Os per second.

transaction

A discrete function performed by an IT service – for example, transferring money from one bank account to another. A single transaction may involve numerous additions, deletions and modifications of data. Either all of these are completed successfully or none of them is carried out.

transition

A change in state, corresponding to a movement of a cyber resilience control, an IT service or other configuration item from one lifecycle status to the next.

transition planning and support

The ITSM process responsible for planning all service transition processes and coordinating the resources that they require.

transport layer security (TLS)

A security protocol similar to secure sockets layer (SSL) that protects information in transit between two communicating points using strong encryption.

underpinning contract

A contract between an IT service provider and a third party. The third party provides goods or services that support delivery of an IT service to a customer. The underpinning contract defines targets and responsibilities that are required to meet agreed service level targets in one or more service level agreements.

urgency

A measure of how long it will be until an incident, problem or change has a significant impact on the business. For example, a high-impact incident may have low urgency if the impact will not affect the business until the end of the financial year. Impact and urgency are used to assign priority.

usability

The ease with which an application, product or IT service can be used. Usability requirements are often included in a statement of requirements.

user

A person who uses an IT service on a day-to-day basis. Users are distinct from customers, as some customers do not use the IT service directly.

utility

The functionality offered by a product or service to meet a particular need. Utility can be summarized as 'what the service does', and can be used to determine whether a service is able to meet its required outcomes, or is 'fit for purpose'. The business value of an IT service is created by the combination of utility and warranty. *See also* service validation and testing.

validation

An activity that ensures a new or changed cyber resilience control, IT service, process, plan or other deliverable meets the needs of the business. Validation ensures that business requirements are met even though these may have changed since the original design. *See also* acceptance; qualification; service validation and testing; verification.

value chain

A sequence of processes that creates a product or service that is of value to a customer. Each step of the sequence builds on the previous steps and contributes to the overall product or service. *See also* value network.

value network

A complex set of relationships between two or more groups or organizations. Value is generated through exchange of knowledge, information, goods or services. *See also* value chain.

verification

An activity that ensures that a new or changed cyber resilience control, IT service, process, plan or other deliverable is complete, accurate, reliable and matches its design specification. *See also* acceptance; validation; service validation and testing.

virtual private network (VPN)

An encrypted connection over a public network that appears to be an extension of a private network, due to the protection of data provided by the encryption.

voice over internet protocol (VoIP)

A method for sending voice traffic using the internet protocol over data networks.

vulnerability

A weakness that could be exploited by a threat – for example, an open firewall port, a password that is never changed, or a flammable carpet. A missing control is also considered to be a vulnerability.

warranty

Assurance that a product or service will meet agreed requirements. This may be a formal agreement such as a service level agreement or contract, or it may be a marketing message or brand image. Warranty refers to the ability of a service to be available when needed, to provide the required capacity, and to provide the required reliability in terms of continuity and security. Warranty can be summarized as 'how the service is delivered', and can be used to determine whether a service is 'fit for use'. The business value of an IT service is created by the combination of utility and warranty. *See also* service validation and testing.

web application firewall (WAF)

A firewall that is able to protect against web-based attacks such as those listed in the OWASP top 10 risks.

WiFi Protected Access (WPA) and WiFi Protected Access 2 (WPA2)

Wireless security protocols based on the IEEE 802.11i standard defined by the WiFi Alliance that protect the confidentiality of information over wireless connections and support strong encryption and authentication. WPA2 is the more secure version of WPA.

wired equivalent privacy (WEP)

A wireless security protocol that protects the confidentiality of information over wireless connections. WEP has been superseded by WPA and subsequently WPA2. WEP is no longer recommended due to its inherent flaws.

workaround

Reducing or eliminating the impact of an incident or problem for which a full resolution is not yet available – for example, by restarting a failed configuration item. Workarounds for problems are documented in known error records. Workarounds for incidents that do not have associated problem records are documented in the incident record.

Index

Index